LEADERSHIP and MANAGEMENT in the HOSPITALITY INDUSTRY

EDUCATIONAL INSTITUTE BOOKS

UNIFORM SYSTEM OF ACCOUNTS FOR THE LODGING INDUSTRY
Eleventh Revised Edition

PLANNING AND CONTROL FOR FOOD AND BEVERAGE OPERATIONS
Ninth Edition
Jack D. Ninemeier

UNDERSTANDING HOSPITALITY LAW
Fifth Edition
Jack P. Jefferies/Banks Brown

SUPERVISION IN THE HOSPITALITY INDUSTRY
Sixth Edition
Jack D. Ninemeier

MANAGEMENT OF FOOD AND BEVERAGE OPERATIONS
Seventh Edition
Jack D. Ninemeier/David K. Hayes

MANAGING FRONT OFFICE OPERATIONS
Eleventh Edition
Michael L. Kasavana

MANAGING SERVICE IN FOOD AND BEVERAGE OPERATIONS
Fifth Edition
Ronald F. Cichy/Philip J. Hickey, Jr.

THE LODGING AND FOOD SERVICE INDUSTRY
Eighth Edition
Gerald W. Lattin/Thomas W. Lattin/James E. Lattin

SECURITY AND LOSS PREVENTION MANAGEMENT
Third Edition
David M. Stipanuk/Raymond C. Ellis, Jr.

HOSPITALITY INDUSTRY MANAGERIAL ACCOUNTING
Ninth Edition
Raymond S. Schmidgall/Agnes L. DeFranco

MANAGING TECHNOLOGY IN THE HOSPITALITY INDUSTRY
Seventh Edition
Michael L. Kasavana

HOTEL AND RESTAURANT ACCOUNTING
Eighth Edition
Raymond Cote

ACCOUNTING FOR HOSPITALITY MANAGERS
Fifth Edition
Raymond Cote

CONVENTION MANAGEMENT AND SERVICE
Ninth Edition
James R. Abbey

HOSPITALITY SALES AND MARKETING
Sixth Edition
James R. Abbey

MANAGING HOUSEKEEPING OPERATIONS
Revised Third Edition
Aleta A. Nitschke/William D. Frye

HOSPITALITY TODAY: AN INTRODUCTION
Ninth Edition
Rocco M. Angelo

HOSPITALITY FACILITIES MANAGEMENT AND DESIGN
Fourth Edition
David M. Stipanuk

MANAGING HOSPITALITY HUMAN RESOURCES
Sixth Edition
Robert H. Woods, William Werner, Seonghee Cho, and Misty M. Johanson

RETAIL MANAGEMENT FOR SPAS

HOSPITALITY INDUSTRY FINANCIAL ACCOUNTING
Fourth Edition
Raymond S. Schmidgall/James W. Damitio

HOTEL INVESTMENTS: ISSUES & PERSPECTIVES
Fifth Edition
Edited by Lori E. Raleigh and Rachel J. Roginsky

LEADERSHIP AND MANAGEMENT IN THE HOSPITALITY INDUSTRY
Third Edition
Robert H. Woods/Judy Z. King

CONTEMPORARY CLUB MANAGEMENT
Third Edition
Edited by Joe Perdue and Jason Koenigsfeld for the Club Managers Association of America

HOTEL ASSET MANAGEMENT: PRINCIPLES & PRACTICE
Third Edition
Edited by Rich Musgrove, Lori E. Raleigh, and A. J. Singh

MANAGING BEVERAGE OPERATIONS
Second Edition
Ronald F. Cichy/Lendal H. Kotschevar

FOOD SAFETY AND QUALITY MANAGEMENT
Third Edition
Ronald F. Cichy and JaeMin Cha

SPA: A COMPREHENSIVE INTRODUCTION
Elizabeth M. Johnson/Bridgette M. Redman

REVENUE MANAGEMENT: MAXIMIZING REVENUE IN HOSPITALITY OPERATIONS
Second Edition
Gabor Forgacs

FINANCIAL MANAGEMENT FOR SPAS
Raymond S. Schmidgall/John R. Korpi

LEADERSHIP and MANAGEMENT in the HOSPITALITY INDUSTRY

Third Edition

Robert H. Woods, Ph.D., CHRE
Judy Z. King

AMERICAN HOTEL & LODGING
EDUCATIONAL INSTITUTE

Disclaimer

ISBN: 978-0-86612-347-1

Printed in the USA

Contents

Preface

Years ago, the field of organizational behavior split roughly down the middle. About half of the academics stuck to the old model, a model that emphasized teaching theories about why people do what they do at work. The rest of the field developed into what have come to be known as "management skills" proponents. There is a substantial difference between these two approaches. A textbook that emphasizes organizational behavior theory will, for instance, describe how motivation works theoretically; however, a management skills book, like ours, shows how motivation works and concentrates on how leaders can better create a motivating environment for everyone in the organization.

Those scholars who moved toward teaching and writing about management skills realized that theory alone did not serve the practical needs of the real world. So, instead of simply teaching theory, management-skills scholars began looking for ways to apply theory to the workplace in practical ways. We believe that practicality is much more important than theory, especially for undergraduate students. Managers and leaders need to learn and know more about how to use practical skills to make their organizations more productive and more enjoyable places to work. We also believe that most people want to do good work, and, when they fall short of that goal, do so because they lack the knowledge and skills they need, not the desire to succeed. This means that we approach work issues from a Theory Y perspective—i.e., that everyone may be ambitious and can exercise self-motivation if given the necessary encouragement by his or her manager. It is our hope that this book will provide current and future hospitality managers and leaders with invaluable, practical assistance in reaching their full potential.

The hospitality industry has entered an interesting phase in its history. Some companies have re-emphasized the important role that management skills play in their organizations. These companies have acknowledged that leadership, people management, interpersonal skills, and attention to quality are critical factors in ensuring their future success. Not all companies have chosen this path, however. Some companies have de-emphasized the role of people management, often outsourcing human resource activities to third parties. These companies have chosen to send the message that people are not very important in their organizations. Time will tell which approach proves to be more effective. We, however, are confident that those companies emphasizing leadership and management skills will be more successful in the long run.

We believe that there is no substitute for ethical leadership and management, grounded in sound principles and practices. The cyclical nature of the hospitality industry, staff turnover at all levels, and frequent changes in ownership provide serious barriers to management excellence on their own; if these factors are compounded by managers and other leaders who blindly follow "fad management," the results are confusion and an inability to perform at high levels. We see the famous line from the Pogo comic strip—"We have met the enemy, and he is us"—as both a warning to hospitality leaders and a call for them to use reliable leadership and management methods for surviving and thriving in the midst of chaotic change. It is our hope that this book will assist readers in making valuable contributions to their organizations and at the same time help them achieve a great deal of personal satisfaction in their work lives.

Acknowledgments

A textbook is always a team effort, and, just as in the workplace, team efforts usually produce the best results. Our two-member team was augmented by several industry experts who took the time to contribute chapters, or revise chapters from previous editions, and we would like to acknowledge their valuable contributions here.

Those individuals who contributed chapters are as follows (in chapter order): Chapter 1, "Managing Organizational Change," was written by Kenneth J. Heymann, Chairman and CEO of UniFocus; Chapter 8, "High-Performance Teams," was written by Sheryl Fried Kline, Associate Dean, College of Hospitality, Retail, & Sport Management, University of South Carolina; "Strategic Career Planning" (Chapter 10) was written by Michael P. Sciarini, Associate Professor, Michigan State University; and Chapter 11, "A Look at Ethics," was contributed by Stephen S.J. Hall, Executive Director, International Institute for Quality and Ethics in Service and Tourism.

Those individuals who revised chapters for this edition or previous editions are as follows (again, in chapter order): "The Quest for Quality" (Chapter 3) was revised by John Mellon, Associate Professor of Business, Misericordia University; "Communication Skills" (Chapter 6) was revised by Robert M. O'Halloran, Professor and Chair, Department of Hospitality Management, East Carolina University; and Chapter 7, "Goal-Setting, Coaching, and Conflict-Management Skills" was revised by Misty Johanson, Associate Professor, School of Hospitality Leadership, DePaul University. The diversity of skills, talents, and backgrounds these individuals brought to the textbook enriched it even beyond our expectations.

Robert H. Woods   Judy Z. King
Las Vegas, Nevada   Hendersonville, Tennessee

About the Authors

Robert H. Woods, Ph.D., CHRE, is a Professor in the William F. Harrah College of Hotel Administration at the University of Nevada, Las Vegas. He is a specialist in management and human resources issues and regularly consults with hospitality organizations and clubs on management, strategic management, service management, human resources, timeshare management, and corporate culture issues. He authored the textbook *Managing Hospitality Human Resources* and *The Job Description Handbook.* He has written more than 150 refereed articles and is the former editor of the *Journal of Hospitality and Tourism Education,* published by the Council on Hotel, Restaurant and Institutional Education. Woods has also written fifteen chapters for various books, including *Ethics in Hospitality Management* and *Contemporary Club Management.* Woods received his Master's degree and Ph.D. from the Hotel School at Cornell University. Before returning to academia, he owned and operated a successful chain of restaurants and a hospitality consulting firm. Among his awards is the 1995 Teacher-Scholar Award, given to a Michigan State University faculty member who excels in both areas. He is the former Hotel Management Department Chair at the University of Nevada, Las Vegas.

Judy Z. King is founder and principal of Quality Management Services. Her areas of expertise include customer service, quality management, team building, operational training and evaluation systems, management development, and strategic planning. King's hospitality industry clients include The Pinehurst Company, MGM Mirage Resorts, Colonial Williamsburg Hotel Properties, Sandestin Resorts, Callaway Gardens, Keystone Resort, Rosewood's Caneel Bay Resort, and Loews Hotels. She has served twice as an Examiner for the Malcolm Baldrige National Quality Award and is a member of the International Society of Hospitality Consultants and an allied member of the American Hotel & Lodging Association. Early in her career, King was the Employee Relations Manager for the Opryland Hotel in Nashville and was responsible for the design, implementation, and management of quality assurance for the hotel. She is a former co-owner of a Shoney's restaurant franchise and developed two stores in Texas and one in Oklahoma. A graduate of the University of Tennessee, she serves as an Adjunct Professor for the Division of Management and Adult Studies of Trevecca Nazarene University in Nashville. She also serves as facilitator for the Leadership and Teams course in Trevecca's doctoral program in Education. King resides in Hendersonville, Tennessee, has three wonderful children, and enjoys life!

Chapter 1 Outline

Characteristics of Change
    External Forces of Change
    Internal Forces of Change
    Fostering Change
Creativity and Change
    What Creativity Is and Is Not
    Creative Organizations
Roles in the Change Process
    Change Sponsors
    Change Agents
    Change Targets
The Change Process
    Planning for Change
    Implementing the Change
    Monitoring the Change
    Continuous Improvement
Cautions and Tips

Competencies

1. Identify the characteristics of internal and external forces of organizational change. (pp. 4–7)

2. Describe the relationship between creativity and change, identify characteristics of creative people and creative organizations, and discuss innovation and "champions" in terms of creativity. (pp. 7–10)

3. Explain the different roles in the change process played by change sponsors, change agents, and change targets. (pp. 10–16)

4. Describe the four major steps of the change process. (pp. 16–37)

5. List cautions and tips for organizations that embark on large-scale organizational change. (pp. 37–38)

1

Managing Organizational Change

IN THEIR BOOK, *Teaching as a Subversive Activity,* Postman and Weingartner suggest an interesting way to look at history, change, and technology.[1] Imagine a clock face. Assume that the 60 minutes represent the three thousand years of history during which people have had access to writing systems. One minute equals 50 years; ten minutes, 500. In this scenario, there were few technological changes in the way we communicate in the first 50 minutes, until the printing press was invented—about 9 minutes ago. The telegraph arrived about 3 minutes ago, the telephone in the last 2 minutes. Television appeared in the last minute, as have computers, lasers, and communication satellites. Virtually everything we consider essential to modern life has come into being in the last 60 seconds. As Postman and Weingartner point out, "Change isn't new; what is new is the degree of change…about three minutes ago there developed a qualitative difference in the character of change. Change changed."[2]

If you were born between 1945 and 1960, you probably grew up with black and white TVs and transistor radios. Boys wore ties to school and girls wore dresses. Only women wore earrings, and only men wore pants. Much of the history you were taught has been revised, and most of the science is outdated. If you were born between 1960 and 1990, you probably grew up with color TVs, stereos, and wore whatever you felt like wearing. Much of the history you were taught is being questioned, and most of the science is outdated. If you were born after 1990, you grew up with cable TV, personal computers, and the Internet. Much of the history you were taught will be questioned, and much of the science is on its way to being outdated. All of the technical knowledge we work with today will represent only a tiny percentage of the knowledge that will be available in 2050.

None of this information is particularly surprising. We all realize that change is an unavoidable fact of life and that the rate at which it occurs continues to accelerate. But few of us are enthusiastic about it. Change means we have to do things differently, learn new ideas, and master new devices. For managers, change means they have to develop new ways of managing ever-changing employees. It's important for managers to remember that they are not alone in dealing with change—all managers face problems in overcoming inertia and implementing innovation and change.[3]

This chapter is devoted to the process of change. First we will look at the characteristics of change, then examine the role creativity plays in change. Next we

---

This chapter was originally written by Kenneth J. Heymann, Chairman and CEO of UniFocus, Carrollton, Texas.

will discuss how change sponsors, agents, and targets affect the change process. Finally, we will review a change-process model, one that will help you understand what must be done to implement large-scale change within an organization.

Characteristics of Change

Organizational change can be as simple as reorganizing an office or as complex as reorganizing an entire corporation. Change is a constant in many, perhaps most, of today's organizations. Some changes are the planned results of management actions. Other changes are unplanned and generally result from management reactions to problems or situations. Unplanned change can have as much impact on an organization as large-scale, planned change.

In instances of unplanned change, management often reacts less to the root cause(s) of change than to the problems and situations that result from the root cause(s). Too often, management sees no need for change—only a need to act and resolve the resultant problems and situations. This, however, is an attempt at a quick fix; after management reacts, the organization is no better off than before. It is, essentially, the same, waiting for the next "cause of change" to trigger yet another reaction from management. This is a picture of an unhealthy organization; however, not all organizations react this way. Sometimes organizations or people in them are change masters—i.e., people or organizations adept at the art of anticipating the need for, and of leading, productive change.[4]

Planned change occurs when an organization recognizes a coming trend or identifies an opportunity that can be seized only by making changes. While one company changes because it sees opportunity, another may change in response to market forces and a sense that change is essential to survival. Then there are companies that either fail to see impending changes or they refuse to change; these companies often fail.[5]

Organizations constantly involve themselves in changes both large and small. People in organizations constantly swap ideas and make small-scale changes because they work closely together. They reorganize their work space to make it easier to get things. Hotel departments reassign work. Housekeepers decide to put bed linen in pillowcases to help with presorting in the laundry. Accounts receivable clerks start meeting with meeting planners to review group bills prior to the groups' departures. All these minor changes occur with little fuss, and are usually well received.

By contrast, management actions leading to large-scale change are typically initiated outside any specific work group. This may be one of the reasons why workers are so resistant to this type of change. This kind of change is often more than just a new solution to a particular problem. Large-scale change is more significant, has greater impact, and, potentially, is riskier for an organization.

External Forces of Change

External forces of change are forces outside management's control to which an organization must react. Managers must be alert to these forces, which is why organizations are always scanning the external environment. Since, however, these external forces are uncontrolled by management, they foster unplanned change in an organization. External forces of change include technological changes, market changes, competitive changes, and work force changes.

Technological Changes. It's difficult to remember what business was like before computers, faxes, modems, cell phones, the Internet, and online social networks. Back then, people sent letters and made land-line telephone calls. Information moved at what, in retrospect, was a leisurely pace. Today, information moves instantaneously. This has had several significant effects on how business gets done. Information is accessible to more people. More information is available, which means there is more to process, digest, and analyze. Nonetheless, perhaps paradoxically, everyone expects quicker decisions and quicker responses. Thus, there is constant pressure to increase the rate of change.

As is clearly evidenced by developments over the past decade, we can be assured that technology will continue to evolve at an ever more rapid pace. If personal computers, cell phones, and the Internet were virtually unimaginable 30 years ago, it is safe to assume that we cannot foresee the technological changes of the next 30 years. And if we can't foresee these changes, we certainly can't foresee their impact on business organizations. New technology will continue to force unplanned changes on businesses, as managers try to adjust their organizations to take advantage of new technology.

Market Changes. Just as technology is changing rapidly, so too are markets. Globally, new markets are opening in Eastern Europe, Asia, and Africa. For example, Vietnam has become a big player in Asian tourism; forty years ago it was a country at war and definitely not a place that tourists wanted to visit. Locally, markets are changing as consumer habits change, and as virtually all businesses work harder to determine what consumers want and what they're willing to pay for in a volatile economy. Managers must continue to react to ever-changing market currents.

Competitive Changes. Business environments are ever more competitive. Technology has enabled companies to enter markets more rapidly. Changes in the financial industry have made it easier for fledgling organizations to acquire start-up capital. Each year, more companies are formed, and more fail. As old competitors change and new competitors come out of the woodwork, managers have to change their own organizations to remain competitive. Only a few years ago, the competitive environment was fairly stable; businesspeople knew all of the players in their particular fields, exactly what they marketed, and to whom. Not anymore.

Work Force Changes. America has always had a diverse work force when one considers the influx of immigrants over the last 150 years. Schools have educated immigrant children and factories have employed their immigrant parents. But there was a time when management was largely made up of white males, and the majority of immigrants were from European cultures. Today, the work force is more diverse. Immigrants come from every continent and enter the work force in a wide range of positions. Each year, more women and minorities graduate from college and enter management. Organizations have found themselves adjusting to employees who speak Spanish, Vietnamese, and Tagalog. Regardless of the type of business, communication is more difficult, and—because of higher employee expectations—it requires more attention from management. One cultural group expects direct and candid communication, while another values subtlety and discretion. Whichever is appropriate, managers are expected to change with the times and acknowledge cultural differences in dealing with the new work force.

Internal Forces of Change

Internal forces of change are the ideas managers and employees have for improving their organizations. These changes are proactive attempts by managers and employees to make their organizations better.

There are many methods managers use to foster change within their organizations. Examples of changes managers control that are used in many organizations today include reinvention, reengineering, and continuous improvement programs.

Reinvention. Reinvention involves more than a few fundamental changes. "Reinvention is not changing what is, but creating what isn't. A butterfly is not more caterpillar or a better or improved caterpillar; a butterfly is a different creature."[6] Reinvention is perhaps the most extreme form of change, because it requires an organization to rethink every aspect of how it conducts business. Nothing is taken for granted or assumed, and "That's the way we've always done it" will not explain or justify anything. Reinvention inevitably involves conflict and confusion because it forces people to start with the most essential question: What business are we in? Reinvention is redefining the organization's task and how it goes about completing that task.

Reengineering. Reengineering involves the complete redesign of a process within an organization, as compared to the redesign of the organization as a whole (reinvention). Reengineering is not an attempt at incremental improvement; the goal is a dramatic improvement, a 20- to 50-percent improvement in the time it takes to complete a task, or a 100-percent improvement in accuracy, and so on. As was the case with reinvention, successful reengineering efforts also require the elimination of assumptions and the ignoring of "the way we've always done it." For example, one hotel recognized an opportunity to improve guest service by combining room service, bell service, and housekeeping deliveries. Realizing that all three departments were involved in delivering things to guestrooms, management determined that this could be done more effectively by creating a new department, called "Service Express," with all personnel trained to provide the appropriate services. Rather than look at how to make three separate areas more effective, management ignored conventional assumptions that the rooms division and the food and beverage division are separate, and looked at desired performance only. Properly managed, reengineering results in significant improvements in quality and efficiency.

Continuous Improvement. Continuous improvement goes by many names—total quality management (TQM), process management, quality improvement programs (QIP), leaning organizations, and knowledge organizations, to name a few.

Regardless of the name, the goal of a continuous-improvement program is to create an organization that is constantly learning and improving.

Fostering Change

There are many reasons why organizations need to change, but without a recognized need, there is no motivation to change. Thus, the first step in any planned change process is to recognize the need for change and begin communicating the need throughout the organization. Thus, as always, recognition of a problem is perhaps more important than the solution.

Good leaders recognize trends and new market forces on the horizon. By communicating a picture of the future to the organization, they can begin the change process. They have the power to make change an organizational imperative.

Sometimes it is not the organization's leaders that first recognize the need for change. Often, people at lower levels within an organization sense the need for change and communicate this need upward. People at lower levels are often closer to customers and trends, or are running into problems that the organization's leaders don't face but that could have a significant impact on the organization.

Crises of various types—a stock market crash, a severe devaluation of real estate, an equipment failure—can stimulate change. These crises may come from inside or outside the organization.

Some organizations are more successful at creating and responding to change than others. Pro-change organizations promote innovation. They tend to encourage the free flow of ideas, have open boundaries, and empower employees. They believe in the slogan, "If it ain't broke, fix it." Anti-change organizations promote turf battles and resist change—they go by the more well-known motto, "If it ain't broke, don't fix it."

Creativity and Change

Creativity leads to innovation; innovation leads to change; change helps foster creativity: it's a constant circle. As Exhibit 1 shows, the creativity-innovation-change cycle never ends. Once started, it tends to build speed as the ability to create, innovate, and change becomes more pronounced. Organizations that embrace this cycle adapt quickly and develop new products or services before others do, while organizations that resist it fall further and further behind. The 3M company is a great example of an organization that pursues this cycle. At 3M, many products are developed through creative accidents—i.e., while trying to develop something else. Post-it Notes, for example, came about while attempting to develop a different kind of glue that would hold when needed but also release easily. In 3M's corporate culture, creativity and innovation are valued. An idea such as the one for Post-it Notes can bring about immediate change, as the company shifts gears to make a brand new, unforeseen product. The more often this happens, the more quickly a company can shift gears as it learns how to react to and embrace innovation and change.

Exhibit 1   The Creativity-Innovation-Change Cycle

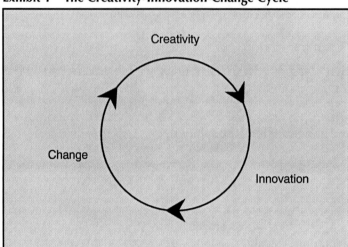

What Creativity Is and Is Not

Being playful and childlike or acting like a slightly crazy person is not the same thing as being creative, and not all creative people behave in those ways. While an inhibited person is not as likely to embrace creativity easily, this does not mean that all uninhibited people are creative. People who stick to logic—perhaps the enemy of creativity—are less likely to create or innovate, because creative or innovative ideas are oftentimes illogical. Creative people and organizations observe things around them; people who observe well are generally more creative than those who do not. While many creative people have a rich fantasy life, this is not a requirement; however, dogmatic people who resist change are generally not creative. If you are concerned with the meanings and implications of problems (not just the problems themselves), you are likely to be creative. Creative people can be nonconformists at times, which reflects a value of independence. Many creative people have a good sense of humor.

While some people seem to have a bent for creativity, this does not mean that the rest of us cannot become more creative. Even though some people may have a predilection for creativity, it can be learned. Managers, leaders, and organizations should strive to be more creative, because creativity gives them the ability to innovate and change—vital attributes in this fast-changing world. Exhibit 2 is a simple test you can take to assess your creativity.

Creative Organizations

Few organizations are creative. As just noted, those that are creative innovate more rapidly. So, what defines a creative organization? One of the major characteristics of creative organizations is that employees are allowed to exercise a great deal of autonomy. Creative organizations also encourage open communication at all levels,

Exhibit 2   Example of a Simple Creativity Test

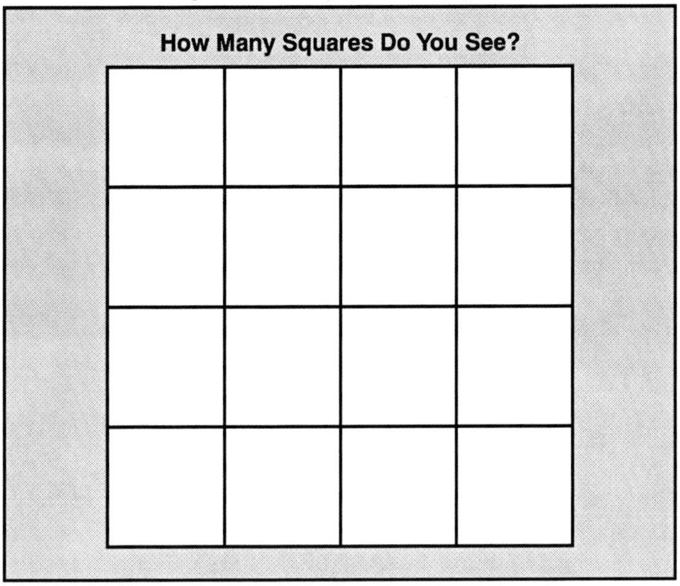

How Many Squares Do You See?

How many squares did you see in this exhibit? Most people see the small sixteen squares first, and, for some people, that is all they see. But then, there is also the big outside square that encompasses the sixteen smaller squares. There are also nine more 2 × 2 squares—that is, squares made up of four of the smaller squares. Finally, some people see the four 3 × 3 squares. How many did you see? Highly creative people see them all.

transcend organizational boundaries and silos, hire people with diverse backgrounds to avoid the potential for groupthink, evaluate ideas on their own merits (not on the status of the ideas' originators), encourage research, allow people to take risks, and often use techniques designed to help people become more creative. Autonomous employees have the freedom to think outside the box and design new and better ways to do things. Open communication allows people to speak their minds, which can spark ideas; entities like departmental silos, on the other hand, inhibit communication and organizational effectiveness. A diverse group of people will come up with more ideas than a homogenous group, simply because the group's range of experiences and understanding is much broader.

Innovation. Creating ideas is the first step in innovation. After organizations or people come up with ideas, they can apply logic to determine which of them might be useful. The key is creating new ideas and then applying logic appropriately, so that both creativity and logic are used. Innovation can be seen as the first commercialization of a creative idea.[7] The person who creates the idea and the person who innovates it may be different people, of course, and an idea may sit around for a while before someone comes up with a way to use it.[8] The role of the innovator is to figure out a way to put the idea into practice.

The Champion. Every new idea needs a champion—someone who will take charge of the idea and bring it to fruition.[9] Picture a champion as someone who stands up and moves forward with the idea while saying, "Follow me!" The champion has to assume responsibility and stick with the idea until it reaches maturity. Getting a new idea started in an organization can be difficult, so tenacity, or the ability to see the idea through its often winding and tortuous road toward implementation, is an absolute must. Champions typically must (1) have a deep and emotional commitment to the idea; (2) be extremely knowledgeable about the issue, product, and/or service in question; and (3) be willing and able to stick with the idea long enough to see it through.[10]

Roles in the Change Process

To understand how change, creative and otherwise, occurs in an organization, three questions must be addressed: Who wants the change? Who is making the change? Who is changing? In his article "Achieving Change in People," Darwin Cartwright answers these questions by defining three groups: change sponsors, change agents, and change targets.[11] The lines between these definitions are not always absolutely clear. A manager who decides to reorganize a department may be both change sponsor and agent, and—ultimately—a change target.

Change Sponsors

Change sponsors are the individuals or groups within an organization that have the power and influence to initiate and implement change. The primary roles of a change sponsor are to envision the needed change, create a **vision statement,** and inspire others with this vision. To carry out this role effectively, change sponsors must:

- Be fully convinced of the need for change.
- Understand the role they have to play in the change process.
- Have a clear vision of the desired outcomes of change.
- Know where the organization is, at present, relative to the desired change.
- Understand the implications of change for managers and employees.
- Be willing to provide the necessary resources to implement the change.
- Create an appropriate time frame for achieving the change.
- Know what the consequences will be if the change does not occur.
- Understand the measurements used to evaluate the success of the change.

When a proposed change has large-scale implications, the change sponsor must occupy a high position within the organization. For example, if the corporate management team of a restaurant chain decides to implement a total quality management system, the appropriate change sponsor would be the president or CEO of the company. Acting alone, the corporate vice president of human resources would not have the amount of power and influence necessary to sustain this kind of change effort throughout the organization. When a proposed change affects the operation of a single division or department, the change sponsor should be the highest manager within that division or department.

The most important task of a change sponsor is to lead, to persuade people to support the change. Change affects how people feel about themselves, their work, the organization, and their place in the organization. Change sponsors must address these issues. Members of the organization expect a change sponsor to set an appropriate example and help them understand the context and the purpose of the change.

Change sponsors choose the change agents, and must support both the change agents and the change targets. This requires guts and leadership.

All change efforts encounter resistance. This is both inevitable and understandable. Inevitable, because the new and unknown lead to insecurity and fear; understandable, because insecurity and fear are typical human responses:

> Without strong leadership from top management, the psychological and political disruptions that accompany...radical change can sabotage the project. Inevitably, managers and employees may feel that their turf, jobs, and organizational equilibrium are under attack. But opposition to the new design can be overcome if top-level managers approach reengineering [i.e., change] as a painful but necessary disruption of the status quo.[12]

Exhibit 3 takes a humorous approach in telling change sponsors what they should avoid doing if they want to successfully implement change.

Change Agents

A **change agent** is a person or group responsible for the day-to-day effort that makes the change happen. Depending on the scope of the change, a change agent may be an individual, an outside consultant, a team, or even several teams scattered throughout the organization. The key is that someone or some group has clear responsibility for the effort.

There are no hard and fast rules as to whether a change agent should be a member of the organization or an outsider. If no credible member of the organization can be assigned to the process, it's best to go outside the organization. Choosing an individual or group with limited credibility instantly damages the change effort. People within the organization quickly decide that the company can't be serious if it's selected someone who doesn't possess the tools to function as a successful change agent.

Unfortunately, many organizations choose individuals with little ability to be change agents because of the fear that the "real work" of the organization will be hampered if top-notch individuals are put in charge of the change effort. In one sense, this mistake is understandable, because the organization must be concerned about its day-to-day performance. But if the change process is to be successful, good people must be put in charge of implementing it and given the time to do so.

To be effective, change agents must:

* Agree with the sponsor's vision statement.

* Be fully convinced of the need for change.

Exhibit 3   A Prescription for Failure

By providing the following prescription for ensuring that change does *not* occur, author Rosabeth Kanter warns change sponsors to avoid certain tactics:

1. Regard any new idea from below with suspicion—because it's new, and because it's from below.
2. Force people who need your approval to do anything to first go through several other levels of managers and get their signatures.
3. Ask departments or individuals to challenge and criticize each others' ideas. (That saves you the job of deciding—you just pick the survivor.)
4. Express your criticisms freely, and withhold your praise. Let people know they can be fired at any time.
5. Treat identification of problems as signs of failure. This discourages people from letting you know when something in their area isn't working.
6. Control everything carefully. Make sure people count anything that can be counted, frequently.
7. Change policies or make reorganization decisions in secret, then spring them on people unexpectedly.
8. Make sure that people fully justify any requests for information; do not give out information freely.
9. Assign to lower-level managers—in the name of delegation and participation— responsibility for figuring out how to cut back on staff, move people around, or otherwise implement unpopular decisions you have made. And make them do it quickly.
10. Above all, never forget that you, the higher-ups, already know everything important about the organization.

Obviously, change sponsors who want to successfully implement change in their organizations would do well to disregard this advice.

Source: Adapted from Rosabeth Moss Kanter, *The Change Masters* (New York: Simon & Schuster, 1984).

- Help develop an implementation plan.
- Know the likely pitfalls of the process and be able to overcome them.
- Appreciate the role of the change sponsor and request support as needed.
- Demonstrate talent and proven credibility within the organization.
- Develop power bases and employ strategies for overcoming resistance to change.
- Be able to refine and use the measurements necessary to evaluate the success of the change.

Effective change agents are highly motivated. Ideally, they are tuned in to informal opinion networks. They must be effective communicators. They must be able to see past short-term setbacks and get past the inevitable obstacles that will arise. Most of all, they must be willing and persistent.

Fifteen Key Competencies of Change Agents

Objectives

1. Sensitivity to changes in key personnel, sensitivity to top management perceptions and market conditions, and sensitivity to the way in which these have an impact on the goals of the project.
2. Ability to set clearly defined, realistic goals.
3. Flexibility in responding to changes without the control of the project manager, perhaps requiring major shifts in project goals and management style.

Roles

4. Team-building abilities, to bring together key stakeholders and establish effective working groups, and to define and delegate respective responsibilities clearly.
5. Networking skills in establishing and maintaining appropriate contacts within and outside the organization.
6. Tolerance of ambiguity, to be able to function comfortably, patiently, and effectively in an uncertain environment.

Communication

7. Communication skills to transmit effectively to colleagues and subordinates the need for changes in project goals and in individual tasks and responsibilities.
8. Interpersonal skills across the range, including selection, listening, collecting appropriate information, identifying the concerns of others, and managing meetings.
9. Personal enthusiasm in expressing plans and ideas.
10. Stimulating motivation and commitment in others involved.

Negotiation

11. Selling plans and ideas to others by creating a desirable and challenging vision of the future.
12. Negotiating with key players for resources, for changes in procedures, and to resolve conflict.

Managing Up

13. Political awareness in identifying potential coalitions, and in balancing conflicting goals and perceptions.
14. Influencing skills, to gain commitment to project plans and ideas from potential skeptics and resisters.
15. Helicopter perspectives, to stand back from the immediate project and take a broader view of priorities.

Source: Adapted from Rosabeth Moss Kanter, *The Change Masters: Corporate Entrepreneurs at Work* (London: Taylor & Francis, 1985).

Change agents can come from any level of the organization. In fact, the broader the scope of the change, the more important it is to have representatives from a variety of organizational levels. A select group of upper-level managers easily overlooks resistance and problems because it tends to be closely knit and shares a vision of change. That's why, in large-scale change efforts, all the organizational constituencies must be considered. The change agents

> must encompass a critical mass of stakeholders—the employees "who really make things happen around here." Some hold sway over key resources. Others are central to informal opinion networks.... The goal is a flywheel effect, where enough key players get involved and enrolled that it creates a momentum to carry the [change] process forward.[13]

Change agents have an ongoing set of responsibilities that must be met to ensure success. They must:

- Establish the context for change and provide guidance.
- Stimulate conversation.
- Provide appropriate resources.
- Coordinate and align projects.
- Ensure congruence of messages, activities, policies, and behaviors.
- Anticipate, identify, and address people problems.[14]

Successful change agents must have the ability to play any of the following roles:

- *Implementer.* Someone who is an effective communicator and an effective motivator.
- *Administrator.* Someone who can control multiple activities, and find and fix problems and bottlenecks.
- *Planner.* Someone who can connect people and resources, and develop guidelines and schedules.
- *Entrepreneur.* Someone who is a risk taker, is future-oriented, and is willing to challenge the organization.
- *System architect.* Someone who is skilled in acquiring, disseminating, and interpreting information.
- *Diplomat.* Someone who sees the organization from a broad perspective and can work with different units within the organization.[15]

In view of the skills and talents suggested in this list, two points should be made. If the scope of change is large enough, a team is needed to meet the needs of the organization. If the scope is small, the organization must decide which of the requisite talents are most important and find someone who possesses them.

While there are innumerable reasons why change fails, poor communication is guaranteed to make change fail. Change agents must fully understand the vision statement and be able to communicate it to the change targets. At the same time, change agents must be sensitive to the various concerns of the targets, and be able to communicate those concerns fairly. More than anyone else, change agents must avoid simplifying the complexities of change. Fostering two-way communication between the change sponsors and the change targets will do far more to make the change successful than can any memo or video from the CEO.

Change Targets

Change targets are individuals or groups within the organization that must change their skills, knowledge, or behaviors because of the planned change. Admittedly, the word "target" has an unappealing connotation; it suggests a passive group that will be the recipient of something, or will have something done to it. However, change targets are active participants in the change process, because they will be the ones doing things differently.

Obviously, the primary resistance to a proposed change comes from the targets. They are the ones who, at first, feel they have the most to lose. If the change targets are not involved in originating the change, it is essential that they understand the need for and purpose of the change. Change agents might communicate the information that has led to the decision to change (poor financial results, new competition, and so on) or paint a bleak picture of the organization's future without the change. In any event, the change targets must have a context that helps them understand the reasons for the change. If they don't know where the organization is going and why it's going there, it will be difficult to get them to go on the trip.

Next, change targets must understand the rewards of the change. At worst, the reward may be as simple as organizational survival. At best, the rewards may be higher wages, more opportunities for growth, or new responsibilities.

All organizations, regardless of how long they have existed, have a culture. It may be explicit in a statement of values or in a mission statement, or it may be implicit and found within the organization's norms and unspoken rules. The more the desired change is consistent with the organization's present values, the more readily it will be accepted. If change targets view the change as a radical departure from the existing culture, they might resist it fiercely. Even if the change is an obvious improvement, it may still be viewed with suspicion. Thus, if the change is not consistent with the organization's values, change sponsors and agents must consistently demonstrate and support the new values.

Change targets are often concerned that the coming change is an indication of poor past performance on their parts. There is no value in lying about or hiding the causes of change. If the change is the result of poor performance, the truth should be told and the concerns addressed. No one is served by being told that everything is great, it just has to be changed. That's a confusing message that doesn't justify change.

Change targets will also be concerned about whether they have the skills and knowledge necessary to implement the change. If new skills and knowledge are necessary, it is the responsibility of the change sponsors and agents to ensure that opportunities to acquire them are made available to the change targets.

Regardless of the scale of change, change targets must perceive solid support for the change from influential individuals in the organization. The change targets must believe that it's okay to take risks and make mistakes. Otherwise, they will avoid trying anything new. If there is a pilot group testing a new approach, the group must be congratulated, even celebrated, for leading the way. If a work group is reengineering a process, it should be encouraged by key individuals within the organization whose opinions are important. If this is not done, the fear of failure will control the change targets' behavior.

Exhibit 4   A Model for Organizational Change

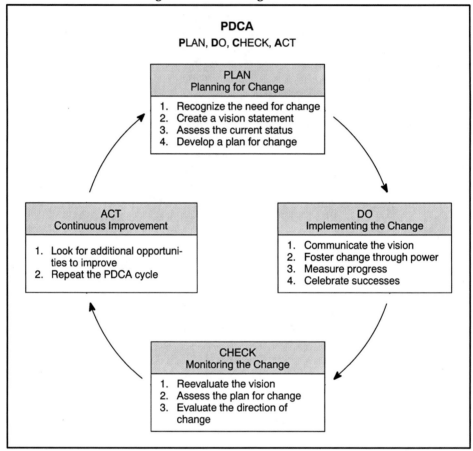

Finally, the change targets must trust and respect the change agents. If they do not, no amount of support from the change sponsor will ensure a successful outcome.

The Change Process

Exhibit 4 presents a model for change that you can use to guide your organization through a major change. This change model is based on the PDCA Cycle. "PDCA" stands for *Plan, Do, Check,* and *Act.* Although studying a model can help us understand the change process, you must remember that change is dynamic. There are multiple activities in any change process, and though breaking up the change process into steps suggests that change processes have clear beginnings and ends, this is not the case. In fact, if change is viewed purely as a set of consecutive activities, change will probably not be successful, because such an approach ignores the complexity of the change process and the interrelationships among its

Exhibit 5   Phase 1 of the Change Model

PLAN Planning for Change
1. Recognize the need for change 2. Create a vision statement 3. Assess the current status 4. Develop a plan for change

components. For example, you should not think that you are finished communicating the vision statement to others once you have done so under Step 1 of the "Do" portion of the change model. As you move through the change process, you will find that the vision must be constantly restated, since resistance will occur at various points in the process and you must continually make the need for change clear.

In the following sections we will take a closer look at each phase of the change model.

Planning for Change

There are four steps in the "Plan" phase of the change model: (1) recognize the need for change, (2) create a vision statement, (3) assess the current status, and (4) develop a plan for change (see Exhibit 5). We will look at each of these steps in the following sections.

Step 1—Recognize the Need for Change. Change occurs when there is a perceived need. The word "perceived" is used because a need becomes a catalyst for change only after someone becomes aware of it. When William Levitt was trying to figure out how to build low-cost houses after the Second World War, he thought of the then-radical notion of constructing nearly identical houses using an assembly-line process. He knew there would be an opportunity for someone who could provide inexpensive housing to the hundreds of thousands of ex-GIs who would be looking to purchase a house. He perceived a need. Kemmons Wilson started building Holiday Inns in the 1950s when he recognized the need families had for convenient and affordable places to stay while traveling.

Need is perceived in many different ways. In the case of Levitt and Wilson, they perceived a need based on thinking about the markets in which they were interested. An organization can define its needs in a more analytical fashion. A SWOT analysis, in which an organization defines *S*trengths, *W*eaknesses, *O*pportunities, and *T*hreats, is one means of defining need. In day-to-day operations recurring problems point to a need for change. On the simplest level, poor financial results can highlight need.

It is preferable to have as many people as possible within an organization understand why changing the organization is necessary. A hotel's general manager can mobilize the initial commitment necessary to begin the change process by helping the hotel's staff develop a shared understanding of what is wrong in the hotel and what can and must be improved. Successful change efforts are built on clearly articulated needs.

Step 2—Create a Vision Statement. A vision statement is the articulation of what the organization will look like after a change is complete. The vision statement defines the organization's response to a perceived need.

It is to the change sponsor that organizations look for vision and leadership. The vision statement sets direction. Specificity is essential. It is not particularly helpful for a change sponsor to say "We need to do better" or "We need to do things differently."

Vision statements range from simple declarations to more detailed descriptions of what is desired and how success will be measured. A well-articulated vision statement clearly communicates the need for change and the direction in which the organization needs to move.

There is no question that there are numerous instances when a vision springs full-grown from the mind of a leader. Many well-known examples of organizational success recount the tale of a single individual's vision (Henry Ford envisioning the assembly line is just one), but creating a vision can also be a group effort. When this is the case, as many people in the organization as possible should be involved, thinking out loud and getting feedback from many different stakeholders. Vision statements tend to be clearer and more understandable when various members or groups in the organization have had an opportunity to contribute. Even when the leader or leadership group has articulated a vision, the rest of the organization needs an opportunity to share in it. To be effective, the vision must have meaning for the change agents and targets as well as the change sponsor. Without a consensus, no vision for change, no matter how brilliant, will succeed:

> The vision must address three fundamental building blocks of all organizations: the technical system—organizing people, capital, information, and technology to produce services or goods; the political system—allocating power, rewards, and career opportunities; and the cultural system—the set of shared norms, beliefs, and values of the organization.[16]

As noted before, people commit to a vision more easily when the vision is consistent with the values held by an organization. Small-scale changes rarely challenge existing values. When large-scale changes call for a new set of values, the vision statement must articulate the desired values, even when this requires repudiating past practices. In circumstances like this, it is essential that the change sponsors, change agents, and other organizational leaders serve as role models for the new, desired values.

Just as the vision statement must address the desired values, it must lay out, at least briefly, the needed changes in structure and resource allocation that will drive the change process.

Articulating a vision for large-scale change that is comprehensible and comprehensive is a daunting task. Resistance is usually encountered on a whole series of levels. Vision must always battle inertia, the tendency of an organization to continue doing what it has been doing. Often, a vision is confronted by cynicism, especially when other change efforts have failed or a management fad has come and gone.

Step 3—Assess the Current Status. Once the need has been realized and the vision articulated, the next step is to determine where the organization is relative to the desired state. Fully understanding the present situation is best accomplished through an analysis that provides as complete a picture of the organization as possible.

The scope of the intended change helps define the scope of the analysis. The more complex the change, the more comprehensive the required analysis. All aspects of the organization are subject to critique: marketing, sales, human resources, operations, finance. No assumptions should be left unquestioned.

Gap analysis. Determining the organization's present status involves measuring present performance and establishing **baseline measurements** of where the organization is now that will later be used to determine the success of the change efforts. For many change efforts, one of the primary causes of failure is the organization's inability to determine what improvements have been made. Without a clear understanding of the present position, it's not possible to assess future success.

Understanding the gap between where the organization is and where it wants to be can begin with some broad measurements. Hotel managers can use market penetration, average rate (both overall and by sub-segment), occupancy percent, labor hours per unit, gross operating profit, or net operating income. These are just a few of the measurements that can be used.

To a large degree, the nature of the change defines the type of analysis that is needed. If, for example, a hotel is trying to reduce its receivables, it may be sufficient to follow the process used, from contract signing through to collection, to determine where breakdowns occur and what steps in the process can be eliminated.

Regardless of the scope of the analysis, it's essential to have appropriate measurements. In the case of a hotel's receivables, the measurements could be percent of receivables, the number of 30-, 60-, and 90-day receivables, receivables as a percent of gross revenues, or even number of days between the departure of groups and the mailing of their bills.

There are far too many methods for conducting analyses to begin an effective review here. The essential point to understand is that determining where "here" is involves establishing appropriate measurement criteria.

Are you ready for change? Before taking the next step—developing a plan for change—now is the time to reassess your organization's readiness for change.

There is never a precise time at which everyone in an organization is ready to embark on a change effort. People generally find it easier to explain why now is not a good time to work at getting better. There are budgets to be done, operational crises to resolve, new staff members to get settled in, and a host of other apparently more pressing problems. As alluded to earlier, a favorite excuse is, "If it ain't broke, don't fix it." This point is usually made when someone is comparing his or her organization's performance to that of competitors and noting that it's not so bad.

If an organization is willing to settle for mediocrity, it probably shouldn't try to change. If an organization is waiting for everyone to demand change for the sake of improvement, then that organization will probably never experience large-scale, planned change. An organization is ready for change only when it recognizes the need for change. Exhibit 6 is a self-assessment tool you can use to gauge your organization's readiness to change.

Step 4—Develop a Plan for Change. You have a clearly perceived need, a clearly articulated vision, and baseline measurements that tell you where the organization is now. To move forward, you must have a coherent plan to create the change you have in mind.

According to Beer, Eisenstat, and Spector, you must start with a plan; you don't start with training:

> It is not an uncommon belief that the place to begin is with the knowledge and attitudes of individuals. Changes in attitudes, the theory goes, lead to changes in individual behavior. And changes in individual behavior, repeated by many people, will result in organizational change. According to this model, change is like a conversion experience. Once people "get religion," changes in their behavior will surely follow.
>
> This theory gets the change process exactly backwards. In fact, individual behavior is powerfully shaped by the organizational roles that people play. The most effective way to change behavior, therefore, is to put people into a new organizational context, which imposes new roles, responsibilities, and relationships on them.[17]

A change plan is a detailed blueprint for putting people into a new organizational context. There are a number of ways to plan change. Change should start with small-scale efforts. Pilot programs and tests help the organization control the change and carefully monitor the success or failure of the various steps. The complexity of the change process generally precludes starting on a large scale because the process can quickly become unmanageable.

Planning change is, ultimately, a management function. Planning is designed to bring about orderly, measurable results. It involves establishing objectives, taking baseline measurements, formulating the criteria for success, and determining the strategies, resources, time frames, and so on needed to achieve the planned change.

Planning tools. Plans must be tailored to the particular circumstances of each organization. No single plan will work in all organizations or under all circumstances. There are a number of ways to plan a change and a variety of tools to use. Tools that we will discuss in this section are force field analysis, critical paths, and action plans.

Force field analysis was developed in the late 1940s by Kurt Lewin, a social scientist. It can be useful both as a means of diagnosing a present situation and as a device for prioritizing activities and developing action plans.

Force field analysis begins with the supposition that any particular situation is the result of dynamic forces that create that situation. Even the status quo is

Exhibit 6   Assessing Your Organization's Readiness to Change

This quiz measures your organization's versatility; the higher the score, the better able your organization is to change when change is needed. The quiz serves a second, equally important purpose: Because it reveals likely causes of failure, it creates an agenda, a list of ways to make a big restructuring or reengineering more likely to be successful in your organization.

This quiz lists 17 key elements of change readiness. Rate your organization on each item. Give 3 points for a high ranking ("We're good at this; I'm confident of our skills here"); 2 for a medium score ("We're spotty here; we could use improvement or more experience"); and 1 point for a low score ("We've had problems with this; this is new to our organization"). Be honest. Don't trust only your own perspective; ask others in the organization, at all levels, to rate the company too.

Readiness Scoring: High = 3; Medium = 2; Low = 1

Category	Score
SPONSORSHIP The sponsor of change is not necessarily its day-to-day leader; he or she is the visionary, chief cheerleader, and bill payer—the person with the power to help the change team when it meets resistance. Give three points— change will be easier—if sponsorship comes at a senior level; for example, CEO, COO, or the head of an autonomous business unit. Weakest sponsors: mid-level executives or staff officers.	
LEADERSHIP This means the day-to-day leadership—the people who call the meetings, set the goals, work till midnight. Successful change is more likely if leadership is high-level, has "ownership" (that is, direct responsibility for what's to be changed) and has clear business results in mind. Low-level leadership, or leadership that is not well-connected throughout the organization (across departments) or that comes from the staff, is less likely to succeed and should be scored low.	
MOTIVATION High points for a strong sense of urgency from senior management, which is shared by the rest of the company, and for a corporate culture that already emphasizes continuous improvement. Negative: traditionbound managers and workers, many of whom have been in their jobs for more than 15 years; a conservative culture that discourages risk taking.	
DIRECTION Does senior management strongly believe that the future should look different from the present? How clear is management's picture of the future? Can management mobilize all relevant parties—employees, the board, customers, etc.—for action? High points for positive answers to those questions. If senior management thinks only minor change is needed, the likely outcome is no change at all; score yourself low.	
MEASUREMENTS Or in consultant-speak, "metrics." Three points if you already use performance measures of the sort encouraged by total quality management (defect rates, time to market, etc.) and if these express the economics of the business. Two points if some measures exist but compensation and reward systems do not explicitly reinforce them. If you don't have measures in place or don't know what we're talking about, one point.	
ORGANIZATIONAL CONTEXT How does the change effort connect to other major goings-on in the organization? (For example: Does it dovetail with a continuing total quality management process? Does it fit with strategic actions such as acquisitions or new product lines?) Trouble lies ahead for a change effort that is isolated or if there are multiple change efforts whose relationships are not linked strategically.	
PROCESSES/FUNCTIONS Major changes almost invariably require redesigning business processes that cut across functions such as purchasing, accounts payable, or marketing. If functional executives are rigidly turf conscious, change will be difficult. Give yourself more points the more willing they—and the organization as a whole—are to change critical processes and sacrifice perks or power for the good of the group.	
COMPETITOR BENCHMARKING Whether you are a leader in your industry or a laggard, give yourself points for a continuing program that objectively compares your company's performance with that of competitors and systematically examines changes in your market. Give yourself one point if knowledge of competitors' abilities is primarily anecdotal—what salespeople say at the bar.	

(continued)

Exhibit 6   *(continued)*

Category	Score
CUSTOMER FOCUS The more everyone in the company is imbued with knowledge of customers, the more likely that the organization can agree to change to serve them better. Three points if everyone in the work force knows who his or her customers are, knows their needs, and has had direct contact with them. Take away points if that knowledge is confined to pockets of the organization (sales and marketing, senior executives).	
REWARDS Change is easier if managers and employees are rewarded for taking risks, being innovative, and looking for new solutions. Team-based rewards are better than rewards based solely on individual achievement. Reduce points if your company, like most, rewards continuity over change. If managers become heroes for making budget, they won't take risks even if you say you want them to. Also: If employees believe failure will be punished, reduce points.	
ORGANIZATIONAL STRUCTURE The best situation is a flexible organization with little churn—that is, reorganizations are rare and well received. Score yourself lower if you have a rigid structure that has been unchanged for more than five years or has undergone frequent reorganization with little success; that may signal a cynical company culture that fights change by waiting it out.	
COMMUNICATION A company will adapt to change most readily if it has many means of two-way communication that reach all levels of the organization and that all employees use and understand. If communications media are few, often trashed unread, and almost exclusively one-way and top-down, change will be more difficult.	
ORGANIZATIONAL HIERARCHY The fewer levels of hierarchy and the fewer employee grade levels, the more likely an effort to change will succeed. A thick impasto of middle management and staff not only slows decision-making but also creates large numbers of people with the power to block change.	
PRIOR EXPERIENCE WITH CHANGE Score three if the organization has successfully implemented major changes in the recent past. Score one if there is no prior experience with major change or if change efforts failed or left a legacy of anger or resentment. Most companies will score two, acknowledging equivocal success in previous attempts to change.	
MORALE Change is easier if employees enjoy working in the organization and the level of individual responsibility is high. Signs of unreadiness to change: low team spirit, little voluntary extra effort, and mistrust. Look for two types of mistrust: between management and employees, and between or among departments.	
INNOVATION Best situation: The company is always experimenting; new ideas are implemented with seemingly little effort; employees work across internal boundaries without much trouble. Bad signs: lots of red tape, multiple sign-offs required before new ideas are tried; employees must go through channels and are discouraged from working with colleagues from other departments or divisions.	
DECISION-MAKING Rate yourself high if decisions are made quickly, taking into account a wide variety of suggestions; it is clear where decisions are made. Give yourself a low grade if decisions come slowly and are made by a mysterious "them," there is a lot of conflict during the process, and a lot of confusion and finger-pointing after decisions are announced.	

IF YOUR SCORE IS

41-51: Implementing change is most likely to succeed. Focus resources on lagging factors (your ones and twos) to accelerate the process.

28-40: Change is possible but may be difficult, especially if you have low scores in the first seven readiness dimensions. Bring those up to speed before attempting to implement large-scale change.

17-27: Implementing change will be virtually impossible without a precipitating catastrophe. Focus instead on (1) building change readiness in the dimensions above, and (2) effecting change through skunkworks or pilot programs separate from the organization at large.

Source: Thomas A. Stewart, "Rate Your Readiness to Change," *Fortune*, February 7, 1994, pp. 109–110. © 1994 Time Inc. All rights reserved.

Exhibit 7   Force Field Analysis

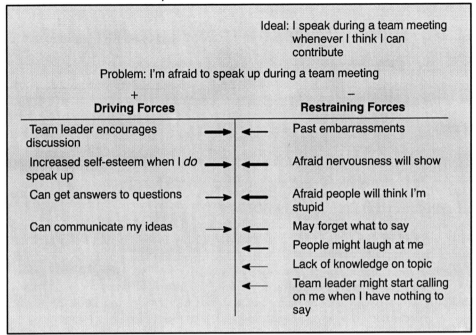

Ideal: I speak during a team meeting
whenever I think I can
contribute

Problem: I'm afraid to speak up during a team meeting

+ Driving Forces		− Restraining Forces
Team leader encourages discussion	→ ←	Past embarrassments
Increased self-esteem when I *do* speak up	→ ←	Afraid nervousness will show
Can get answers to questions	→ ←	Afraid people will think I'm stupid
Can communicate my ideas	→ ←	May forget what to say
	←	People might laugh at me
	←	Lack of knowledge on topic
	←	Team leader might start calling on me when I have nothing to say

ultimately the result of a particular dynamic. Any situation is the result of various forces acting upon that situation, creating a particular balance.

There are two types of forces acting upon any situation. **Driving forces** encourage a particular direction; **restraining forces** inhibit movement in that direction. The interaction of these forces creates an equilibrium, which is perceived as a static situation. Change occurs when adjustments are made to any of the driving or restraining forces, thus altering the equilibrium.

For a simple example of how force field analysis works, suppose that Chris, a dining room manager, wants to figure out why she is reluctant to speak up during meetings of the continuous-improvement team that she's a member of. She draws a large "T" on a sheet of paper, and labels the left side "plus" or driving forces, the right side "minus" or restraining forces (see Exhibit 7). Above the "T" she writes the problem she is analyzing, and the solution to the problem or the ideal she would like to strive for. Under "driving forces," she lists those forces that are driving her toward the solution or ideal; under "restraining forces," she lists those forces that are holding her back from attaining the solution or ideal. The thickness or thinness of the arrows indicates the strength of the forces; a thick arrow indicates a strong force, a thin arrow indicates a weaker force. (The lengths of the arrows, or a number assigned to each arrow—a range of 1 to 5, with 1 indicating "very weak," 5 indicating "very strong," for example—can also be used to indicate relative strengths.) As you can see, at present the restraining forces are stronger than the driving forces, so Chris is not likely to voluntarily contribute ideas or comments during team meetings until she can strengthen the driving forces or weaken or remove some of the restraining forces.

Another example: suppose that long lines frequently form in a hotel restaurant. The driving forces creating long lines would be short-term high demand (a lot of people want to eat at the same time), shortage of tables, occasional staff shortages, and so on. The restraining forces, which keep the lines from being even longer, are availability of alternative food and beverage outlets at the hotel, a buffet in the restaurant, and groups having banquets. Adjust any of these factors, and you will affect the line length.

Imagine that a company is dealing with a high turnover rate. The driving forces that contribute to people leaving include poor training, limited advancement opportunities, and unsatisfactory pay levels. The restraining forces that keep the turnover rate from being higher include pleasant working conditions and friendly co-workers. As with the other examples, working on any or all of the separate forces will affect the turnover rate.

Force field analysis makes it clear that change is initiated by making adjustments to any of a number of driving and restraining forces. Lewin described this as "unfreezing" the present situation. Adjustments to the forces create a new dynamic, which becomes the new state of equilibrium. This state can then be frozen, so that the change is stabilized. As will be discussed later, there are many instances when organizations backslide and return to the original state.

A **critical path** is a series of activities or steps that guide the change process. Exhibit 8 is an example of a critical path developed for the change effort of a small hotel group. The effort's change sponsor is the vice president of operations, and a project coordinator was selected as the change agent. The perceived need was to establish service consistency among the group's properties in order to stabilize the organization's position in the market.

Action plans outline the tasks to be completed for each step in the critical path. A basic action plan will have the following sections: the task to be completed, who is responsible for completing the task, a list of obstacles (obstacles in the broadest sense—such a list could include needed resources, time from another individual, etc.), a target date or deadline, and the date the task is actually completed. Exhibit 9 shows sample action plans for tasks 1 and 2 listed as part of the critical path in Exhibit 8.

Implementing the Change

Once the change has been planned, the plan must be implemented. It is primarily the change agent who is responsible for implementing the change process. Depending on the scope of the desired change, the change agent may be an individual or a group. Individuals can manage the change process at a single unit, assuming the change sponsor provides appropriate support. For change that spans multiple units, groups tend to be necessary to cope with and manage all the issues that need to be addressed in various locations.

Jeanie Duck proposes the use of a "transition management team (TMT)" for large-scale change. "The TMT oversees the large-scale corporate change effort; it makes sure that all the change initiatives fit together. It is made up of 8 to 12 highly

Exhibit 8   Sample Objectives and Critical Path

Objectives

- To develop a series of operating standards that will establish minimum performance levels for all Hotel Company properties.
- To develop these standards in a manner that avoids the historical approach of top-level management developing standards that are then imposed upon the properties.
- To develop appropriate systems and mechanisms that will ensure Hotel Company's ability to monitor and manage the consistent achievement of the standards.
- To maintain an annual occupancy growth of 2 points.

Critical Path

Task	Responsibility	Obstacles	Deadline	Completion
1. Conduct planning session.				
2. Gather appropriate data (quantitative and qualitative) from transient and group guests. Collate/organize results.				
3. Gather qualitative data from employees and collate/organize results.				
4. Benchmark performance relative to other firms.				
5. Develop preliminary standards and review.				
6. Conduct necessary studies to assess present performance levels.				
7. Implement standards.				
8. Assess validity and verify with guests.				
9. Make any necessary adjustments to standards.				
10. Develop tools for monitoring performance on an ongoing basis.				
11. Determine information system flow, from unit level to corporate.				
12. Final review and implementation of standards and assessment tools.				

talented leaders [change agents] who commit all their time to making the transition a reality."[18] A TMT is different from a steering committee in that members of a TMT work on the change effort full-time, while change agents on a steering committee convene periodically to review progress and provide guidance. However,

Exhibit 9 Sample Action Plans

Critical Path

1. Conduct planning session.

Action Plan

Task	Responsibility	Obstacles	Deadline	Completion
a. Lay out the time frames for the process.				
b. Determine data collection methods for gathering information about desired standards: • Develop questions for use with customer focus groups. • Develop questionnaire for meeting planners and/or major corporate clients. • Develop methods for ensuring employee participation via question-naires or focus groups.				
c. Establish criteria for determining success of the process.				
d. Determine how best to establish baseline measurements of the hotel's current performance.				
e. Determine what organizations, if any should be used to develop benchmarks for service standards.				
f. Develop means of coordinating information gathered to develop standards.				
g. Determine how best to prepare all hotel properties for the impending changes.				

2. Gather appropriate data (quantitative and qualitative) from transient and group guests. Collate/organize results.

Action Plan

Task	Responsibility	Obstacles	Deadline	Completion
a. Develop survey instrument.				
b. Develop cover letter for distribution with survey.				
c. Distribute survey.				
d. Contact and invite potential focus group participants.				
e. Organize focus groups.				
f. Summarize survey responses.				
g. Conduct focus groups.				
h. Summarize focus group results.				

Exhibit 10   Phase 2 of the Change Model

DO Implementing the Change
1. Communicate the vision 2. Foster change through power 3. Measure progress 4. Celebrate successes

steering committees can be successful if the members have the necessary authority and work well with the change agent.

Another approach that can be effective involves putting together a cross-functional team, with members from different disciplines. This approach involves individuals who dedicate an agreed-on portion of their time to the change process. In essence, this is a compromise between a steering committee and a TMT. The team members still have operating responsibilities in their designated areas, but also have direct responsibility for managing key components of the change process.

The key issue for determining how many change agents are needed to implement the change is the size of the change. Large-scale, organization-wide change is effectively managed by a TMT. Unit-level change can be managed by a steering committee or cross-functional team. Small-scale change can be managed by an individual or department head.

The steps of "Implementing the Change" are (1) communicate the vision, (2) foster change through power, (3) measure progress, and (4) celebrate successes (see Exhibit 10).

Step 1—Communicate the Vision. People in the organization may need to hear the vision repeated over and over before they believe that, this time, the call for change is not just a whim or a passing fad. It takes time for people to hear, understand, and believe the message. If they don't particularly like what they hear, then it takes them even more time to come to terms with the concept of change.[19]

Because change sponsors and agents work on the vision well before they begin to communicate it, it quickly seems old to them. But it's not old to the people who must achieve it. To them, it is new, and they need time to get used to it, understand it, and buy into it.

Everything the leaders in the change process do, and don't do, sends a message. If change agents distribute the vision statement in a memo and don't refer to it again, the vision will be filed away and forgotten along with the memo. When managers and staff can repeat and explain the vision statement, the organization has begun the journey:

Once top-level managers have resisted the temptation to stick with the status quo and have dedicated themselves and their best performers to the project, they must take a final—and crucial—step. By communicating openly, using a variety of methods, managers will encourage frank discussion, build consensus and commitment, ensure a common understanding of the need for change, foster participative problem solving, celebrate and reinforce accomplishments, and make continuous improvement a company value.[20]

One of the keys to communicating the vision is communicating the facts and circumstances that require the change. Virtually no one will willingly change for the sake of change. People will change when they understand why they have to. Thus, the vision must be given a context. Whatever information or circumstances created the need, these should be communicated. One of the change sponsors' and agents' key roles is to ensure that everyone is educated about the need that inspired the change and the vision statement.

Organizations experiencing severe operating problems are certainly more open to change than those that appear to be doing well. Generally speaking, the better the condition of the organization, the harder it will be to communicate the vision and convince company staff of the need for change.

Step 2—Foster Change Through Power: The Politics of Change. "The politics of change" refers to the use of power to implement new ideas in an organization. Change agents must understand the operation of power and politics in organizations. To deny the reality or importance of power and politics is to deny the reality of the way organizations really function. Change sponsors and agents must develop power bases if they want the change effort to be successful.

Organizations undergoing change often become political arenas with individual managers jockeying for power and influence. Change agents must acknowledge the presence and importance of power. In fact, power and its use should not be viewed with discomfort or embarrassment. First, power is a fundamental attribute of any organization. It is there, regardless of whether it's a force for improvement or a force for decline. Properly used, power is what moves organizations forward and keeps them growing. Top managers who do not recognize their power are fooling themselves. No matter how much power resides at the top, organizations have pockets of power throughout.

Keeping in mind that implementing change involves the appropriate use of power, a change agent's ability to be effective is a function of four factors:

1. *The change agent's own power bases.* With whom is the change agent closely allied? How much power and influence do these people have?

2. *The power bases of others.* With whom are these other people allied? How much power and influence do these people have?

3. *Situational awareness (appropriate organizational behaviors).* How attuned is the agent to day-to-day organizational pressures? If a change agent insists on meeting with the chef while the kitchen is, literally, on fire, the agent needs to be more situationally aware.

4. *Personal awareness (strategies that work well for a particular person).* Ideally, you should be able to discuss anything with anybody at any time, but the real world doesn't work that way. Some people are best approached at certain times or under certain circumstances. Effective change agents recognize this.

Power bases. Earlier, the importance of dealing with resistance was discussed. Effective change management requires making plans to determine the sources of resistance and deal with them. There also are people who are open to new ideas and new approaches. These people, brought together, can form an effective power base. In large, multi-unit organizations, these innovators may come from different units. At the single unit level, they may come from various departments.

Joseph M. Juran, one of the pioneers of the quality management movement, describes three primary positions taken by people when an organization undertakes large-scale change:

- *Explorers.* These people are aware of the need for change and are open to new ideas. They provide the testing ground for new approaches. Rosabeth Moss Kanter, author of *The Change Masters*, defines "change masters" as those people and organizations that are adept at the art of anticipating the need for, and of leading, productive change. They tend to share several characteristics. They're enthusiastic. If they're unhappy, they speak out, but don't spend a lot of time whining and muttering. They tinker with new approaches and discuss new ideas. They tend to be leaders of their work group, regardless of titles. These people are rare.

- *Conservatives.* These people are wary of change, but don't oppose change on principle. They're willing to change once it's been demonstrated that the change produces good results. As a rule, their objections are logical. Most people fall into this group.

- *Inhibitors.* These people are not convinced by logical reasons or demonstrated results. They do not like change and are absolutely unwilling to participate in it. They accept change only because they do not want to openly remain in a small minority, or because they believe that their jobs are threatened.

One of the major mistakes some organizations make when they try to implement long-term change is to choose a manager who is an inhibitor to lead the effort. The strategy behind this approach is, "If it works with Joe, it will work with everybody." Of course, Joe makes sure it doesn't work, because he doesn't want it to. He then claims to have proof that change cannot be successful. The organization is left to pick up the pieces of Joe's failed effort.

While this is the wrong way to embark upon change, it's still fairly common. Asking inhibitors to pilot a change process is a lot like asking an early twentieth-century railroad president to help prove that airplanes can be used for commercial travel. It's not very surprising when the president says it just won't work.

The key is to find the innovators and make them the champions of the change process. These are the people, scattered throughout the organization, who will help sow the seeds of success. They are the ones who are not afraid to fail. Change agents must create success with them first. Only then can the organization begin working with the conservatives. Conservatives won't be won over right away, but ignoring them creates unnecessary opposition. Allowing them to be involved makes it easier for them to jump on the bandwagon when they see it gaining momentum. Change agents should deal with inhibitors last.

Power strategies. There are no absolute rules as to how you should behave when implementing change. But there are a number of useful guidelines that address issues of power and politics within an organization:

1. *Present a nonthreatening image.* If you are a change agent, it is important for you to be perceived as conservative and essentially nonthreatening to existing organizational activities. Learn your organization's repertoire of acceptable arguments and cast change proposals within these terms. The point is not that you shouldn't rock the boat, because that is precisely what you are trying to do. But the boat can be rocked without personally offending anyone, and without being disdainful of the organization's history or previous efforts.

2. *Deal with conflict.* Rather than stifle opposition, diffuse it through an open discussion of ideas. Left unaddressed, conflict invariably intensifies.

   People can use any of five approaches to deal with conflict. They can collaborate, compete, accommodate, compromise, or avoid. *Collaboration* is the most productive approach to conflict management. With collaboration, the conflicting parties develop an approach or solution together. It is the most effective way to ensure commitment and buy-in from everyone. Many people, especially those in authority, are prone to *compete* when confronted with conflict. There are times when competition is an appropriate approach, especially when dealing with inhibitors. But competition usually creates alienation, and should only be used after other alternatives have been explored. *Accommodation* is a highly useful approach on issues of little importance, or that have no long-term impact. It's natural to want to win all points, but sometimes it's useful to simply let the other person or group have their way. *Compromise* is, unfortunately, far too common an approach to conflict management. Compromise means that each party gets a little bit of what it wants, but not all. Compromise can be useful as a final means of moving forward, but is not as effective as collaboration. *Avoidance* is the worst approach to take in dealing with conflict, because it doesn't deal with the conflict at all. Avoidance is not the same as putting off dealing with something until a later time. This is an appropriate strategy under certain circumstances, but permanently avoiding dealing with issues will inevitably damage the change process.

3. *Align with a powerful other.* Gain top management approval. Even more effective are alliances with line or operating managers who will be directly affected by the change.

4. *Touch bases.* Keep top-level people informed of the change, especially if it's going to have an impact on them at some later point. While it's important to stay out of ivory towers, it's equally important to make sure that the folks in the towers know what's going on so they don't suddenly get the urge to pour boiling water on anyone's head.

5. *Trade off.* Your ability to introduce change programs may hinge on the amount of stature you have. Your stature can be enhanced by first attending to projects or programs designed to meet people's immediate needs. For example, during one change effort, an executive housekeeper didn't want to implement a new program for inspecting guestrooms because she was battling the laundry over linen supplies and distribution, and didn't feel she had the time to properly oversee the new program. Once the change agent helped her resolve the linen supply problem to her satisfaction, she implemented the new inspection program.

6. *Strike while the iron is hot.* Follow up a successful program with a request for approval to implement a somewhat unpopular or less-well-understood program.

7. *Inch along.* Achieving change in small increments is preferable to an "all-or-nothing" stance.

8. *Withdraw.* If you're not getting anywhere, or someone else or some other group is trying to lead the effort and you can't work with them, leave the field of play.

Step 3—Measure Progress. Although measurement is often seen as the province of accountants and controllers, its usefulness in managing the change process transcends merely keeping score. Measurement, made visible and public, plays an essential role in the change process.

Probably many baseline measurements were defined during the planning process, but only a few of them can be considered key measurements. Change agents should regularly communicate these key measurements to staff. Whenever possible, employees should participate in measuring, especially when the item being measured is one over which they have considerable or total control and influence. Whatever measurements are used, they should be understood by the largest number of employees possible.

Accurate and well-communicated measurements are particularly important once the change process is under way. People are far more likely to stay the course if the measurements help them understand that they are actually making progress. If they have no evidence of progress, they are far less likely to support change efforts.

There are many potential forms of measurement. The following is a partial list of those that would be suitable for a hotel:

- Increased occupancy percentage
- Increased average daily rate (ADR)
- Increased market penetration
- Increased rate yield
- Increased gross operating profit
- Increased net operating income
- Increased sales dollars per hour
- Lower unit cost

- Reduced dollar expenditures
- Lower cost per occupied room
- Lower cost per cover
- Fewer FTEs (full-time equivalent employees)
- Fewer shifts per day
- Shorter cycle time for work processes
- Higher rate of return customers
- Better comment card scores
- Higher inspection scores
- Fewer guest complaints
- Lower recovery costs (fewer meals or drinks given free to dissatisfied customers)

These are just a few of the measures that can be used. Regardless of the measurements used, it is important that they be valid indicators of progress and that change agents take them and communicate them on a regular basis.

Step 4—Celebrate Successes. Celebrating successes gives change sponsors and agents opportunities to restate and reemphasize the vision statement. Because change is difficult, it's important to recognize successes when they occur. This is not to suggest that change efforts are well served with a lot of cheerleading and phony congratulations, and celebrating success does not require throwing a party every Friday. Celebrating success does require that change sponsors and agents regularly make the organization aware of improvements, both big and small.

Celebrating involves recognizing. Recognizing the change, recognizing the improvements, and—most of all—recognizing the people who made it happen. From minor pats on the back to more formal awards, change sponsors and agents have many ways to acknowledge and celebrate the accomplishments of participants.

It is important to focus the recognition on results, not just hard work. Many change programs fail even though everyone's been congratulated for a lot of hard work. This is where measurement can play an essential role. You should celebrate accomplishments, not just involvement.

In multi-unit organizations, newsletters should have a section devoted to the change effort. This gives people involved in the process a place to look for the latest news. In some organizations, special recognition programs have been developed, such as "Change Master" clubs. At the unit level, recognition can be delivered via staff meetings, the unit's newsletter, a monthly manager's meeting, or any of a variety of available methods.

In certain circumstances, financial rewards such as bonuses or compensatory time (where legal) provide an appropriate means of celebration. Rewards can also come in the form of gifts or the use of facilities. When providing rewards, it's important to ensure that the reward is one that the recipient will value and feel comfortable with.

Exhibit 11 Phase 3 of the Change Model

CHECK
Monitoring the Change

1. Reevaluate the vision
2. Assess the plan for change
3. Evaluate the direction of change

Monitoring the Change

The third phase of the change model involves three steps: reevaluating the vision, assessing the plan for change, and evaluating the direction of change (see Exhibit 11).

Step 1—Reevaluate the Vision. Since the change vision was driven by a perceived need, you should start reevaluating the vision by revisiting the circumstances or situation that created the need in the first place. Are the circumstances moving in the expected direction? Have any new variables been introduced? Has business been getting better or worse? Many organizations abandon change efforts when they see an improvement in business. Short-term improvements do not mean that the circumstances that caused the need for change are no longer valid and the change process should be abandoned.

If the organization has followed the change process well to this point, everyone involved should understand the vision. This can easily be verified through discussion with people at various levels in the organization. Do they know what the vision is? Is it current and meaningful, or has it been superseded by a new directive?

Perception is everything. If people think the change vision has been forgotten by upper management or was just a passing phase, then the change effort is in trouble. If the vision has been forgotten, it's important to find out what happened. Was it something the change sponsors did, or more probably, didn't do? Were the change agents ineffective? Were department heads less than supportive?

By now, everyone should be so familiar with the vision that any questions about objectives and goals should be easily related to it. Any activity should be critiqued within the context of the vision. If people aren't sure that they're working toward the vision, they probably aren't.

Step 2—Assess the Plan for Change. If there are problems with the change process, they probably originated in the planning phase. Simple mistakes can hamper progress or even lead to failure. If the organization isn't where it expected to be, and the consensus is that everyone's expectations (in terms of progress) were in sync, you need to assess the mistakes made in planning.

It's easy to establish unrealistic time frames when planning. People tend to overestimate how many projects can be accomplished in a given period. When deadlines are constantly missed, frustration sets in, and all the tasks involved in implementing the change become more daunting.

Did people lack needed knowledge or skills? Or did they overestimate their knowledge or skills? Just as people are prone to say that something can be done in a week when they need three weeks, they are also likely to say "Oh sure, I know how to do that" when they don't.

Were resources that you planned on not provided, for financial or other reasons? Were there unexpected obstacles that were not foreseen when the plan for change was put together?

These are just a few of the potential problems that may be encountered. None of them are easy to solve, but all must be dealt with, which means the change plan may have to be adjusted.

Step 3—Evaluate the Direction of Change. The more frequently the organization measures progress, the less susceptible the process is to break down. Yet, many change sponsors and agents shy away from measurement, for fear that it will demonstrate that progress isn't being made. This is absurd. If measurements reveal that change efforts undertaken thus far have not moved the organization forward, this gives change sponsors and agents a chance to reevaluate efforts and make adjustments. If measurements indicate progress, all involved can be reassured that what they're doing has value.

Sometimes the wrong measurement is selected, or the measurement used is not easily related to the change effort undertaken. For example, choosing to measure the success of an employee training program by whether gross operating profit (GOP) increases would be a mistake. Too many other factors might influence GOP: decreased competition, overall improvements in area ADR and occupancy, reductions in supply costs, and so on. But the success of the training program can be tied to reductions in employee turnover, reductions in service errors, or increased compliments on guest comment cards.

At this point in the change process, an organization has lived with its change effort for some time, and measurements should reveal the direction in which the organization is headed. Chances are, measurements will reveal that the organization is headed in one of three directions: failure, plateau, or success.

The path to failure. Many change efforts fail, some miserably. For various reasons, people reject the change or deny that it's needed. When the path to failure is pursued, the next step is breakdown. Resources devoted to change are rechanneled. The vision is changed or denied (a common occurrence when new executives take over) and the organization returns to what we simply call "point zero." Basically, things go back to the way they were.

Failure can occur for many reasons:

1. The change wasn't well-planned.

2. The measurements weren't valid or the expected improvements weren't achieved. If there are no tangible results that management can point to promote further change efforts, there will be no further efforts.

3. Change targets resist the change because its impact on their work relationships was not accounted for in the planning and implementation phase, and they perceive the change as disruptive or even dangerous.

4. Change agents are preoccupied with the technical challenges presented by the change and neglect the human element. They're so busy saving the organization that they forget about the people in the organization.

5. Change agents overlook input from the change targets and don't demonstrate enough respect for them.

6. Change agents are too interested in "owning" the idea and don't allow others to contribute to it.

7. Change sponsors and agents want too much credit for improvements, and don't want to share accomplishments with others.

8. Change sponsors and agents are too dependent on complex explanations and formulas for justifying the change, and treat their knowledge as a secret domain. As a result, the change targets don't understand the reason for the change, and resist it. If it's not rocket science, don't treat it like rocket science.

9. Change agents "go native." This is the opposite of change agents who are too aggressive and unsympathetic. In this instance, the agents are so sympathetic, complimentary, and tentative that the change targets believe that they're doing very well and that there's no need for change.

10. Change sponsors get hesitant or fearful about the planned change. Or, as is often the case, the change sponsors believe that, while change will affect everyone else, they can get on with business as usual. If the change sponsors are not part of the solution, they will end up as part of the problem.

The path to plateau. Plateauing occurs when small changes with limited long-term impact are made, but the most important aspects of the change plan are neglected or put aside—for example, when a gainsharing program results in improvements in a single department, but the program isn't shared with other departments.

Sometimes, people who sincerely believed that they wanted change find that there's too much change, too soon. They discover that they don't adapt as well as they'd expected to new responsibilities and new structures. So they stop and retain some of the preliminary work that's been done, but don't implement the rest of the plan. Other times, an organization decides that it has gone far enough and wants to let the change "settle in"—but "forgets" to go forward.

Plateaus can be reached for other reasons. The organization misplanned the use of resources needed to create further change, and has to slow down or stop. The original change sponsor is transferred, and the new leader wants to review everything or take a different tack. Whatever the cause of the plateau, the organization retains what has been done to date, as compared to going back to the way things were before, but makes no further effort to carry out the plan. In essence, it stops in the middle of the critical path and stays there. Some vestiges of the new systems or structures remain, which leads some organizations to think they've made progress. They're fooling themselves, however. If you're standing still, you're really moving backward, because most of your competitors are moving forward.

The path to success. An organization on the path to success views implemented changes as successful and beneficial. More changes are made, and the organization begins to do business in a new fashion and moves to the next phase of the change process—commitment to continuous improvement.

A key to success is trust among the change sponsors, agents, and targets. If the change sponsors support change efforts in public, but question them in private, eventually the private message will most likely become public. If the change agents constantly question the commitment of the change sponsors, the change targets will lose faith. Change agents and sponsors must be seen as predictable. In other words, change targets must feel that they know what responses they can expect:

> Predictability consists of intention and ground rules: what are our general goals and how will we make decisions? The more leaders clarify the company's intentions and ground rules, the more people will be able to predict and influence what happens to them—even in the middle of a constantly shifting situation.[21]

The following are some indications that your organization is on the path to long-term success:

- Early events and people disappear into the background as later events and people come forward. People actually begin to create a little mythology by telling stories of the early days of the change effort.

- Conflict is less frequent and consensus more common. Managers who previously fought over their turf and protected what they perceived to be the interests of their departments now recognize the interests of the entire organization.

- Alternatives that seemed equally plausible, creating uncertainty, give way to obvious choices that are seen as consistent with the desired goals.

- Accidents, uncertainties, and muddle-headed confusion disappear into clear-sighted strategies.

- Changes that seemed tentative become part of the routine, and new systems and structures are viewed as essential.

An organization is following the path to success when the changes are no longer seen solely as an end unto themselves, but as the means to new ends. Properly managed, the culture that supports the change effort becomes fully integrated into the organization's total culture, thus supporting new changes and new improvements.

Continuous Improvement

"Continuous improvement" is the final phase of the change model. It consists of two steps: (1) look for additional opportunities to improve, and (2) repeat the PDCA Cycle (see Exhibit 12).

After you have gone through the change model for the first time and have successfully implemented a large-scale organizational change, the work to improve the organization is not finished. Invariably, there will be another organizational change that will suggest itself to someone or some group within the organization.

Exhibit 12   Phase 4 of the Change Model

ACT Continuous Improvement
1. Look for additional opportunities to improve 2. Repeat the PDCA cycle

This change could have something to do with the large-scale change the organization just put into place; perhaps some aspect of the change is causing problems and needs to be adjusted. Or, someone might think of an entirely unrelated large- or small-scale change that could improve the organization. The important thing is for everyone to keep looking for improvements and make positive change a way of life for the business.

The good news is that the next go-round through the change model should be easier. Lessons learned during the first large-scale change can be applied to new challenges. Managers and employees now have valuable strategies for overcoming barriers and resistance. Having gone through one large-scale change, the organization should be more flexible and responsive during the next. A sensitivity to the necessity for change and a process for achieving change is now part of the corporate culture.

Once the need for another change has been recognized, the organization has completed the first step of the planning phase of the PDCA Cycle. It only remains to complete the cycle again, armed with new skills and behaviors, and with valuable experience to build on.

Cautions and Tips

Change can be difficult. While much has been written about change, and more is yet to come, there are no perfect prescriptions for success, nor any guaranteed methods that will work in all organizations in all circumstances. One-size-fits-all approaches ignore the unique circumstances and histories of organizations. A good change plan must acknowledge this uniqueness.

Change sponsors and change agents should be careful of excessively logical "how-to" approaches to managing change. Change involves human beings and there are no one-two-three guides to follow. There are only roles people play, and various strategies to use. Style, especially in the early part of the process, is just as important as substance.

It is not uncommon for companies to start change programs because upper management believes that a new approach will help the organization do better. Upper management thinks that the organization just needs a little fine-tuning, and the change program is started half-heartedly. If change is to be taken seriously, and if change is to take hold, it can't be part of a CEO's effort to prove that everything is already pretty good. If the organization is not serious about improvement, it should do nothing. Dabbling in new ideas can be more harmful than doing nothing, because it creates instability without any gain.

Companies should also avoid change if they don't expect to see any results for three to five years. Given the rate of change, no one can comfortably predict what business will be like in five years. Successful change programs, no matter how large in scope, should start generating noticeable improvements in six to twelve months.

Effective change is time consuming. It requires that people work in different ways and adjust to a different organization. But, successfully implemented, change is invigorating and motivating. Most importantly, the more effectively a company manages change, the more it becomes the kind of organization that has the flexibility and adaptability to constantly renew itself and maintain a strong position in a rapidly changing, ever more competitive world.

Endnotes

1. Neil Postman and Charles Weingartner, *Teaching as a Subversive Activity* (New York: Dell Publishing, 1960), p. 10.

2. Postman and Weingartner, p. 10.

3. Charles A. O'Reilly III and Michael L. Tushman, "Ambidextrous Organizations: Leading Evolutionary and Revolutionary Change," *California Management Review* 38, no. 4 (1996): 8–30.

4. Rosabeth Moss Kanter, *The Change Masters: Corporate Entrepreneurs at Work* (London: Taylor & Francis, 1985).

5. Michaela Driver, "From Loss to Lack: Stories of Organizational Change as Encounters with Failed Fantasies of Self, Work and Organization," *Organization* 16, no. 3 (2009): 353–369.

6. T. Goss, R. Pacale, and A. Athos, "The Reinvention Roller Coaster: Risking the Present for a Powerful Future," *Harvard Business Review*, November–December 1993, p. 98.

7. Everett Rogers, *Diffusion of Innovations*, 4th ed. (New York: Free Press, 1995).

8. Eric von Hippel, *The Sources of Innovation* (New York: Oxford University Press, 1988).

9. Thomas J. Peters and Robert H. Waterman, *In Search of Excellence: Lessons from America's Best-Run Companies* (New York: HarperCollins, 2004).

10. Morgan W. McCall Jr. and Robert K. Kaplan, *Whatever It Takes: Decision Makers at Work* (New Jersey: Prentice-Hall, 1985).

11. Darwin Cartwright, "Achieving Change in People," *Human Relations* 4, no. 4 (1951).

12. G. Hall, J. Rosenthal, and J. Wade, "How to Make Reengineering Really Work," *Harvard Business Review*, November–December 1993, pp. 119–120.

13. Goss, Pacale, and Athos, p. 105.

14. Jeanie Daniel Duck, "Managing Change: The Art of Balancing," *Harvard Business Review*, November–December 1993, pp. 117–118.

15. Gordon Lippitt, *Organization Renewal* (Englewood Cliffs, N.J.: Prentice-Hall, 1982), p. 118.

16. Noel M. Tichy, "Revolutionize Your Company," *Fortune*, December 13, 1993, p. 118.

17. M. Beer, R. Eisenstat, and B. Spector, "Why Change Programs Don't Produce Change," *Harvard Business Review*, November–December 1990, p. 159.

18. Duck, p. 116.

19. Duck, p. 116.

20. Hall, Rosenthal, and Wade, p. 131.

21. Duck, p. 115.

Key Terms

action plan—An outline of the tasks to be completed for each step in a critical path.

baseline measurement—A measurement used as a basis for comparisons or for control purposes; a beginning point in an evaluation of output observed over a period of time. A baseline measurement represents how a process performs prior to any improvement effort.

change agent—A person or group responsible for the day-to-day effort that makes an organizational change happen.

change sponsor—An individual or group within an organization that has the power and influence to initiate and implement change. The primary roles of a change sponsor are to envision a needed change, create a vision statement, and inspire others with this vision.

change target—An individual or group within an organization that must change skills, knowledge, or behaviors because of a planned organizational change.

critical path—A planning and control technique that graphically depicts the relationships between the various activities of a project; used when time durations of project activities are accurately known and have little variance.

driving force—A force that tends to encourage change in a particular direction.

force field analysis—A planning technique that helps you identify and visualize the relationships of significant forces that influence a situation, problem, or goal.

reengineering—An organizational change that involves the complete redesign of a process within the organization, the goal of which is to achieve a dramatic improvement.

reinvention—An extreme organizational change requiring an organization to rethink every aspect of how it conducts business.

restraining force—A force that tends to keep a situation from changing in a particular direction.

vision statement—An overarching statement describing an ideal future state for an organization, unit, department, or functional area.

 **Review Questions**

1. What are some of the external and internal forces of change faced by hospitality organizations?

2. What are some of the characteristics typically attributed to creative people? to creative organizations?

3. What is the role of the change sponsor in the change process?

4. What role does a change agent play in the change process?

5. How can an organization plan change?

6. What is a force field analysis?

7. How can an organizational change be implemented?

8. What are three positions, identified by Joseph M. Juran, that individuals may take when an organization undergoes large-scale change?

9. What are some of the power strategies change agents can use when implementing change?

10. How can an organization monitor an organizational change?

11. What steps are part of the "continuous improvement" phase of the change model?

Chapter 2 Outline

Competencies

1. Describe the traditional functions of management (planning, organizing, coordinating, staffing, directing, and controlling), and explain why a gap exists between them and the actual behavior of managers. (pp. 44–50)

2. Describe the various interpersonal, informational, and decisional roles managers fulfill, and explain how managers can benefit from thinking about their jobs in terms of these roles. (pp. 50–54)

3. Explain the traditional theory of management skills and why it fails to accurately reflect the work of managers, supervisors, and employees in many of today's hospitality organizations. (pp. 54–56)

4. Identify characteristics and applications of the three traditional management styles and describe factors that limit an individual's flexibility in adopting different management styles for different situations. (pp. 57–60)

5. Describe the dominant contemporary views of leadership. (pp. 60–64)

2

The Changing Nature of Leadership and Management

APPROACHES TO MANAGEMENT and leadership change constantly. So do prevailing views of which approach is best. A good leader or manager should understand both the most modern and prevailing methods as well as the outdated and ineffective methods. Knowing how the methods work and being able to draw effective tools from them—even the outdated and ineffective ones (sometimes just knowing what doesn't work is valuable)—will enhance a manager's or leader's ability to do things right.

Management and leadership are very different. A management role typically emphasizes control and production, whereas a leadership role focuses on creating a vision and inspiring others to follow. Managers often get employees to perform by using rewards and punishments. While this can work in the short run, it is not likely to produce optimum long-term results. All managers should strive to be leaders, not only because leaders occupy the top rungs of any given organization, but also because effective leadership will always produce better results than effective management. Leaders get people to perform by inspiring the best out of them.

Over the past several decades, hundreds of books and thousands of magazine and journal articles have been written about the nature of leadership and management. Prompting this explosion of new organizational theories and managerial practices is the ever-increasing acceleration of change. For example, technological changes have not only increased the speed with which information flows through organizations, these changes have also permanently altered the structure of many companies. As the structure of a company changes, so does the nature of leadership and management within that organization.

Not so long ago, management information systems in the hospitality industry were cumbersome and often ineffective. Information flowed up an organization to its corporate offices through a series of manual and automated reports issued by layers of managers within the hierarchy. It often took corporate headquarters so long to collect, assemble, and distribute data back down through the organizational chain that the usefulness of the information expired before general managers received it at the property level. With today's electronic information management systems, however, information can be distributed throughout an organization from any point within the organization at the very moment it is collected.

This tremendous change in management information systems, coupled with equally significant changes in business conditions and the expectations of guests and employees, has opened new opportunities for company leaders to rethink, and, in some cases, to reinvent, the way they do business. Many of today's hospitality companies have seized the opportunity to flatten their organizational structures, redistribute power and responsibility, and release decision-making authority to the lowest possible level within their organizations. These changes have redefined the roles, responsibilities, and competencies of managers at every level.

Getting a management job today and keeping that job tomorrow requires a willingness to change. Successful managers have the motivation and flexibility to respond to the changing needs of their organizations. This means taking personal responsibility for acquiring new skills, developing new talents, and committing to a journey of life-long learning.

This chapter provides a framework for new and experienced managers and for students considering hospitality careers to grasp the changing nature and scope of leadership and management. The beginning sections of the chapter evaluate traditional approaches to management and focus on the traditional ideas, concepts, and practices that are most relevant to today's managers. Each management approach provides a manager with a broad perspective for examining his or her job. However, the management approaches vary in relation to how helpful they are to today's managers, who live and breathe the realities of today's pressures, demands, and responsibilities. The final sections of the chapter outline the fundamental skills that continue to shape the contemporary scope of leadership and management in the hospitality industry.

From Traditional to Contemporary Principles of Management

Traditional management principles date back to the work of Henri Fayol (1841–1925), a French mining engineer who became the head of a major mining group.[1] Writing about his own successful practices, Fayol suggested broad, general guidelines for the effective management of any kind of business. His ideas had their greatest impact 25 years after his death. This is partly explained by the fact that his work was not generally available until its second translation into English in 1949. His work in identifying basic management principles provided the foundation for many approaches to management since the 1950s.

Fayol's management principles have been interpreted, rephrased, and added to over time. Some principles that reflect Fayol's early work are described in Exhibit 1. Compare these principles to the realities of business today to see how much has changed.

Fayol often stressed that managers should be flexible when applying management principles. Principles are general guidelines, not rigid blueprints, for success. Knowing when *not* to apply a principle, or how to adjust its application to fit specific circumstances, is just as important as understanding the principle itself.

Many of Fayol's management principles make the most sense in companies with tall organizational structures where power and decision-making authority is

Exhibit 1   Traditional Principles of Management

Common Good
   The interests of the organization are more important than those of any individual or group within the organization.

Centralization
   Decision-making authority should rest at the top levels of an organization.

Unity of Direction
   One plan should be used for a group of activities that has the same goal or objective.

Unity of Command
   Each employee should receive orders from only one boss.

Span of Control
   The number of employees that report to a manager or supervisor should be limited. Also called span of management.

Scalar Chain
   The line of authority and formal communication should run from top management down to the lowest organizational levels.

Authority Commensurate with Responsibility
   Managers should have the amount of formal (positional) authority necessary to do their jobs.

Division of Labor
   Employees should specialize in specific work tasks.

Compensation
   The organization should have a fair wage and salary administration plan.

Staff Stability
   High management and employee turnover rates lead to inefficiency.

Matching
   Employees should be placed in the positions most suitable for them.

Discipline
   Employees should respect rules and policies that govern the organization.

Employee Initiative
   Employees should be given some freedom to develop and implement plans.

Esprit de Corps
   The organization benefits from teamwork that builds harmony and unity.

centralized at top management levels. For example, centralization, unity of command, scalar chain, and division of labor best fit a vertical or tall organizational structure, as shown in the top portion of Exhibit 2. These same principles have very different applications for a company with a horizontal or flat organizational structure in which power and decision-making authority are decentralized and released to lower management levels, as shown in the bottom portion of Exhibit 2. Notice the difference between hierarchical and horizontal structures. Horizontal

Exhibit 2   Vertical and Horizontal Organizational Structures

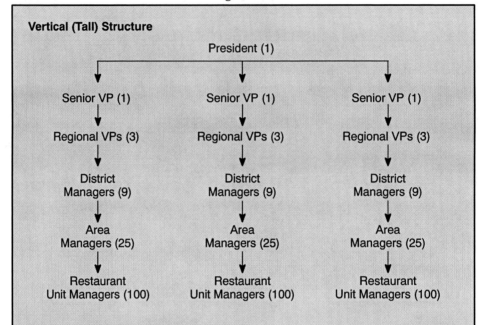

Vertical (Tall) Structure

President (1)

Senior VP (1)   Senior VP (1)   Senior VP (1)

Regional VPs (3)   Regional VPs (3)   Regional VPs (3)

District Managers (9)   District Managers (9)   District Managers (9)

Area Managers (25)   Area Managers (25)   Area Managers (25)

Restaurant Unit Managers (100)   Restaurant Unit Managers (100)   Restaurant Unit Managers (100)

Horizontal (Flat) Structure

President (1)

Senior VP (1)

Regional VPs (8)   Regional VPs (8)   Regional VPs (8)

Restaurant Unit Managers (100)   Restaurant Unit Managers (100)   Restaurant Unit Managers (100)

structures can obviously respond to change much quicker, as communications up and down the corporate ladder are streamlined.

Many of today's hospitality companies are decentralizing—releasing power and decision-making authority to the lowest possible level within their organizations. Lines of authority and communication are changing from a top-down direction to bottom-up and lateral directions. The impact of computerized information management systems has dramatically increased the span of control exercised by top managers. Many companies are redefining the division of labor by cross-training employees and developing cross-functional managers.

Exhibit 3   Management Functions as a Rational Process

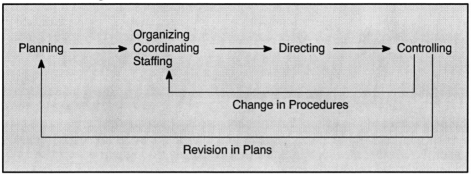

The New Context for Traditional Management Functions ——

Henri Fayol also studied management by grouping the many different activities that managers perform into a few conceptual categories that are now referred to as *management functions*. While Fayol defined five conceptual categories (planning, organizing, commanding, coordinating, and controlling), many of today's management texts identify as few as four or as many as seven. In this section, we'll look at six management functions:

- Planning
- Organizing
- Coordinating
- Staffing
- Directing
- Controlling

Exhibit 3 diagrams these six functions as a rational process of managing an organization, division, or department.

Planning. Planning establishes goals and objectives to pursue during a future period. The planning function spans all levels of management. Top managers are involved in strategic planning that sets broad, long-range goals for an organization. These goals become the basis for short-range, annual operational planning, during which top and middle managers determine specific departmental objectives that will help the organization make progress toward the broader, long-range goals. Operations budgeting is another example of planning that involves top and middle managers. Planning at the supervisory level may include such tasks as developing employee work schedules and preparing for employee performance appraisals.

Organizing. Organizing typically follows planning and reflects how the organization tries to accomplish its goals and objectives. In relation to the structure of a company, organizing involves the assignment of tasks, the grouping of tasks into departments, and the allocation of resources to departments. Organizing also involves establishing the flow of authority and communication between positions and levels within the organization. These organizing activities are performed by top managers. Middle managers and supervisors organize by grouping similar tasks to create positions within their departments. Job analysis and job design activities are organizing functions.

Coordinating. The management function of **coordinating** refers to management activities related to achieving an efficient use of resources to attain the organization's goals and objectives. Servicing the needs of a large convention group in a hotel requires coordinating materials and staff members from several departments. Interfacing electronic point-of-sale terminals throughout a resort or club operation is also a coordinating activity.

Staffing. The **staffing** function refers to the fundamental cycle of human resources activities: determining human resource needs, and recruiting, selecting, hiring, training, and developing staff members.

Directing. Also referred to as leading, **directing** involves influencing divisions, departments, and individual staff members to accomplish the organization's goals and objectives. In this context, directing means communicating goals and objectives throughout the organization and striving to create an environment that encourages everyone to perform at the highest level.

Controlling. Managers performing the **controlling** management function translate organizational goals and objectives into performance standards for divisions, departments, and individual positions. Controlling also involves assessing actual performance against standards to determine whether the organization is on target to reach its goals, and taking corrective actions as necessary. Managers practicing the evaluative component of controlling assess how well the organization has achieved its objectives. This analysis provides feedback for planning as managers revise goals and objectives or develop new ones.

Management Functions versus Management Behavior

Management studies from 1965 to 1985 attempted to rank management functions in relation to the amount of time spent on each by different levels of management.[2] These studies seemed to consistently find that top managers spent relatively more time with planning and organizing functions than did middle managers and supervisors, and that middle managers and supervisors spent more time directing their departments and employees than top managers spent directing their divisions and organizations. Despite these research findings, it would seem that characterizing management as a set of functions imparts a false sense of logic and rationality to a manager's job—as if a manager's activities could be easily pigeon-holed into separate functions.

In practice, management functions cut across most managerial activities. For example, is it simply a planning function when supervisors develop work schedules for their employees? Or, is it more of an organizing activity, a coordinating activity, a staffing activity, or a controlling activity? Each of these functions could apply in a significant way to the specific task of scheduling employees to work. Clearly, the usefulness of the functional approach to understanding management diminishes as you try to apply the functions to individual management activities and tasks.

In his classic article, "What Effective General Managers Really Do,"[3] John P. Kotter notes that the daily activities of most general managers seem to have little to do with textbook management functions such as planning, organizing, staffing, etc. In fact, Kotter found that a large gap exists between the traditional management functions and actual managerial behavior.

Observing the day-to-day activities of successful general managers from different types of companies, Kotter compiled notes similar to daily logs, listing actual events as they happened and recording time frames for each event. Kotter found that the general managers spent 70 to 90 percent of their time in brief, fragmented conversations with others on virtually anything and everything even remotely associated with their organizations.

The people that the general managers talked with went well beyond those directly reporting to them. In fact, Kotter found that general managers regularly ignored the formal chain of command and talked directly with many managers and employees that were several levels below them in the management hierarchy. During their conversations, the general managers asked a lot of questions but rarely made any "big" decisions. Discussions were often full of joking and kidding, usually on non-work-related issues. In these conversations, the general managers rarely gave orders; instead, they would either react to what others said or use persuasive techniques to influence others to take some kind of action. Perhaps Kotter's most interesting findings were:

- The typical general manager's day was unplanned.

- Most of a general manager's time with others was spent in short, disjointed conversations.

- Discussions of a single question or issue rarely lasted more than ten minutes.

On the surface, Kotter's findings seem to be textbook examples of exactly how not to behave as a general manager. How are planning and organizing functions applied in unplanned days full of short, disjointed conversations? Kotter concluded that, below the surface, these functions still existed, but that general managers applied them through unique forms of agenda-setting and network-building.

Kotter noted that a general manager's agenda, or plan, was usually different from the formal plans or strategies of the organization. He found that these agendas covered a broad range of loosely connected issues and goals and that they spanned very different time horizons. Some agenda items were very specific; others were vague and ambiguous.

Kotter also noted that a general manager's network was very different from the organizational structure of the company. The networks that general managers built were cooperative relationships among those people whom they felt were essential to accomplishing goals and items on their unique agendas.

It sounds as if successful general managers found ways to get things done by avoiding the formal planning processes of their companies and by ignoring their organizational structures as well. They succeeded in spite of the formal planning and organizing functions within their organizations. The big question is why?

Kotter insightfully addressed this as well. He noted that to understand the agenda-setting and network-building behavior of successful general managers, you first need to recognize the unique types of challenges and dilemmas found in most of their jobs. He describes the challenge met by agenda-setting as: "Figuring out what to do despite uncertainty, great diversity, and an enormous amount of potentially relevant information." He also describes the dilemma of network building as: "Getting things done through a large and diverse set of people despite having little direct control over most of them." These are the challenges and dilemmas faced by today's top-, middle-, and lower-level managers.

Corporate offices of lodging and food service chains (and management companies as well) are releasing more responsibility and authority to individual properties and business units to meet and exceed their guests' expectations within their unique competitive environments. There are fewer and fewer corporate directives and formulas to guide business decisions at the property level. Instead, corporate offices are supplying more and more data and information for general managers to analyze in the context of their own business situations. As a result, general managers find themselves with more freedom to act and with greater accountability for the results of their actions. Faced with new decision-making situations, today's general managers are, indeed, charged with "figuring out what to do despite uncertainty, great diversity, and an enormous amount of potentially relevant information." The success of today's general manager in meeting these new challenges may depend a great deal on the individual's agenda-setting and networking abilities. As general managers release more decision-making responsibility down through the levels of their organization, department managers and supervisors also face similar types of challenges.

Traditional Management Roles

Much in the same vein as Kotter, Henry Mintzberg looked at what managers actually do in their jobs and found that Fayol's management functions were inadequate descriptions of managerial work. In his classic business article, "The Manager's Job: Folklore and Fact,"[4] Mintzberg suggested that planning, organizing, etc., were at best only vague objectives that managers have as they work. Their actual behavior is better characterized by brevity, variety, fragmentation, and oral communication. The appendix to this chapter presents a day in the life of Hans Willimann, the general manager of the 343-room Four Seasons in Chicago. The activities of his day reflect the behavior described not only by Mintzberg, but by Kotter as well.

In particular, Mintzberg noted that managers are not reflective, systematic planners. The managers he studied invariably preferred action to reflection. When those managers did plan, they didn't retreat to a solitary state of reflection with an abstract planning process. Rather, they planned in the context of their daily actions, and their plans existed mainly in their heads as flexible, but specific, intentions.

Mintzberg proposed that a manager's job is better described in terms of various "roles," or organized sets of behaviors appropriate to management positions, than in terms of the "tasks" that Fayol used to describe management. Mintzberg

Exhibit 4   Traditional Management Roles

Categories	Roles
Interpersonal Roles	**Figurehead** Performs ceremonial or symbolic acts as the formal representative of an organization or department.
	Leader Acts to create a productive atmosphere in the workplace.
	Liaison Networks with peers and others outside the organization's vertical chain of command.
Informational Roles	**Monitor** Gathers information from both formal and informal channels within the organization.
	Disseminator Passes information on to staff members who otherwise would not have access to it.
	Spokesperson Sends information through speeches, letters, reports, or memos to people outside the department or organization.
Decisional Roles	**Entrepreneur** Initiates change within a department or organization.
	Disturbance Handler Resolves conflicts among staff members and problems that arise in day-to-day operations.
	Resource Allocator Distributes resources to achieve organizational goals and departmental objectives.
	Negotiator Bargains with unions, contracts with suppliers, and sets goals with individual staff members.

identified three major role categories—interpersonal, informational, and decisional—and described ten roles that formed an integrated whole making up the job of an effective manager. Exhibit 4 identifies these categories and briefly outlines the ten roles.

While these roles are inseparable from every manager's job, different management positions tend to emphasize different sets. For example, interpersonal roles are more central to the job of a sales manager, informational roles are more central to staff managers such as controllers or human resources managers, and decisional roles are more central to executive-level managers or production managers like executive chefs or catering managers.

Interpersonal Roles

A manager performs **interpersonal roles** when acting as a figurehead, leader, or liaison. As a **figurehead,** a manager performs numerous ceremonial or symbolic acts as the formal representative of an organization or department. For example, the general manager of a hotel acts as a figurehead when hosting a luncheon of community leaders. Upper managers, department managers, and supervisors act as figureheads when they entertain important customers, present awards to employees, or even attend the wedding of a member of their staff. Of course, the way this figurehead role is carried out differs among organizations.

As a **leader,** a manager acts to create a productive atmosphere in the workplace. A leader not only exercises human resource duties such as hiring, training, appraising, and so on, but also acts to encourage and motivate employees by helping to align their individual needs with the overall goals of the department and organization.

A manager acts as a **liaison** by networking with peers and others outside the organization's vertical chain of command. Mintzberg notes that managers typically spend as much time with peers and other people outside their departments or functional areas as they do with their own staff members. (Mintzberg also noted that managers spend surprisingly little time with their own bosses.) Departments within an organization can act almost independently, rarely consulting with or seeking advice from other departments. These "silos" work against company objectives. Managers acting as liaisons can break down the barriers between siloed departments.

Informational Roles

A manager performs **informational roles** when acting as a monitor, disseminator, or spokesperson. Mintzberg found that managers spend a great deal of their time developing and maintaining information networks because most of a manager's access to information, in spite of electronic information systems, is through personal contacts in the form of oral and written communications. In many ways, it's possible to see every manager's job as primarily communication.

Managers act as **monitors** when scanning the environment for information, questioning personal contacts in other departments, or listening to members of their own staff. Much of the monitor role involves dealing with unsolicited information coming from a network of personal contacts. This information is usually obtained though conversations and often involves gossip, hearsay, and speculation.

Acting in the role of **disseminators,** managers relay information to members of their staff who otherwise would not have access to it. This is not referring to passing on rumors or speculation to staff members. It involves communicating the efforts of other departments that directly or indirectly affect the manager's department or the overall organization. At times, disseminators also serve to maintain important facets of the corporate culture.

As a **spokesperson,** a manager sends information through speeches, letters, reports, or memos to people outside the department or organization. For example, a front office manager acts as the department's spokesperson when sending reports to the sales department or to the general manager. A general manager acts as a spokesperson when speaking at a city council meeting or when lobbying for the organization.

Decisional Roles

When performing interpersonal and informational roles, managers enhance their ability to make sound decisions affecting a department, division, or organization. A manager acts in **decisional roles** as an entrepreneur, disturbance handler, resource allocator, or negotiator.

Acting in the role of an **entrepreneur,** a manager initiates change within a department or an organization. The agenda-setting behaviors of general managers that Kotter studied are examples of managers acting in the entrepreneur role. These managers juggle a number of ideas and plans. At times, one idea gets more attention and energy than the others, but all of the ideas are somehow in motion and at various stages of implementation.

Acting as **disturbance handlers,** managers react to changes and conditions that are beyond their control. Despite thorough planning and careful organization, managers cannot anticipate every contingency. A disturbance handler resolves conflicts among staff members and fights "fires" that come up in the course of day-to-day operations.

As a **resource allocator,** a manager is responsible for distributing resources to achieve organizational goals and departmental objectives. These resources include staff members, money, time, work procedures and methods, energy, materials, and equipment. Allocating resources also includes designing the structure of an organization or department and establishing the chain of command.

In the role of a **negotiator,** a manager's job may include bargaining with unions, contracting with suppliers, selling to customers, or setting goals with individual staff members.

From Management Roles to Practical Skills

Much of the value of Mintzberg's work lies in providing managers with tools for gaining insight into their own work. A manager's performance often depends on how well he or she understands and responds to the pressures and dilemmas of the job. All managers, but especially new managers, benefit from knowing that effective performance in decisional roles depends largely on contacts and information obtained by performing interpersonal and informational roles.

The interpersonal roles stress that much of a manager's time and effort is devoted to people. Especially in the hospitality industry, managers constantly interact with guests, employees, peers, and their bosses. An area often overlooked by new managers is what Mintzberg describes as the liaison role. People that are new to managerial jobs tend to focus almost exclusively on their departmental leader roles, feeling that other departments and functional areas are not their concern. Actually, new managers need to take the time and make the effort to establish a network of contacts with peers in other departments. Otherwise, they will not develop the wider perspective needed to make effective decisions within their own areas and the company will develop silos.

The informational roles emphasize the importance of formal and informal channels of communication. Again, most of a manager's daily activity is taken up with communicating. It's important for new managers to realize that they shouldn't leave meetings, hang up the telephone, or brush people out of their office in order to get back to work. Meetings, phone calls, interactions, and even interruptions by others are to a large extent part and parcel of their jobs as managers.

In attacking the traditional view of management as a logical series of functions, Mintzberg's managerial roles focus on the practical side of a manager's job and introduce a number of skills that managers need to perform effectively. These skills include:

- Developing peer relationships

- Carrying out negotiations

- Creating an atmosphere for a self-motivated staff

- Resolving conflicts

- Establishing information networks

- Disseminating information

- Making decisions in conditions of extreme ambiguity

- Allocating resources

These are all skills emphasized by a managerial-skills approach to teaching management. Mintzberg's focus on specific, practical skills runs counter to the prevailing notion of traditional management skills.

Traditional Management Skills

While the functions of management attempt to categorize the many activities associated with a manager's job, another approach to management focuses on the skills that managers need to carry out their jobs effectively. Robert L. Katz offered a view of management in relation to three skills:[5]

- Technical skill

- Human relations skill

- Conceptual skill

Technical skill involves specialized knowledge of tools, techniques, methods, procedures, or processes associated with a specific type of activity. Executive chefs, chief engineers, marketing specialists, controllers, and other types of hospitality managers apply a unique set of technical skills to their particular jobs. **Human relations skill** is the ability of a manager to work effectively with people at every level in the organization. Managers need interpersonal skills that enable them to relate to guests, bosses, peers, and employees. **Conceptual skill** involves a manager's ability to see beyond the technical aspects of his or her position. It includes recognizing the interdependence of various departments and functional areas within the organization as well as seeing the bigger picture of how the organization fits into the structure of the industry, the community, and the wider world at large.

Katz first proposed this "three skills" approach to management in 1955, when the vast majority of businesses and corporations were structured as centralized hierarchies with multiple management layers. At that time, he concluded that the relative importance of these skills to a manager varied in relation to the manager's level within the organization. Managers in the lower levels of an organization, such as supervisors, had the greatest need for technical and human relations skills. The effectiveness of middle managers, such as department heads, depended largely on human relations and conceptual skills. Conceptual skill was seen as most important for top managers, such as general managers and corporate executives. In fact, Katz felt that, at the top level of an organization, managers needed few, if any, technical skills. They could perform effectively if their human relations skills and conceptual skills were highly developed. The top portion of Exhibit 5 diagrams the relative importance of these traditional skills to different levels of management in the late 1950s.

However, in 1974, Katz proposed a slightly different picture. He suggested that technical skills were more important at top management levels than he had originally proposed—especially in relation to managers within small companies. This certainly rings true in relation to hospitality businesses. The manager of a restaurant unit, department managers in a hotel, and even corporate division managers need a solid base of technical skills to model the behaviors they expect from their staff. When a restaurant is short-staffed, the manager serves guests, operates a point-of-sale terminal, fills in at the broiler, or even works the dishline.

Today, the relative importance of Katz's three skills to different levels of management is becoming more and more difficult to determine. For example, hospitality supervisors need conceptual skills as much as they require expertise in technical skills. In order to make the right day-to-day operational decisions, supervisors need to understand how their actions affect the overall financial situation of the business. Two books—*The Great Game of Business*, by John Stack, and *Open-Book Management: The Coming Business Revolution*, by John Case—explain how involving employees at all organizational levels in key decision making can dramatically and positively affect organizational outcomes, including the bottom line.

Decentralization, flatter organizational structures, cross-functional managers, empowered employees, and team-based work processes are fast redistributing the emphasis on each skill throughout many hospitality organizations. The lower portion of Exhibit 5 diagrams the relative importance of traditional management skills at different levels within today's flatter, more decentralized organizations.

Katz's early work seemed to suggest that employees simply needed technical skills to perform their jobs. This has never been true in the hospitality business. Employees in high guest-contact positions have always needed human relations skills, also called interpersonal skills, to communicate with guests and satisfy their needs. In today's empowered workplace, hospitality employees will need greater conceptual skills as they solve problems, make decisions, and take actions to meet or exceed guests' expectations.

Exhibit 5   Traditional and Contemporary Management Skills

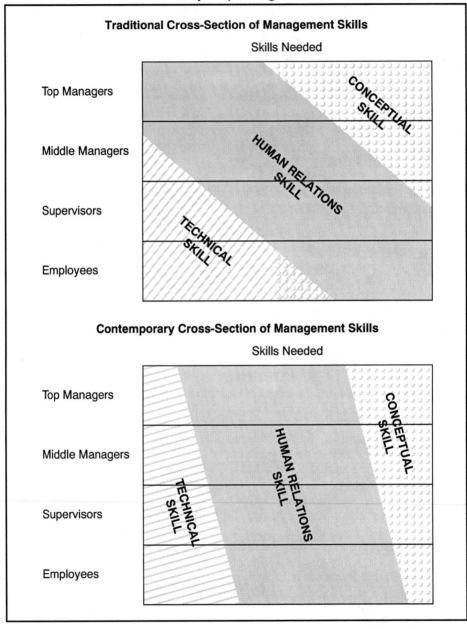

Knowing about traditional management skills enables individuals within an organization to think about the broad demands that their jobs place on them. However, the general skills identified by Katz are not very helpful to managers, supervisors, or employees in the everyday realities of work today.

Traditional Management Styles

As traditional management skills became less and less applicable to contemporary managers, more recent approaches to management have focused on various styles by which managers achieve results through people. Management styles are patterns of behavior managers use to interact with other managers and with their staff. Three traditional management styles are those of the autocratic manager, the bureaucratic manager, and the democratic manager.

The Autocratic Manager. Autocratic managers stress immediate, short-term results over concerns about people in a department or organization. They generally give orders without explanations, and expect those orders to be obeyed without question. These are "my way or the highway" managers. They make decisions without input from their staff and are usually unwilling to delegate work to employees under their supervision, often because they do not trust them. This type of manager believes in Theory X—that people have to be controlled or they will do wrong. Often, a structured set of rewards and punishments is used to ensure employee compliance. Autocratic managers assume that employees put in time for a paycheck, and money is the only reward that will motivate them. Their assumptions about employees generally become self-fulfilling prophecies. Employees often become extremely dependent on the autocratic manager—they do what they are told, no more and no less. Work gets done when the manager is present, but things fall apart when the manager is absent. Since employees are given little, if any, discretion about how to perform their jobs, they learn to suppress their initiative and simply follow orders—that is, they learn behaviors that match their bosses' expectations. The end result of this approach is that employees learn to wait for their autocratic boss to tell them what to do. This does not work well in hotels, restaurants, and other service environments, because employees are seldom empowered enough to satisfy customer needs or expectations.

The Bureaucratic Manager. Bureaucratic managers make decisions by enforcing rules, regulations, policies, and procedures that are already in place. Concerns for results and for people take a back seat to the way things have always been done. Bureaucratic managers resist change and act as caretakers of the status quo. They rely on higher levels of management to make decisions about issues not covered "by the book." Like the employees created by autocratic managers, employees under the thumb of bureaucratic managers quickly learn to suppress their initiative and simply follow the rules. When no rule seems to apply to a situation, employees cease to act and call the bureaucrat. This approach is often widely associated with military or government agencies, in which people must always check with their boss before changing anything.

The Democratic Manager. The **democratic manager** is almost the reverse of the autocratic manager. Democratic managers tend to focus more on a participative process than on short-term, immediate results. They take the time to keep employees informed on matters directly affecting their work, and often use delegation as an opportunity for employees to develop higher levels of job satisfaction. Democratic managers share decision-making and problem-solving responsibilities

Exhibit 6   Traditional Management Styles

high	Democratic Managers	Most-Effective Managers
Concern for People		
low	Bureaucratic Managers	Autocratic Managers
	low high	
	Concern for Results	

with their staff. Open to new ideas, democratic managers often foster and champion change within their departments and organizations. These managers want employees to be less dependent on them, to willingly accept responsibility, and to take the initiative to get things done themselves.

Flexibility and the Three Traditional Management Styles. Exhibit 6 diagrams the three traditional management styles along two dimensions: concern for people and concern for results. The upper-right quadrant of the diagram represents the challenge facing management today—how to simultaneously maximize concerns for people and for results. We have dubbed this quadrant "Most-Effective Managers" to emphasize its importance. The big question is whether this can be accomplished with a single management style. More recent trends seem to suggest that today's managers need the flexibility to adopt different styles for specific circumstances.

While many find the democratic style most appealing, this style—when taken to extremes—can stifle an organization as quickly as bureaucratic red tape. Paralysis by analysis, wasted time in unproductive meetings, abdication under the excuse of delegation—these mark the potential abuses and negative aspects of an extreme democratic style.

Most people consider the autocratic manager to be a dinosaur from the past without a place in today's work world. However, there are situations in which a manager or leader may need to play this role. This is often the case in times of great stress, because the most effective approach in a crisis is often autocratic. This is true in the case of very large, atypical crises, such as the 9/11 terrorist attacks in the United States, as well as in small, everyday crises. Consider what happens when twice the expected number of guests needs to be served at lunch, for example. There simply isn't time for everyone to meet the usual standards of service, so "service by the book" goes out the window. Nor is there time for the manager to always consult with the staff. The manager must make quick, autocratic decisions to coordinate the staff's actions and deal with the crisis.

Similarly, every management position has some bureaucratic functions. For example, legal issues relating to hiring and firing require managers to strictly adhere to established policies and procedures. In these situations, reckless autocratic or democratic decisions could result in expensive lawsuits.

Other Management Styles. Throughout the last quarter of the twentieth century, dozens of management styles were popularized in journals and trade magazines, such as "management by committee," "management by intimidation," "management by deadline," "management by example," "management by objectives," "management by walking around," "management by inspiration," etc. Many of these styles were variations on or parts of the three traditional styles just described. Some were touted as panaceas for managerial problems, but most were simply offered as tools—styles to adopt for different situations. From these various management styles, situational and contingency leadership theories emerged, advocating flexible managers capable of adopting very different management styles as warranted by specific circumstances.

Factors Affecting Management Styles

Three of the most important factors limiting a manager's flexibility in adopting different management styles are the manager's personal background, the characteristics of the organization's or department's employees, and the culture of a given organization.

The personal background of a manager includes personality, knowledge, attitudes, feelings, values, and experiences. These factors shape a manager's willingness and ability to move easily among radically different management styles. Some managers feel comfortable in freely delegating work and recognize the need to involve employees in a team approach to defining and resolving problems. Other managers prefer to do almost everything themselves. The success that managers achieve with a particular management style also affects their willingness to adopt a different style.

The characteristics of employees often limit the management styles that a manager can successfully adopt. Autocratic and bureaucratic styles might be more successful in departments with a large number of new and inexperienced employees who do not know what to do. A bureaucratic style might also be useful when a company needs to "stay its course." A democratic style may work best in departments with knowledgeable and experienced employees who are capable of greater independence and decision-making responsibility.

Perhaps the greatest limiting factor of a manager's choice of management styles is the structure and culture of the organization. Managers court disaster when they adopt styles that run counter to the traditions and values of their organizations, or when they attempt to do something without the right employees in place for the job. For example, consider three basketball coaches who each coach different teams. One team is tall, another is fast, and the third is known for its "smarts." To effectively coach these teams, the coach must adapt his or her style to the skills of the players, much like a manager must adapt to the skills of his or her employees.

The autocratic style is traditionally associated with classical command and control cultures that are characteristic of vertically structured, highly centralized organizations with many levels of management. The bureaucratic style also fits this type of culture and often prevails in stale, decaying organizations that suffocate under mountains of red tape. Unchecked, an entire culture of bureaucratic managers tends to foster little empires within an organization, and turf wars persist across department boundaries. The democratic style fits well with cultures that are highly decentralized with relatively few levels of management.

Given these constraints, it's easy to see that while a manager may recognize the need for flexibility and be knowledgeable about alternative management styles, actually adopting different management styles for different situations can be extremely difficult.

Leadership in the 21st Century

One of greatest shortcomings of traditional theories of management is the alarming absence of any discussion of customers or guests. Most of these theories seem to suggest that management activities occur in a vacuum of internal operations. Contemporary leadership and management practices focus first and foremost on the customer/guest. Today, virtually every major hospitality company is reevaluating, restructuring, or reengineering its organization to meet and exceed the expectations of their guests. The resulting organizational changes create new duties and responsibilities for managers, supervisors, and employees alike.

Caught in the midst of these larger changes, managers try to do things right, but few can say for sure if they're actually doing the right things. As we've seen in this chapter, the traditional approaches to defining the job of management no longer provide a straight and narrow path for professional growth and development. Many of today's managers find themselves lost in a bewildering maze of contradictory functions, roles, skills, and styles. While there are no textbook answers to the contemporary challenges of leadership and management, a new direction for managers is emerging from the practices of today's successful hospitality companies. These practices encourage a balance of the focus of management with the vision of leadership.

Exhibit 7 outlines some of the seemingly contradictory responsibilities that managers need to balance. It's important for managers to continue to do things right, but they must constantly ask themselves whether they are actually doing the right things. For example, managers direct operations, but they learn what to direct and how to direct by monitoring guest expectations. Managers must enforce policies and rules, but they must create within their staff an understanding of "Why these particular policies?" and "Why these rules?" by communicating a vision of the organization and the values that drive that vision. Managers must work with their staffs to design procedures and tasks in their areas, but they must also manage the broader systems and processes of which those procedures and tasks are a part. Managers are responsible for the results of their operational areas, but they

Exhibit 7   Balancing Management and Leadership

The Focus of Management		The Vision of Leadership
Do things right	vs.	Do the right things
Direct operations	vs.	Monitor guest expectations
Enforce policies and rules	vs.	Communicate vision and values
Design procedures and tasks	vs.	Manage systems and processes
Control results	vs.	Support people
Foster stability	vs.	Engage in continuous improvement

achieve results by supporting the efforts of people in their departments. Managers are responsible for fostering stability within their areas, but stability does not necessarily mean preserving the status quo—it can very well mean creating a learning environment by fostering change and engaging in continuous improvement efforts. In short, managers must also be leaders; the following chart illustrates the differences between the two:[6]

Leadership	**Management**
Is an influence relationship	Is an authority relationship
Is done by leaders and collaborators	Is done by managers and subordinates
Is an episodic affair	Is done continuously
Does not require a position from which to operate	Requires position power from which to operate

What Is Leadership Today?

After thousands of studies, all we know for sure about leadership is that it is complicated, managers can exercise their leadership talents in a variety of ways, and leadership takes on different forms at different times. The following characteristics describe the ideal for today's twenty-first century leaders[7] (past views have been listed in the first column for comparison purposes):

Leadership Yesterday	**Leadership Today**
Commerce	Compassion
Work	Balance life and work
Answers	Questions
High-tech	High-touch
Directives	Participation
Rationalism	Spirituality
Serious	Fun
Independent	Interdependence
Exclusive	Inclusive
Return-on-investment	Human worth
Directives	Conversations
Homeostasis	Ambiguity

Company goals	Self-knowledge
Conventional	Unconventional
Speaks	Listens
Objective	Relational
Colloquial	Global

Vision plays an especially important role in leadership. All great leaders need a clear vision of where their organizations should be heading. The vision must be attractive and compelling—a long-term dream that stretches and motivates. To be effective, it should reach hearts and minds, raise ambitions, and be a catalyst for action. To act as a catalyst, a vision must be owned by as many people as possible. Essentially, a vision is a shared view of the future. A vision is not static; it lives, grows, and evolves. It can never be "reached." Without a vision, a leader cannot move an organization forward. However, a vision in itself is little more than an empty dream until it is widely shared and accepted.

Leadership Theories

Four leadership theories are most dominant today. These theories vary considerably; all have merit. The key for hospitality managers is to decide which leadership approach best suits their knowledge, skills, and abilities, and which fits best in their organization.

Personality-Based Leadership. Throughout history, many people have believed that only charismatic individuals can be good leaders. That is not true. Many people who are not charismatic are good leaders—Bill Gates of Microsoft, for example, who would seldom be called a charismatic leader.

Six qualities are normally associated with charismatic leaders: vision and articulation, sensitivity to others' needs, environmental sensitivity, unconventional behavior, taking personal risks, and upsetting the status quo. Charismatic leaders also have something else in common; they inspire intense feelings on the part of followers. These feelings include loyalty, respect, affection, acceptance, an increased sense of personal power, and excitement.[8]

Situational Leadership. Situational leadership has been viewed by many as a very good way to apply leadership skills.[9] This approach does not attempt to define what a good leader is from a personality standpoint. Instead, situational leadership uses supportive and directive behaviors to create four leadership styles that are appropriate at various times, depending on the situation and the developmental level of an employee or work group. Situational leaders recognize that the best leadership style will vary, depending on the situation. For example, in an emergency, or when someone is learning a skill for the first time, it is better to be more directive (spell out tasks and goals very clearly) than it is to be supportive.

The situational leadership scale is useful in helping people understand how to lead others effectively. The scale is most easily pictured on a continuum:

Directing ⟶ Coaching ⟶ Supporting ⟶ Delegating
(Dependent)   (Independent)

When people take on a new task, they begin on the dependent end of the continuum and need more direction from a leader. Then, moving at different speeds (depending on the person's experience, ability, and sense of self-worth, as well as the responses he or she gets from the leader), a person begins to move along the scale toward independence. When independence is reached, the leader can delegate tasks rather than direct tasks. A situational leader must be sensitive enough to move along the continuum as he or she leads, depending on the person and the situation.

Transactional Leadership. Transactional leadership is sometimes called "bartering" or "leader-follower exchange."[10] Transactional leadership is based on an exchange of services. Workers exchange levels of performance for certain types of rewards (such as salary, bonuses, time off, and so on). The rewards come from the leader, who controls all rewards in this system. Practicing transactional leadership involves giving out rewards to workers in exchange for compliance or good performance, or giving out punishments for non-compliance or non-performance.

Transformational Leadership. To understand the transformational approach to leadership, you need to know about Type A and Type Z organizations and their differences.[11] Type A organizations are those where leaders make the decisions and workers follow. The capital letter "A" (smaller at the top than the bottom) illustrates how a small number of leaders at the top direct a large number of workers below them in the organization. Type Z organizations, in contrast, are those wherein the differences in status between workers and managers are less pronounced and decision-making takes on a participative tone. In this type of organization, "consensual" or "facilitative" power is most useful. This power is manifested *through* workers, rather than from above them, as in Type A organizations. The letter "Z" illustrates an organizational decision-making structure in which many people at different organizational levels might participate in deciding what to do and how to do it. Transformational leaders involve their staff members in collaborative goal-setting and share leadership with others by delegating power.

Transformational leaders communicate a vision that inspires and motivates people to achieve something extraordinary. Effective transformational leaders typically have the ability to align people and systems with their vision. These leaders pay attention to the concerns and developmental needs of their staff members. They assist staff members by helping them to look at old problems in new ways. They are able to excite, arouse, and inspire workers to put out extra effort to achieve group goals. In the final analysis, staff members adopt the transformational leader's vision as if it were their own. After the transformational leader leaves, staff members continue the effort to achieve the now-shared vision.

As you can see, transformational leaders are more visionary and inspirational in their approach than situational leaders. They can inspire intense emotions in their followers. Rather than handing out rewards for performance, as transactional leaders do, transformational leaders attempt to build within their staff members a sense of ownership of the vision by involving them in the decision-making process.

Leaders as Storytellers

Storytelling has always been an integral part of the human experience.[12] From early childhood to adulthood, stories are an important means of learning and communication. When we are children, our parents relate fairy tales and other stories to us as a form of entertainment, as well as a way of teaching us about morals, our culture, and acceptable standards of behavior and conduct. Listening to stories and learning from them is a skill we learn early in life that remains important throughout our lives. The same is true in organizations. Stories about organizational "deviates" tell us what we *should not* do, while stories about organizational heroes tell us what we *should* do.

Throughout history, political and religious leaders have used storytelling as a powerful motivational tool, particularly during times of uncertainty and change or in response to crises. Even in today's high-tech world, the art of storytelling is still an essential leadership skill. In fact, the rapid dissemination of information today may make online storytelling a very powerful tool.

Many leaders use storytelling as the primary means by which they communicate their vision to their followers. The telling of stories provides listeners with mental "maps" that allow them to know what is important and how things are to be achieved. For instance, a story about a manager or employee who achieved great things often describes more about acceptable and expected behaviors than any number of rules or policies. The most powerful communication is still face-to-face dialogue. Political and business leaders still meet face-to-face to discuss important issues.

Storytelling provides a useful means for understanding life within organizations and helps define individual and corporate values. An important component of many stories is the hero, who acts as a role model of integrity, courage, and goodness. People admire organizational "heroes" who are perceived to possess similar qualities.

Organizational leaders can use storytelling to paint the big picture, to teach management values, and to tap into and change the company's culture. Memorable stories can also act as potent change mechanisms because they generate belief. They can encourage behavioral and attitudinal mind-shifts. Clearly, storytelling should be part of any leader's communication repertoire. Fortunately, if one does not already have the ability to tell stories effectively, like other communication skills, it can be developed through training and practice.

Endnotes

1. Derek S. Pugh and David J. Hickson, *Writers on Organizations* (Sage Publications, Inc., 2007).

2. T. A. Mahoney, T. H. Jerdee, and S. J. Carroll, "The Job(s) of Management," *Industrial Relations* 4, no. 2 (1985): 103.

3. John P. Kotter, "What Effective General Managers Really Do," *Harvard Business Review*, November–December 1982, pp. 156–167.

4. Henry Mintzberg, "The Manager's Job: Folklore and Fact," *Harvard Business Review*, July–August 1975, pp. 49–61.

5. Robert L. Katz, "Skills of an Effective Administrator," *Harvard Business Review,* September–October, 1974, pp. 90–02.

6. Greg Blanch, "When the Topic Turns to Leadership, Most Educators Miss the Mark," *Journal of Hospitality & Tourism Education* 10, no. 3 (1998): 14–18.

7. Melissa Horner, "Leadership Theory: Past, Present, and Future," *Performance Management* 3, no. 4 (1997): 270.

8. Ron Cacioppe, "Leadership Moment by Moment!" *Leadership & Organization Development Journal* 18, no. 7 (1997): 335–345.

9. Some of the information in this section was adapted from John R. Schermerhorn, "Situational Leadership: Conversations with Paul Hersey," *Mid-American Journal of Business* 12, no. 2 (Fall 1997): 5–12.

10. First developed by James Burns, *Leadership* (New York: Harper & Row, 1979); Dong I. Jung, "Transformational and Transactional Leadership and Their Effects on Creativity in Groups," *Creativity Research Journal* 13, no. 2 (2001): 185–195; Timothy R. Hinkin and Chester A. Schriesheim, "A Theoretical and Empirical Examination of the Transactional and Non-Leadership Dimensions of the Multifactor Leadership Questionnaire (MLQ), *The Leadership Quarterly* 19, no. 5 (2008): 501–513; Carl P. Borchgrevink and Franklin J. Boster, "Leader-Member Exchange in a Total Service Industry: The Hospitality Business," in George B. Graen, *New Frontiers of Leadership* (Information Age Publishing, Inc., 2004).

11. J. M. Howell and B. J. Avolio, "Transformational Leadership, Transactional Leadership, Locus of Control, and Support for Innovation: Key Predictors of Consolidated-Business-Unit Performance," *Journal of Applied Psychology* 78, no. 6 (1993): 891–902; Bernard M. Bass and Ronald E. Riggio, *Transformational Leadership,* Psychology Press (2005); Anoop Patiar and Lokman Mia, "Transformational Leadership Style, Market Competition and Departmental Performance: Evidence from Luxury Hotels in Australia," *International Journal of Hospitality Management* 28, no. 2 (2009): 254–262; Mark R. Testa, "National Culture, Leadership and Citizenship: Implications for Cross-Cultural Management," *International Journal of Hospitality Management* 28, no. 1 (2009): 78–85.

12. Some of the information in this section was adapted from Nick Forster et al., "The Role of Story-telling in Organizational Leadership," *Leadership & Organization Development Journal* 20, no. 1 (1999): 11–17.

Key Terms

autocratic manager—A manager who typically stresses immediate, short-term results over concerns about people in a department or organization.

bureaucratic manager—A manager who typically makes decisions by enforcing rules, regulations, policies, and procedures that are already in place.

conceptual skill—An ability to see beyond the technical aspects of a job. Conceptual skills include recognizing the interdependence of various departments and functional areas within the organization and understanding how the organization fits into the structure of the industry, the community, and the wider world at large.

controlling—The traditional management function of assessing actual performance against standards to determine whether the organization or a staff member is on target for reaching goals, and taking corrective actions as necessary.

coordinating—The traditional management function of using resources efficiently to meet organizational goals and objectives. Coordinating typically consists of assigning work and organizing people and resources.

decisional role—A traditional management role performed when a manager acts as an entrepreneur, disturbance handler, resource allocator, or negotiator.

democratic manager—A manager who tends to focus more on a participative process than on short-term, immediate results.

directing—The traditional management function of influencing divisions, departments, and individual staff members to accomplish the organization's goals and objectives. Also referred to as leading.

disseminator—A traditional management role in which a manager passes information along to members of his or her staff who otherwise would not have access to it.

disturbance handler—A traditional management role in which a manager resolves conflicts among staff members and solves problems that arise in day-to-day operations.

entrepreneur—A traditional management role in which a manager initiates changes within a department or an organization.

figurehead—A traditional management role in which a manager performs ceremonial or symbolic acts as the formal representative of a department or an organization.

human relations skill—An ability related to working effectively with people at every level in the organization.

informational role—A traditional management role performed when a manager acts as a monitor, disseminator, or spokesperson.

interpersonal role—A traditional management role performed when a manager acts as a figurehead, leader, or liaison.

leader—A traditional management role in which a manager acts to create a productive atmosphere in the workplace. A leader encourages and motivates staff members by helping to align their individual needs with the overall goals of the department and organization.

liaison—A traditional management role in which a manager networks with peers and others outside the organization's vertical chain of command.

monitor—A traditional management role in which a manager scans the environment for information, questions personal contacts in other departments, or listens to staff members.

negotiator—A traditional management role in which a manager bargains with unions, contracts with suppliers, or sets goals with individual staff members.

organizing—The traditional management function of assembling limited resources to attain organizational goals. It involves establishing the flow of authority and communication among people.

planning—The traditional management function of creating goals and objectives, as well as programs of action to reach those goals and objectives.

resource allocator—The traditional management function of creating goals and objectives, as well as programs of action to reach those goals and objectives.

spokesperson—A traditional management role performed when a manager sends information through speeches, letters, reports, or memos to people outside the department or organization.

staffing—The traditional management function of completing the cycle of human resources activities: determining human resource needs and recruiting, selecting, hiring, training, and developing staff.

technical skill—Specialized knowledge of tools, techniques, methods, procedures, or processes associated with a specific type of activity.

 # Review Questions

1. How did Henri Fayol contribute to management theory?

2. What are the six traditional management functions and how do managers fulfill those functions?

3. What did John P. Kotter's study of general managers reveal?

4. What are the interpersonal, informational, and decisional roles of management?

5. How do technical, human relations, and conceptual skills help managers do their jobs?

6. What are the characteristics of the autocratic manager? the bureaucratic manager? the democratic manager?

7. What factors affect a manager's choice of management styles?

8. What is one of the greatest shortcomings of traditional management theories?

9. What four leadership theories are most dominant today?

Chapter Appendix

One Day in the Life of Hans Willimann

Hans R. Willimann, general manager of the 343-room Four Seasons Chicago, is a 13-year veteran of Four Seasons Hotels and Resorts, Toronto. Previously, he was the general manager of Four Seasons hotels in Boston and Houston.

7:11 A.M.

Our doorman stands in the middle of the street frantically waving down any taxi that would be so good as to dignify us with its presence. How many angry guests, I ponder, are going to call me this morning because even the doorman's aggressive hustling didn't get them their timely cabs? I contemplate giving cabbies a free car wash voucher if they respond to our doorman's lively trilling.

As I pull into the hotel, I see the milk truck is obstructing the entrance to and from the garage. I also see that the dock master is yelling; the department store truck cannot exit the receiving turntable, and the grease truck is on the wrong dock.

7:15 A.M.

The milk truck finally leaves, and I ascend to the eighth floor in the parking garage. Through the guest elevator I finally enter my serene and elegant hotel lobby. The oversized flower arrangement of snow-white daisies greets me. I make a mental note not to forget to spray the lobby with floral scent to complete our guest's impression of a multi-sensual experience.

My first concern is with room service. We are running a full house of demanding radiologists in town for meetings.

Pandemonium. Two waiters called in sick. One elevator is broken down. The repair service was notified at 6:15 A.M., but their voice mail directed us to press the right extension or the pound sign. We do not know the right extension and are pounding the phone. The service contract covers us only for the hours of 8 A.M. to 6 P.M. Anything before or after those appointed hours costs us $150—for starters.

7:20 A.M.

Where is the food and beverage director? Oh, I forgot. He worked the Governor's function last night until the wee hours, and I told him he should sleep in. So I call Banquets to check if they can help us out. Yes, two waiters are on their way.

Taking the emergency stairs, I huff and puff up to Housekeeping. The Executive Housekeeper's face seems flushed. I worry that she is close to a coronary.

"How do you expect me to make up the rooms?" she queries. "What's wrong with the emergency stairs?" I timidly ask. "Have you ever carried a bucket, vacuum cleaner, assorted sheets, pillow cases, soaps, shampoos, not to mention 12 terry-cloth bathrobes up three flights of stairs without a cart?" she answers. What can I say?

7:25 A.M.

My telephone rings. "Are you the manager?" "Yes sir. My name is—" "I don't care about your name. Just tell me why it should take 31 minutes for a lousy slice of dry toast and lukewarm coffee to be delivered to my room. Do you know how to run a luxury property? My corporation will never again stay in any of your miserable establishments." "Please, sir. I would like to apologize for the lapse in service." Too late; he hangs up. I remind myself that the customer is always right.

I check with room service. Yes, Room 4305 was very angry and did not leave a tip. I check with the Front Desk. Yes, they know the gentleman in 4305. He didn't have any credit cards, and when the assistant manager tried to get cash in advance, he could not be found. I check with Security. Yes, the gentleman in 4305 has his car in the garage—a 1978 Nova filled to the brim with wallpaper sample books. This guest arrived on our doorstep at 11:00 last night, relocated from another hotel. I call the doorman. "Do not deliver Room 4305's car without my personal approval or the guest's full payment on his account."

7:51 A.M.

The chief engineer is calling to inform me that the couple in Room 3802 seems to prefer taking a shower outside the bathtub, and the people in Room 3702, directly underneath, are complaining that their bathroom ceiling is leaking. "How could this happen in a luxury hotel?" they ask. "Did you use a cheap plumbing contractor?"

7:57 A.M.

Finally I head for breakfast. I order my usual fare—carrot juice to lower my cholesterol, yogurt with fresh berries, and our alternative cuisine bran/carrot muffins. Twenty minutes later my healthy victuals have not yet arrived at my table. The maitre d' informs me that the new pantry cook, who just arrived, had no idea how to squeeze a carrot. I settle for orange juice, and make a mental note to talk to the human resources director about taking pictures of all the menu items for new staff members.

8:23 A.M.

The Planning Committee is meeting with all division heads. I am late. The director of human resources reports that at the end of our first operating year, of the 18,000 individuals screened and interviewed, we hired 532. Our full-time head count is 498, and 76 positions have turned over and over and over. Should we increase our wages or contract this service? The Americans with Disabilities Act (ADA) mandates new employment practices that require rewriting all of our job descriptions.

The controller says we are surpassing our advertising budget, and the marketing director notes that the direct-mail campaign brought us only weekend business with a quadruple occupancy. We need to purchase more rollaway beds, and the guests all think the bathrobes and hair dryers are freebies.

I report that the Mayor and Alderman are very grateful for our participation in the Clean Sweep Program for Chicago. Could we also participate in the Adopt-a-Street Program and donate items for the annual food drive? By the way, the City Council passed a resolution to increase the room tax and the telephone tax.

The fire alarm interrupts the briefing. We spring to action, dispersing to our assigned emergency stations. The fire trucks come howling down the street. Guests file down staircases and out doorways. The fire fighters storm up to the 36th floor with fire axes in hand. Only then do we discover that a young child pulled the fire alarm by mistake.

People are upset, yelling about incompetent management. And—you guessed it—they threaten to stay at the venerable hotel across the street. "It doesn't happen over there," says one. "I'm going to miss my million-dollar merger meeting," says another. "You will certainly hear from my lawyer." "I want a rebate." I humbly beg their pardon, hand out my business card, and the beat goes on.

9:53 A.M.

Back to the meeting. We are going through the high balance report on all the guestrooms. And here's our old friend in Room 4305. Seems he called room service again, but this time he ordered $400 worth of champagne and caviar, with no credit cards. Let's call the police before this bird flies the coop.

10:29 A.M.

Eleven messages wait on my desk and one is holding. A prominent charity in town wants what every other charity in town wants—a weekend for two at the hotel. Naturally, they note in their very pleasant letter, it's tax deductible.

Here's a note from my very best friend, Don Schmo. "Remember me? We met in the St. Louis airport four years ago when our planes were delayed. You gave me your card and said that if I need a room in Chicago…" Funny, I've never been to St. Louis, and even if he were my best friend, we are 40 rooms overbooked due to a computer breakdown. But, he insists, don't GMs always have a room up their sleeves?

11:06 A.M.

The chef wants to resign. He has had it with the menu changes in our lounge—three times in two days. And a regular guest sent back her hamburger saying that she wanted it cooked black and blue, not bloody.

Speaking of employment, an executive search firm has been calling for the last three days wanting to know if I'd be interested in working in Hong Kong at twice my salary, living in. I decline, but make a mental note of their number.

12:00 noon

The vintner's luncheon is 30 minutes late. We will be doing a vertical tasting of the most exciting Cabernet Sauvignons. I hope to make it through without going horizontal.

My wife calls to remind me that I promised to baby-sit the kids at 8 P.M. while she attends a parent-teacher association meeting. And could I donate a raffle prize for the teacher's union? "Does that guarantee that my 7-year-old's teacher will not go on strike?" I snap.

12:15 P.M.

I am scanning the 15 guest comment cards. Twelve guests find that the attitude and service at the hotel is exceptional. One guest didn't like the decor, and one guest is allergic to feather pillows. I make a note to include the guest's wishes in our guest history.

12:30 P.M.

The press and the vintner are waiting for me. So is the goose liver and port luncheon. Into the third course, all the problems of the day seem so far away. However, by dessert, reality looms. My guilt button triggers remorse for not having worked out today, and I drag myself back to my office.

3:30 P.M.

The Regional VP invites me on an inspection tour of all guest corridors. Carpets need shampooing, walls need touch-up, baseboards could do with repair, and the sand in the ash urns needs to be changed. And whoever puts the hotel logo in the sand needs to press a little harder. The Regional VP mentions the impending inspection of the Area VP. "Do I have to be more explicit?" he hints with one eyebrow raised.

4:16 P.M.

I start working on the profit-and-loss statement for the last month. The cash flow is terrific. The bottom line has increased, and our guest retention is starting to become acceptable.

7:11 P.M.

The Mayor is supposed to arrive at the hotel. Could I escort him up to the dinner party? I am delighted. How many members of the press are waiting at the front door?

7:45 P.M.

The Sheik would like to extend his visit one more week. He needs 20 rooms. We're sold out. I start calling my hotel colleagues to round up some empty rooms.

8:15 P.M.

I am going through my mail and see my medical report. I need to lose 10 pounds, have excessive cholesterol, and should exercise at least three times a week for 50 minutes. Further, I should cut out sodium if I would like to see my children reach age 20.

8:25 P.M.

I leave the hotel and by 8:55 P.M. find my way back home, seeing all the morning sights in reverse. I pull into the garage, walk through the kitchen door, and wham. If looks could kill, I'd be one dead GM.

"What have I done?" I ask my wife in all innocence. "Remember that PTA meeting? Remember the raffle prize for the teacher?" she says.

I slink into the den and turn on CNN. Che, my golden retriever, looks at me with sad and knowing eyes and signals to me that he is looking forward to fetching the paper at 5:30 A.M.

Source: Adapted from Hans R. Willimann, "One Day in the Life of Hans Willimann," *HOTELS* 26, no. 8 (August 1992): 63–64.

Chapter 3 Outline

Competencies

1. Describe the rationale for and evolution of quality management. (pp. 75–77)

2. Summarize W. Edwards Deming's 14 points for management. (pp. 77–83)

3. Discuss Joseph Juran's approach to quality management. (pp. 83–87)

4. Explain the contributions made by Walter Shewhart, the Shewhart Cycle, and the IDEAL^{SM} Model to quality management. (pp. 87–88)

5. Identify ISO and explain how it can contribute to a business's quality-management efforts. (pp. 88–93)

3

The Quest for Quality

This chapter was revised for this edition by John Mellon, Associate
Professor of Business, Misericordia University, Dallas, Pennsylvania.

Quality is never an accident; it is always the result of intelligent effort.
—John Ruskin, 19th-century reformer[1]

QUALITY IS EXTREMELY IMPORTANT in the hospitality industry. To better understand this, we can contrast the hospitality industry with other industries, such as those in manufacturing. One of the biggest differences between a manufacturing organization and a hospitality organization is that workers in manufacturing are aware that they are doing their part to make something that somebody will see, feel, and use. In contrast, hospitality employees are typically not aware that they are "manufacturing" a product, but they are: that product is service. Often, hospitality employees have no perception of their work being a product or that their jobs have an impact on the success of the property.[2]

In this chapter, we will take a look at the rationale for and evolution of quality management. Next we will examine the quality-management contributions of two giants in the field, W. Edwards Deming and Joseph Juran. Deming provided a new and comprehensive theory for managing organizations; Juran provided an analytical approach to managing for quality. The quality-management methods of Walter Shewhart (who influenced Deming) and the IDEAL[SM] model (which is based on Shewhart's work) are covered next. Finally, the chapter concludes with a discussion of ISO—the International Organization for Standardization—and its contribution to the quest for quality among businesses throughout the world.

The Rationale for Quality Management

Service always involves the guest as part of a transaction, and the goal of high-quality service is to ensure a satisfied guest. A high-quality service is one that meets or exceeds the guest's expectations. The components of perceived service quality have been identified as:

1. *Reliability:* the ability to provide a service as expected by the guest.

2. *Assurance:* the degree to which the guest can feel confident that the service will be correctly provided.

3. *Tangibles:* the quality of the physical environment and materials used in providing the service.

4. *Responsiveness:* the ability of the service provider to respond to the individual needs of a particular guest.

5. *Empathy:* the courtesy, understanding, and friendliness shown by the service provider.[3]

One of the best ways for managers in the hospitality industry to distinguish their properties from others is to provide excellent service to guests. Hospitality managers want every employee to provide high-quality service to every guest, every time. Just as with companies in other industries, hospitality companies are under pressure to be profitable and keep costs down. However, in most situations it is money well spent to implement quality-management principles and strategies, because where they are present, guests get the best service and employees are treated with the respect they deserve.[4] This view is embodied in the company motto that the quality-conscious Ritz-Carlton hotel chain teaches to every staff member in the organization: "We Are Ladies and Gentleman Serving Ladies and Gentleman." Giving guests great service and treating employees well are critical factors in maintaining a healthy bottom line.

A big challenge for hospitality industry managers is to ensure that service standards are communicated, understood, and maintained throughout their organizations.[5] Hotel employees hear all about quality standards from the general manager and other managers, but it's not until managers demonstrate and live out those standards that employees really learn what quality service means. The behavior of managers is more closely observed by employees than managers may realize, and it is their behavior that determines to a great extent how the members of an organization behave.[6] In short, quality management is not simply a management tool to be added on to other management tools, but an overall way of managing that managers must embody and model.

In today's highly competitive business environment, high levels of quality are becoming requisites for staying in business. Thus, the goal of quality management is to deliver the highest value for the guest at the lowest cost while achieving profits and economic stability for the hospitality operation.

While quality management is vital to an organization's success, it can be difficult to achieve. It is not just a way to deliver higher-quality products and services; it is also a way to change how people think, work, and relate to other people. Quality involves improving everything an organization does. Managing for high quality is stressful and demanding, loaded with surprises and problems, and is constantly challenging—especially for the head of the hospitality operation.[7]

Hospitality operations need to focus their strategies, their operations, and their employees on their customers and create a quality-service culture with high employee participation. To do this, top management must commit to a vision and train employees to accomplish a common mission. Another important principle in implementing quality management is to incorporate a system to measure quality improvement in every product, process, and service. This must be established as a prime organizational operating principle and never made subservient to costs.[8] Achieving and maintaining long-term relationships with customers, employees, and suppliers should be management's focus rather than short-term profits.[9]

To establish a connection between quality management and financial success, research on the relationship between quality and financial performance began in the 1970s with studies associated with the Profit Impact of Market Strategy (PIMS) project. PIMS project researchers looked into the effects of various marketing strategies on financial performance at corporations and found a strong link between service quality and financial success. Quality-management gurus have always assumed that improving product quality would improve profitability, and it turns out they were correct.[10]

The Evolution of Quality Management

The past several decades have seen the rise and fall of many approaches to quality. Quality control, quality assurance, quality circles, total quality management (TQM), and continuous improvement are just a few of the quality movements that captured the interest of hospitality business leaders who saw a need to change the way their organizations conducted business. One of the most important lessons learned from these movements is that quality is a journey, not a destination.

Quality, in fact, is a moving target. The hospitality industry, buffeted by the winds of change that rule the marketplace and the overall economy, must continually search for the most effective leadership and management systems in its quest for quality—quality as defined by the ever-changing wants and needs of guests and the offerings of competitors.

The discipline of quality management has its roots in agriculture. In the early 1900s in Great Britain, R. A. Fisher conducted statistical research to assist farmers in understanding how to optimally plant and rotate crops. This work inspired Walter Shewhart, whose work subsequently motivated W. Edwards Deming to devote his life to the teaching and improvement of quality methods. Deming became the best-known quality expert of his day, although Joseph Juran ran a close second in prestige and respect in the field.[11] Both men helped improve quality in private and public organizations in manufacturing, services, education, and government. Many credit these two quality pioneers for the recovery of Japanese industry after World War II, and that country's subsequent success in world markets. The once-radical ideas of Deming and Juran are now part of the everyday language of business. In the following sections, we will explore many of the concepts advanced by these two men, concepts that can be used by hospitality organizations to meet the challenges of global competition.

W. Edwards Deming and Quality Management

W. Edwards Deming is considered by many to be the father of quality management. Deming was a philosopher who desired to provide a new way to view the world and advocated returning the quality control function to the worker. Deming was a mathematician and physicist by training, and his contributions range from detailed applications of statistical quality techniques to unrelenting criticism of traditional management methods. Deming's contention that managers should be helpful rather than authoritarian reflects the position of numerous historical management theorists, including Likert, Maslow, McClelland, and Herzberg.

Exhibit 1   Deming's 14 Points for Management

1. Create constancy of purpose.
2. Adopt the new philosophy.
3. Cease dependence on inspection to achieve quality.
4. End the practice of awarding business on the basis of price tag.
5. Improve constantly and forever the system of production and service.
6. Institute job training.
7. Institute leadership.
8. Drive out fear.
9. Break down barriers between departments.
10. Eliminate slogans.
11. Eliminate work standards (quotas).
12. Remove barriers that rob employees of pride of workmanship.
13. Institute a vigorous program of education and self-improvement.
14. Put everybody in the company to work to accomplish the transformation.

Source: W. Edwards Deming, *Out of the Crisis* (Cambridge, Mass.: Massachusetts Institute of Technology, Center for Advanced Engineering Study, 1982), pp. 23–24.

Deming's 14 Points

Perhaps the most widely known feature of Deming's work is his "**14 points for management**" (see Exhibit 1). The short sections that follow focus on these points, which summarize core features of Deming's approach to quality and his ideas for reforming the nature of leadership and management.

Point 1: Create Constancy of Purpose. That is, create a dedication for innovation and continuous improvement in quality that stretches into the future. This implies a strategic plan that identifies resources needed for quality improvement. In essence, Deming called for companies to take a long-term view. Often he found managers directing their time and energy almost exclusively toward achieving immediate financial goals. Deming suggested that the future success of a business depends on whether it has a clear purpose and a core set of values that do not change over time. A business with a constancy of purpose is more likely to innovate, invest in research and education, and continuously search for ways to improve. Within the hospitality industry, Ritz-Carlton is a conspicuous example of a company with long-term goals and a core set of values.

Point 2: Adopt the New Philosophy. Transform the organization, Deming said, starting at the top, toward continuous quality improvement. Instill the idea that mistakes are not the natural course of production.

In today's fiercely competitive markets, new management practices have emerged from the realization that long-term success is only achieved by consistently meeting or exceeding the expectations of customers. The new management philosophies and practices are based on quality, not quantity; repeat business, not one-time sales.

This point emphasizes that management must lead the way in the quality-improvement revolution. In fact, Deming stated that, in his mind, point 2 calls for a "transformation of management" in which managers become committed to the quality-improvement program. Management involvement is critical to the success of any quality-management effort.

Point 3: Cease Dependence on Inspection to Achieve Quality. Deming said that the American tradition of mass inspection implied that the production process was inherently flawed. Historically, American workers focused on the quantity produced, with the knowledge that quality-control inspectors would identify mistakes. But Deming recognized that the work involved in trying to salvage defective products discovered during the inspection process is very costly. Quality comes from improvement of the process, not inspection, Deming maintained.

As a practical matter, Deming acknowledged that a certain amount of inspection is always needed, if only to monitor progress toward organizational goals and evaluate individual performance. In the hospitality industry, for example, inspection of incoming food products is always necessary to determine which suppliers provide the highest quality and to prevent problems in food production areas.

What Deming rejected, however, is the notion that inspection of the final result of a process creates a quality product or service. For example, inspecting prepared menu items before servers deliver them to waiting guests may catch errors and defects in orders, but this type of inspection will do nothing to improve the process so that errors are not made in the first place. In fact, this kind of inspection seems to expect defects and may encourage a lax attitude on the part of cooks and servers.

Deming maintained that you cannot inspect quality into a product or service. Just because a hotel manager insists that every guestroom be inspected before front desk agents can issue room keys does not guarantee quality (that is, well-cleaned) guestrooms. No amount of inspection after the fact will improve the output of a guestroom-cleaning process. In Deming's view, such an inspection program only adds layers of housekeeping inspectors and encourages an attitude of indifference on the part of housekeepers. Why take pride in your work when someone else is paid to find mistakes? Why worry about the quality of the guestroom when "quality" is someone else's job? Inspection does not create quality; it only finds defects.

Point 4: End the Practice of Awarding Business on the Basis of Price Tag. The lowest-price bidder usually has not emphasized quality. Instead, a business should cultivate a long-term relationship with one or two reliable suppliers who emphasize quality, Deming said.

Purchasing agents must learn how the materials they order are actually used in production processes and service-delivery systems. Always selecting the lowest-priced items may cause considerable problems, making simple tasks difficult or lowering the quality of service. Controllers often pit several vendors against one another and do business only with the vendor with the lowest prices. Over time, this practice may actually raise the cost of doing business. Not only does it increase the paperwork and time necessary to keep track of constantly changing suppliers, it may also drive good vendors out of business.

Deming suggested that purchasers and suppliers should have more cooperative and less adversarial relationships. According to Deming, a long-term relationship of loyalty and trust with a single vendor will benefit a company more than the immediate savings of buying from the lowest bidder. When suppliers are assured of long-term contracts, they are more likely to invest time and money in improving their products and services. Also, with long-term relationships, suppliers might become more flexible in the timing and frequency of deliveries—an important factor to many hospitality businesses.

Point 5: Improve Constantly and Forever the System of Production and Service. Quality must be built into the process. Quality is continuously monitored by statistical control techniques, so that a problem can be corrected as it occurs, not after the fact. Deming emphasized that quality improvement is not a one-time effort and is not limited to solving problems. Problem-solving "puts out fires" but usually results in putting a process back to where it was in the first place. Deming asserted that the real task of management is to look for ways to improve the process itself. Perhaps work flow can be redesigned or some parts of the process can be automated, thus eliminating certain opportunities for error.

Point 6: Institute Job Training. The foundation and prerequisite for any quality-improvement effort is job training. Variations in production and service systems often result from managers and employees who have not been properly or fully trained. Therefore, managers and employees should be given formal job training. Such training should provide employees with the tools they need to do their jobs correctly, and provide managers with the tools they need to evaluate processes and improve systems within the company.

Point 7: Institute Leadership. Management must lead by focusing on improvement, removing barriers to improvement, and managing the system rather than supervising the day-to-day activities of workers. Deming stressed that managers must remove the barriers that prevent employees from taking pride in their work. Employees are usually well aware of these barriers, which sometimes take such forms as:

- Pressure to perform without concern for quality—when managers purposely short-staff a shift, for example.

- An overriding emphasis on numbers—when managers demand that each housekeeper clean 14 rooms a day, regardless of the types of rooms or the number of guests staying in those rooms.

- Poor tools—when vacuum cleaners often break down in housekeeping or when spotted silverware is always stocked at server stations in the dining room.

- Deaf ears to suggestions—when employees recommend improvements to managers and the managers refuse to listen or take action.

Managers must act on the information they gather and remove the obstacles that prevent their employees from performing at their best.

Point 8: Drive Out Fear. Many workers are afraid that if they report problems or suggest improvements, they will rock the boat and lose their jobs. Management must drive out sources of fear and focus on fostering a positive acceptance of change. Deming constantly stressed that people cannot perform to the best of their ability unless they feel secure. When the managers of an organization lack leadership ability and the employees are poorly trained, fear rules the workplace. Deming recognized this fear as a primary cause of quality and productivity problems. Little can be done to improve quality when people in the organization are afraid to point out problems. Employees and managers alike won't express new ideas, ask for assistance, or even complain about broken equipment when they fear reprisals from above. As managers create more open and less threatening work environments and take their quality-management responsibilities seriously, employees develop the confidence to contribute new ideas and make suggestions for improvement.

Point 9: Break Down Barriers Between Departments. Traditionally, workers identify with their specializations and distrust those from other areas. They often set up competing goals that generate conflicts. Cross-functional teams must be set up to break down barriers between departments and set up areas of cooperation.

In some cases, barriers are erected because managers are more concerned with building empires than fostering cooperation with other departments. Supervisors and line employees take up arms and fight their managers' turf battles, often blaming other departments for their own problems or for problems experienced by guests. Guest complaints are handled with phrases like:

- "That's housekeeping's fault."

- "Don't ask at the front desk, they never help anyone."

- "Sorry about the mix-up and the delay—the cooks are always making mistakes."

Guests become unsympathetic victims of these internal turf battles. While individual departments might win an occasional battle, the entire organization loses the war when guests depart the property unhappy.

To prevent these kinds of problems, each department must know not only how its work affects guests, but how its work affects other departments or areas within the organization as well. Cross-functional teams can break down barriers and set up areas of cooperation among departments.

Point 10: Eliminate Slogans. Slogans exhorting workers toward improvement are worthless, Deming said, because they do not give any direction on how to improve. Empty slogans usually suggest that performance would improve if employees just tried harder. Slogans, banners, buttons, or balloons cannot sustain a quality-improvement effort. They are usually aimed at motivating people to work faster and produce more. Deming stated that slogans actually have a negative impact on productivity and quality. Employees perceive slogans as signs that management not only doesn't understand their problems, it doesn't care enough to find out what their problems are. Deming also claimed that slogans represent the hope that workers could, simply by some additional effort, accomplish the goals set by management. But a goal without a method for reaching it is useless.

Managers must learn that the responsibility for improving the system is theirs, not their employees'.

Point 11: Eliminate Work Standards (Quotas). Quotas focus on quantity instead of quality. Deming argued that quotas ignore quality issues, such as guest expectations, and are typically based simply on what managers have concluded is necessary to achieve the goals of the operation. For example, consider the practice of a restaurant manager who sets service quotas (number of guests served, or tables turned) based on a predetermined average performance, rather than on the individual talents of each server. If the quotas are too low, the above-average servers may quit to go work at other restaurants where they can make more money and management may take greater pride in their abilities. If the quotas are too high for the below-average servers, these servers are pushed beyond their skill levels, often at the expense of guests.

Deming maintained that this kind of practice not only lowers morale and encourages shoddy performance; it actually creates inefficiencies and leads to higher costs. Deming suggested that the key to productivity and quality improvement is for managers to identify the different levels of skill and talent among members of their staffs and then plan the work to make the most of those differences, thus improving overall performance.

Point 12: Remove Barriers that Rob Employees of Pride of Workmanship. Most people want to do a good job and are frustrated when barriers block them from accomplishment. Typical barriers are misguided supervisors, faulty machines, and poor material. Performance appraisals and merit pay are also barriers, Deming said, because they focus on individual performance when, in actuality, many aspects of an individual's overall performance are largely out of the control of the individual worker.

Deming suggested that employees are often evaluated on outcomes over which they have little control. The desire and ability of an employee is not enough to overcome problems and barriers caused by inadequate systems, poor training, and improper tools. It's management's job to create the systems, provide the training, and furnish the tools that will enable employees to give their best performance and produce work they can take pride in.

Managers can start removing barriers that hinder employees by asking such basic questions as the following:

- Do my employees understand what their jobs are?

- Do my employees know what level of work is acceptable?

- Have my employees been adequately trained?

- Is the equipment my employees use in good condition? Is it the right equipment for the job?

- Are all of my employees getting the assistance they need from me and from other managers?

- How can my employees report problems or suggestions?

- What is my response time to problems or suggestions offered by employees?

In order to achieve quality, Deming insisted that all employees must be given the tools and training they need to perform well and take pride in their work. This often requires that managers first listen to employees and then act on their suggestions and requests. Listening and following up take time and effort. Upper-level managers must encourage and reward all managers in the organization to listen to employees and remove the barriers to pride of workmanship.

Point 13: Institute a Vigorous Program of Education and Self-Improvement. Workers require continuous self-improvement opportunities in teamwork and statistical procedures in order to make suggestions for continuous improvements in quality. It's no longer sufficient to simply have good people in the right positions. All employees must be ready, willing, and able to acquire new knowledge, skills, and competencies to deal with the fast-paced changes in market demands and technological advances.

Point 14: Put Everybody in the Company to Work to Accomplish the Transformation. Deming's 14 points do not offer a specific blueprint for change. There are no predetermined actions to guide hospitality organizations in the implementation of a quality-improvement process. Deming firmly insisted that each company must work out its own adaptation of the previous thirteen points—an adaptation suitable to its own particular mission, culture, and markets. Everyone within an organization must work together in developing a mutual understanding of Deming's points, then set appropriate goals and create action plans to achieve those goals. Without this organization-wide understanding, departments and individuals may spin their wheels, travel in different directions, or work at cross-purposes and undercut each other's efforts.

Joseph Juran and Quality Management

Joseph M. Juran had an approach to quality that agrees with many of the fundamental ideas and concepts of W. Edwards Deming. However, Juran delved much more deeply into the mechanics of actually implementing a system of quality improvement within an organization. He emphasized the need for a common language of quality. He offered some basic terms and definitions that he felt were essential to the success of any quality improvement effort, but he advised each organization to also compile and distribute its own glossary of quality terms.

For Juran, the term "product" included both goods and services and is defined as the output of a process; "process" is defined as a set of organizational activities that, taken together, produce a result that is of value to a customer. Products and processes are not confined to the work of a single department. The process that creates a product may well include several departments and areas within an organization. For example, a clean guestroom is primarily the output, or product, of a cleaning process within a hotel's housekeeping department. A guestroom available for sale, on the other hand, is the output of a larger process that includes the work of several hotel departments. Certainly housekeeping must clean the room, but the preventive maintenance and repair work of the engineering department also contributes to the room's availability for sale. Housekeeping could clean a room and engineering could perform repairs to the room, but the room might not be

Exhibit 2   Juran's Ten-Step Quality-Improvement Process

1. Build awareness of the need and opportunity for improvement.
2. Set goals for improvement.
3. Organize to reach the goals.
4. Provide training throughout the organization.
5. Carry out projects to solve problems.
6. Report progress.
7. Give recognition.
8. Communicate results.
9. Keep score.
10. Maintain momentum by making annual improvement part of the regular systems and processes of the company.

sold because of communication breakdowns between housekeeping, engineering, and the front desk. If housekeeping or engineering fails to report the readiness of a room to the front desk, the room does not become available for sale and the hotel could lose revenue for each night the room goes unsold. Front office activities that make a guestroom available for sale are also part of this particular process.

Juran defines the quality of a product in terms of its "fitness for use." This definition focuses on the perspective of the product's end-user: the customer. A customer is anyone affected by a product or by the processes that create the product. In this sense, customers can be either external or internal. In the hospitality industry, **external customers** are defined as guests; **internal customers** are staff members of the hotel or other hospitality business who must cooperate with each other to deliver a product or service to external customers. For example, the guest is housekeeping's external customer, but front desk staff and engineering department personnel are housekeeping's primary internal customers.

Juran's ten-step quality-improvement process (see Exhibit 2) provides general quality-improvement directions for hospitality operations.

Quality as Product Features

Juran identified one form of quality as making sure the features of a product or service meet the needs of customers. The key to ensuring this form of quality is keeping in touch with the changing needs of customers and providing those product features that create customer satisfaction. To maintain and increase revenues, hospitality companies continually create new product features and new processes to produce those features.

There is no universal unit of measurement for this form of quality. Most hotels and restaurants have formal systems for collecting and analyzing feedback from guests. Companies analyze information from guest surveys and comment cards, customer focus groups, and other sources to identify which features of their current products or services are important to their guests. This information is also used to identify new features to develop and, thereby, raise the level of guest satisfaction. For example, over the past several years many hotels have dramatically reduced the amount of time that guests spend checking in or checking out. This quality improvement began with hotels finding out that a speedy check-in and an even faster check-out were important criteria consistently used by guests to evaluate the quality of their stay.

Quality as Freedom from Defects

Juran argued that creating higher quality by reducing defects significantly lowers the costs of doing business. Lower costs result from reductions in error rates, rework, waste, inspections, and service-recovery expenses (such as providing complimentary meals to angry restaurant guests). To keep costs competitive, companies must continually reduce the level of product defects as well as defects in the processes used to produce their products.

For example, on a monthly basis, a hotel might want to measure the quality of its guestroom cleaning process in terms of the amount of rework needed after rooms have been reported as ready and available for sale. In this case, the numerator (frequency of defects) might be the number of times each day, week, or month hotel staff members must respond to guest requests for items (such as towels, soap, glasses, room amenities, and so on) that housekeepers should have stocked when cleaning the room but didn't. The denominator (opportunities for defects) might be the total number of items that housekeepers stock in each room, multiplied by the number of occupied rooms for the day, week, or month. If the **defect ratio** for housekeeping rework is unacceptable, managers and staff can work to eliminate the causes of the defects and, thereby, improve the process.

The value of the "freedom from defects" approach to quality is that it awakens managers to unnecessary costs of doing business and enables them to understand the importance of setting quality-improvement goals.

Quality Planning and Control

Juran proposed that quality planning and control are fundamentally similar to financial planning and control. Quality planning should also be a company-wide effort to determine specific, measurable quality objectives for areas within the organization. These objectives can then be coordinated with the company's overall quality goals. For example, a hospitality company might determine that an overall quality goal is to achieve a ten-percent improvement in guest service ratings by the end of the first business quarter. Department managers and staff then identify the actions they will take to improve guest service. Once actions are approved, a measurement system is devised as a quality-control tool that managers can use to monitor performance. As the business quarter progresses, managers receive weekly, or perhaps daily, summaries of quality ratings from guests. Just as they do with financial control processes, managers note variances between actual and targeted performance, and take corrective action as necessary. And, just as financial planning and control are not one-time activities (budgets are reforecasted as business and market conditions change), so quality planning and control are continuous activities within the organization.

Quality Improvement

For Juran, quality planning and control mainly focus on customer satisfaction, and include activities related to enhancing product features to meet customer needs. Quality *improvement*, on the other hand, concentrates on avoiding guest dissatisfaction by eliminating defects in products or services as well as in the processes used to make products and deliver services. Juran defines quality improvement as the reduction of defects on an unprecedented scale, which leads to **breakthrough performance**—measurable results producing previously unattainable savings in the cost of doing business.

Organizing for Quality Improvement. According to Juran, quality improvement should be mandated, not left to the whims or initiatives of individual managers. Quality-improvement efforts should be coordinated as an integral part of a company's business plan, with specific, measurable quality-improvement targets. This kind of annual quality-improvement process represents a new management responsibility and radically changes the focus of business operations.

For Juran, the first step in mobilizing for quality is to establish the organizational infrastructure needed to secure annual quality improvement. Infrastructure needs vary tremendously from one organization to another. What works well for one company might be disastrous for another. Each hospitality company must assess its own unique organizational needs in relation to its quality goals, size of operation, expertise of management and staff, and other factors. The infrastructure Juran recommends includes the formation of a **quality council** (also called a quality-improvement council, quality committee, quality steering committee, and other titles). The basic responsibility of a quality council is to launch, coordinate, and institutionalize quality-improvement efforts throughout the organization.

Members of the quality council are drawn from the ranks of senior managers. Juran noted that limiting membership to lower-level managers and staff sends a message throughout an organization that quality improvement is not a high-priority item for the company. For Juran, the value of a quality council made up of senior managers lies in such a council's ability to identify specific issues and problems, schedule them for solution, and assign responsibility to individuals or, as necessary, to interdepartmental teams. The council is also responsible for changing the prevailing reward system, which more than likely reinforces the actions of individuals in meeting operating goals instead of encouraging teamwork and progress toward quality improvements. Additional quality council responsibilities may include the following:

*   Establishing a process for identifying issues and problems that need quality-improvement efforts.

*   Determining the process for establishing quality-improvement teams.

*   Providing needed resources such as training, time for working on quality-improvement projects, and other forms of support.

*   Assuring that project solutions are implemented.

*   Designing tools for measuring quality improvement, **benchmarking** against competitors and others, and evaluating the performance of managers and staff.

- Coordinating quality-improvement projects, reviewing progress, and providing recognition.

Juran suggested that an organization's first quality-improvement effort should focus on a major issue or problem that holds a high probability for successful resolution. He recommended the following criteria for selecting the first quality-improvement project:

- Focus on a chronic issue or problem—one that is perceived and understood by many people in the organization and one that they have wanted to solve for some time.

- Select a project with a feasible solution—there should be a strong likelihood of successfully completing the project within a relatively short time frame (no longer than a few months).

- Make sure that the issue or problem is significant—people within the organization must be able to recognize a successful effort as meaningful to their departments or to the organization as a whole.

- Measure the results—in financial terms as well as in other terms that people throughout the organization will understand and appreciate.

Criteria for selecting later quality-improvement projects include factors such as return on investment, amount of potential improvement, urgency, ease of technological solution, and the amount of change suggested by probable solutions.

Life Cycle of a Quality-Improvement Project. In Juran's scheme, once a project is selected by the quality council, the project's parameters are defined in a mission statement and the project is assigned to a project team. The team usually meets for an hour once a week. At each meeting, the team reviews progress since the previous meeting, agrees on the actions to be taken before the next meeting, and asks individual members to accept responsibility for completing those actions. Actions include defining the issue or problem at hand, identifying root causes of the problem, determining solutions, selecting and implementing the best solution, and establishing controls to monitor success.

As the team progresses with its project, it issues periodic reports to team members, upper management, and others. Upper managers can use these reports to review the team's progress. A final report by a quality-improvement team generally summarizes the results achieved and provides a brief description of the activities that led to the results. Juran encouraged teams to also include a section on "lessons learned" that describes methods, procedures, or techniques for improving quality that the teams learned during their projects—lessons that can be applied elsewhere in the company.

Other Quality-Management Models

The work of Deming and Juran is of enduring value. Both men provide a deeper understanding of management problems and enable managers to take more effective actions for planning, initiating, and studying changes for improvement, and then acting on what they observe after the changes have been initiated. Of course, theirs are not the only quality-management approaches. In this section we will take a brief look at the work of Walter Shewhart and his Shewhart Cycle, along with an offshoot of the Shewhart Cycle—the IDEAL[SM] Model.

Walter Shewhart and the Shewhart Cycle

Walter Andrew Shewhart (March 18, 1891–March 11, 1967) was a physicist, engineer, and statistician, and is known as the "father of statistical quality control."[12] The American Society for Quality's first honorary member, he successfully brought together the disciplines of statistics, engineering, and economics.[13]

Shewhart realized that a continual adjustment during the production process in reaction to non-conformance actually decreases quality. In 1924, Shewhart framed the problem in terms of assignable-cause and chance-cause variation, and introduced the control chart as a tool for distinguishing between the two. His monumental work, *Economic Control of Quality of Manufactured Product*, published in 1931, is regarded as a complete and thorough exposition of the basic principles of quality control.[14] Shewhart also authored *Statistical Method from the Viewpoint of Quality Control* (published in 1939) and *Industrial Quality Control* (published in 1949).

Shewhart developed the Shewhart Learning and Improvement Cycle (see Exhibit 3), which combines creative management thinking with statistical analysis. This cycle contains four steps: Plan, Do, Check, and Act (it is also commonly known as the "Plan-Do-Check-Act" or PDCA Cycle). The steps in this cycle, Shewhart believed, ultimately lead to total quality improvement as the cycle is repeated. The cycle draws its structure from the notion that constant evaluation of management practices—as well as the willingness of management to disregard unsupported ideas—are keys to the evolution of a successful enterprise.[15] The cycle originated with Shewhart and was subsequently modified and applied to management practices by Deming.[16]

The IDEAL[SM] Model

The IDEAL[SM] model (see Exhibit 4) was created by the Software Engineering Institute (SEI) and is an adaptation of the Shewhart Cycle. It is an organizational improvement model that serves as a roadmap for initiating, planning, and implementing improvement actions. The IDEAL[SM] model is named for the five phases it describes: Initiating, Diagnosing, Establishing, Acting, and Learning. It originally grew out of a model for software process improvement, but, recognizing that the model had great potential outside of the software arena, SEI revised the model for broader application.[17]

ISO and the Quest for Quality

ISO—the International Organization for Standardization—is an international standard-setting body with a membership of more than 100 countries. Headquartered in Geneva, ISO was founded in 1947 to encourage worldwide industrial and commercial standards. Because "International Organization for Standardization"

Exhibit 3   The Shewhart Learning and Improvement Cycle

Plan

1. Study the process.
2. Recognize the opportunity:
   Define the opportunity.
   Define the theory on how to realize the opportunity.
3. Choose between several suggestions.
4. Predict the outcome—form a hypothesis.

Do

1. Test the theory to achieve the opportunity,
2. Preferably on a small scale,
3. According to the plan.
4. Test on customers to:
   Increase satisfaction by educating them.
   Improve your understanding of customers' expectations.

Check

1. Observe the test results.
2. Use statistical methods where possible.
3. Do they correspond with hopes and expectations?
4. How does it affect your ability to predict tomorrow's results?

Act

1. Three options:
   Adopt the change.
   Abandon the change.
   Modify your prediction or rerun the cycle with different variables.

would be abbreviated with different letters in different languages, "ISO" was chosen as the standard short form of the organization's name, a decision reflecting the standardizing spirit of the organization itself. "ISO" is derived from the Greek "isos," meaning "equal," which echoes the organization's goal of equalizing or standardizing business specifications and processes worldwide. ISO's philosophy is that standards facilitate quality, and international standards make products and services better for consumers and facilitate trade between countries.

ISO publishes quality standards for voluntary adoption by businesses throughout the world. Governments sometimes use ISO standards when creating laws to regulate businesses; in other instances, ISO standards are incorporated into international treaties. ISO 9000 and 14000 quality standards represent an effort by ISO to endorse and encourage a quest for quality by hospitality and other businesses. ISO 9000 standards constitute a widely accepted definition of

Exhibit 4   The IDEAL℠ Model

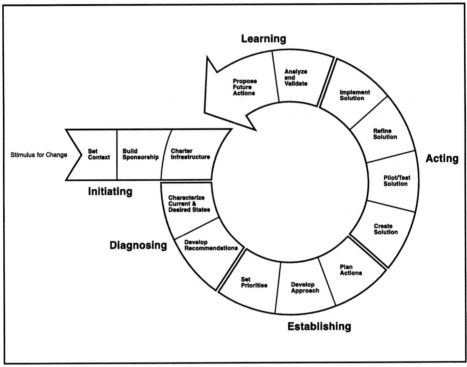

Source: The "IDEAL Model Graphic," copyright 2007 by Carnegie Mellon University, is reproduced with special permission from the Software Engineering Institute.[18]

the basic features of an effective quality-management system. ISO 9000 consists of twenty clauses that govern in minute detail all of the requisites for an ISO-certified quality-management system. These clauses cover the various areas and procedures of a well-run business, including detailed descriptions of management responsibility, the quality system, and purchasing, to mention just three. ISO certification comes via inspection by an outside body that examines an organization wishing to be ISO 9000 accredited.

ISO 14000 environmental management standards were developed to meet the demand for a single international standard for businesses that wish to reduce their environmental footprint by decreasing the pollution and waste they produce. ISO 14000 standards were developed through consensus by an international technical advisory committee of industry professionals, government officials, consumer interest groups, and the general public.

Strongly favored and supported by European companies, ISO 9000, though a voluntary standard, became a presupposition for most international companies that wished to do business in Europe. It is anticipated that a similar process will take place regarding the ISO 14000 environmental standards, and that most international companies will require that their suppliers be ISO 14000 certified.[19]

ISO Certification

To qualify for either ISO 9000 or 14000 certification, a company must write a specific, step-by-step guide for complying with ISO's standards, and then demonstrate that it does indeed follow the standards. John Huey learned just how involved the process was when he directed the ISO 14000 certification process for the division of Delaware North Companies that manages guest services in tourist spots like the Yosemite and Sequoia national parks. First, Huey drafted an environmental-management policy. Then he documented the company's environmental impact, tracking water use, energy use, and food recycling. Next, he devised a plan to reduce waste, researched legal requirements, trained employees, brought in a consultant to prepare for the compliance audit, and conducted his own preliminary audit. And still, there was more work to be done. Huey shipped 300 pages of documents to a third-party auditor for a "desk audit" (ISO doesn't certify companies itself—750 or so independent firms handle that), then flew the auditor to each of the five sites he was certifying. The auditor spent a day or so at each site, interviewing employees, reviewing Delaware North's adherence to ISO standards, and noting infractions. Two months later, Huey had to fly the auditor in again to re-interview staffers, take another look at the documentation, and confirm that the infractions had been corrected. Finally, eighteen months and about $115,000 later, the sites were certified.

Many companies, such as Delaware North, that have implemented an ISO 9000 quality-management system have realized significant improvements, but many object to the burdensome documentation requirements. The authors of the ISO 14000 standards took this into account, and asked for written documentation of policy and/or procedures in only four or five instances. Those companies that put document control and recordkeeping systems in place to comply with ISO 9000 are at a major advantage in implementing ISO 14000.[20]

Advantages of ISO Certification. Hospitality organizations that have implemented ISO 9000 have gained such benefits as reduced staff turnover, waste reduction, and favorable publicity. One study also cited positive changes in operational factors, customer satisfaction, and employee turnover, enthusiasm, cooperation, and communication. ISO 14000 certification typically is pursued to enhance a corporation's image and community relations, improve the environment, and secure marketing advantages.

Disadvantages of ISO Certification. The disadvantages of ISO certification for hospitality firms are similar to the disadvantages experienced by other businesses—namely, ISO certification reduces a business's flexibility and is time-consuming, expensive, and bureaucratic to achieve. The cost of implementing an environmental-management system that meets ISO 14000 standards, for example, can be expensive; a range of costs between $15,000–$150,000 per site have been reported, depending on the size and complexity of the operation. Obtaining ISO certification requires codifying nearly every aspect of a business's operations—something that runs counter to the style of fast-moving entrepreneurial organizations. But if companies do not go through the process, they often can't work for big corporations that require or prefer that the companies they hire be ISO certified.

Integrating Quality Management into Hospitality Operations

The hospitality industry is too complex to be handled by any single approach to quality. There are many roads to nurturing a quality-driven business culture. The road that works best for a particular hospitality business is the one that runs straight through its own unique organization. Therefore, as you might expect, no two hospitality businesses adopt, create, or use quality-management systems in exactly the same way. Some use or adapt for their own needs Deming's 14 points for management, others are drawn more to Juran's approach to quality, still others may use the Plan-Do-Check-Act Cycle or IDEAL^{SM} model. Many high-performance, quality-driven hospitality companies focus on three quality-management components: (1) the importance of establishing and using standards, (2) the need for quality teams or circles, and (3) the value of empowering employees. As you can see, there are many quality approaches to choose from. Whatever approach is used, however, all quality-management systems are founded on the same major tenet, which is that customers are vital to any business and, consequently, it should be the primary aim of all managers and employees to keep customers satisfied by providing quality service.

In today's highly competitive global environment, hospitality operations must address the key issues that will distinguish successful companies from the unsuccessful. Fundamental quality principles that hospitality managers can use to attract and keep guests include:

1. *Get back to the basics.* Make sure the hospitality operation is clean and comfortable and that everything is in working order. When something goes wrong during a guest's stay, processes must be in place to correct the deficiency quickly and with minimal impact on the guest.

2. *Use quality-management technologies.* Many can help track guest complaints or log incidents, but the challenge is to find technology that gets staff members working better, smarter, and faster.

3. *Make guests feel special.* Luxury hotel brands have long understood that a personal, high-touch approach yields repeat business. Knowing guest histories, issues, and preferences is especially vital to wowing customers in this segment. But hospitality organizations in every segment can strive to provide the type of product and service quality that their guests expect. The right quality-management tools will help managers and employees anticipate guest needs rather than react to them. Computer technology can be used to communicate knowledge about guests throughout an organization.

4. *Be consistent.* The final step in implementing quality basics is to apply quality-management concepts and processes to the entire enterprise. Giving hospitality operations and personnel the tools they need to deliver the service promise is vital.

As we have seen, quality management is not a short-term approach to doing business. Instead, it is a road map that, when followed, allows hotels and other hospitality operations to achieve the highest possible customer and employee satisfaction. Quality revolves around knowledge of what guests want. Quality standards are set, ultimately, by guests; hotels and other hospitality businesses must then find ways, through the use of quality-management systems and other means, to deliver the quality that their guests desire.

Endnotes

1. *Cornell Hotel and Restaurant Administration Quarterly*, Vol. 3, Issue 3, May 1992, p. 51.

2. Ian W. Saunders and Mary Ann Graham, "Total Quality Management in the Hospitality Industry." *Total Quality Management*. Vol. 3, Issue 3, May 1992, pp. 243–256.

3. Ibid.

4. Judi Brownell and Daphne Jameson, "Getting Quality Out on the Street—A Case of Show and Tell." *Cornell Hotel and Restaurant Administration Quarterly*, Vol. 37, Issue 1, February 1996, pp. 28–33.

5. Thomas J. Cartin, *Principles & Practices of TQM* (Milwaukee, Wisconsin: ASQC Quality Press, 1993), p. 29.

6. Ibid., p. 31.

7. Jeremy Main, *Quality Wars: The Triumphs and Defeats of American Business* (New York: Macmillan, 1994), p. ix.

8. Cartin, p. 31.

9. Peter Capezio and Debra Morehouse, *Taking the Mystery Out of TQM—A Practical Guide to Quality Management* (Hawthorne, New Jersey: Career Press, 1993), p. 1.

10. Sheryl E. Kimes, "How Product Quality Drives Profitability: The Experience at Holiday Inn," *Cornell Hotel and Restaurant Administration Quarterly*, Vol. 42, Issue 3, June 2001.

11. www.vanderbilt.edu/Engineering/CIS/Sloan/web/es130/quality/ iqi1.htm

12. http://en.wikipedia.org/wiki/Walter_A._Shewhart.

13. www.asq.org/join/about/history/shewhart.html.

14. http://en.wikipedia.org/wiki/Walter_A._Shewhart.

15. www.skymark.com.

16. www.vanderbilt.edu/Engineering/CIS/Sloan/web/es130/quality/ iqil.htm.

17. www.sei.cmu.edu/ideal.

18. Any Carnegie Mellon University and Software Engineering Institute material contained herein is furnished on an "as-is" basis. Carnegie Mellon University makes no warranties of any kind, either expressed or implied, as to any matter including, but not limited to, warranty of fitness for purpose or merchantability, exclusivity, or results obtained from use of the material. Carnegie Mellon University does not make any warranty of any kind with respect to freedom from patent, trademark, or copyright infringement. The Software Engineering Institute and Carnegie Mellon University do not directly or indirectly endorse this publication. AH&LA Educational Institute is responsible for the accuracy and interpretation of the translated IDEAL^SM Model graphic.

19. Ionnis Boudouropoulos and Ionnis Arvanitoyannis, "Potential and Perspectives for Application of Environmental Management System (EMS) and ISO 14000 to Food Industries," *Food Reviews International*, Vol. 16, Issue 2, 2000, pp. 177–237.

20. Susan Graff, *ISO 14000: Should Your Company Develop an Environmental Management System?* Environmental-Expert.com.

Key Terms

benchmarking—The process of establishing standards to drive continuous-improvement efforts. Benchmarking often involves adapting and applying within a company the best practices of other companies.

breakthrough performance—The achievement of previously unattainable savings in the cost of doing business through reduction of defects on an unprecedented scale.

defect ratio—A measurement of the number of defects in a product or service, generalized by the following formula: defect ratio = frequency of defects ÷ opportunities for defects.

Deming's 14 points for management—The core features of William Edwards Deming's approach to quality and a summary of his ideas for reforming the nature of leadership and management.

external customer—People outside an organization who purchase a product or service produced by the organization.

internal customer—A staff member of a department or functional area who is affected by processes that contribute to the making of a product or the delivery of a service.

quality council—A committee, usually made up of senior managers, whose goals are to launch, coordinate, and institutionalize quality improvement efforts throughout the organization.

Review Questions

1. What are Deming's 14 points?
2. In Deming's view, what role does inspection play in improving quality?
3. Why should companies refrain from automatically awarding business to the supplier with the lowest bid?
4. What are some common barriers that prevent employees from taking pride in their work?
5. How does Juran define quality?
6. What is Juran's process to achieve quality planning and control and improve quality?
7. What is ISO, and how may it contribute to a business's quality-management efforts?

Internet Sites

For more information, visit the following Internet sites. Remember that Internet addresses can change without notice. If the site is no longer there, you can use a search engine to look for additional sites.

The IDEAL^{SM} Model
www.sei.cmu.edu/ideal

Juran Institute
www.juran.com

International Organization for Standardization (ISO)
www.iso.org

The W. Edwards Deming Institute
www.deming.org

Chapter Appendix

Practices of High-Performance Companies: A Checklist

While the following checklist is not a definitive assessment tool, it can be used by anyone in an organization to evaluate how closely the organization's workplace practices model those of high-performance companies.

SKILLS AND INFORMATION

Training and Continuous Learning

- Does your organization invest a higher proportion of its payroll in employee training and development than its competitors do?
- Are there programs to support continuous, life-long learning (job rotation and cross-functional team training, for instance)?
- Are training expenditures balanced among the company's entire work force?
- How effective are company training programs? How is effectiveness measured?

Information Sharing

- Do all workers receive information on the company's operating results, financial goals, and organizational performance? How?
- How are employees trained to apply the financial information that they receive about the company?
- Are there multiple mechanisms by which internal communication occurs so that information flows up, down, and across the organization?

PARTICIPATION, ORGANIZATION, AND PARTNERSHIP

Employee Participation

- Are workers actively involved in continuously improving their work processes and redefining their jobs?
- Can workers rapidly modify their work processes to correct quality, safety, or other problems?
- Are employees actively involved in problem-solving, selecting new technology, modifying the product or service they provide, and meeting with customers?
- When individuals or teams make suggestions, do they always receive feedback about their suggestions?

Organizational Structure

- Has the organization made an effort to reduce layers of management recently? Why or why not?
- Are most workers organized into work teams that enjoy substantial autonomy?

- Are there cross-functional teams and other company mechanisms for sharing innovative ideas across organizational boundaries?

Worker-Management Partnerships

- Are workers and their representatives partners with management in decision-making on a range of issues traditionally decided solely by managers (for example, new technology, quality, and safety)?
- If the company is unionized, has the union-management relationship moved toward joint participation and decision-making?
- Is collective bargaining based on interest-based techniques and cooperative problem-solving?
- Have the company and the union engaged in innovative collective bargaining arrangements?

COMPENSATION, SECURITY, AND WORK ENVIRONMENT

Compensation Linked to Performance and Skills

- Does the company's incentive system incorporate new ways of rewarding workers?
- Do individual workers or work teams receive financial rewards when they improve products or work processes, or make other improvements?
- Is individual compensation tied to both individual and company performance?
- Is executive pay tied to company (or business-unit) performance?

Employment Security

- Are there comprehensive employment planning strategies and policies to minimize or avoid laying off workers?
- If layoffs have occurred in recent years, did the company actively help laid-off workers find new jobs? How?
- Is there a stated company policy ensuring that workers will not suffer adverse effects from suggestions that result in productivity gains?

Supportive Work Environment

- Does the company attract and retain a talented work force? What is the annual turnover rate? Why do people leave?
- Are there policies and programs in place to encourage better staff morale and greater staff commitment to the company?
- What practices are in place to ensure that all problems with staff morale are promptly and systematically addressed?
- Are employees actively involved in designing and implementing health and safety policies and programs?
- Are accident rates in this organization below the industry average?
- Are family-supportive policies, such as flexible work schedules, child care, and elder care, in place?

- Does the organization actively hire, train, retain, and promote a diverse work force?

PUTTING IT ALL TOGETHER

- Does the company fully integrate its human resource policies and workplace practices with other essential business strategies?
- Are quality and continuous improvement efforts meshed with training, work organization, employee involvement, and alternative compensation programs?
- Are workers involved in the design and purchase of new technologies?
- Do workers have the opportunity to regularly modify the technologies they use (for example, modifying the program of a machine tool, or writing macros in a word processor)?
- Do employees receive adequate training to use new technologies effectively?

Source: *Road to High-Performance Workplaces: A Guide to Better Jobs and Better Business Results* (Washington, D.C.: U.S. Department of Labor, Office of the American Workplace, 1994), pp. 21–24.

Chapter 4 Outline

The Quality Movement in the Hospitality
    Industry
    Six Sigma
A Continuous-Improvement Process
    Target an Opportunity for
        Improvement
    Analyze the Area Targeted for
        Improvement
    Develop and Implement
        Improvements
    Evaluate Improvements
Tools Commonly Used in Continuous-
    Improvement Processes
    Tools for Generating Ideas
    Selection Tools
    Tools for Analysis
    Data-Gathering Tools
    Tools for Displaying Data

Competencies

1. Discuss continuous improvement, distinguish incremental improvement from breakthrough improvement, and describe the quality movement in the hospitality industry. (pp. 101–105)

2. Describe the four fundamental steps of a continuous-improvement process. (pp. 105–113)

3. Identify and describe tools commonly used in continuous-improvement processes. (pp. 113–132)

4

Continuous Improvement— Process and Tools

CONTINUOUS IMPROVEMENT is a concept that has been discussed in various ways since people have been contemplating the meaning of management. The effective management of resources, such as people, materials, time, and energy, requires managers to make decisions so that resources are used efficiently and outcomes satisfy customers. In the hospitality industry, managers strive to improve productivity, resource-allocation, and customer-service processes. The concept of **continuous improvement** has emerged from management's quest to make processes faster, better, and less expensive while continuously striving to deliver products and services when, where, and how the customer desires their delivery.

Continuous improvement refers to both incremental improvement and breakthrough improvement. **Incremental improvements** are the most common, as teams and individuals regularly develop simple solutions to resource-use, process, and service challenges. For example, a hotel facing an unusually large number of arrivals could resign itself to long lines, or could try an incremental improvement such as having its front desk agents operate temporary check-in kiosks in the lobby, using laptop computers hooked to the hotel's wireless network. In this example, technology and thinking outside the normal mode of operations resulted in an extraordinary improvement in guest satisfaction, dramatically decreasing the check-in time for arriving individuals and groups, and reducing errors in the check-in process.

Breakthrough improvements include redesigned work processes that result in new levels of quality, speed, and savings. An example of breakthrough improvement relates to the time-honored method of guestroom cleaning—consecutive, task-by-task work performed by one room attendant per guestroom. The Ritz-Carlton Hotel in Dearborn, Michigan, has implemented a breakthrough improvement with a team approach to guestroom cleaning that coordinates simultaneous work activities of three room attendants cleaning a single guestroom. The new process increased productivity from 13 to 15 guestrooms per room attendant. Previously, three room attendants working alone cleaned 39 rooms per shift. With the improved process, three room attendants working together clean 45 rooms per shift. In addition, the new process reduced the housekeeping cycle time by 50 percent. That is, rooms were cleaned and ready for sale by the front desk in 50 percent less time than they were with the previous guestroom cleaning process. The new work process resulted in unprecedented levels of quality, speed, and savings.

101

Incremental or breakthrough improvements usually do not happen overnight, and they often result from the efforts of a team. The first section of this chapter takes a brief look at the quality movement in the hospitality industry and examines fundamental features of a continuous-improvement process that can help individuals think through a problem or work process and can help organize the efforts of improvement teams within or across departments. The second section of the chapter presents continuous-improvement tools that individuals and groups or teams can use to generate ideas, gather facts, make decisions, and evaluate progress. There are dozens of continuous-improvement tools. This chapter examines only some of the most commonly used ones.

The Quality Movement in the Hospitality Industry

From the beginning of the quality movement, hoteliers and restaurateurs have experimented with a variety of tools and techniques to improve the guest experience and increase profitability. Many of the tools were developed in the manufacturing sector and subsequently adapted to the hospitality industry.

Karou Ishikawa and Genichi Taguchi are two of the fathers of the quality movement. Their early work included identifying defects in the production process and implementing a quality control phase with the goal of preventing defects by applying problem-solving and process-assessment techniques. Ishikawa promoted the idea that quality control groups should be empowered to work independently on solving job-related problems and to recommend to management solutions that relate to root causes of problems. In turn, Taguchi developed a formula to calculate the costs associated with poor quality. Taguchi's intent was to demonstrate that poor quality had a cost associated with it that, when factored into the costs of production, could actually result in cost overruns. Examples of these "hidden" costs include, for example, lost productivity, lost time, customer dissatisfaction, employee discontent, unnecessary use of resources, and reduced employee morale.

Tools such as statistical charts, cause-and-effect diagrams (first promoted by Ishikawa), flow charts, histograms, pareto charts, and scatter diagrams are now common methods employed by quality teams using continuous-improvement processes.

An early innovator who brought the concepts of quality to the hospitality industry was Price Gibson, a consultant who understood how to employ quality circles in the problem-solving process. Quality circles are small groups of employees (between eight and ten is ideal), typically from the same department, that are charged with solving job-related problems. Price Gibson worked first in the manufacturing field, but was ultimately employed as a consultant by some leading hotels that were interested in implementing the concepts of quality improvement in their organizations. Some of the first hotels included the Opryland Hotel in Nashville, Tennessee, and the Waldorf=Astoria in New York City. Gibson and his associates worked with these hotels and others in the late 1980s, testing the concepts of quality he had learned and further developed in the manufacturing sector. These early adopters met numerous barriers, perhaps the greatest of which was endemic to the hospitality industry: the simultaneous nature of production and consumption, coupled with the fact that hotels deliver an intangible product or experience. These two variables make continuous-improvement processes very challenging to implement in the hospitality industry.

As the early hospitality quality managers worked closely with Gibson to customize quality processes to fit the unique characteristics of the industry, success became common. The main features of the continuous-improvement process incorporated the ideas of early quality gurus such as Ishikawa, Taguchi, Philip Crosby, Joseph Juran, and William Edwards Deming, and included such activities as collecting data, creating cross departmental teams, focusing on customer needs, and enlisting support from top management.

Gibson developed a very structured approach to adopting the quality culture. He believed that structure provided clarity and accountability. The structure began at the top, with executive commitment to creating a parallel organization that focused on quality service. This parallel system included a steering committee that consisted of people at various levels of the organization, from top management to line employees.

In the 1980s and early 1990s, the quality assurance and continuous-improvement processes pioneered by those who followed Gibson were streamlined, eliminating the often very time-consuming nature of quality circles. With more emphasis on employee empowerment and the advent of computerized property management systems that could track and compile data on all aspects of an operation, managers were able to get to the bottom of problems more quickly. Teams were taught to identify barriers to guest satisfaction and solve problems for guests immediately. New systems for analyzing problems, identifying problems to solve, and for developing innovative solutions and strategies for improving quality were rapidly developed.

Six Sigma

Today, Starwood Hotels & Resorts Worldwide leads the way in continuous improvement with a program called Six Sigma. Six Sigma streamlines and institutionalizes the quality improvement models of the 1980s by assigning roles and responsibilities to process managers. Extensive training of these key quality managers provides them with the tools and knowledge to integrate problem-solving into the daily operation by empowering associates with information and skills designed to aid the process managers in eliminating defects that lead to guest dissatisfaction. Six Sigma was first developed by Motorola Corporation. It is a data-driven approach to continuously improving a process by reducing defects and barriers to customer satisfaction.

The central idea behind Six Sigma is that if you can identify defects in a process, you can systematically figure out how to eliminate them and get as close to zero defects as possible. As a practical tool, Six Sigma is used to focus Starwood on the customer, using a systematic method of integrating data collection and guest feedback into quality improvement and problem-solving activities. This should lead to innovative solutions, elimination of defects, and ultimately improved profitability.

Key Concepts. Customers value consistent and, therefore, predictable services and products of high quality that are delivered through a stable process. This is what organizations with Six Sigma programs strive to achieve. Six Sigma focuses first on reducing process variation and then on improving process capability. At its core, Six Sigma revolves around these key concepts:

1. Identifying the core attributes of the guest experience that are critical to guests' perception of quality.

2. Identifying defects in the delivery process that lead to guest dissatisfaction.

3. Understanding what the process is ultimately capable of delivering when zero defects are the norm—in other words, finding the optimum capability of the guest service systems in order to strive for perfection each and every time.

4. Identifying variation in the system in order to find opportunities to remove defects and ultimately improve guest satisfaction.

5. Developing a stable operation where ensuring consistent, predictable processes to improve the customer experience is the focus of every employee.

Six Sigma is a systematic methodology utilizing tools, training, and measurements to enable organizations to design products and processes that meet customer expectations and can be produced at Six Sigma–quality levels.

Six Sigma is implemented by teams of staff members and managers with the goal of improving processes by eliminating unproductive steps and barriers to quality service. It is also a system for designing innovative business solutions. Tools employed in the Six Sigma improvement process include the following:

- Control charts—used to monitor variance in a process over time and alert the business to unexpected variances that may cause defects.

- Defect measurement—accounting for the number or frequency of defects that cause lapses in product or service quality.

- Pareto diagrams—used to focus efforts on the problems that have the greatest potential for improvement by showing relative frequency and/or size in a descending bar graph. Pareto diagrams are based on the idea that 20 percent of the sources cause 80 percent of any problems.

- Process mapping—using illustrated descriptions of how things get done, which enables participants to visualize an entire process and identify areas of strengths and weaknesses.

- Root cause analysis—studying the original reason for nonconformance in a process. When the root cause is removed or corrected, the nonconformance will be eliminated.

- Statistical process control—applying statistical methods to analyze data, and study and monitor process capability and performance.

- Tree diagrams—used to graphically show any broad goal broken into different levels of detailed actions. They encourage team members to expand their thinking when creating solutions.

Many of these tools will be discussed in more detail in the following sections as we look at one continuous-improvement process and the tools and techniques managers and their staffs can use in their quest for continuous improvement.

A Continuous-Improvement Process

Leadership is an essential component of the quality-improvement process. Quality in high-performance organizations begins at the top when leaders focus attention on continuous improvement as a strategic initiative. With this focus, everyone in the organization can be put to work improving product and service quality, resulting in greater guest satisfaction, elimination of waste, and, ultimately, greater profitability.

Once leadership has set the direction for quality improvement, tactics for responding to process problems can be developed. Some process problems may be addressed by an executive team, while others may be addressed by a line-level cross-functional team. The type of team that is assigned to a problem depends on the problem itself. If, for example, a budget problem is identified where responsibility lies with management, teams composed of the managers responsible for the budget area would be best suited to solve the problem. If, however, a problem was identified in the check-out process of a hotel, then the persons best suited for solving this process problem may be a functional or cross-functional team that is responsible for the check-out process.

Once an organization establishes methods for collecting information that helps identify problems, a system for assigning the people responsible for solving problems can be put into place. The common sources of data that help identify process-related problems include: (1) external customer feedback, (2) innovative ideas and suggestions from employees, (3) employee satisfaction assessments, (4) supplier feedback, and (5) performance indicators.

While there are a variety of continuous-improvement approaches used throughout the hospitality industry, the process presented here focuses on four fundamental steps:

1. Target an opportunity for improvement

2. Analyze the area targeted for improvement

3. Develop and implement improvements

4. Evaluate improvements

Exhibit 1 outlines each of these steps as they are discussed in the following sections.

Target an Opportunity for Improvement

In years past, areas for improvement were commonly discovered in a haphazard way when problems would come to the forefront based on customer complaints or perhaps after managers and employees became frustrated with barriers to success such as resource waste, low productivity, poor staff performance, or ineffective work procedures. Poor performance is often a result of variation in work

Exhibit 1   Steps in a Sample Continuous-Improvement Process

> **1. Target an opportunity for improvement**
>   Keep track of data
>   Write problem statements
>   Develop selection criteria
>   Select an area for improvement
>
> **2. Analyze the area targeted for improvement**
>   Establish baseline measurements
>   Analyze processes
>   Identify potential causes
>   Determine the root cause(s)
>
> **3. Develop and implement improvements**
>   Identify potential solutions
>   Select the best solutions
>   Conduct a trial test
>   Develop an action plan
>
> **4. Evaluate improvements**

processes. When guest experiences become unpredictable, then there is increased likelihood that quality will be variable. For example, if a guest arrival forecast is inaccurate and more guests than predicted arrive on a Friday night, the check-in system may experience stress, because not enough guest service agents were scheduled. A breakdown in one aspect of the guest service system will have potentially great ramifications. A continuous-improvement process, therefore, strives to identify areas for improvement before they become a sore spot for guests, employees, and managers.

A variety of methods are used by managers and employees to identify areas for improvement. Methods include:

- Analyzing guest feedback results from guest comment cards, surveys, and interviews.

- Analyzing data collected by employees pertaining to productivity.

- Reviewing organizational processes to identify waste in the system.

- Reviewing organizational goals and objectives as outlined in annual business plans.

- Discussing problems and challenges in staff meetings.

- Using idea logs and employee suggestion boxes. Staff suggestions can also be gathered online.

Keep Track of Data. A key to any continuous-improvement process is to collect pertinent data. Tools used to keep track of employee performance and other data include checklists, frequency charts, timing devices, and control charts. For example, in the reservations area of an independent ski resort, each phone call could be timed and sales successes and failures could be tracked for each reservation agent. This information could be used to determine training needs and areas for productivity improvement.

Many departments keep track of various data such as uniform counts, laundry usage, sales, rooms out of order, etc. These reports can be used in monitoring work processes. Creating control charts for these reports so that managers and staff know when red flags should go up is relatively simple. For example, if a housekeeping department keeps track of uniforms and guest apparel that goes out for cleaning, a control chart can be created that tracks missing items. If the number of missing items goes below one or above four, one might say that the system is out of control, if "in control" or normal has been defined as between one and four missing items. For example, at the Hyatt Regency Crystal City, an employee in the laundry area keeps track of all uniforms and guest laundry that goes out for washing. When the laundry is returned, it is checked against the outgoing list to be sure that nothing is missing. Sometimes more than 20 pieces are missing. This might be considered out of control and, if it occurs frequently, a problem-solving team may want to figure out a way to bring it back into control.

Room attendants are checked frequently by housekeeping inspectors on the quality of their work as well as on their productivity. Checklists are employed to ensure that all details of the room-cleaning regimen are attended to. If the head supervisor were to compile all of the checklists to determine which items are left unattended to on a consistent basis, these points would be a good target for a control chart and attention from a housekeeping problem-solving team. For example, if coffee pots were improperly cleaned more often than acceptable, then a team would identify the problem and follow the problem-solving process to develop a viable, long-term solution. The solution could easily be tested to determine if adherence to the control points became consistent or continued to go beyond the controls set by management.

Front desk agents at a center-city hotel might be responsible for keeping track of guest requests. Guest requests could then be categorized and analyzed for frequency. If certain requests are commonplace, then the hotel management could take action to ensure that the item or service requested is inserted into the product/service mix for the hotel wherever possible. Frequency of guest complaints about food quality can be tracked using comment cards in the restaurant. If an employee team determines that guests complain frequently about a certain menu item, then this can become an area for possible improvement.

Identifying areas for improvement is frequently the purview of an employee problem-solving team. Teams take on various members, depending on the philosophy of the organization, the purpose of the team, and the organizational level of problem-solving.

For problems relevant to a specific department, departmental teams are adequate, but interdepartmental teams may become necessary when problems cross boundaries.

Write Problem Statements. Problem statements are developed in an evolutionary process from initial brainstorming to a careful review of each word to ensure objectivity and accuracy in stating the problem. This process is important, because

---

Managing the Continuous-Improvement Process

Leading hotel companies employ managers whose primary responsibility is to oversee the continuous-improvement process. At The Ritz-Carlton Company, for example, an important management position is that of Process Manager. At Starwood Hotels and Resorts, Inc., a manager of Six Sigma oversees the quality-improvement system. These managers, and often the entire hotel staff, are involved in employing techniques and tools for identifying areas for improvement, analyzing the area targeted for improvement, developing and implementing improvements, and evaluating improvement strategies and tactics.

---

the first statement resulting from a brainstorming process might be a symptom of the problem rather than the actual problem. For example, the statement that "hand towels in the guest bathrooms are often frayed" may be a symptom of a larger problem that may have to do with the budget or the purchasing function. In order to get to the actual problem, the team leader or an individual working alone should ask the question, "Why is this a problem?" The answer might come back, "Because we don't have a full stock of acceptable hand towels." "Why?" would be the follow-up question. Answer: "Because the rooms division manager wouldn't let us purchase any new hand towels for the high season." "Why is that?" would be the next question. "Because the housekeeping budget wasn't completed in time and we didn't have the funds." So the problem statement should actually read, "Hand towels are frayed in guestrooms because the housekeeping department failed to meet the deadline for budget requests." As a result of this clear statement, the team may tackle this problem or pass it on to the director of housekeeping or the purchasing manager to determine a solution.

After clearly and correctly describing the problem, people will actually be solving the problem rather than a symptom of the problem. If in this example the housekeeping department simply ordered new hand towels, the problem could happen again in the next budget cycle.

Ideas for writing problem statements. Ideas about the problem, especially those generated in team brainstorming sessions, are usually expressed in short phrases or statements. The different perspectives that people bring to a brainstorming session can shape their understanding of problem areas. For example, a problem idea brainstormed by an improvement team at a hotel might be phrased as: "Too many convention team billing errors." Individual team members might have very different interpretations of this expression of the problem:

Team Member	Interpretation
Director of Sales	"We'd better fix this fast so the hotel doesn't lose future business."
Rooms Manager	"If we cleared up the confusion about complimentary rooms before guests arrive, we'd be more accurate with their bills when they leave."

Convention Services Manager	"Almost every convention team wants to change something once they're here at the hotel. We need a more flexible billing process that keeps up with us as we scramble to meet the changing needs of our guests."
Banquet Manager	"What do you expect when Banquet Event Orders never match up with original contracts?"
Controller	"We'll never have accurate convention team billings when everyone is authorized to negotiate charges."

Everyone on the team wants to improve the billing process, but each person reacts to the idea "too many convention team billing errors" with a natural bias related to his or her function and responsibilities at the hotel. Before selecting one idea as the best or most appropriate problem or improvement opportunity to work on, a team must clarify all of its ideas, so everyone involved has the same understanding of what the short phrases or statements that represent the ideas actually mean. The best way to clarify improvement ideas is to transform them into specific, objective problem statements.

Teams are often tempted to jump beyond an objective description of a problem and embed causes or solutions in their problem statements. Causes and solutions should be addressed in later steps of the continuous-improvement process. The time taken now to clarify problem statements will save a great deal of time later. Well-written problem statements specify areas for improvement, prevent misunderstandings, and form the foundation for objective analyses of problems and processes.

Develop Selection Criteria. Once a team has a list of specific problem statements, the next step in targeting an opportunity for improvement is to decide on the selection criteria the team will use to choose one problem to work on. **Selection criteria** are factors a team uses to assess and rank a list of choices—in this case, the choices are problems to work on. Examples of selection criteria a team might use to help it choose a problem to work on include the following:

- *Importance to guests.* If guest surveys, interviews, or comment cards indicate high levels of guest dissatisfaction with a current situation outlined by a problem statement, then that particular problem takes on a degree of seriousness and urgency and is more likely to be chosen than a problem that is unimportant to guests.

- *Importance to management.* When a problem relates to goals outlined in the company's business plan, management is likely to provide the needed support and encourage the cooperation necessary for success.

- *Importance to staff.* If staff surveys, interviews, or other feedback channels indicate high levels of staff dissatisfaction with a current situation outlined in a problem statement, then that problem takes on a degree of seriousness and urgency and is more likely to be chosen than a problem that is unimportant to staff members.

- *Stability of the improvement area.* For obvious reasons, team members should not choose to work on a hotel area or work process that is unstable—that is, an area or process that is currently changing, or is scheduled to change, due to new equipment, training, renovation, and so on.

- *Availability of resources.* A team should not choose a problem to work on unless it has the people, time, money, and equipment to deal with it effectively.

- *Probability of timely success.* This criterion balances a sense of urgency with the perceived difficulty of solving a problem or improving the work process.

The factors chosen as selection criteria vary with circumstances. The critical point here is that everyone on the team should understand and agree with each of the selection criteria it will use.

Select an Area for Improvement. After achieving consensus on selection criteria, teams generally conduct whatever fact-finding searches they deem appropriate before selecting a problem to work on. When selecting a problem, there are many tools and methods a team can use, such as priority determination charts, selection matrixes, and weighted selection matrixes. These tools are discussed in detail later in the chapter.

Analyze the Area Targeted for Improvement

Now that the team has decided on one problem to work on, it must analyze the area targeted for improvement. The length and depth of this analysis will depend on the nature and scope of the area selected for improvement. Some problems will need less analysis than others, but all problems will need some analysis.

Analyzing an area targeted for improvement involves four steps:

1. Establishing baseline measurements
2. Analyzing processes
3. Identifying potential causes
4. Determining the root cause(s)

Establish Baseline Measurements. Baseline measurements result from fact-finding efforts in relation to analyzing the area targeted for improvement. The problem identified in the previous example, "too many convention team billing errors," needs to be stated with greater precision. After all, how many is "too many"? With fact-finding research efforts, the team could find out how many convention team billing errors actually occur. The team could designate a reasonable time period for the duration of the fact-finding effort, ensuring that the time period takes into account fluctuations in business that may affect the problem. The result could be a baseline measurement such as: "over the past three months, 20 percent of convention team billings contained errors."

Baseline measurements become a standard against which to gauge the effectiveness of solutions developed and implemented by the team in later steps of the continuous-improvement process. At this stage of the process, the baseline measurements help the team to visualize the nature and scope of their task in relation to closing the gap between actual current conditions and future desired results.

While baseline measurements are important and should be carefully taken, fact-finding should be conducted in the shortest amount of time possible. How short is "short"? The length of time and the amount of effort a team spends on fact-finding will vary in relation to circumstances surrounding the targeted area for improvement and are ultimately determined by the common sense and good judgment of the team. The important point is not to bog down the continuous-improvement process in an unnecessarily detailed research effort. Teams should not let a drive for perfection get in the way of doing sufficiently good research and analysis.

Analyze Processes. Analysis begins by documenting exactly what happens in the process responsible for producing the problem. Documenting exactly what happens focuses a team's attention on work processes. Team members benefit from detailing the relevant processes with flow charts, because flow charts enable the team to visualize the actual sequence of steps and decisions made in the processes.

Identify Potential Causes. At this point in analyzing the area targeted for improvement, a team brainstorms potential causes of the problem. A cause-and-effect diagram is an analytical tool a team can use to structure brainstorming and organize many potential causes of a problem.

Determine the Root Cause(s). The next step is to pare down the number of causes the team brainstormed to the vital few major causes that produce the majority of the problem, and then trace the major causes to their roots: 80 percent of a problem is usually produced by 20 percent of the brainstormed causes. **Root causes** are where the problem starts.

A technique a team can use to determine root causes is to select one of the few major causes and ask "Why does this happen?" The answer will be an "underlying" cause. The same question is then asked about this underlying cause, and the answer may lead to another even more underlying and more important cause of the problem. Asking "why" at least five times (the "Five Whys Technique") generally leads the team to root causes. The team can then verify root causes by conducting appropriate fact-finding efforts. Think of this verification as analyzing the strength or power of root causes by measuring how each root cause affects the area targeted for improvement.

Develop and Implement Improvements

At this stage of the continuous-improvement process, teams usually have little trouble coming up with potential solutions. In fact, there is usually a pent-up supply of ideas because, so far in the continuous-improvement process, team members have been suppressing their urge to jump to conclusions and solutions. However, even here—perhaps especially here—teams are still inclined to jump too quickly and act on imprecise solutions.

A team can develop and implement solutions by following these steps:

1. Identify potential solutions
2. Select the best solution(s)
3. Conduct a trial test
4. Develop an action plan for implementation

Identify Potential Solutions. Improvement teams often use brainstorming to identify potential solutions. Before conducting a brainstorming session, teams review the verified root causes of the problem. After the brainstorming activity, the team can focus on the root causes and baseline measurements while specifying solution ideas in written improvement statements. Well-written improvement statements clarify solutions by setting goals that solutions aim to achieve and by indicating how achievement can be measured in relation to baseline measurements established previously. If the team is improving a work process, the improvement statement could be attached to a flow chart of the newly designed work process that will be tested and compared with the old work process.

Select the Best Solution(s). After developing a list of potential solutions, the team can prepare to choose the best solution(s) by developing selection criteria. It's helpful at this point for the team to turn back to the selection criteria used earlier to assess and rank problems. Some of these selection criteria can be used again to help the team select the best solution(s) to the problem. Selection criteria for choosing the best solution(s) might include such factors as:

- Acceptance by guests.
- Acceptance by management.
- Acceptance by staff.
- Cost effectiveness.
- Timeliness of implementation.
- Practicality of implementation.

The factors chosen as selection criteria vary with circumstances.

Conduct a Trial Test. When possible, a team should test a solution on a limited, trial basis before implementing it. During the test period, the team can conduct fact-finding efforts that measure the solution's success in eliminating root causes of the problem. The baseline measurements established earlier now serve as "before" pictures that can be compared to the "after" pictures—the measurements taken during the trial test. Usually, a trial test of a solution uncovers additional items that the team must resolve before fully implementing the solution.

Develop an Action Plan. The results of a trial test indicate whether the solution(s) should be implemented throughout the area targeted for improvement. With large-scale improvements that affect many people and several different work areas, completing an action plan worksheet, like the one shown in Exhibit 2, may help the team organize and schedule the necessary activities. The worksheet can be adapted to meet those situations in which the nature and scope of an improvement are more focused and more limited. The important point is for the team to have a time-based plan that assigns specific responsibilities to the people who will carry out the solution(s).

Evaluate Improvements

After implementing solutions and standardizing new processes, the team should evaluate their effectiveness and, when necessary, take corrective action to ensure

Exhibit 2 Sample Action Plan Worksheet

ACTION PLAN WORKSHEET					
ACTION ITEM	STEP(S) TO BE TAKEN	PERSON RESPON.	TODAY'S DATE	TARGET DATE	COMPLETION DATE

continued improvement. Teams track improvements by periodically measuring the results of whatever new processes or solutions they put in place to solve the problem. These measurements are the same measurements established during the trial test. These fact-finding efforts track results on weekly, monthly, or quarterly bases until the area targeted for improvement stabilizes and the improvement goal is reached.

In evaluating their improvement efforts, teams may also gather feedback from guests, managers, and staff members. Depending on the nature and scope of the improvement, teams may discover:

- Higher guest satisfaction levels in comment card reports and survey results.
- Progress toward management goals outlined in the company's business plan.
- Higher levels of staff satisfaction in employee survey results.

Over time, these more general indicators of success measure the value of the continuous-improvement process as it becomes standardized throughout the organization.

As you can see, the continuous-improvement process has come full circle. At the beginning of the process, teams relied on feedback from guests, managers, and staff members to help them target an opportunity for improvement. Now, the team again must listen to guests, managers, and staff members to determine how successfully its solution worked.

Tools Commonly Used in Continuous-Improvement Processes

There are many tools individuals or teams can use to help them improve a company's products, services, or work processes (see Exhibit 3). Some tools can help

Exhibit 3   Tools Commonly Used in a Continuous-Improvement Process

PROCESS STEP	TOOLS USED
I. Target an Opportunity for Improvement	Guest Feedback Business Plan Goals
1. Identify improvement ideas	Staff Feedback Brainstorming
	Fact-Finding Planning Sheet
2. Write problem statements	Brainstorming
3. Develop selection criteria	Selection Matrix Priority Determination Chart
4. Select an area for improvement	
II. Analyze the Area Targeted for Improvement	Check Sheets Bar, Pie Charts
1. Establish baseline measurements	Line Graphs
	Flow Chart
2. Analyze processes	Cause-and-Effect Diagram
3. Identify potential causes	Five Whys Technique
4. Determine the root cause(s)	
III. Develop and Implement Improvements	Brainstorming
1. Identify potential solutions	Selection Matrix Priority Determination Chart
2. Select the best solution(s)	Fact-Finding Planning Sheet
3. Conduct a trial test	Action Plan Worksheet
4. Develop an action plan for implementation	
IV. Evaluate Improvements	

you generate ideas; some can help you make a selection from among a number of items; some can help you gather data; and some can help you display data. Among the most commonly used tools are the following:

• Brainstorming

• Priority determination charts

• Selection matrixes

- Weighted selection matrixes
- Flow charts
- Cause-and-effect diagrams
- Fact-finding planning sheets
- Check sheets
- Bar charts, pie charts, and line graphs

Although most of these tools can be used by individuals as well, in the following sections, we will discuss them as they are used in team settings.

Tools for Generating Ideas

Several tools exist to help teams come up with ideas, but one of the most commonly used—and perhaps the easiest to use—is brainstorming.

Brainstorming. Brainstorming uses team interaction to generate as many ideas as possible. Brainstorming taps into the collective brainpower of the team and yields greater results than could be achieved if each individual in the team worked alone. It stimulates creativity, promotes participation, and develops a team spirit among team members, which can heighten their commitment to the continuous-improvement process.

Some teams conduct a brainstorming session, then let some time pass (from a few hours to a few days) to let team members think about the ideas generated during the first session before calling the team together again for a second brainstorming session. There are also brainstorming methods for individuals to perform alone. The important common denominators among all brainstorming methods are the following: try to generate lots of ideas, think creatively, do not criticize or evaluate ideas during the initial listing phase, and (in team situations) build on the ideas of others.

What follows are some basic steps for conducting a brainstorming session:

1. Appoint a session leader. This person will write down the team's ideas and facilitate the session.

2. The session leader should write (on a chalkboard or flip chart, for easier viewing by the team) the purpose of the brainstorming session and make sure that everyone on the team understands it.

3. Team members should be creative and unconventional in their thinking; the goal is to come up with as many ideas as possible. At this stage it is quantity, not quality, that counts.

4. The team should take a few minutes to think silently about the question or problem.

5. Before beginning the session, the session leader should remind team members that at first the goal is simply to list ideas. There should be no discussion of ideas, and team members should not express approval or disapproval of any ideas, although it is okay to build on the ideas of others. Team members

should state their ideas quickly and succinctly so that the team can move rapidly from idea to idea.

6. To begin the first round, the session leader should ask each member of the team in turn to share one idea only. This makes it harder for an individual to dominate the discussion or discourage others from contributing. Team members should simply state their idea, not explain it. The session leader should record each idea exactly as it was stated by the team member. After the first round, team members should again take turns stating one idea at a time.

7. If a team member does not have an idea, he or she should simply say "Pass" and let the next member state an idea. The session leader should call on this team member during the next round when it becomes his or her turn again, because the member might have thought of an idea while other team members were contributing.

8. The brainstorming session ends when all the team members pass during one go-round of the team.

9. The team should go over each idea; team members should clarify those ideas that are not understood by everyone on the team. The team should then combine similar ideas.

Brainstorming sessions allow a team to come up with many possible problem statements, solutions to problems, or other ideas in a short amount of time.

Selection Tools

The selection tools discussed in this section are priority determination charts, selection matrixes, and weighted selection matrixes. Each of these tools can help a team make a selection from among a list of options; the best tool to use depends on the team's selection goals.

Priority Determination Charts. Priority determination charts are useful whenever a team wishes to rank an entire list of items in order of importance. In this case, the goal is not simply to eliminate items until the team is left with two or three to debate, but to determine the relative importance of each item to all of the others. With this technique, a team starts out with a list of randomly ordered items, and ends up with a list that still has all of the items on it, but has the most important item (as determined by the team) at the top, the second most important item listed second, the third most important item listed third, and so on. A priority determination chart is useful when a team has decided that it will eventually work on all of the problems it has listed. It doesn't want to remove any items from the list, but wants to rank the entire list in order of importance so that the team knows in what order to work on the problems.

A priority determination chart helps a team quickly evaluate the importance of each item on a list in relation to all of the other listed items. An example of a priority determination chart is shown in Exhibit 4. In this case, a team brainstormed a list of six selection criteria ("Importance to Guests," "Importance to Management," and so on) and then wanted to rank them in order of importance.

Exhibit 4 Sample Filled-Out Priority Determination Chart

Items to Prioritize	Circle the Most Important Item in Each Vertical Column	Number of Times Circled	Final Priority Ranking
1. Importance to Guests		5	1
2. Importance to Management	① 2	1	5
3. Importance to Staff	①② 3 3	0	6
4. Control Over the Improvement Area	①②③ ④ 4 4	3	3
5. Availability of Resources	1 2 3 ④ 5 ⑤⑤ 5	2	4
6. Probability of Timely Success	① 2 3 4 5 6 ⑥⑥⑥⑥	4	2

As you can see, the team has ranked each criterion against all the others (as recorded by the circled numbers in the second column), counted the number of times each item to prioritize was circled (recorded in the third column), and has assigned a final priority ranking accordingly (fourth column). This team decided that "Importance to Guests" was the most important criterion, "Importance to Staff" was the least important.

To begin, the team wrote out the chart's major headings—"Items to Prioritize," "Circle the Most Important Item in Each Vertical Column," "Number of Times Circled," and "Final Priority Ranking." Then the team listed the six selection criteria in random order.

To complete the chart, team members were asked to make a series of forced choices between two of the listed criteria. The session leader began by asking one person in the team to compare the second criterion on the list to the first one: "Which is the more important criterion, Number 2—'Importance to Management,' or Number 1—'Importance to Guests'?"

The session leader wrote down the numbers of these items ("1" and "2") in the second column, opposite the second item listed, and circled the number that corresponded to the person's response. Then the session leader asked the team if it agreed with the person's response. If the team agrees with a response, then the session leader can continue the process by moving down to the third item listed and asking a different team member to compare the third item to the first two. (If the team does not agree with the team member's response, the team should discuss the rating until it can reach an agreement.) In the case of Exhibit 4, the session leader moved on by asking a second team member these questions:

• "Which is the more important item, Number 3—'Importance to Staff,' or Number 1—'Importance to Guests'?"

• "Which is the more important item, Number 3—'Importance to Staff,' or Number 2—'Importance to Management'?"

Again, the session leader wrote the numbers of these items in the third column and circled the numbers that corresponded to the second member's response. The team agreed with the second member, so the session leader asked another team member to compare the fourth item to the first three.

Although this process is a bit cumbersome to describe on paper, in reality it can move quite quickly, since the session leader simply moves down the list of items and asks team members to compare each item to the ones listed above it.

When the last item was compared, the team completed the third column of the priority determination chart ("Number of Times Circled") by recording how many times the number of each item listed in the first column was circled in the second column. The item with the highest number of circles in column two becomes the most important item or, in the case of our example, the most important selection criterion. The item with the second highest number of circles is the second most important item, and so on. As you can see, the team that filled out the priority determination chart in Exhibit 4 ranked their items in this way:

Ranking	Items (Criteria)
1	Importance to Guests
2	Probability of Timely Success
3	Control Over the Improvement Area
4	Availability of Resources
5	Importance to Management
6	Importance to Staff

The team, which wants to use these criteria to help it make a decision, now knows which criteria team members think are more important than others. This information can be valuable, depending on the complexity of the decision to be made.

Selection Matrixes. As mentioned earlier in the chapter, a selection matrix is a decision-making tool that teams can use to rank opportunities for improvement. Selection matrixes can also be used to rank other lists of choices.

What follows are some basic steps a team can use for setting up a selection matrix. Using a dry-erase board or flip chart, the session leader should write, along the top of the board or chart, the list of items the team wants to rank, then write each criterion along the left side of the board or chart.

Exhibit 5 presents a sample selection matrix. In this example, the team first brainstormed three improvement opportunities—"numerous convention team billing errors," "slow room service," and "not enough clean rooms for arriving guests." Which improvement opportunity should the team work on first? Rather than simply voting, the team brainstormed a list of criteria that it felt should be taken into consideration when it made its choice. How can the team effectively and quickly use these criteria to help it make its decision? By creating a selection matrix.

To create the selection matrix shown in Exhibit 5, the team wrote the three improvement opportunities ("numerous convention team billing errors," "slow room service," and "not enough clean rooms for arriving guests") along the top of

Exhibit 5   Sample Selection Matrix

Criteria	Items to be Ranked		
	Numerous Convention Team Billing Errors	Slow Room Service	Not Enough Clean Rooms For Arriving Guests
Importance to Guests	10	7	10
Importance to Management	10	4	10
Importance to Staff	8	3	8
Control Over the Improvement Area	5	10	8
Availability of Resources	8	2	6
Probability of Timely Success	9	5	6
Totals	50	31	48

the flip chart, then the list of criteria the team had brainstormed ("Importance to Guests," "Importance to Management," and so on) along the left side of the chart.

Then the team rated each improvement opportunity according to each criterion, using a scale from 1 to 10, with 1 as the lowest score, 10 as the highest. The opportunity with the highest score ("numerous convention team billing errors") becomes the opportunity targeted for improvement.

An efficient way to complete a selection matrix in a team setting is for the session leader to ask a member of the team to rate the first item to be ranked on the first criterion, then ask if anyone in the team disagrees with the rating. If the team agrees, the session leader should move on to the next criterion and ask a different team member to rate the first item on the second criterion, and so on around the team with the rest of the criteria. Whenever there is disagreement with a suggested rating, a brief but focused discussion should resolve the disagreement. After all of the items to be ranked have been rated against all of the criteria, the items' ratings should be totaled. The item with the highest total is the one that the team should work on first.

Sometimes it is best to create a separate matrix for each item the team wants to rank, then have the team fill out each matrix *without totaling the score*. (In the Exhibit 5 example, three matrixes would be created and filled out—one for "numerous convention team billing errors," one for "slow room service," and one for "not enough clean rooms for arriving guests.") After all of the matrixes have been filled out, the session leader can then go back and total the score for each matrix. In this way, no one knows how any of the items to be ranked scored until the end of the process, which avoids situations in which some team members might try to unfairly affect the outcome of the process.

Weighted selection matrixes. A more sophisticated version of a selection matrix is a weighted selection matrix. Sometimes a team feels that the criteria it has brainstormed are not of roughly equal value. Therefore, the team may decide that the most important criteria should be given more influence or weight in determining the ranking of items.

A team can simply weight criteria based on the intuitions or "gut feelings" of the team members. This method can work well if there are only a few criteria to weight. If there are just two criteria to weight, for example, a team might easily come to an agreement that "the first criteria listed is more important than the second," and give it more weight than the second one.

When there are more than just a few criteria to rank, and when the ranking is not as obvious to the team, a priority determination chart can help the team weight its selection criteria. As you probably noticed, the priority determination chart in Exhibit 4 rated the selection criteria used in the unweighted selection matrix shown in Exhibit 5. As you recall, the priority determination chart in Exhibit 4 yielded the following ranking of criteria:

Ranking	Criteria
1	Importance to Guests
2	Probability of Timely Success
3	Control Over the Improvement Area
4	Availability of Resources
5	Importance to Management
6	Importance to Staff

Now that the criteria have been ranked in order of importance, how does the team assign weights to them? A simple technique is to assign a weighting value in relation to the total number of criteria used. If there are six criteria, the most important criterion is assigned a value of six, the next most important criterion is assigned a value of five, and so on, with the least important criterion assigned a value of one:

Ranking	Criteria	Weighted Value
1	Importance to Guests	6
2	Probability of Timely Success	5
3	Control Over the Improvement Area	4
4	Availability of Resources	3
5	Importance to Management	2
6	Importance to Staff	1

As shown in the sample weighted selection matrix presented in Exhibit 6, the weighting value is used as a multiplying factor. The criteria ratings the team gave to each improvement opportunity are multiplied by each criterion's weight value before each improvement opportunity's figures are totaled. Once again, the opportunity with the highest score becomes the opportunity targeted for improvement.

Why would a team use a weighted selection matrix instead of a simpler unweighted matrix? Sometimes an unweighted matrix does not differentiate the team's list of items enough for the team to make a decision. Or, as stated previously, the team might decide to use a weighted selection matrix because it thinks that some of the listed criteria are more important than others, and therefore the team cannot make an accurate or "good" decision unless the most important criteria are assigned more weight or influence than the less important criteria.

Exhibit 6   Sample Weighted Selection Matrix

Criteria	Items to be Ranked		
	Numerous Convention Team Billing Errors	Slow Room Service	Not Enough Clean Rooms For Arriving Guests
Importance to Guests	10 × 6 = 60	10 × 6 = 60	10 × 6 = 60
Probability of Timely Success	9 × 5 = 45	5 × 5 = 25	6 × 5 = 30
Control Over the Improvement Area	5 × 4 = 20	10 × 4 = 40	8 × 4 = 32
Availability of Resources	8 × 3 = 24	2 × 3 = 6	6 × 3 = 18
Importance to Management	10 × 2 = 20	4 × 2 = 8	10 × 2 = 20
Importance to Staff	8 × 1 = 8	3 × 1 = 3	8 × 1 = 8
Totals	177	142	168

Tools for Analysis

Flow charts and cause-and-effect diagrams are effective, easy-to-use tools for analyzing a problem, process, or situation.

Flow Charts. A **flow chart** is a step-by-step pictorial representation of activities and decision points in a work process. Exhibit 7 defines the most common symbols used in creating a flow chart. Think of these symbols as the words of a special "process language" that people can use to quickly and efficiently communicate movement, flow, activity, and relationships. What could easily take several pages of narrative description can be flow charted on a single page—proving, once again, that a picture is worth a thousand words.

When a team creates a flow chart to analyze a work process, it is important for the team to document what actually happens—not what policy and procedure manuals state should happen, not what managers think happens, and not what the staff wants to happen. The objective is to analyze the process "as it is," not as it should be, might be, or could be.

The best people to create an "as it is" flow chart are those who actually perform the steps of the current process. Exhibit 8 presents a sample flow chart created by staff members of a restaurant bar. The flow chart diagrams the popcorn preparation process that the staff currently follows. The analysis may have been prompted by guest complaints about stale-tasting popcorn, staff dissatisfaction with annoying aspects of the process, or any number of other types of problems. As you can see, the major steps of the process—"Gather Supplies," "Cook Popcorn," and "Store Items and Clean Up"—were placed in double rectangles. Each major step's sub-steps were listed below it.

An efficient procedure a team can use to create a flow chart includes the following five steps:

1. Brainstorm and sequence the major steps of the process.
2. Brainstorm the sub-steps within each major step of the process.

Exhibit 7   Commonly Used Flow Chart Symbols

The most commonly used flow chart symbols have fairly standard meanings and are as follows:

An oval, or "terminal symbol," signifies the beginning or end of a process. Inside the oval, the instruction "Start" or "End" is written.

Major process steps should be written inside a double rectangle. A double rectangle should have one arrow flowing into it and one arrow flowing out.

Arrow

An arrow shows the direction of the process flow. Arrows signify that something— information, a person, paper, supplies, etc.—is traveling from one point to another.

Rectangle

A rectangle is the symbol for an activity. A brief description of the activity should be written in the rectangle. A rectangle may have more than one arrow flowing into it, but only one arrow flowing out.

A diamond is used for those steps in a process where a decision must be made. A diamond will usually have one arrow flowing in, but two or more arrows flowing out. A question is written in the diamond, and the number of "out" arrows will depend on the question. Usually, teams try to use only questions that can be answered "yes" or "no," so that there are no more than two arrows leading out of a diamond. This simplifies the flow chart.

3. Sequence the sub-steps of each major step.

4. Identify the appropriate flow chart symbol for each sub-step.

5. Diagram the flow chart and verify its accuracy.

A team can create a flow chart during a brainstorming session, using a flip chart and packs of self-stick notes. With the name of the process written at the top of the flip chart, the team can brainstorm the major steps of the process and record them, from left to right, across the flip chart directly under the name of the process. For more complicated processes, the team might want to write the major

Exhibit 8   Sample Flow Chart

Popcorn Preparation Process

Start → Gather Supplies → Cook Popcorn → Store Items and Clean Up → End

Gather Supplies
- Estimate amount of supplies needed
- Turn on cooker
- Check amount of supplies in concession stand
- Adequate for day?
  - Yes → Collect supplies for the day
  - No → Check supplies in back storage → Available?
    - Yes → Restock concession stand supplies → Collect supplies for the day
    - No → Notify manager → Manager secures supplies and delivers to concession stand → Restock concession stand supplies

Cook Popcorn
- Measure ingredients and place in cooker
- Pop the popcorn
- Season the popcorn
- Bag some popcorn for sale
- Check popcorn level periodically
- Enough?
  - Yes → Use up remaining popcorn
  - No → (return to Measure ingredients and place in cooker)

Store Items and Clean Up
- Is popcorn left over?
  - Yes → Is popcorn fresh?
    - Yes → Bag popcorn in storage bags → Place bags in concession stand bins → Store supplies
    - No → Throw popcorn out → Store supplies
  - No → Store supplies
- Store supplies → Clean measuring cups, spoons, machine, and counter → Store cups and spoons

steps on self-stick notes as they are brainstormed. This allows the team to easily re-sequence the major steps as more steps are identified.

Here it should be noted that the major steps on a flow chart are supposed to be just that—major. Most work processes can be flow charted with six or fewer major steps. If a team has more than six, it should reexamine its major steps; perhaps several of the "major" steps are really sub-steps under other major steps.

Why should a team bother to flow chart all of the sub-steps under each major step? If only the major steps of a process are flow charted, it is difficult for the team to fully understand or improve the process, since many activities are hidden within each major step. Breaking out the sub-steps for each major step reveals the intricacies of the work process and helps the team identify problems.

After the major steps of a process are listed in sequence, a team brainstorms the sub-steps and lists them under the major step they belong to. Helpful questions to ask when sequencing sub-steps are:

- What really happens next?
- Does anyone make a decision before this activity is completed?
- Are approvals required before going to the next sub-step?
- Have we overlooked anything in this sequence of tasks?

Keep in mind that too much detail defeats the team's purpose. A flow chart big enough to cover an entire wall is more a hindrance than a help. In such a huge chart, the critical sub-steps in the work process are lost. Teams new to the continuous-improvement process can easily go overboard at the decision points in their flow charts. All teams—especially inexperienced ones—should complete the "yes" path after a decision point first and work out the "no" path second. When trying to work out the "no" path, it's easy for inexperienced teams to get caught up in "What if?" types of speculation and create a monstrous flow chart.

At this point, the sub-steps can simply be listed on the flip chart in the order in which the team thinks of them. Trying to correctly sequence the sub-steps as each of them is identified defeats the purpose of brainstorming, which is to generate as many ideas/items as possible in as short a time as possible.

After the brainstorming is completed, the team can go back to each major step, review the list of sub-steps under it, and place the sub-steps in the proper order. If the team used self-stick notes to record sub-steps, the sub-steps can be moved easily to reflect the correct sequence. If the team wrote the sub-steps down on the flip chart, the team can re-order the sub-steps by assigning numbers to them.

After identifying the appropriate flow chart symbol for each step and sub-step, the team should create a rough draft of the flow chart and check for errors. If necessary, the team can test the flow chart by working through the process exactly as it is drawn. If a step was left out, or if two steps are in reverse order, these errors can be corrected.

Once the team identifies major steps and sub-steps, puts them in the proper sequence, and assigns flow chart symbols to them, a final version of the "as it is" flow chart can be created with arrows drawn between steps and sub-steps. Once the team is satisfied that the flow chart accurately reflects the process as it is currently performed, the flow chart can be used as a tool to evaluate the current process.

A flow chart can help a team pinpoint steps or sub-steps in a work process that are especially critical to success. Steps or sub-steps that pose problems or erect barriers to great performance can also be spotted. Viewing a work process in its entirety enables the team to streamline and improve the process by combining or eliminating sub-steps, or turning decision points into activities. A completed flow chart also helps ensure that all team members know the nature and scope of the work process it has targeted for improvement.

Cause-and-Effect Diagrams. As mentioned earlier, a **cause-and-effect diagram** (also called a fishbone diagram because of its shape) is an analytical tool that a team can use to structure a brainstorming session.

To create a cause-and-effect diagram, the team's leader can write the problem to be analyzed at the top of a dry-erase board or flip chart and draw a box around it. The team leader can then draw a large arrow pointing to the box, with branches off the arrow indicating the main or general categories of causes of the problem. The team can brainstorm the titles of these main/general categories, or use five categories that are commonly used with cause-and-effect diagrams:

*   **People**—customers, staff, and others (if applicable) who interact within the process

*   **Methods**—current procedures governing relevant tasks, activities, or relationships

*   **Equipment**—machines, tools, computers, and so on that are used in the process

*   **Materials**—supplies or things used in the process

*   **Environment**—the environment of the work place or area in which the process occurs, including such things as temperature, lighting, noise levels, and so on

Exhibit 9 presents a sample cause-and-effect diagram used by the XYZ Hotel's service and kitchen staff to brainstorm causes of dirty and spotted silverware found at service stations in the dining room. The problem to be analyzed, "Dirty Silver," is listed at the top of the diagram (at the fish's head). Branches off the central arrow indicate main categories of causes. As you can see, this team chose to use the five commonly used main categories—people, methods, equipment, materials, and environment. As the team brainstormed potential causes, it listed them as branches off the main categories.

The purpose of the main categories is to help make the task of brainstorming potential causes manageable. For most problems, three to six main categories are sufficient. Teams new to the continuous-improvement process are often tempted to add a new main category each time an idea comes up that fails to fit neatly into one of the already established main categories. Just as a flow chart with too many main steps can be confusing and perhaps inaccurate, a cause-and-effect diagram with too many main categories can confuse a team and slow the continuous-improvement process down.

Exhibit 9 Sample Cause-and-Effect Diagram

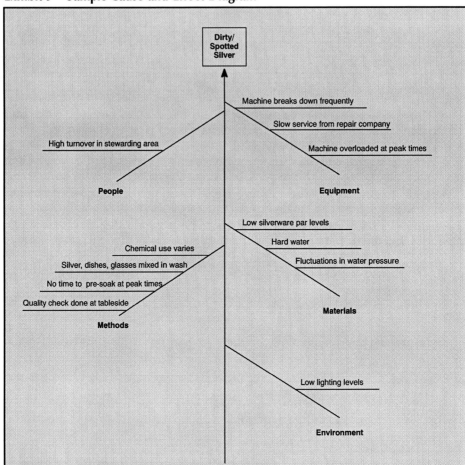

The main categories also help team members to more completely analyze a problem by prompting them to consider potential causes they might otherwise have overlooked. If the team seems to reach an impasse in brainstorming potential causes, the main categories can be turned into "who, what, where, when, and how" types of questions that might stimulate more ideas:

- **People**—"*How* do we know that all the right people are involved? Are key staff people left out of the process and that's what is contributing to the problem?"

- **Methods**—"*What* current procedures may be causing the problem? Does it matter *when* procedures are carried out? Is the timing of the work a cause of the problem?"

- **Equipment**—"Does it matter *who* operates the equipment?"

Analyzing Processes in a Hotel

The rooms-not-available problem-solving team at the Rose Hotel realized that guests checking into unclean rooms cost the hotel hundreds of thousands of dollars each year. The Rose Hotel is a corporate-owned luxury hotel located in a major American city. It has 1,500 guestrooms and two fine-dining restaurants. The hotel hosts elegant banquets for the city's elite and plays host to high-end meetings and conferences. In order to determine the root cause of the problem, the continuous-improvement team developed a process flow analysis. The guest's steps from arrival to actually entering the guestroom were documented. The steps in the check-in process included the following:

1. A guest with a reservation arrives and requests a room for the night.
2. The guest is told that a room is not available immediately.
3. The guest is provided with some options and a time when the room will be available. The options include:
   a. Waiting on-property in a public area such as a café or lounge.
   b. Storing luggage and returning at a later time.
   c. Checking into another room type if available.
4. The guest returns when the room is clean and ready for occupancy.

Each of the options provided to the guest while waiting for the room to become available has a cost associated with it. Some of the costs are direct and some are hidden and/or indirect. Costs associated with each option may include the following:

- *Waiting on-property.* The front desk may provide a voucher for a beverage or even a light meal in the lounge. This has a real, direct cost.
- *Storing luggage.* There is labor involved in storing the luggage, and space is used that could have been used for other guest needs. These may be viewed as direct or hidden costs.
- *Checking into another room type.* If the guest is upgraded at no additional cost, or if the guest is downgraded at a discounted rate, the costs associated are direct as the hotel is losing potential revenue. A room upgrade could cost dearly if the room could have been sold to another guest and it may even take more labor to clean.

Additional hidden costs associated with this problem but that are difficult to measure include:

- Dissatisfied guests who may not return after this stay.
- Frustrated staff whose morale declines or productivity decreases.
- Wasted time for staff members who deal with the problem.
- Negative word of mouth passed on by dissatisfied guests.

After reviewing the potential costs of the problem, the problem-solving team determined that it was important to identify causes of rooms not being available upon check-in. The check-out process flow was analyzed to determine whether the root cause of the problem originated in the check-out process. Steps in the check-out process included:

1. A guest decides to check out either by check-out time or as a late check-out.
2. The guest proceeds with luggage to front desk, uses express check-out, requests a bellperson to take the luggage to the front desk, and checks

(continued)

(continued)

out. The guest may also decide to leave the property without formally checking out.

3. After formally checking out, the guest may return to the room after a time to gather his or her belongings.
4. The guest proceeds to leave the property.

After reviewing the possible flow of the guest check-out process, the cross-functional problem-solving team then analyzed the processes hotel employees go through during the guest check-out phase. These processes included the following procedures:

1. The front desk formally checks a guest out and alerts housekeeping of a vacant/dirty room.
2. The front desk formally checks a guest out, but neglects to alert housekeeping of a vacant/dirty room.
3. A bellperson assists a guest with luggage and alerts the front desk that the guest has gone directly to his or her vehicle.
4. A bellperson assists a guest with luggage, but doesn't let the front desk know that the guest went directly to his or her vehicle without stopping at the front desk.
5. A guest checks out late, but housekeeping has already completed the guest-room floor and the staff is too busy to revisit the floor in a timely manner to clean the room.
6. A guest checks out, returns to a clean room after breakfast, and doesn't let the front desk know that the bathroom, for example, was used again after the housekeeper cleaned.

Determining Root Causes and Problem Cause Analysis

The problem-solving team realized a number of things after carefully considering the variables associated with the check-out process:

1. Late check-outs were frequent among foreign guests.
2. When bellpersons neglected to alert the front desk of a check-out, delays in cleaning the rooms were common.
3. When guests went back to their rooms after checking out, housekeeping found it challenging to return to the guestroom block in a timely manner, and often the rooms were forgotten until after housekeeping went home for the evening.

Root Causes. Late check-outs among foreign guests was a serious issue that prompted further investigation. It turned out that many of these foreign guests didn't speak English well and the front desk personnel were providing information about check-out times to these guests in English. A large market segment that had recently been attracted to the hotel was of Japanese origin.

Possible Solutions. One possible solution developed by the rooms-not-available team seemed simple enough. Information regarding check-out would be printed in both English and Japanese. This information would be given to guests upon check-in, and would also be included in the written materials provided in the hotel room.

The second possible solution was to develop a formal communication system between bellpersons and the front desk so that when bellpersons took luggage directly to transportation for a guest, they would alert the front desk that a particular room was being vacated. This simple communication process would inform the front desk that a guest was checking out and that housekeeping could be alerted.

Exhibit 10   Sample Fact-Finding Planning Sheet

Problem: Dirty silverware at service stations

What do we want to know?	How and where do we get the facts?	Who will get the facts?	When do we need the facts?
1. How many racks of silverware are returned for rewashing each week?	Use a check sheet to keep track	Entire team	1 month
2. How often does the dishwashing machine break down?	Check with Engineering Records	John	1 week
3. a. Does the water pressure fluctuate? b. How much? How often?	a. Check with Engineering b. Have a check sheet	a. George and Ann b. Entire team	1 week 1 month
4. Where do we buy our soap and chemicals? Who else uses them?	Interview Manager Interview Vendor	Invite to team meeting	2 weeks
5. a. What is the rated capacity of the dishwashing machine? b. How often do we exceed it?	a. Ask managers or engineers b. Use a check sheet to keep track	a. Ralph b. Entire team	3 weeks 3 weeks
6. What is the proper procedure for using the dishwashing machine? Does every one understand and use it?	Survey other Stewards	Susan, Tommie, Eddie, Gina	6 weeks

- **Materials**—"Is there something about *where* the supplies are stored that causes the problem?"
- **Environment**—"*How* does the work station affect this problem?"

Just because a "who, what, where, when, or how" question is based on a particular main category doesn't mean that the answers to that question should be listed under that same category. For example, in answering the "Equipment" question ("Does it matter *who* operates the equipment?"), a team might produce answers or ideas that belong not under the "Equipment" main category, but under some other main category on the diagram, such as "People."

If a team tried to collect data on each potential cause listed on its cause-and-effect diagram, the continuous-improvement process would be very time-consuming. To gain speed and efficiency, teams need to make reasonable judgments as to the major causes of the problem, determine the underlying or root causes of these causes, and conduct just enough fact-finding to verify their judgments.

Data-Gathering Tools

Tools commonly used by individuals or teams requiring more information to tackle a problem include fact-finding planning sheets and check sheets.

Fact-Finding Planning Sheets. A fact-finding planning sheet (see Exhibit 10) can help a team in planning and carrying out appropriate fact-finding tasks.

Fact-finding planning sheets pose critical questions a team should answer before it begins to gather data:

- What do we want to know?
- How and where do we get the facts?
- Who will get the facts?
- When do we need the facts?

Determining when facts are needed involves determining deadlines for collecting data as well as establishing the duration or time periods over which the data is collected. Cooperation and advice from others can save a team a great deal of time and energy in planning and carrying out fact-finding efforts. By filling out a fact-finding planning sheet, a team may discover, for example, that it does not have to spend time and energy to collect some of the data critical to measuring the extent of the problem it has chosen to work on, because this data already exists in the form of accounting records, customer and staff survey results, departmental reports, computer printouts, and so on.

Check Sheets. Teams should devise simple, easy-to-use tools for collecting facts, such as **check sheets** for recording observations. Check sheets are also used as data-gathering tools to record how frequently something occurs. The second column in Exhibit 10 mentions check sheets three times, showing that the service and kitchen staff of the XYZ Hotel plans to use check sheets for recording:

- The number of silverware racks returned for rewashing each week.
- The amount and frequency of fluctuations in water pressure.
- The number of times that the rated capacity of the dishwashing machine is exceeded.

Check sheets should be simple to use and easily understood. It's often wise to collect a small amount of data with newly designed check sheets and revise them, if necessary, before using them to collect data over a long period of time. Also, for team members trying to design simplicity and clarity into a check sheet, it's helpful to imagine someone picking up the check sheet five years from now and having no difficulty immediately understanding what the check sheet was intended to do.

Tools for Displaying Data

After fact-finding efforts are completed, teams can use bar charts, line graphs, or pie charts to visually display the data they collected. As shown by Exhibits 11, 12, and 13, graphic displays enable team members to see the significance of data much more easily and more quickly than if they had only columns of numbers to review.

Team members should not spend an excessive amount of time and effort trying to create professional-looking computer-generated graphics. In many cases, hand-drawn graphic displays are all that the team needs to understand the data and move on in the continuous-improvement process.

Bar Charts. Bar charts show relationships among two or more items. Exhibit 11 displays data showing the frequency of dessert sales by five servers for a particular Saturday dinner shift.

Exhibit 11   Sample Bar Chart

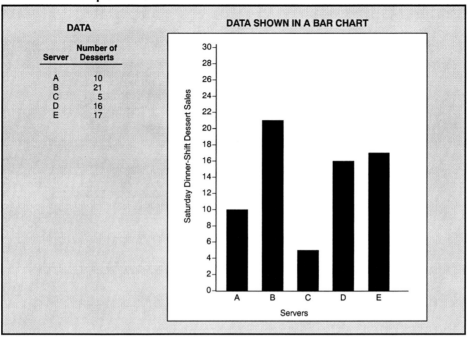

Exhibit 12   Sample Line Graph

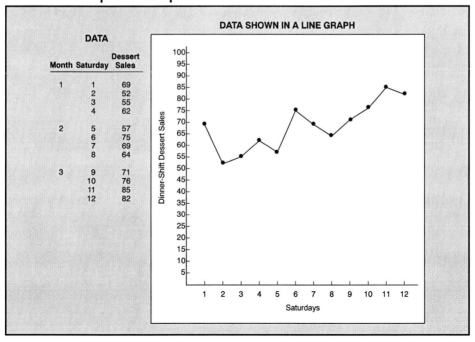

Exhibit 13   Sample Pie Chart

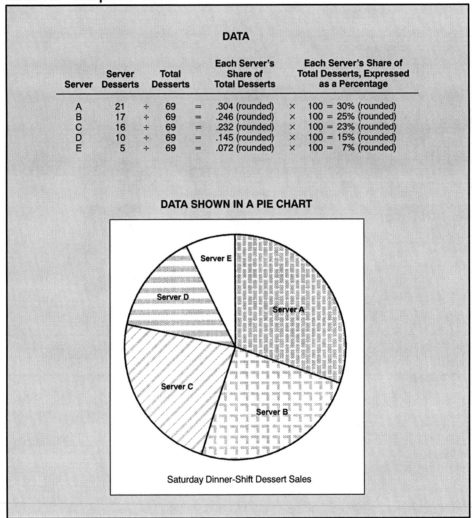

DATA

Server	Server Desserts		Total Desserts		Each Server's Share of Total Desserts			Each Server's Share of Total Desserts, Expressed as a Percentage
A	21	÷	69	=	.304 (rounded)	×	100 =	30% (rounded)
B	17	÷	69	=	.246 (rounded)	×	100 =	25% (rounded)
C	16	÷	69	=	.232 (rounded)	×	100 =	23% (rounded)
D	10	÷	69	=	.145 (rounded)	×	100 =	15% (rounded)
E	5	÷	69	=	.072 (rounded)	×	100 =	7% (rounded)

DATA SHOWN IN A PIE CHART

Saturday Dinner-Shift Dessert Sales

Line Graphs. Line graphs show a data pattern over time. Exhibit 12 quickly shows whether dessert sales on Saturday dinner shifts are growing or declining.

Pie Charts. Pie charts show relationships among two or more items and are most useful when you want to show how *all of something* can be broken down into percentages of the whole. Note that in the case of Exhibit 13, if there were more than five food servers on the Saturday dinner shift, the pie chart, labeled "Saturday Dinner-Shift Dessert Sales," would be inaccurate, because the percentages shown would not be of total dessert sales, but only of the dessert sales contributed by the five food servers.

 **Key Terms** ——

bar chart—A graphic representation using rectangles to show quantitative relationships among two or more items. Also called a bar graph.

baseline measurement—A measurement used as a basis for comparisons or for control purposes; a beginning point in an evaluation of output observed over a period of time. A baseline measurement represents how a process performs prior to any improvement effort.

brainstorming—An idea-gathering technique that uses team interaction to generate as many ideas as possible within a given time period. Brainstorming taps into the collective brainpower of the team and yields greater results than could be achieved if each individual in the team worked alone.

breakthrough improvement—The achievement of previously unattainable savings in the cost of doing business through reduction of defects on an unprecedented scale.

cause-and-effect diagram—An analytical tool used to structure brainstorming and to organize many potential causes of a problem. Also called a fishbone diagram because of its shape.

check sheet—A data-gathering tool commonly used to record how frequently something occurs.

continuous improvement—The ongoing efforts within a company to meet the needs and exceed the expectations of customers by changing the way work is performed so that products and services are delivered better, faster, and at less cost than in the past.

flow chart—A pictorial representation of steps in a process.

incremental improvement—Activities designed to enhance or streamline current work processes within a company, department, or work area, resulting in limited but steady gains in quality, speed, and/or savings.

line graph—A chart in which points showing a data pattern over time are connected by lines.

pie chart—A circle cut into segments showing the quantitative relationships among two or more items. Pie charts are most useful for showing how *all of something* can be broken down into percentages of the whole. Also called a circle graph.

priority determination chart—A tool used to rank items in order of importance; individuals or teams make a series of forced choices among the items to determine their ranking.

problem statement—A phrase or sentence that describes an area for improvement as clearly and as objectively as possible.

root cause—A primary contributor to a problem.

selection criteria—Factors used to assess and rank a list of choices.

selection matrix—A decision-making tool that uses established criteria to rank a list of choices.

? Review Questions

1. What are the differences among continuous improvement, incremental improvement, and breakthrough improvement?

2. What are some techniques teams can use to target an opportunity for improvement?

3. What are some of the ways teams can analyze an area targeted for improvement?

4. Why should a team conduct a trial test of its solution to a problem?

5. What are some basic steps for conducting a brainstorming session?

6. What is a priority determination chart?

7. What is the difference between a selection matrix and a weighted selection matrix?

8. Why is a flow chart useful to a team studying a work process?

9. What is a cause-and-effect diagram?

10. What are some data-gathering tools?

11. What are some tools for displaying data?

Chapter 5 Outline

Competencies

1. Define power and empowerment, and describe how these concepts tend to play out in centralized and decentralized organizations. (pp. 137–141)

2. Explain why the authority of managers should be commensurate with their level of responsibility. (pp. 141–142)

3. Describe the types and sources of organizational and personal power, the typical responses to each type of power, and methods to enhance power and build alliances. (pp. 142–147)

4. Define power tactics, and describe eight techniques managers can use to influence the behavior of others. (pp. 147–149)

5. Describe four basic communication styles, and explain why effective managers need flexibility in their communication style as they influence the behavior of others. (pp. 149–154)

6. Identify the challenges a manager can face when sharing power with others through delegation, and describe the steps involved in effective delegation. (pp. 154–157)

7. Explain what an organization must do to empower its managers and staff. (pp. 157–158)

5

Power and Empowerment

EMPOWERING STAFF MEMBERS can be a viable solution for hospitality companies as they search for ways to excel while dealing with a variety of challenging issues, such as the need to meet and exceed the rising expectations of guests, do more with less, address staff shortages, comply with increased regulations requiring significant dedication of resources, and meet the needs of staff members who want to be involved in problem-solving and decision-making. True empowerment prompts a decentralization of power and redefinition of responsibilities for managers, supervisors, and employees.

In this chapter, **power** is defined as the ability to influence the behavior of others. Within organizations, a manager's power is a function of responsibility, authority, and accountability. **Empowerment** is defined as the redistribution of power within an organization that enables managers, supervisors, and employees to perform their jobs more efficiently and effectively. The overall goal of empowerment is to enhance guest service and increase profits for the organization by releasing decision-making responsibility, authority, and accountability to the lowest levels within the organization.

This chapter begins by comparing centralized and decentralized hospitality organizations in terms of power structures and empowerment issues. Next, organizational and personal sources of a manager's power are described, as well as strategies by which managers can enhance their power within an organization. Power tactics and power communication styles are presented as techniques managers can use to influence the behavior of their employees, peers, and supervisors. Power sources, strategies, tactics, and styles are not presented as techniques for managers to use to manipulate others or to carve out personal empires within their organizations. Rather, managers are encouraged to use these techniques as diagnostic tools to assess their current interpersonal skills and the structure of power within their organizations. The chapter also looks closely at delegation as a power-sharing technique and describes steps for effectively delegating work to others. The final section focuses on what managers can do to empower their staff.

Centralization versus Decentralization

Centralized organizations have power structures that place most decision-making authority at top management levels. **Decentralized organizations** have power structures that place decision-making authority at the lowest organizational levels.

The degree of centralization or decentralization within a company is not determined by how tall or how flat a company's structure appears on an organization chart. Large companies with tall structures are not necessarily highly centralized organizations. The key determinant is where decisions are made—at corporate headquarters or at the unit level. Some large restaurant chains, for example, may give unit managers broad decision-making powers in matters that affect their restaurants. Conversely, small organizations with flat structures can be highly centralized. The organization chart of a mid-size hotel may be flat, but power may be centralized in the general manager's position, especially if he or she micromanages every department and functional area.

A number of factors influence the degree of centralization within an organization. In times of financial crisis, a high degree of centralization may be most appropriate; investors, creditors, and the managers and staff of a financially troubled organization generally expect top managers to take control of the situation and work out the crisis. Decentralization may be most appropriate for organizations that face stiff competition in fast-changing market or business conditions. Decentralized organizations can usually respond more quickly and effectively to change than centralized organizations.

The culture of an organization also affects how power is distributed. Changing the structure of power within an organization can be difficult. When companies become more centralized, power is taken away from middle and lower management levels and given to top-level managers, and the former group may resent the loss of power, status, and prestige within the company. The top-level managers may become frustrated with the additional duties that accompany their increased power. When companies become more decentralized, power is taken from higher-level managers and given to middle and lower managers. In this case, top managers may feel threatened by their loss of power, while middle and lower-level managers may be intimidated by their new responsibilities.

The downsizing or "rightsizing" efforts of many hospitality companies are primarily attempts to reduce costs. However, to be effective, downsizing must be more than just cutting staff—it must include a real redistribution of power and decision-making responsibility.

Centralization and Learned Helplessness

Excessively centralized organizations are generally characterized as top-down, command-and-control systems with multiple levels of management. At each level, managers report to the managers above them and closely monitor the actions of the managers below them. Information moves upward through the organization, and directives are issued downward. Each manager has a limited, well-defined area of responsibility and a relatively narrow span of control, usually with three to seven managers reporting to him or her from below. Decision-making can be a slow and cumbersome process, as several levels of approval are usually required before lower-level managers, supervisors, or employees can initiate action on even the simplest issues, such as implementing obvious solutions to everyday operational problems.

In such organizations, managers and employees can become so narrowly focused on their specific duties and tasks that they lose sight of the fundamental values, mission, and goals of the organization. When the general manager micromanages hotel operations, department heads tend to simply carry out directives and scrutinize the activities of the supervisors below them. Likewise, supervisors follow orders and constantly loom over the shoulders of their staff members. Staff members, in turn, simply do what they are told. Everyone becomes so concerned with doing things right that they rarely question whether they are actually doing the right things. In other words, everyone is so concerned with pleasing the general manager that no one stops to wonder if they are actually pleasing the guests.

Strangled by limited responsibility and the seemingly endless details of standard operating procedures, managers and employees of overly centralized organizations simply go through the motions of serving guests. Procedures established by upper management start to control not only the actions of staff members, but their thoughts as well, a phenomenon known as **learned helplessness.** The comical series of notes presented in the chapter appendix illustrates the learned helplessness of the housekeeping staff in an excessively centralized hotel. In this series of exchanges, the employees are determined to meet the expectations of management, no matter what the guest wants. The housekeeping staff members are unable to see beyond their required tasks to the fundamental reason they stock guestrooms with soap in the first place: to serve the guest. Eventually, the guest simply gives up.

Over-centralization can breed an organization of individuals paralyzed by learned helplessness. When the general manager is the only one in the hotel who sees the entire picture of operations, department managers can't see beyond the edges of their boxes on the organization chart. Focusing solely on the activities of their own departments, department managers lose the wider perspective needed to identify and solve problems that cut across functional areas; such problems always seem to belong to someone else. Each department "makes do" or simply works around the problems.

The following example is adapted from a story told by Horst Schulze, the former president and COO of The Ritz-Carlton Hotel Company, about a command-and-control general manager of a large downtown hotel. The hotel constantly received guest complaints about room service: while the food was superb, the service took forever. The GM issued a directive to the room service manager to increase the speed of service. Service improved over a month or two but then declined again. The GM fired the room service manager, hired another, and issued the same directive—reduce the time from room-service order to delivery. The directive produced the same results: for a month or two, guest complaints about the speed of service subsided but then rose to previous levels. Once again, the GM fired the room service manager, hired another, and reissued the same directive. When nothing changed, the GM finally asked the new room service manager why deliveries took so long. The manager replied that the elevators were too slow. This was the poorest excuse the GM had heard yet.

The GM decided to take matters into his own hands—he personally assessed the room service process by timing each task, from taking the order to delivery. Nothing seemed out of the ordinary until he accompanied a room service attendant delivering an order to a room on the 28th floor. The elevator stopped at the 2nd floor, and a houseperson entered with an armload of sheets. At the 4th floor, the houseperson left the elevator, and another one entered carrying an armload of towels. This houseperson got off on the 6th floor. At the 8th floor, another houseperson entered the elevator burdened with bed linens and towels; he got off at the 12th floor. The parade of housepersons, sheets, and towels continued up to the 28th floor and all the way back down to the lobby.

The current room service manager was right—the slowdown in the room service process was taking place at the elevators. But why? Before returning to the lobby, the GM asked a houseperson why he was delivering linen at that hour, as procedures dictated that linen deliveries be made at specific times that would not interfere with the needs of guests or other operations—like room service deliveries. The houseperson replied that the standard procedures were being followed, but that none of the housepersons ever received enough sheets and towels to properly service their areas. Thus they were constantly raiding the linen closets on each others' floors to provide enough linen for the room attendants in their respective areas.

The GM finally discovered the real cause of the problem—room service was slow because linen pars were too low. But why didn't the room service manager make the same connection? Why didn't room service attendants ask the housepersons what they were doing? Why didn't the housepersons inform their supervisors of the linen shortages? Why didn't the executive housekeeper put in a request to the purchasing department for more linen? Because the entire staff was stuck in a mire of learned helplessness. No one looked beyond his or her narrowly defined responsibilities. The staff was not only powerless to change the situation, but unconcerned by it as well. They "made do" and simply worked around inadequate linen pars—resulting in slow room service and guest complaints.

Decentralization and Empowerment

Highly decentralized organizations are typically characterized as bottom-up, leadership-and-support systems with relatively few levels of management. Managers have broad areas of responsibility and, in many large organizations, they have wide spans of control, with eight or more managers reporting to them. Reporting and monitoring functions are designed to support the initiatives of lower-level managers rather than direct and control their actions. Instead of numerous and detailed directives moving downward through the organization, needs and requests are communicated upward, and information flows freely in every direction.

Decentralization and empowerment begin with changes in the leadership roles of top managers. The president, the CEO, and other high-level managers must spend less time controlling the activities of lower-level managers and more time communicating their shared vision of the company. The vision of leadership should include where the company is today, where it is going tomorrow, why it is heading in that direction, and how it will get there. Top managers influence others to accept the responsibility of power by gaining their commitment to the fundamental values, mission, and goals of the organization. They must ensure that everyone understands how their work contributes to the success of the company and fits into the overall vision of the organization.

Decentralization can create an organization of empowered managers and staff members who have an understanding of the entire operation. Department managers learn to see and think beyond the boundaries of their boxes on the organization chart and to cooperate with other departments. Focusing on the values, mission, and goals of the organization as a whole, they work together to identify and solve problems that cut across functional areas—an approach critical to organizational success.

Fundamentals of Power and Authority

The fundamentals of power and authority apply equally to centralized and decentralized organizations. Power is the ability to influence the behavior of others. **Authority** is the formal power granted by the organization to a management position. An important aspect of authority is that the power is vested in the position, not the individual. A manager exercises authority when making decisions, issuing orders, and using resources to achieve departmental and organizational goals.

In addition to power, authority carries with it responsibility and **accountability,** which means that managers with authority accept responsibility for their decisions and must justify their actions to those above them in the chain of command. The **chain of command** is represented on an organization chart by an unbroken line of authority linking all positions within the organization and specifying formal reporting relationships. Managers placed high in the chain of command carry more responsibility and greater authority than managers below them.

Authority Commensurate with Responsibility

A manager's authority should be commensurate with the responsibility of his or her position within the organization. When managers are given responsibility for achieving certain goals but have insufficient authority to take the necessary steps toward achieving them, their jobs become very difficult, if not impossible. They must rely on the authority of other managers higher in the chain of command to get the job done. In such situations, work becomes a stressful source of frustration.

Consider the fictional case of the Scalar Center Plaza, a large convention hotel. Susan is a salesperson and reports to Pablo, the director of sales, who in turn reports to Maximillion, the general manager. Susan is responsible for booking a specific number of room nights each month, but she does not have much authority to negotiate with meeting planners. Virtually every item on each draft of a contract—and all subsequent changes—must be passed on to Pablo for approval, and Pablo must get Maximillion's blessing on each item before giving his response to Susan.

Susan feels she is more like a gofer ("go for" this, "go for" that) for Pablo than a professional salesperson. Anything she does on her own is interpreted as subverting the structure of authority and bypassing her manager. At the same time, Pablo feels like a paper-shuffler and wonders what sales directors do at other organizations. And all the while, the hotel loses business. Some meeting planners distrust Susan, believing that her need to "talk to her manager" is simply a cheap negotiating trick. Other meeting planners wonder if this is the kind of runaround they can expect when their groups stay at the hotel. Bookings decrease, Maximillion dumps on Pablo, Pablo dumps on Susan, Susan quits, and Pablo updates his résumé.

Conversely, when the authority of managers exceeds their responsibility departments can become empires and the organization embroiled in turmoil, with constant in-fighting and turf wars. Consider the fictional case of the Can-Do/No-Win Convention Center, a competing hotel across town from the Scalar Center Plaza. The general manager, Arjun, orders the director of sales, Mika, to do whatever it takes to increase occupancy—or else. Mika authorizes her sales representatives to find ways to exceed their monthly quota of room sales. The sales reps negotiate lower function prices and sweeten deals with offers of free coffee breaks and fully stocked complimentary hospitality suites. Tentative bookings increase dramatically.

Meanwhile, Arjun meets with David, the executive chef, and yells at him for exceeding budgeted expenses. He orders David to do whatever it takes to reduce food costs—or else. David meets with his food and beverage managers and tells them to do whatever is necessary to bring food costs in line with the budget.

Neither Mika nor David are aware of each other's meetings with Arjun. When the sales contracts are reviewed at an executive committee meeting, David and Mika jump at each other's throats. If the "sweet deals" Mika authorized are accepted, food costs will go through the roof and David will look like a fool to his staff. However, if the deals are renegotiated, meeting planners will be upset, room nights will be lost, and Mika will look like a fool to *her* staff.

While there are several leadership and management issues involved in the previous scenarios, in both cases the general manager is at fault for not ensuring that the authority of the managers is commensurate with their responsibility. At the Scalar Center Plaza, Maximillion narrowly defined responsibility and withheld virtually all authority from the director of sales and the sales reps. With so little responsibility, and less authority, how could Pablo or Susan be held accountable for sales? And at the Can-Do/No-Win Convention Center, Arjun failed to involve his department heads in a collaborative goal-setting effort. Instead, he gave both the director of sales and the executive chef seemingly boundless authority. It's no wonder the staff meeting turned into a battle.

Types and Sources of Power

Power—and its source—may be either organizational or personal. Exhibit 1 outlines both organizational and personal sources of power.

Power based on organizational sources includes position power, reward power, and coercive power. **Position power,** also referred to as **legitimate power,** stems from the formal authority granted to a position within the hierarchy of an organization. For example, general managers, department managers, and area supervisors have varying degrees of power due to their positions in a hospitality organization. Employees generally accept position power as legitimate and therefore comply with a manager's work-related directives. **Reward power** results from a manager's authority to provide rewards for employees; managers influence the behavior of others by providing formal rewards such as pay increases, promotions, bonuses, days off, and so on. They can also influence behavior by providing informal rewards such as attention, praise, and recognition. **Coercive power** stems from a manager's or supervisor's authority to withhold rewards or inflict punishment. Managers exercise coercive power when they influence behavior by denying pay increases or reprimanding, demoting, or firing employees.

Exhibit 1 Sources of Power

Types of Organizational Power	Source
Position Power	Authority granted to a position within the hierarchy of an organization
Reward Power	Authority to provide rewards
Coercive Power	Authority to withhold rewards or administer punishment
Types of Personal Power	**Source**
Expert Power	Specialized knowledge, skill, or expertise
Referent Power	Personal characteristics admired and respected by others

Personal sources of power include expert power and referent power. **Expert power** stems from an individual's special knowledge or skill in relation to tasks performed by members of his or her staff. For example, kitchen employees may follow many of the executive chef's recommendations simply because they trust his or her superior knowledge of cooking. In the hospitality industry, supervisors have often been promoted to their supervisory positions because of their mastery of basic skills. Their expertise may become a source of expert power enabling them to influence staff members. **Referent power** results from the admiration and respect that others have for an individual's personal characteristics and interpersonal skills. For example, the front desk staff of a hotel may admire the way that their manager relates with them, as well as with guests. Their admiration becomes a source of referent power for the manager, as the staff wishes to follow his or her example when interacting with guests and each other.

There are three general responses to a manager's use of power: commitment, compliance, and resistance. Generally, a manager seeks *commitment* from staff members, demonstrated when they agree with the manager's point of view, adopt his or her suggested plans of action, and enthusiastically carry out new instructions. Expert power and referent power—power from personal sources—are most likely to produce staff commitment. Position power and reward power are most likely to generate staff *compliance:* staff members may state agreement with the manager's point of view, help implement his or her plans, and carry out new instructions, but they may also harbor personal reservations about the manager and his or her directives. Coercive power most often generates staff *resistance*—staff members may openly state their opposition to the manager's plans, ignore instructions, and openly disobey orders.

While enthusiastic commitment from others should be the goal behind every manager's use of power, given the realities of hospitality operations, compliance may be the optimum result in some situations. Consider the manager's role in influencing the behavior of staff members as an organization downsizes. Downsizing inevitably means eliminating positions and redistributing work throughout the organization. While upper managers may be enthusiastically committed to doing more with less, staff members may feel frustrated, overworked, and under-appreciated. Personal sources of power may be of little use to middle managers as they implement the initial phases of a downsizing plan; early actions may rely heavily on position power and reward power. Later, as the restructuring effort takes effect and others see how the company and staff benefit from the downsizing, a manager's expert power and referent power might regain their effectiveness.

Enhancing Position Power. Successful managers make the most of formal and informal opportunities to expand their spheres of influence by increasing their position power. Building upon the formal authority granted to their positions within the hierarchy, managers can enhance their power by:

- Increasing the flexibility of their jobs

- Becoming an important part of the organization's information loop and thereby increasing their visibility

- Promoting the importance of their work

Position power can diminish when the vast majority of a manager's time is taken up with routine activities. Managers need flexibility in their work schedules so they can be available to participate in task forces within the organization or initiate projects on their own. These types of activities enhance a manager's position power.

With greater job flexibility, managers can become more aware of the important issues facing the organization and work toward gaining greater access to the flow of critical information through the organization. The more a manager is part of this "information loop," the more others see and acknowledge his or her position power. Laboring in isolation does not enhance power; being recognized for one's efforts does.

Managers working to increase their activities and visibility within an organization must take care to maintain their performance of regularly assigned duties and responsibilities—the foundation of a manager's position power. When managers become overly concerned with increasing their importance and position power, they may find that others in the organization perceive them as power-hungry. The best way for managers to be noticed is to promote the importance of their *fundamental* responsibilities and make sure that others in the organization know about the excellent performance of their staff members.

Enhancing Personal Power. Managers can enhance their personal power by promoting their current achievements and abilities, by refining their interpersonal skills, and by obtaining more specialized knowledge. A manager's expert power increases as it makes him or her more useful—and thereby more visible to others in the organization. Staff members, peers, and superiors recognize the abilities of a manager when they experience firsthand how those abilities help them achieve their own goals and objectives. Likewise, obtaining more specialized knowledge or skills increases a manager's expert power as long as the new knowledge or skills meet the needs of the organization.

Let's look at a simple example. Mary is the convention sales executive for a mid-size upscale resort. In addition to her sales skills and specialized knowledge of markets, Mary has excellent computer skills. For the past several months, she has downloaded customer data supplied by the accounting department into database and spreadsheet programs that she purchased from a local software outlet. At a recent business planning meeting, Mary used a number of colorful and informative charts and graphs that made immediate visual sense out of data that in the past was presented in the form of long, confusing columns of numbers. Mary's expert power increased dramatically. While her basic computer skills were well below those of professional information specialists, they far exceeded those of the other managers at the resort. After the meeting, other department heads—and the general manager—sought her advice and assistance on everything from basic spreadsheets to print designs for menus. A skill marginal to Mary's position as convention sales executive enhanced her credibility in the eyes of both her peers and her supervisor. Her expert power increased dramatically because her newly recognized computer skills met important needs of the organization.

Enhancing Power Through Alliances with Others. Another important way that managers can enhance their personal power and increase their spheres of influence within an organization is to tap the power of others by forming strategic alliances. Power alliances are effective when a plan of action requires that managers in several areas work together to influence the behavior of others. Such alliances are often necessary, for example, when planning budgets or implementing components of a marketing plan.

The importance of alliances is illustrated by the following example. Vincente, the new food and beverage director of a large convention hotel, wants to reposition one of the property's restaurants. The strategy calls for an overhaul of the menu, some redecorating, and changes in service standards. Vincente works for weeks on the details of the plan and consults periodically with the marketing executive and the dining room manager. Menu possibilities, guest preferences, and cost components of the plan are finally established. With the homework done and the numbers crunched, Vincente proudly presents the plan at an executive staff meeting.

The general manager and other executive team members carefully review the plan's executive summary, praise Vincente for his diligent work, and then decide to table discussion and action until some unspecified future point in time. The committee moves on to other matters. Vincente is stunned and wonders what went wrong.

What did go wrong? New to the organization, Vincente naturally wanted to further the success of the hotel, show his commitment to his job, and demonstrate his talents and abilities. But Vincente failed to forge alliances with key power figures within the hotel. If he had taken the time to assess the power centers of the organization, he would have found that three key people on the executive committee—the general manager, the executive chef, and the controller—have the personal power to influence virtually every decision made by the executive team. If he had formed alliances with at least two of these people, he would have vastly increased the chance that the team would have devoted serious discussion to his proposal.

Exhibit 2 presents a worksheet that can be used to assess the power centers of an organization. Vincente might have benefitted from using this worksheet to assess his own power. Then he could have filled it out on other managers in the

Exhibit 2   Assessing Organizational Power

Person Being Rated: _____

Organizational Power	**Power Scale**
Position Power	1 2 3 4 5 6 7 8 9 10
	No power Great power
Instances of Use	_____
	_____
	_____
	_____
	_____
Reward Power	1 2 3 4 5 6 7 8 9 10
	No power Great power
Instances of Use	_____
	_____
	_____
	_____
	_____
Coercive Power	1 2 3 4 5 6 7 8 9 10
	No power Great power
Instances of Use	_____
	_____
	_____
	_____
	_____

Personal Power	**Power Scale**
Expert Power	1 2 3 4 5 6 7 8 9 10
	No power Great power
Knowledge/Skills List	_____
	_____
	_____
	_____
	_____

Exhibit 2   *(continued)*

Referent Power	1 2 3 4 5 6 7 8 9 10
	No power Great power

Personal Characteristics   **Respected by**

_____   _____
_____   _____
_____   _____
_____   _____
_____   _____
_____   _____
_____   _____

organization to help him gauge, as best he could, the power of others within the organization. The worksheet is by no means an objective measurement of power, but it does offer a way of thinking about an organization's corridors of power and estimating the sphere of a particular individual's influence. This enables a manager to identify powerful allies to recruit as needed.

Identifying powerful individuals can also help a manager identify a possible mentor. A mentor can increase a manager's sphere of influence simply because others perceive that the manager has the ear of someone who commands high organizational and personal power. A mentor can help a new manager get noticed, make the right decisions, and avoid unnecessary conflicts. A manager's mentor should be, and usually is, his or her immediate supervisor. When this is not the case, managers must take care that their relationship with their mentor does not affect their loyalty to their supervisor.

An alliance becomes a disruptive faction when it is formed with the intent to fight turf wars with other departments, plan an end-run around another manager, or sabotage the efforts of peers. From time to time, these hardball power games are played at some level within almost every organization. However, there are usually no winners—and many losers—because these factions arise from narrow personal agendas and rarely serve the interests or support the goals of the organization.

Power Tactics

Power tactics are the methods by which managers use the five sources of power to influence the behavior of their employees, peers, and supervisors. There are eight common ways that managers try to influence the behavior of others: consultation, reasoning, inspirational appeal, ingratiating appeal, peer pressure, bargaining, pulling rank, and upward appeal (see Exhibit 3). The differences among these power tactics are best illustrated with examples of each.

Exhibit 3   Common Power Tactics

Consultation

Involving the other person in decisions that directly relate to the desired behavior.

Reasoning

Influencing behavior by presenting facts and appealing to logic.

Inspirational Appeal

Generating enthusiasm and commitment by appealing to the other's values or emotions.

Ingratiating Appeal

Winning approval through the use of praise or flattery.

Peer Pressure

Enlisting an individual's peers to support the need for the desired behavior.

Bargaining

Offering rewards or favors to achieve the desired behavior.

Pulling Rank

Using the authority of position power to order the desired behavior.

Upward Appeal

Referring to others with greater position power and authority who support the desired behavior.

Consider the case of Anja, an executive housekeeper, whose goal is to influence the behavior of Bill, the houseperson on the afternoon shift. The hotel lobby is generally well-kept under current public-area cleaning routines, but Anja feels that an additional touch-up in the late afternoon and early evening would be an improvement and would please arriving guests. Given current staffing levels within the department, Bill is the only person that Anja can assign additional duties. What follows are eight ways that Anja could go about influencing Bill:

- *Consultation:* Anja could ask Bill for ideas on how to make the lobby sparkle for arriving guests and then ask him how he could help or contribute.

- *Reasoning:* Anja could describe her reasons for touching up the lobby and explain to Bill that he is the only person available to make it happen.

- *Inspirational appeal:* Anja could refer to Bill's sense of teamwork and his past willingness to help others while the department is short-staffed.

- *Ingratiating appeal:* Anja could ask Bill to touch up the lobby, commenting on the pride he takes in his regular work.

- *Peer pressure:* At a department meeting, Anja could explain the situation and ask the other staff members if they feel Bill could do the job.

- *Bargaining:* Anja could offer an exchange—Bill touches up the lobby in exchange for three Saturdays off each month.

- *Pulling rank:* Anja could simply use the authority of her position and order Bill to touch up the lobby twice during his shift.

- *Upward appeal:* Anja could tell Bill that the general manager wants him to touch up the lobby twice during the afternoon shift.

Which tactic should Anja use? The answer depends on a variety of factors: Anja's feeling about each alternative, her predominant management style, how well she understands what motivates Bill, the organizational culture, and so on. The answer also depends on the type of message Anja wants to send while influencing Bill's behavior. Every use of power sends a message about the person exerting the power. In pulling rank and making upward appeals, for example, Anja sends a message that says, "Bill, I know you don't want any more work, but I'm going to get you to touch up the lobby anyway"—that is, Anja will exercise her power based in the organization to get things done. Ingratiating appeal, peer pressure, and bargaining send a similar but less explicit message: that Anja will use referent and reward power to get things done. Consultation, reasoning, and inspirational appeal send messages that appeal to Bill's reason, values, and emotions. Such power messages depend greatly on Anja's interpersonal skills, and success with them may help Anja build more of a referent power base within her own department.

Experienced managers are usually prepared to use two or three power tactics in any given situation. First, they try the tactic that they feel will work best—the one they believe will be the least threatening to the other person. If that fails, they try their second choice. Inexperienced managers seldom realize the options available to them. Many new managers rely solely on their position power to get things done and constantly pull rank when attempting to influence members of their staff. When challenged by their staff, their standard reply is, "I'm your supervisor and I'm telling you to do it." While this tactic may achieve compliance in a given situation, over time it may provoke resistance and perhaps even create confrontational situations. And it does not generate the peak performance that results from real staff commitment.

Power and Communication Styles

Communication styles are important aspects of power. Since every use of power is an attempt to directly influence the behavior of others, the way a manager communicates can significantly affect the outcome of a power-related situation. The communication model illustrated in Exhibit 4 can help managers become more aware of how they use power in specific situations and enable them to develop more effective ways of influencing others. The model diagrams four basic communication styles—emotive, directive, reflective, and supportive—along two dimensions: dominance and sociability.

Exhibit 4   Power Communication Styles

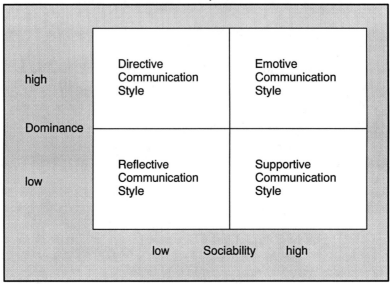

Source: Adapted from Gerald L. Manning and Barry L. Reece, *Selling Today: A Personal Approach*, 6th ed., p. 98. © 1995. Reprinted by permission of Prentice-Hall, Upper Saddle River, New Jersey.

Emotive. Managers displaying an **emotive communication style** combine high levels of dominance with high levels of sociability. They are action-oriented and seem constantly on the move. They prefer informal interactions and usually approach others on a first-name basis. These managers also seem naturally persuasive because they find it easy to express their points of view both forcefully and dramatically. A manager with an excessively emotive communication style is likely to:

• Express opinions in a highly emotional manner

• Use exaggerated gestures and facial expressions

• Appear outspoken, almost to the point of being offensive

• Seem unwilling to listen to the views of others

Directive. Managers with a **directive communication style** combine high dominance with low sociability. They are typically frank, demanding, assertive, and determined, and they usually project a take-charge, no-nonsense attitude. They express their opinions strongly through gestures or tone of voice. The speed and efficiency by which these managers approach power situations lead them to prefer brief, formal interactions with others. Managers who have an excessively directive communication style are likely to:

• Exhibit a determination to come out on top

• Rarely admit to being wrong

- Seem cold and unfeeling in dealing with others
- Appear arrogantly and stubbornly assertive

Reflective. Managers displaying a **reflective communication style** combine low dominance and low sociability; they are usually orderly, deliberate, and seemingly under control at all times. To others, these managers may seem aloof, preoccupied, and hard to get to know. They seldom seem rushed or in a hurry and prefer formal, orderly situations in which they can control the interaction. A manager with an excessively reflective communication style is likely to:

- Avoid making decisions
- Seem overly interested in details
- Appear stiff and formal when dealing with others
- Avoid displaying emotions

Supportive. Managers with a **supportive communication style** combine high sociability with low dominance; these managers are usually sensitive, patient, and good listeners. They often prefer nonthreatening, informal interactions in which they actively listen to the other's point of view. Managers who have an excessively supportive communication style are likely to:

- Attempt to win approval by always agreeing with others
- Appear insecure by frequently seeking reassurance
- Are reluctant to take a strong stand
- Seem unnecessarily apologetic

The communication styles characterized by high dominance—directive and emotive styles—are used by managers who are generally strong-willed and assertive and who actively seek to influence others. Styles characterized by low dominance—supportive and reflective styles—are usually employed by managers who are less assertive and more cooperative and who eagerly seek to assist others rather than order them about. The two styles characterized by high sociability—supportive and emotive—are typically used by managers who are open and outgoing and who freely express their thoughts and feelings. Styles characterized by low sociability—reflective and directive—predominate among managers who are less talkative and more reserved and who prefer formal relationships with their employees, peers, and supervisors.

Exhibits 5 and 6 are rating sheets by which managers can subjectively measure the degree of dominance or sociability that characterizes their own behavior when attempting to influence others. Comparing self-ratings to those completed by co-workers can help a manager become more aware of how his or her actions are perceived by others. The rating sheets can also be used to gain a better understanding of the behaviors of their peers and supervisors. There are no "correct" ratings, of course, and it is not necessarily good or bad to score high or low on any one of the factors; the rating sheets are simply tools to gauge tendencies. However, if the overall pattern of responses indicates a very high level of dominance, the manager may need to develop greater flexibility when communicating in power-related situations.

Exhibit 5   Dominance Rating Sheet

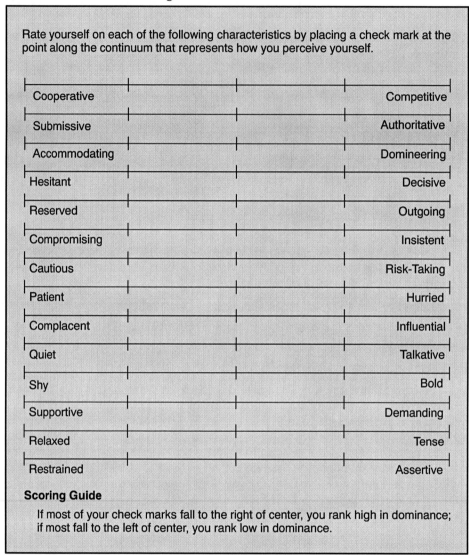

Rate yourself on each of the following characteristics by placing a check mark at the point along the continuum that represents how you perceive yourself.

Cooperative	Competitive
Submissive	Authoritative
Accommodating	Domineering
Hesitant	Decisive
Reserved	Outgoing
Compromising	Insistent
Cautious	Risk-Taking
Patient	Hurried
Complacent	Influential
Quiet	Talkative
Shy	Bold
Supportive	Demanding
Relaxed	Tense
Restrained	Assertive

Scoring Guide

If most of your check marks fall to the right of center, you rank high in dominance; if most fall to the left of center, you rank low in dominance.

Source: Adapted from Barry L. Reece and Rhonda Brandt, *Effective Human Relations in Organizations*, 4th ed., p. 126. Copyright © 1990 by Houghton Mifflin Company. Reprinted with permission.

Conversely, if the overall pattern indicates a very low level of dominance, the manager may need to learn how to be more assertive. If the overall pattern of responses indicates a very high level of sociability, the manager may need to learn how to curb his or her emotional enthusiasm when communicating in power-related situations. And if the overall pattern indicates a very low level of sociability, the manager may need to learn how to be more open and expressive.

Exhibit 6   Sociability Rating Sheet

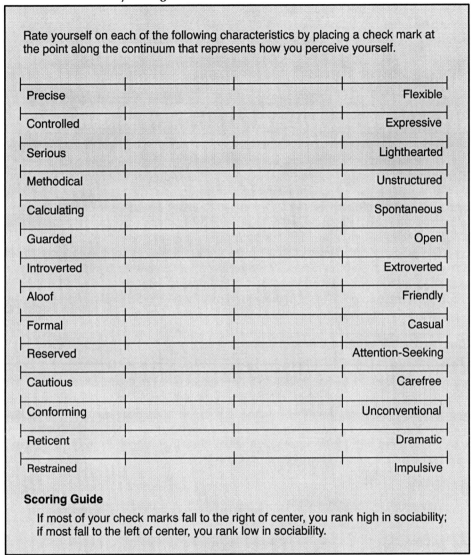

Rate yourself on each of the following characteristics by placing a check mark at the point along the continuum that represents how you perceive yourself.

Precise	Flexible
Controlled	Expressive
Serious	Lighthearted
Methodical	Unstructured
Calculating	Spontaneous
Guarded	Open
Introverted	Extroverted
Aloof	Friendly
Formal	Casual
Reserved	Attention-Seeking
Cautious	Carefree
Conforming	Unconventional
Reticent	Dramatic
Restrained	Impulsive

Scoring Guide

If most of your check marks fall to the right of center, you rank high in sociability; if most fall to the left of center, you rank low in sociability.

Source: Adapted from Barry L. Reece and Rhonda Brandt, *Effective Human Relations in Organizations*, 4th ed., p. 129. Copyright © 1990 by Houghton Mifflin Company. Reprinted with permission.

Flexibility and Communication Styles

A rigid, inflexible communication style will not help a manager deal effectively with the many different kinds of power situations that arise in hospitality organizations. Effective managers adopt communication styles that are appropriate to the circumstances of each specific situation: they may be emotive when communicating the vision and values of the organization, supportive when empowering their staff to assume greater responsibilities, reflective when evaluating the performance of the organization, and directive when taking corrective actions. Flexibility and good judgment are the keys to successful communication in power-related situations.

Sharing Power Through Delegation

Delegation is the process of assigning responsibility and granting authority to employees to perform tasks or make decisions for which the manager is still accountable. It is a difficult skill to master, yet essential for managerial success.

Perhaps the greatest obstacle to delegation is the belief held by many managers that they can do the work better and more quickly than their employees. Not only is this usually untrue, it also begs the question of whether the manager should be doing the work in the first place and ignores the question of what the manager could be doing instead. Quality and speed are not necessarily the primary objectives in delegating work to others. If this were the case, few managers would delegate much more than boring, unpleasant, and relatively simple tasks.

The primary objectives of delegating work should be to develop the abilities and talents of staff members. Managers who delegate effectively share power with their staff members and provide the training and coaching needed for their employees to succeed. These managers typically outperform and outlast those managers who burn out trying to do everything themselves.

Barriers to Delegation

Managers, not employees, build most of the barriers to delegation. Some managers are reluctant to delegate because they lack confidence in their employees' abilities. Others wish to avoid risk: they refuse to delegate because an employee's failure might reflect poorly on their own managerial capabilities. Still other managers are insecure and fear being outshined by their employees; they want the credit for the accomplishment of important tasks. Other reasons that managers may be uncomfortable with delegation include:

- Lack of experience
- Lack of organizational skills
- Fear of being disliked by employees
- Reluctance to spend the time it takes to train employees
- Failure to establish effective control or follow-up procedures

Exhibit 7 presents a self-assessment questionnaire with which managers can measure their comfort level with delegating work to others.

A manager's staff can also present barriers to delegation. Employees may not want the responsibility and authority delegated to them, or they may lack self-confidence and fear failure. The manager on their previous job might have controlled everything, and they might have been rewarded only for following specific instructions. The best way to overcome these barriers is to clarify with the employee exactly how much authority he or she will have to carry out a task.

Exhibit 7   Self-Assessment Questionnaire Concerning Delegation

Answer the following statements with a "yes" or "no":

1. I enjoy being personally involved with the details of every project.
2. I'm more committed to the success of this organization than others on my staff are.
3. My boss expects me to know all the details of my job.
4. I'm managing activities and solving problems similar to those I had before my last promotion.
5. I often have to rush to meet deadlines.
6. I don't mind assigning members of my staff new responsibilities, but I'm uncomfortable with relinquishing authority.
7. I need to be in control of activities for which I am held accountable.
8. I get impatient with members of my staff when they take longer to complete a task than I would.
9. I tend to be a perfectionist.
10. It's unfair to have my success depend on someone else's performance.

Scoring Guide

If you answered "yes" to more than three of these questions, you may have trouble delegating work to others.

Generally speaking, there are three levels of delegation. By making it clear which level employees will operate on, the manager can reduce employees' feelings of uncertainty and increase their willingness to accept new responsibilities. The three levels are as follows:

- *Level 1:* Full authority is given to the employee to take whatever actions are necessary to carry out the assignment without consulting or reporting to the manager.

- *Level 2:* The employee has the same authority as in Level 1 but must keep the manager informed of actions taken.

- *Level 3:* Limited authority is given to the employee to take specific kinds of actions. In relation to other aspects of the task, the employee makes recommendations and takes action as advised by the manager.

Steps in Effective Delegation

There are many ways to delegate effectively; managers must develop their own styles and adapt them to the specifics of the work to be done and the abilities and motivation levels of their staff. The following sections outline the general steps involved in delegating work to others (see Exhibit 8).

Exhibit 8   Steps in Effective Delegation

Step 1
Think the project through.

Step 2
Set a tentative deadline.

Step 3
Choose an employee.

Step 4
Meet with the employee.

Step 5
Monitor progress, provide assistance, and praise the
employee.

Think the Project Through. Before assigning a project to an employee, the manager should think through each facet of the project. What are the desired results?
What materials or other resources are needed? Does the employee need to work
with others? What options does the employee have to get the job done? Options
increase the decision-making power of the employee: the more options at the
employee's disposal, the more he or she acquires a sense of responsibility and
ownership of the project.

Set a Tentative Deadline. Managers should set realistic deadlines for projects
delegated to employees. Whenever possible, the employee performing the work
should help set the deadline for its completion. Inexperienced managers sometimes set target dates that can't possibly be met, just to impress their supervisors.
However, when the deadline passes with much work yet to be done, supervisors
are not impressed. Other managers try to impress their supervisors by setting
deadlines that can be met too easily, but supervisors soon learn which managers
pad wasted time into project schedules. The best approach is to consistently establish realistic deadlines and meet them most of the time. Managers who develop
reputations for getting things done close to schedule are in better positions to
negotiate with their supervisors for more time when a project takes longer than
anticipated to complete.

   If a project deadline is set by higher-level managers, the delegating manager
and the employee must do everything they can to meet it. If more time is needed,
the delegating manager can try negotiating with his or her supervisor. If a project
must be completed on a less-than-realistic schedule, delegation may not be the
best course of action.

Choose an Employee. A manager must make sure that the employee chosen for
a project has the time and the skills to get the job done. Factors that managers

should consider when selecting an employee include the employee's abilities and workload, the importance of the project to be delegated, and projects that will be coming up in the near future.

Meet with the Employee. When meeting with the employee, the delegating manager should fully explain the project and its importance. During the meeting, the manager should encourage the employee to ask questions and should actively listen to the employee's ideas on how to approach the task. The manager should also tell the employee what level of authority he or she will have to get the job done and, together, they should agree on a realistic schedule and a firm deadline for completion. The manager should also point out any obstacles the employee might face and suggest ways to overcome them. The meeting should end only when the manager and the employee are in complete agreement on how the project will be completed. The manager should express confidence in the employee and be available if questions or problems arise.

Monitor Progress, Provide Assistance, and Praise the Employee. As the project moves forward, the manager should check on the employee's progress from time to time. Despite a manager's best efforts, sometimes employees misunderstand what is expected of them. It is especially important to monitor progress early in the project. The manager should be friendly and helpful and avoid the appearance of constantly looking over the employee's shoulder.

If the employee gets stuck or goes off in the wrong direction, the manager should provide just enough help to get the project back on track. The manager should avoid the appearance of being condescending or sarcastic and should take control of the project only under the most extreme circumstances.

Throughout the project, the manager should praise the employee's efforts and build the employee's self-confidence. At the end of the project, the manager should ensure that the employee receives the proper recognition for the work. Nothing is more discouraging to employees than when their supervisors take all the credit for a delegated accomplishment.

Empowering Others

Empowering others is itself a use of power—it is influencing others to accept greater responsibility and exercise more control over the way they perform their jobs. Empowering others must start with an organization's highest-level leaders. For empowerment to work, top-level managers must influence others to accept the new responsibilities that accompany increases in power. Top-level managers do this by involving managers, supervisors, and employees in defining the fundamental values, mission, and goals of the organization. Linking others with a shared vision involves showing them how their work contributes to the success of the company and achieves the overall goals of the organization. Without direction and support from an organization's leaders, empowerment efforts are bound to fail.

Once the message is out, leaders provide the necessary training, coaching, and support for members of their management team. Organizations have found that it is more effective to empower managers before asking managers to empower their staffs. Managers and supervisors learn how to accept greater responsibility, adopt new roles, access more information, solve larger problems, and take meaningful risks at reasonable costs before they empower their staff. Department managers learn how to think "outside their boxes" and cooperate with other departments in identifying and solving problems that cut across functional areas. Upper managers need to reward the new forms of cooperation and teamwork that they expect from empowered managers.

When empowering their staff, managers employ the same leadership skills that top-level managers used in empowering them. Line-level employees need to know how their work contributes to the overall success of the company. Managers share business-related information with their staffs and explain the important ways in which line-level performance helps the company succeed. If the past culture of the organization bred learned helplessness in the staff, the first step toward empowering employees may be to raise their level of self-esteem. Before exercising more control over their jobs, employees may need assurances from management that the organization values their ideas, has confidence in their judgment, and will support their efforts.

🔑 Key Terms

accountability—A manager's acceptance of the responsibility that accompanies authority and the need to justify his or her actions to higher-level managers in the organization.

authority—The formal power granted by an organization to a management position.

centralized organization—An organization with a power structure that places most decision-making authority at top management levels.

chain of command—A series of management positions in order of authority. An organization's chain of command is represented on an organization chart by lines of authority linking all positions within the organization and specifying formal reporting relationships.

coercive power—A form of organizational power stemming from the authority to withhold rewards or administer punishment.

decentralized organization—An organization with a power structure that gives the lowest organizational levels decision-making authority.

delegation—The process of assigning responsibility and granting authority to staff members to perform tasks or make decisions for which the delegator is still accountable.

directive communication style—A communication style that combines high dominance with low sociability, characterized by frankness, determination, and a no-nonsense approach.

emotive communication style—A communication style that combines high dominance with high sociability, characterized by expressiveness and an informal, emotional approach.

empowerment—The redistribution of power within an organization that enables managers, supervisors, and employees to perform their jobs more efficiently and effectively, with the overall goal of enhancing service to guests and increasing profits for the organization by releasing decision-making responsibility, authority, and accountability to every level within the organization.

expert power—A form of personal power stemming from an individual's special knowledge or skill in relation to tasks performed by members of his or her staff.

learned helplessness—An attitude common among managers and staff members in overly centralized operations. It occurs when people have lost sight of the broader goals of the operation and blindly follow standard operating procedures to please upper management.

legitimate power—A form of organizational power stemming from the formal authority granted to a position within the hierarchy of an organization. Also referred to as position power.

position power—A form of organizational power stemming from the formal authority granted to a position within the hierarchy of an organization. Also referred to as legitimate power.

power—The ability to influence the behavior of others.

power tactic—A way in which managers use a source of power to influence the behavior of their employees, peers, and supervisors.

referent power—A form of personal power resulting from the admiration and respect that others have for an individual's personal characteristics.

reflective communication style—A communication style that combines low dominance and low sociability, characterized by a preference for an orderly, controlling, and formal approach.

reward power—A form of organizational power resulting from a manager's authority to provide rewards for staff members.

supportive communication style—A communication style that combines high sociability with low dominance, characterized by sensitivity, patience, and a preference for informal interactions.

Review Questions

1. What are the characteristics of a centralized organization? a decentralized organization?

2. What is "learned helplessness"?

3. What sorts of problems can occur when managers have more responsibility than they do authority? when their authority exceeds their responsibility?

4. What three types of power are given to a manager by his or her organization?

5. How does expert power differ from referent power?

6. How can managers increase their position power? their personal power?

7. What are eight common strategies managers use to influence the behavior of others?

8. What are the differences among the emotive, directive, reflective, and supportive communication styles of managers?

9. What are the general steps involved in successfully delegating work to others

Chapter Appendix
Learned Helplessness in Housekeeping

Dear Maid,

Please do not leave any more of those little bars of soap in my bathroom, since I have brought my own bath-size Dial. Please remove the six unopened little bars from the shelf under the medicine chest and the three in the shower soap dish. They are in my way. Thank you.
S. Berman

Dear Room 635,

I am not your regular maid she will be back tomorrow (Thurs) from her day off. I took the 3 hotel soaps out of the shower soap dish as you requested. The 6 bars on your shelf I took out of your way and put on top of your Kleenex dispenser in case you should change your mind. This leaves only the 3 bars I left today which my instructions from the management is to leave 3 soaps daily. I hope this is satisfactory. If anything else comes up please call Mrs. Korm in the linen room.
Kathy (relief maid)

Dear Maid (I hope you are my regular maid),

Apparently Kathy did not tell you about my note to her concerning the little bars of soap. When I got back to my room this evening I found you had added 3 little Camays to the shelf under my medicine cabinet. I am going to be here in the hotel for two weeks and have brought my own bath-size Dial so I won't need those 6 little Camays which are now on the shelf. They are in my way when shaving, brushing teeth, etc. Please remove them.
S. Berman

Dear Mr. Berman,

My day off was last Wed so the relief maid left 3 hotel soaps which we are instructed by the management to leave. I took the 6 soaps which were in your way on the shelf and put them in the soap dish where your Dial was. I put the Dial in the medicine cabinet for your convenience. I didn't remove the 3 complimentary soaps which are always placed inside the medicine cabinet for all new check-ins and which you did not object to when you checked in last Monday. Also I placed 3 hotel soaps on your shelf as per my instructions from the management since you left no instructions to the contrary. Please let me know if I can be of further assistance or call Mrs. Korm in the linen room. Have a pleasant stay.
Your regular maid, Dotty

Dear Mr. Berman,

The assistant manager, Mr. Kensedder, informed me this A.M. that you called him last evening and said you were unhappy with your maid service. I have assigned a new maid to your room. I hope you will accept my apologies for any past inconvenience. If you have any future complaints please contact me so I can give it my personal attention. Call extension 1108 between 8 A.M. and 5 P.M. Thank you.
Elaine Carmen, Housekeeper

(continued)

Dear Mrs. Carmen,

It is impossible to contact you by phone since I leave the hotel for business at 7:45 A.M. and don't get back before 5:30 or 6 P.M. That's the reason I called Mr. Kensedder last night. You were already off duty. I only asked Mr. Kensedder if he could do anything about those little bars of soap. I did not want a new maid. The new maid you assigned me must have thought I was a new check-in today, since she left another 3 bars of hotel soap in my medicine cabinet along with her regular delivery of 3 bars on the bathroom shelf. In just five days here I have accumulated 24 little bars of soap. I'm beginning to dread the next 9 days. Why are you doing this to me?
    S. Berman

Dear Mr. Berman,

Your maid Kathy has been instructed to stop delivering soap to your room and remove the extra soaps. If I can be of further assistance, please call extension 1108 between 8 A.M. and 5 P.M. Thank you.
    Elaine Carmen, Housekeeper

Dear Mr. Kensedder,

My bath-size Dial is missing. Every bar of soap was taken from my room, including my own bath-size Dial. I came in last night and had to call the bellhop to bring me a bar of soap so I could take a shower. He brought me 4 little Cashmere Bouquets.
    S. Berman

Dear Mr. Berman,

I have informed our Housekeeper, Elaine Carmen, of your soap problem. I cannot understand why there was no soap in your room since our maids are instructed to leave 3 bars of soap each time they service a room. The situation will be rectified immediately. Please accept my apologies for the inconvenience. If you prefer Cashmere Bouquet to Camay, please contact Mrs. Carmen on extension 1108. Thank you.
    Martin L. Kensedder
    Assistant Manager

Dear Mrs. Carmen,

Who the *%#@ left 54 little bars of Camay in my room? I came in last night and found 54 little bars of soap. I don't want 54 little bars of Camay. I want my 1 *&%# bar of bath-size Dial. Do you realize I have 58 bars of soap in here? All I want is my bath-size Dial. Give me back my bath-size Dial.
    S. Berman

Dear Mr. Berman,

You complained of too much soap in your room so I had them removed. Then you complained to Mr. Kensedder that all your soap was missing so I personally returned them; the 24 Camays which had been taken and the 3 Camays you are supposed to receive daily. I don't know anything about the 4 Cashmere Bouquets. Obviously your maid Kathy did not know I had returned your soaps so she also brought 24 Camays plus the 3 daily Camays. I don't know where you got the idea that this hotel issues bath-size Dial. I was able to locate some hotel-size Ivory which I left in your room. We are doing our best here to satisfy you.

> Elaine Carmen, Housekeeper

Dear Mrs. Carmen,

Just a short note to bring you up-to-date on my latest soap inventory. As of today I possess:

> On shelf under medicine cabinet: 18 Camays in 4 stacks of 4 and 1 stack of 2.
>
> On Kleenex dispenser: 11 Camays in 2 stacks of 4 and 1 stack of 3.
>
> On bedroom dresser: 1 stack of 3 Cashmere Bouquets, 1 stack of 4 hotel-size bath-size Ivory, 8 Camays in 2 stacks of 4.
>
> Inside medicine cabinet: 14 Camays in 3 stacks of 4 and 1 stack of 2.
>
> In shower soap dish: 6 Camays (very moist).
>
> On northeast corner of tub: 1 Cashmere Bouquet (slightly used).
>
> On northwest corner of tub: 6 Camays in 2 stacks of 3.

Please ask Kathy when she services my room to make sure the stacks are neatly piled and dusted. Also, please advise her that stacks of more than 4 have a tendency to tip. May I suggest that my bedroom window sill is not in use and will make an excellent spot for future soap deliveries. One more item. I have purchased another bar of bath-size Dial which I am keeping in the hotel vault in order to avoid future misunderstandings.

> S. Berman

Source: Adapted from Shelley Berman, *A Hotel is a Place…* (Los Angeles: Price/Stern/Sloan Publishers, Inc., 1972), pp. 95–101. Reprinted by permission of Price Stern Sloan, Inc. © 1972, 1985 by Price Stern Sloan, Inc.

Chapter 6 Outline

Competencies

1. Provide a definition of effective business communication, and identify seven myths about communication. (pp. 165–167)

2. Outline the communication process. (pp. 167–170)

3. Describe upward, downward, and lateral communication, and explain how managers can improve their skills in these three types of communication. (pp. 170–172)

4. Identify barriers to effective communication. (pp. 173–178)

5. Describe the importance and nature of nonverbal communication, explain how managers can effectively use body language, and identify four types of interpersonal space. (pp. 178–181)

6. Explain the importance and nature of strong speaking and presenting skills, and give examples of presentation delivery tips. (pp. 181–186)

7. Define "feedback" and describe six characteristics of effective feedback. (pp. 186–188)

8. Describe three types of listening and common obstacles to listening, and list techniques managers can use to improve their active listening skills. (pp. 188–195)

9. Explain why writing is an important skill for managers, summarize guidelines for better business writing, and describe writing tips and formats for memos, business letters, and e-mails. (pp. 195–205)

6

Communication Skills

This chapter was revised for this edition by Robert M. O'Halloran, Ph.D., Professor and Chair, Department of Hospitality Management, East Carolina University, Greenville, North Carolina.

COMMUNICATION IS THE LIFEBLOOD that flows through the veins of organizations. It is the critical element in helping employees learn the skills that will help them contribute to their organizations and understand the reasons behind organizational changes. Effective communication is the lubricant that allows organizations to smoothly and productively operate. The payoff for effective communication in hotels and restaurants is that managers and employees who develop strong communication skills are usually strong performers on the job.

In a study examining essential competencies for hospitality managers and leaders, communication skills were prominently highlighted as keys to success.[1] The study noted that interpersonal communication skills were rated highly and indicated that a manager needs to be effective both in written and oral communication. Interpersonal communication skills include listening skills, face-to-face communication skills, and oral communication skills as well as the ability to resolve conflicts positively. (Listening skills were rated most important.) These communication skills are essential for any hospitality manager in any functional area. Given the people-intensive nature of the hospitality industry, it can be argued that the most important strength for a manager is his or her ability to deal with employees, guests, suppliers, and others one-on-one. In fact, managers spend as much as 80 percent of their day communicating with others.[2] How effective they are in communicating often determines success or failure for managers.[3]

Managers are always communicating; communication skills are used in every important managerial activity. Recruiting, interviewing, training, motivating, evaluating, coaching, counseling, leading, interacting with guests, and many other managerial responsibilities require communication skills. Yet many managers are not proficient in this important area. While most managers believe that they communicate well, in many cases they do not. Communication research found that while 95 percent of managers believe that they have good interpersonal communication skills, only 30 percent of their employees agreed. This research also reported that managers and employees often could not even agree on whether they had met during the current week.[4] Clearly, the communication skills that managers think they have are not working effectively for many of them.

Successful communication is a message that a speaker or writer sends and a listener or reader receives and that both parties understand and act on. Knowing how to effectively communicate is very important for managers and leaders because it often determines the extent to which the information that they think they have communicated to others is actually understood.

To define communication in a hospitality organization, we offer this conceptual definition of effective business communication: Effective business communication is the ability of a sender to get his or her message across to the intended receiver through oral, physical, and/or written methods. The sender also must follow up with the receiver to check for receipt and clarity of the message, which completes the communication loop.

This chapter will help you learn how to communicate more effectively. It begins by examining some common communication myths and pointing out barriers to communication, including personality differences, prejudices, and poor listening habits. The chapter then explains how you can improve your communication skills by using effective nonverbal communication, speaking, presenting, listening, and writing techniques.

Myths About Communication

Before discussing how the communication process works, let's examine seven myths about communication:[5]

1. *We communicate only when we want to communicate.* This is not true. We communicate all day, every day, often without realizing it. For example, suppose you are listening to a report in a staff meeting. You are tired because you were up late last night. Without realizing it, you yawn several times, even though you are interested in the report. The other people in the meeting do not know you are tired, so they conclude that your yawning is a signal that you are bored. Inadvertently, you sent an incorrect message to the others in the meeting.

2. *Words mean the same to both the speaker and the listener.* Words hold different meanings for different people, based on their various experiences, perceptions, and biases. For example, when you tell an employee that her work is "above average," you may mean that she is doing extremely well and you believe that she has great potential. However, your employee may have always perceived herself as a hard worker and a high achiever, and to her "average" means "merely acceptable," so your "above average" comment means to her that you believe she is just above "merely acceptable." As a result, your well-intentioned comment may actually deflate the employee, and her morale and performance may suffer.

3. *We communicate chiefly with words.* In reality, most communication is nonverbal. We may say one thing but reveal another through our facial expressions, tone of voice, gestures, eye contact, or how we sit or walk. For example, another manager may tell you that her new assignment is going well, but as she does so she frowns, looks tired and worried, and jiggles her pen nervously. As you observe her, you believe what her facial expression and mannerisms are telling you more than her words. This is because it is harder to lie with our faces and bodies than with our words.

4. *Nonverbal communication is silent communication.* Some people believe that all nonverbal communication can be seen but not heard. This is not true, because we can hear laughter, weeping, or the tone of voice in which something is said. If you hear co-workers whistling as they go about their jobs, you naturally assume that they are having good days.

5. *Communication is a one-way street between an active speaker and a passive listener.* This myth assumes that all speakers talk *at* listeners rather than *with* them. In reality, communication is better when both parties participate actively. Participation is heightened when a listener provides feedback to a speaker through verbal and nonverbal communication. Often, shaking your head or furrowing your brow is a stronger indication that you do not understand something than what you actually say in response.

6. *The message we communicate is the message that the listener receives.* Managers often assume that others receive their messages exactly as they intended them. Suppose that your boss gives you an assignment on Monday and states that it is due "soon." You look at your schedule and decide that you can work on it Thursday and get it to your boss first thing Friday morning. On Tuesday your boss asks you for the completed assignment. In this case, "soon" meant "tomorrow" to your boss, while it meant "sometime this week" to you.

7. *There is no such thing as too much information.* Both too little and too much information can be bad. Few employees need to know every little detail about an assignment, and a manager can easily overload an employee with needless information. In many cases, even if we had all of the information available to us, we would not have the time to hear it, read it, or listen to it all. Since information overload is common in organizations, it is important for managers to concentrate on the quality of their communications as much as the quantity of them.[6]

The Communication Process

Even the simplest communication is a relatively complex process. The **sender-receiver model** depicted in Exhibit 1 shows how communication between two people works. When two people communicate, a sender must initiate a thought or feeling, encode it into words, then transmit it to the other person. The receiver must decode the message, assign thoughts and feelings to a response, encode a response, and send a message back. Communications in which three or more people are involved become increasingly more complex. Exhibit 2 shows another interpersonal communication model that reflects more of the complexities within the communication process.

Poor communication can have unfortunate consequences. Consider the following example: A motorist is driving on a freeway when his engine stalls. Another motorist stops to help.

"My car has a manual transmission," the first motorist says, "so you'll have to get up to 30 to 35 miles an hour to get me started."

Exhibit 1   Sender-Receiver Model

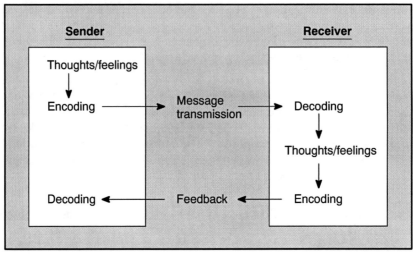

Source: Chad T. Lewis, Joseph E. Garcia, and Sarah M. Jobs, *Managerial Skills in Organizations*, p. 18. © 1990. Reprinted by permission of Prentice-Hall, Upper Saddle River, New Jersey.

The second motorist nods and walks back to his car. The first motorist waits and waits for his rescuer to pull up behind him. Finally, he turns around just in time to see the second motorist bearing down on his car at 35 miles per hour![7]

Miscommunication in a hospitality business can also result in disaster. For example, consider this true story: After interviewing a female applicant for a server's position, the manager, who happened to be male, handed her a uniform and said, "Try this on right away. I want to make sure we have a uniform in stock that will fit you." He turned away to retrieve a file, and when he turned around he discovered that the applicant was disrobing right in front of him. The manager had intended that the applicant go to a dressing room to try the uniform on, but had not said so. The nervous applicant assumed that she was being asked to disrobe immediately and, needing the job, intended to comply fully and without question. Luckily, the manager stopped the applicant before she had gotten very far and explained that he did not mean for her to try on the uniform in his office. She apologized and retired to the dressing room, and the incident passed with no harm done except for some embarrassment for both parties. Such a communication mix-up could have led to serious problems for the manager and the company, however.

Communication Within an Organization

Managers must effectively communicate upward to their boss, downward to their staff, and laterally (or across) with fellow managers. Managers and employees can be seen as a network of linking pins. Line employees are linked to their managers through supervisors, while managers serve as linking pins for supervisors and

Exhibit 2   A Model of Interpersonal Communications

1. **Speaker begins by:** Thinking about the message he or she is about to send

2. **The speaker sorts and selects from:** Knowledge / Past experience / Feelings / Attitudes / Emotions

3. **The speaker puts the message into:** Words / Actions / Signs / Symbols

4. **The speaker sends the message to the listener by:** Speaking / Acting / Writing

5. **The listener:** Receives the message

6. **The listener begins by:** Thinking about the message and reacting to it

7. **The listener sorts and selects from:** Knowledge / Past experience / Feelings / Attitudes / Emotions

8. **The listener puts the message and his or her reactions into:** Words / Actions / Signs / Symbols

9. **The listener sends feedback to the speaker by:** Speaking / Acting / Writing

10. **The speaker:** Receives feedback from the listener

11. **The speaker begins again by:** Thinking about the feedback he or she receives from the listener

12. **The speaker sorts and selects from:** Knowledge / Past experience / Feelings / Attitudes / Emotions

13. **The speaker responds to feedback from the listener by putting a message into:** Words / Actions / Signs / Symbols

14. **The speaker sends a message to the listener by:** Speaking / Acting / Writing

15. **The listener:** Receives the response from the speaker

16. **The listener begins again by:** Thinking about the speaker's response to his or her feedback

17. **The listener sorts and selects from:** Knowledge / Past experience / Feelings / Attitudes / Emotions

18. **The listener responds to feedback from the speaker by putting his or her reactions into:** Words / Actions / Signs / Symbols

19. **The listener responds to the speaker by:** Speaking / Acting / Writing

20. **The speaker:** Receives the listener's response

Source: Stephen J. Shriver, *Managing Quality Services* (Lansing, Mich.: American Hotel & Lodging Educational Institute, 1988), p. 191.

department heads; department heads, in turn, are linked to division heads, and so on. Peers in the organization are linked to each other. As a manager, you play an important role that links line employees and upper management and that links you to the organization's other managers. These links are strengthened through good communication or weakened if communication is poor. Therefore, your own performance, as well as that of your organization as a whole, often depends on the extent to which this network of linking pins facilitates communication.

Managers can become better at upward, downward, and lateral communication by using the tips presented in the following sections.

Upward Communication. A successful manager knows that communicating with his or her boss is very important. However, **upward communication** takes care and planning. Some tips to help you communicate better with your boss include the following:

- Be sure your message is important; your boss's time is limited.

- Be sure the information is accurate and complete.

- Be brief.

- Communicate both good and bad news.

- Communicate regularly.

- When you present a problem, suggest potential solutions.

- Make an agenda; some bosses appreciate receiving a list of topics you will discuss in advance so that they, too, can be prepared.

- Be sure your timing is right; trying to present information to your boss at the wrong time can derail the communication process.

- Establish clear objectives; know in advance what you want to accomplish during your talk with your boss.

- Don't go over your boss's head unless it is absolutely necessary.

Downward Communication. Developing effective **downward communication** skills helps managers identify potential problems, gain staff commitment, and gather information for making decisions. However, managers must work hard to establish an effective downward communication style. Some tips to help you develop better downward communication skills include the following:

- Maintain an open-door policy, and let employees know they can come to you with problems.

- Listen attentively and objectively to your employees' concerns and contributions.

- Don't react emotionally or critically when someone brings you bad news. Becoming angry at the message bearer will cut off communication in the future.

Peter Drucker on Workplace Communication

Because hospitality is a people-oriented business, it is easy to see that hospitality managers should be good communicators and that hospitality organizations need to create a good environment for communication. Peter F. Drucker, a noted expert on management and author of the classic *Management: Tasks, Responsibilities, Practices* and scores of other books on management and business, highlights four fundamentals of communication:

- Communication is perception.

- Communication is expectation.

- Communication makes demands.

- Communication and information are different yet interdependent.

According to the "perception" fundamental, before managers communicate, they need to ask if this communication is within the recipients' range of perception—that is, can they receive and understand it? If the receivers cannot understand the message, the best efforts of any sender are lost.

In terms of communication as expectation, people want to be prepared for communication. Typically, people at least believe they know what is coming. Drucker argues that the unexpected is not received at all and that the human mind attempts to fit impressions and stimuli into a frame of expectations. For hospitality managers, this means that when someone—a guest, an employee, a colleague—hears or reads something unexpected, he or she will need more time to process that information.

To understand how communication makes demands, one must realize that communication always asks that the recipient do something or believe something; communication typically expects an action or reaction to the sent message. Even if the message is informational, there was an objective to send it that at some point will require thought and action on the recipient's part.

According to Drucker, communication and information are different, and communication may not depend on information. Indeed, the most perfect or pure communication may be shared experiences that require no words at all. Not all workplace communication need be work-related; even in the workplace, casual communication is important for building and maintaining a positive environment.

Finally, Drucker states that there can be no communication if it is conceived as going from the "I" to the "thou." Communication works only from one member of "us" to another. Communication is vital in any management process. The development of individual communication skills and styles enhances a manager's opportunities to successfully conduct business. More than individual managers, however, must pay attention to communication skills. A hotel, restaurant, club, or other hospitality business must visualize itself as a communication organization and focus on the "us" in communicating.

- Use active listening skills (active listening will be discussed later in the chapter).

- Be sure that employees know that you care about their opinions and suggestions.

Communication Styles

Communication skills are a key part of a manager's package of talents. Managers need to assess their overall communication skills, so they are in a better position to enhance their skills and develop their own communication style.

The hospitality industry's management pool is diverse, and managers' individual communication styles differ because of such factors as gender, race, educational background, and so on. For example, men, in some situations, may try to use a blustering physical presence and loud vocal tones to communicate; in the same situations, women might take a more persuasive approach. Additionally, a manager's rank and the authority that he or she has within the organization has an impact on the manager's communication style.

All in-person communication includes the words spoken, vocal tones and intonations, and the visual cues (smiling, frowning, raised eyebrows, and so on) that senders use to add emphasis to their points. The way in which a manager uses and blends all of these factors defines a manager's personal communication style.

When developing a communication style, managers often will emulate or mimic an effective style they have seen. That benchmark may be a good place to begin, but no two individuals communicate in exactly the same way. For example, a tall, imposing manager will have different communication strengths and challenges than a small, demure person will have. When managers develop their communication style, it is important that they customize it to fit their personal strengths.

Lateral Communication. Communicating effectively with other managers helps ensure that information will continue to flow your way and enhances your career opportunities. Tips that can help you develop better **lateral communication** skills include the following:

- Get to know as many managers in the organization as you can.

- View peer communication as a chance to establish relationships that work for both parties.

- Share information; nobody wants to talk to someone who doesn't share in return.

- Constantly look for overlapping areas of responsibility or interests that might help improve your interaction with other managers.

- Take a "big picture" perspective and communicate about issues that might help the whole organization, not just your part of it.

- Give sincere and positive feedback when asked.

- When appropriate, offer your help.

- Use positive body language when communicating.

- Work a day or two in another department to help you understand some of the problems and issues your peers are discussing.

Barriers to Effective Communication

Many barriers can interfere with a manager's ability to communicate. For example, some clearly stated and well-intended messages can still come across as insensitive or abrasive. The result is that the message itself is not heard or understood. Sometimes a manager tries to get across an idea using the wrong words. For example, in a meeting to discuss potential sales promotion ideas, a dining room captain suggested that the restaurant could increase sales by providing complimentary meals to front desk agents in local hotels who send guests to the restaurant. The restaurant's manager responded with, "I don't know; I think we should concentrate on long-term solutions rather than wasting our time on quick fixes." What the restaurant manager was trying to say was, "I'd prefer it if we concentrated on another type of sales approach." However, what the dining room captain heard was, "I think your idea is stupid." In this exchange, the restaurant manager demoralized the dining room captain without meaning to.

Before you read the rest of this section on barriers to interpersonal communication, it might be helpful to complete the Interpersonal Communication Self-Analysis form in Exhibit 3. Barriers to effective interpersonal communication include:[8]

- Misinterpretation
- Evaluation of sender
- Projection
- Stereotyping
- Arrogance and superiority
- Defensiveness
- Inarticulateness
- Hidden agendas
- Status
- Environment
- Emotions
- Differences in backgrounds
- Poor timing
- Personality conflicts[9]

Let's take a brief look at each of these barriers in the following sections.

Misinterpretation. People receiving a message must interpret the message and the intent of the sender. Since many messages are ambiguous or incomplete, it's easy to jump to inaccurate conclusions about what is being said. For example, a manager who believed that an employee who enthusiastically agreed to work late was greedy for overtime pay instead of simply being willing to help out could seriously misjudge the spirit and intent of the employee.

Exhibit 3   Interpersonal Communication Self-Analysis Form

Find out how good your interpersonal communication skills are by completing this self-assessment. Put a number next to each of the following statements, using the scale below:

1—Seldom   2—Sometimes   3—Often   4—Usually

_____ 1. I adjust my vocal and body communication to fit what I'm saying.

_____ 2. I coach my staff to use positive vocal and body communication.

_____ 3. I can tell how people *feel* about what they are saying.

_____ 4. When talking with people of different cultures, I adjust my vocal and body communication to match theirs.

_____ 5. I try to avoid giving negative vocal and body messages to people I don't care for.

_____ 6. I don't let guests' or employees' emotional behavior distract me from the point they're making.

_____ 7. I use simple and clear language when I speak.

_____ 8. People do not ask me to repeat or clarify what I say.

_____ 9. My employees follow my directions.

_____ 10. When I speak, I know when to use examples or repetition.

_____ 11. I emphasize to my staff why it is important to do certain things.

_____ 12. When giving a message to guests or employees, I check to see if they understand it.

_____ 13. I have time to listen to employees and guests.

_____ 14. I wait until a person finishes speaking before I make my point.

_____ 15. When I don't understand a person's message or if I want more information, I ask questions.

_____ 16. I check to see if I understand people's messages by briefly repeating to them what I hear them say.

_____ 17. I avoid giving advice when employees come to me with personal problems.

_____ 18. I use different listening skills according to the type of listening situation I'm in.

_____ 19. I have no problem getting my boss to listen to me.

_____ 20. I know when I should take information to my boss.

_____ 21. I make myself available to my employees so they can talk to me.

_____ 22. My employees hear bad news from me before they hear it from anyone else at the property.

_____ 23. I consult other managers when I need help or advice.

_____ 24. I willingly offer help or advice to other managers when appropriate.

Add the numbers you wrote next to the self-assessment statements, then put a check mark in the box below that corresponds to your total.

72-96: Congratulations! You manage your interpersonal communication effectively.

48-71: Careful! Your interpersonal communication skills may be affecting your work performance and your personal relationships.

24-47: Warning! You need to significantly improve your interpersonal communication skills.

Source: Adapted from *Hospitality Management Skill Builders: Interpersonal Communication* (Lansing, Mich.: American Hotel & Lodging Educational Institute, 1994), pp. 4–7.

Evaluation of Sender. People commonly make evaluations of those who send them messages, and these evaluations influence how they interpret the messages. For example, it is not uncommon for receivers to decide a message is right or wrong based solely on their evaluation of the sender. Managers sometimes have unrealistically positive or negative impressions of others. When managers see everything someone does as positive—a phenomenon called the **halo effect**—they often interpret that person's messages in a positive way no matter what the messages are. The opposite is true when managers hold a negative opinion of a sender—the **devil's horns effect**. Suppose an employee tells his manager that he made a minor error while running the cash register earlier in the evening. A manager who sees the employee with a halo will probably dismiss the mistake as no big deal. If the manager sees the employee with devil's horns, she might view this confession as proof that the employee constantly makes mistakes.

Projection. It's natural to assume that others feel or perceive things the same way you do. Yet, **projecting** your own attitudes, assumptions, or beliefs into messages often leads to misunderstandings. The most common example is the simple statement, "I know how you feel." In reality, we often do not know how the other person feels, and by saying so we are dismissing the importance of the sender's statement.

Projection can also occur when one person assumes that the other holds the same intentions. An ambitious manager might assume that all other managers are ambitious, too. Such a manager might hear all messages from other managers as evidence of ambitious actions.

Stereotyping. People who hold preconceived opinions about others based on their ethnicity, gender, age, national origin, class, or sexual orientation are guilty of stereotyping. For example, someone who stereotypes older people may interpret everything seniors say in terms of his or her preconceived notions about older people. Suppose you are a server at an upscale hotel restaurant and all of your friends are either servers or bartenders. You shun dishwashers and buspersons because you believe they represent a lower class of people. In this case, you are missing the opportunity to communicate with others simply because you hold a stereotypical bias against them.

People who are effective listeners make no assumptions about someone's attitudes, perceptions, or abilities. Instead, they make a conscious effort to discover the other person's values and attributes. Viewing people as individuals and giving them an opportunity to show their strengths allows managers to overcome the barrier of stereotyping.

Arrogance and Superiority. Arrogance and superiority prevent communication because they cause people who feel this way to assume that others have little to offer. Constantly interrupting others, refusing to talk to "inferiors," and dominating conversations are examples of how someone with an arrogant and superior attitude inhibits communication.

Defensiveness. People sometimes have insecurities and can become protective of actions they take or projects they complete. Suppose a manager who is defensive is questioned about his report on room sales to conventioneers. While the questioner may simply have wanted more information, the manager interpreted the question as a challenge to his report.

Inarticulateness. Not all people express themselves clearly at all times. An inability to say what you mean inhibits communication. One of the best ways to avoid this problem is to follow the KISS rule: keep it short and simple. Most people can organize and present short messages better than they can complex ones.

Hidden Agendas. Senders who are perceived to have **hidden agendas** are generally thought of as deceptive. Receivers who have hidden agendas often do not hear the sender's intended message because they see everything in relation to their own agendas. For example, a front office manager may believe that gaining more power and prestige for her department will lead to promotions or pay raises. Therefore, many of her actions are devoted to ensuring that the front office is seen in a positive light. As a result, she may not hear correctly what others are saying about the department or may send messages about the department that others distrust.

Status. When a manager talks to an employee, many employees are thinking something along the lines of, "This is my manager talking, so I had better listen and do what I'm told." Some employees are so eager to do a good job that they may not listen to the entire message the manager is sending—they hear the first part and immediately start thinking of how they are going to perform that part of the task and miss the rest of the message. Sometimes an employee may believe that because he and the manager hold different positions, they are at odds with one another. In this case, when the manager is talking, the employee may be thinking, "The same old song and dance. I'll listen but I don't really have to do all of this." The employee may hear only what he wants to hear. This is especially true if the manager has a reputation of not following up on his or her instructions or suggestions.

Environment. Noisy, hot, cold, or otherwise distracting environments make it difficult to communicate. It's usually not a good idea for a manager to tell cooks frantically working on the line that they need to remember to clean the fryers tonight, for example. Or, one of your best employees might come to you with a personal problem, since you have always assured your employees that you have an open-door policy. However, telephone calls, noise from outside, and comments from others who stick their heads in the door during your conversation all create an environment that is not conducive to good communication.

Emotions. Either the sender's or receiver's emotions can create communication barriers. For example, you schedule a performance evaluation meeting with an employee in which you suggest that the employee's job performance must improve. While you may do this calmly and expect that the employee will receive the message calmly, this might not be the case. The employee might become angry, which in turn might make you angry. What started out as a positive communication experience could deteriorate rapidly. You cannot be angry and either speak or listen effectively at the same time.

Differences in Backgrounds. Differences in education, experience, age, knowledge, and other background variables may impede communication. An employee with minimal education may not fully understand a message sent by a manager with more education, for example. A recent graduate from a hotel school might try to tell an "old" manager how to run things, and find out that the message, while well-intentioned, upset the manager.

Poor Timing. People sometimes say things in haste or anger that they later regret. Or, communication may not occur because one party is distracted or unwilling to listen. The best communication takes place when both the speaker and the listener are ready.

Suppose that you call Sharon, one of your best housekeepers, in for a meeting about how to help new housekeepers clean rooms effectively. You want to hear Sharon's ideas. However, Sharon appears distracted and unwilling to help. Her reluctance may not be because she is unwilling. Instead, Sharon's reaction may be because she is preoccupied with a family problem or some other issue. To overcome this obstacle, you will probably have to reschedule the meeting.

Personality Conflicts. Sometimes people do not get along with each other because of personality conflicts, and this can influence how senders and receivers communicate. If David, an employee whom you do not like, comes to you for assistance, unless you are careful it is likely that your communication with David will be influenced by your dislike of him.

Although the list of communication barriers we've just discussed contains some of the most important barriers, there are certainly many other behaviors that also block effective communication. For example, each of the following behaviors might negatively affect either the sender, the receiver, or both:

- Allowing others to interrupt

- Interrupting others

- Talking too much

- Talking too little

- Arguing

- Over-generalizing

- Blaming others

- Commenting or judging too soon

- Using sarcasm

- Speaking, listening, or writing poorly

- Having no interest in the subject

- Thinking of what to say before the speaker finishes

- Pretending to understand

Other communication problems are listed in Exhibit 4.

Exhibit 4   Common Communication Errors

First Impression Errors
  Basing communication opinions on your first impressions of a sender or receiver

Similarity Errors
  Favoring those who we believe are like us

Contrast Errors
  Ranking people by comparing them with others we know

Leniency or Severity Errors
  Being overly lenient or severe in our opinions of others

Overweighing Negative Information Errors
  Hearing more of the negative than we do the positive

Faulty Listening or Memory Errors
  Mishearing or incorrectly remembering what someone says

Recency Errors
  Remembering only the most recent behaviors or communication signals

Central Tendency Errors
  Viewing everyone as about the same

Nonverbal Cues Errors
  "Listening" more to nonverbal cues than to what is actually said

Nonverbal Communication: Body Language

Nonverbal communication has a powerful impact in the workplace. It certainly makes a difference in how you feel if your boss shows up for work with a scowl rather than a smile on her face. As one manager noted, "You can spend 15 seconds first thing in the morning making a good impression or the rest of the day undoing a negative one."

Nonverbal communication is powerful because we spend so much time doing it. Only a small portion of communication is expressed in words. On average, you spend 15 to 20 minutes a day speaking; the rest of the time you are communicating nonverbally.[10] People usually consider the *way* something is said as much more important than *what* is actually said. When there appears to be a discrepancy between verbal and nonverbal communication, we tend to believe the nonverbal message 90 percent of the time.[11] In fact, research has indicated that only about 7 percent of a message is expressed verbally, while facial expressions and posture account for about 55 percent, vocal intonation and inflection about 38 percent.[12]

Body language can be expressed through our facial expressions, eyes, posture, gestures, and body movement. Understanding body language is not easy. Eye contact is a good example of how confusing body language can be. For example, while eye contact is generally considered to be a positive nonverbal cue, too much of it can make people nervous. There is a considerable difference between staring at someone (which sends a negative message) and merely looking at someone.[13]

Facial Expression. By far the most common body language, facial expressions often reveal a great deal. Think about how much more difficult it is to listen to someone when you can't see his or her face. Not knowing whether the speaker is smiling, frowning, staring off into space, and so on inhibits our ability to understand and interpret the message.

This does not mean that managers should base all of their decisions on the facial expressions they see. It is relatively easy for someone to "put on a face" for a conversation. Poker players do it all the time when they maintain a "poker face" during a game. In fact, we all are guilty at times of purposefully misleading a listener through our facial expressions.

Eyes. When someone catches your eye, you are more apt to listen to him or her. Speakers who make eye contact are often considered better speakers than those who do not make eye contact. We usually suspect that people who won't make eye contact are either insincere or nervous.

Posture. A person's posture conveys a lot. Slumped shoulders might indicate boredom, tiredness, depression, or disinterest. Shifting around can indicate nervousness or anxiety. Arms crossed over the chest might indicate an unwillingness to communicate. Rapid eye movement may indicate tenseness. On the other hand, a comfortable and upright seating position with open arms or hands often indicates a willingness to communicate.

Gestures. Gestures are a very telling form of body language. Playing with a paper clip, for example, can indicate disinterest, while chewing on your lips or fingernails or folding and unfolding your arms might indicate uneasiness. Most repetitive gestures (drumming fingers, chain smoking, and so on) indicate impatience or disinterest.

People convey both intended and unintended messages through gestures. Rubbing your neck, for example, might have different meanings depending on whether you did it intentionally or unintentionally. Intentionally rubbing your neck might signal that you are considering something carefully; unintentionally doing so might be an indication of uncertainty.

Body Movement. Body movement can send a variety of signals. Nodding during a conversation signals agreement. When a speaker steps toward the audience, it reinforces what he or she is saying; if the speaker steps away, it de-emphasizes the importance of what is said.

Using Body Language Effectively

Judi Brownell provided a list of basic, positive body language strategies that managers should try to use as often as possible (see Exhibit 5). To this list can be added a short list of cautions that might help you use body language effectively:

Exhibit 5   Positive Body Language

- Be physically alert.
- Maintain eye contact (but don't stare).
- Use an open, relaxed body posture.
- Minimize gestures and random movement.
- Show the speaker that you are actively listening (for example, by nodding your head).

Source: Judi Brownell, *Building Active Listening Skills* (Englewood Cliffs, N.J.: Prentice-Hall, 1986), p. 249.

- *Nonverbal communication is easily misunderstood.* To ensure that their nonverbal communication is not misunderstood, managers should involve the other party in active listening. Active listening (discussed in a later section) allows the sender to get feedback from the receiver to confirm that the message was correctly understood.

- *Verbal and nonverbal communication can easily send mixed signals.* As mentioned earlier, when the verbal message and the nonverbal message don't match, the listener usually believes the nonverbal message. Managers can reduce this problem by making sure that their facial expressions, eye contact, posture, and gestures all send the same message that their words send.

- *Negative body language tells others that you are either not interested or distrustful.* On the other hand, positive body language sends the message that you are trying to communicate. Maintaining positive body language can convince listeners that you care about what they are saying and that you are sincere in what you say.

- *Some forms of body language send different messages in different cultures.* Many hospitality managers find themselves managing diverse work forces or interacting with guests from other cultures. Therefore, it is important to ensure that your body language is sending the right message. In some cultures, for example, it is considered improper to show the bottoms of your feet while sitting. In others, direct eye contact is considered a challenge. People in some cultures consider it an unclean practice to touch others with your left hand.

While it is more important for managers with international assignments to learn the appropriate body language for the culture they are visiting, managers in the United States must also be keenly aware of the body language they use in multicultural environments.

Using Space Effectively

The amount of space we maintain from others is also a form of nonverbal communication. There are four types of space people typically maintain from one another, depending on the circumstances and the people involved: public space, social space, personal space, and intimate space.[14]

Public space is 12 or more feet (3.7 or more meters) between you and the person or persons you are communicating with. Speakers often maintain this space during group presentations, for example. Most business communication takes place within the **social space**, which ranges from 4 to 12 feet (1.2 to 3.7 meters). In comparison, **personal space** ranges from 2 to 4 feet (.6 to 1.2 meters), and **intimate space** is 2 feet (.6 meters) or less. Managers must maintain the proper distance when communicating or they risk sending an unintended message. For example, a hotel manager who moves uncomfortably close to an employee—definitely inside 18 inches (46 centimeters), and often inside 3 feet (approximately 1 meter)—is sending a very different message than one who stands 4 or more feet (1.2 or more meters) away to communicate.

Speaking and Presenting Skills

Most of the communicating managers do is face to face. Whether you are having a conversation or making a presentation to a group, much of the oral communication you engage in consists of three parts (formally, in the case of presentations; informally, in the case of conversations): some sort of introduction, the main body of your message, and a conclusion. In regard to presentations, some presentation experts put it this way: tell them what you are going to tell them, tell them, then tell them what you told them.

In this section, we will review tools and techniques that can help you become a better communicator when speaking to individuals, small groups, or large audiences. Exhibit 6 also presents tips for effective speaking.

Oral Communication

Oral communication is the most common method of communication in most hospitality operations. Managers interact with employees, guests, vendors, and others many times each day. How well managers communicate face to face with people can make the difference in whether or not they accomplish their goals. Oral communication involves the following factors:

- *Verbal:* These are the words spoken by the sender to communicate the message.

- *Vocal:* The vocal factor involves the tone, pitch, and changes in intonation that a speaker uses in the communication process.

- *Volume:* Volume refers to the loudness or softness of speech and its ability to provide emphasis.

- *Rate:* Rate refers to the speed with which one speaks.

- *Articulation:* Is the speaker understandable? Are the words clearly enunciated?

- *Vocal variety and pauses:* Do the vocal sounds change and are pauses or "dead air" used to emphasize a point?

Exhibit 6   Tips for Effective Speaking

The following guidelines can help most speakers present their points more effectively to individuals or groups.

Identify Your Main Point in the Introduction

Most ideas can be communicated in a single sentence. If the message is too complex for one sentence, it should either be put in writing or broken down into steps.

Use Repetition or Examples

Repeating or providing examples that illustrate your main idea is especially useful for complex messages.

Use Concrete Language

"Erudite verbiage obfuscates cognition." That is, big words make a message hard to understand. Keep the language simple, use jargon sparingly or not at all, and explain terms that your audience may not understand.

State Things Positively

When the manager told the employee, "Don't fill out the form with a pen," she thought the message was clear. However, the employee only remembered the words "form" and "pen" and filled out the form with a pen. Whenever possible, state the message positively. The manager would have been better off saying, "Use a pencil to fill out the form."

Tell Why the Message Is Important

The message is not important to everyone just because it's important to you. Tell listeners why the message is important to them and why they should pay attention to it. They will take your message more seriously.

Check for Understanding

The number one reason that employees fail to carry out a manager's message is that they do not understand it. However, it probably won't do any good to ask employees if they understand; they often answer "yes" even when they don't understand. Sometimes they believe that they understand when in fact they don't; other times, they simply do not want to look stupid. Look for nonverbal clues that illustrate understanding. Ask specific questions about the message, and ask listeners to repeat the message in their own words to make sure they understand.

- *Vitality:* Vitality is the component speakers use to show listeners their interest and enthusiasm for what they are communicating.

    Another factor for success in face-to-face communication is described as "verbal intimacy." Verbal intimacy refers to spoken behaviors that increase psychological closeness and provide for more effective communication.[15] Verbal intimacy factors include:

- Praise

- Using people's names

- Humor

- A willingness to be engaged in conversation
- A willingness to self-disclose
- Asking questions

Formal Presentations

Formal presentations require planning and organization. Many managers start planning their presentations by asking themselves *what* they want to say. This is usually a mistake. Instead, presenters should begin by asking themselves *why* they want to make a presentation. This way, they can identify what they want the presentation to accomplish.

Presentations can be informative, persuasive, or anything in between. Persuasive presentations are used to sell an audience on something; informative presentations are used to explain a topic. Determining whether you want to persuade or inform helps you prepare the right material for your presentation.

Different types of audiences require different presentation approaches. The following are four items to remember when analyzing your audience:

- What *values* are important to your audience?
- Why does the audience *need* the information you want to present?
- What *constraints* exist that would hold audience members back from doing what you want them to do or understanding what you want them to understand?
- What is your audience's *demographic profile?*

Each of these four factors might greatly influence how you should approach preparing for and delivering your presentation.

The Introduction. Your introduction should (1) get the attention of your listener(s); (2) obtain the interest of your listener(s); and (3) communicate your purpose for speaking. You can begin a presentation in many different ways. Each of the following methods is appropriate at times:

- Show how the information relates to the audience.
- Establish your competency as a speaker on the subject.
- Use humor to "warm up" the audience.
- Refer to the unusual to capture the audience's attention.
- Refer to the familiar to establish a bond between you and the audience.
- Reassure the audience about the importance of what you have to say.
- Shock the audience to capture their attention immediately.
- Use a quotation from someone else to focus attention on your topic.

While we have discussed the introduction first, good presenters do not necessarily begin preparing a presentation by writing the introduction. Instead, an introduction is often derived from materials that went into the main body of the presentation. Therefore, it is good practice, when preparing a presentation, to work from the center outward—that is, from the main body to the introduction and conclusion.

The Main Body. The main body of a presentation is used to present information in a logical sequence. Each point mentioned in the main body should support your purpose for speaking. Information that does not support your purpose will detract from your presentation. The main body also includes references to any benefits the audience is likely to experience as a result of accepting your presentation.

Good speakers summarize information from time to time during the main body. These are called internal summaries. While some speakers prefer to summarize only at the end of their talk, in the conclusion, others find that summarizing points during the presentation's main body helps prepare their audience to accept their conclusions.

The Conclusion. The conclusion is used to summarize the presentation for your audience. It is not appropriate to introduce new information or material during a conclusion.

Visual Aids. Visual aids can add substantially to a presentation if used properly. Many managers use too many visual aids or make them too complicated. You should follow these guidelines when preparing visual aids:

- *Use the KISS system.* Keep your visual aids short and simple.

- *Use visual aids sparingly.* The rule of thumb is a maximum of one visual aid for every two minutes of speaking.

- *Use graphics.* Graphs, pictures, flowcharts, and so on make better visual aids than words on a page.

- *Make text and numbers legible.* For most presentations, 18-point is the minimum font size you should use. Before your presentation, go to the back of the room in which you will be presenting and see for yourself whether you can read the visual aids.

- *Use color sparingly.*

- *Graph data.* Graphed data is easy to read.

- *Use bullets.* If you use a visual aid to present written ideas, set off the important points with numbers, indents, or some other method.

- *Develop titles for visual aids.* Your audience is more likely to remember a visual aid if it has a title.

- *Use overlays when possible.* Most people dislike the "hide and peek" method of revealing portions of a visual aid as you go. Instead, develop a series of overlays.

Controlling the Presentation Environment

A poor environment has ruined many an otherwise good presentation. Before you begin a presentation, make sure that the environment is properly prepared.

Following a few suggestions will help ensure that the presentation environment will not be a distraction:

- *Equipment:* Test overhead projectors, computers, slide projectors, and other equipment in advance. Have spare bulbs and software ready.

- *Flip charts:* Make sure you have ample paper and pens on hand.

- *Handouts:* Make sure handouts are easily accessible and can be easily distributed.

- *Pointers:* Make sure a pointer is easily accessible if you plan to use one.

- *Microphone:* Test the microphone in advance. (Presentations to more than 75–100 people will likely require a microphone.)

- *Lighting:* Determine how to turn lights on or off if you need to during your presentation. Leave some light on when using overheads or slides; speaking in a completely dark room is disconcerting.

- *Seating arrangements:* Arrange seating in the room appropriately.

Presentation Delivery Tips

How you deliver your presentation is often the key to success. Tips that can help you deliver your presentations more successfully include the following:

- *Posture:* Your posture should be relaxed and erect. Evenly distribute your weight, and don't shift back and forth from one foot to the other.

- *Movement:* Moving nearer the audience emphasizes main points. If you are using a lectern, move out from behind it occasionally. Avoid staying frozen in one spot or moving too rapidly or too much. The audience is also aware of hand movements. Wringing your hands or keeping them in your pockets, "handcuffed" behind your back, or folded in front of you all detract from your presentation.

- *Orientation:* Speakers who keep their shoulders turned toward their audiences often find that they are considered more engaging. Speaking while facing away from the audience is disconcerting to listeners.

- *Gestures:* Many people "talk with their hands" when speaking. Gestures are an important form of nonverbal communication when used appropriately. However, quick hand movements, nervous tics, and other visual signs of anxiety detract from presentations.

- *Eye contact:* You should make eye contact with the audience to reinforce your message. If the group is too large for you to make eye contact with each individual, it is okay to focus on those immediately in front of you while you speak. Eye contact of from one to three seconds is considered appropriate.

- *Volume, pitch, tone, and pace of speaking:* If your voice is too loud, listeners may decide that you are pushy or overbearing; conversely, speaking too quietly signals sheepishness or nervousness. Strive to speak at a medium volume. The pitch of your voice is most effective when it comes naturally to you. Your voice's tone should change according to the situation; monotones bore audiences. Speaking at a moderate pace is usually best. A quick pace generally sends the message that you are trying to get through too much material or are nervous. Speaking slowly gives listeners the opportunity to absorb your words, but some listeners may become bored or distracted. Remember, your audience can listen to twice as many words a minute as you can say.

To assess their presentation skills, managers should use a video camera to tape themselves and actually see what they look and sound like when they are making a presentation. This will allow them to make sure that their body language and voice dynamics reinforce the message rather than detract from it. Some people jingle the change in their pockets while they speak; men with facial hair may repeatedly stroke their beards while speaking; some women play with their hair or items of jewelry while making presentations. All of these actions can distract listeners from the message, and presenters may not even be aware that they are doing them until they see themselves on videotape.

Feedback Skills

An important part of every manager's job is providing feedback to others, especially those on his or her staff. "**Feedback**" can be defined as any communication in which a person provides information about some aspect of another's message, motivation, or behavior.[16] Feedback directly influences an employee's motivation to perform.[17] Stephen P. Robbins pointed out that feedback works in several different ways. Feedback helps employees establish goals, for example. Feedback also helps employees understand how well they are accomplishing their goals. Feedback can also suggest means for employees to perform better by helping them attain, increase, or enhance their goals.[18]

Managers should maintain a record of the feedback they provide to each employee during a coaching or performance evaluation session. One way to do this is to maintain a checklist in each employee's file detailing the topic, date, and expected outcome of each coaching/evaluation session with an employee. An example of such a checklist is provided in Exhibit 7.

Positive versus Negative Feedback. Positive feedback is readily accepted by most employees; negative feedback is not. Most people like to hear good news, but they tend to block out bad news. This does not mean that managers should never give negative feedback. Sometimes it's necessary to point out performance problems to employees. A bell captain who is offending guests, for example, has to hear that information in order to understand why additional training is necessary.

While managers typically believe that their employees know what is expected of them, often this is not true. In fact, many employees learn what is and is not acceptable only when they break a rule and are reprimanded. Therefore, it is important for managers to clearly state and constantly reinforce what is and is not acceptable behavior.

Managers who take the time to tell employees exactly what is expected of them generally find that their employees do the right thing more often than not. One effective way to coach employees about what is and is not acceptable is for

Exhibit 7   Sample Feedback Checklist

Name _____ Evaluation by _____				
Date Discussed	Topic Discussed	Expectations	Date Reviewed	Progress Notes

managers to make two lists, one containing acceptable or desired behaviors, the other containing unacceptable behaviors. By providing these lists to employees, a manager clearly communicates the behaviors that he or she deems either desirable or undesirable. By providing such lists, managers are, in effect, coaching their employees to display desirable behaviors.

Feedback Techniques. Several techniques are available to managers who want to improve the feedback they provide to employees. Robbins summarized several characteristics of effective feedback. Effective feedback:

- *Is immediate or well-timed.* Feedback is most effective if there is a very short interval between someone's behavior and the receipt of feedback. Ken Blanchard, author of *The One Minute Manager,* advises managers to catch employees doing something good and praise them immediately as a means of establishing rapport and encouraging positive performance.

- *Is specific.* Specific feedback helps employees understand exactly what behaviors are required. Generalized feedback usually ensures that an employee will not understand what is expected.

- *Considers the needs of the receiver.* Some employees need constant feedback; others require very little. Managers must decide which approach is best for each employee. Generally speaking, poor performers or new employees will probably need frequent feedback, while good performers and employees with more experience will probably need less.

- *Focuses on behavior rather than personality.* Feedback that is impersonal, descriptive, and job-related will lead to desired outcomes more often than feedback based on personalities.

- *Is emotionally controlled.* It is tempting for managers who observe an employee performing poorly to immediately say something that they may regret later. While timeliness and immediacy are important concepts in feedback, sometimes it is better to take a moment to control your emotions and think of the best way to provide negative feedback to an employee.

- *Is two-sided.* Asking an employee how he or she feels about what you've said can improve the feedback you provide. Employees usually view one-way communication as negative, two-way communication as positive.

No matter how clear feedback may sound to a manager, an employee may not understand it. Asking an employee to restate the main points you made during the feedback session is a good way to make sure you and the employee understand each other.

Listening Skills

Listening skills are crucial to a manager. While many managers think they are good listeners, many—perhaps most—are not. Research conducted by Brownell found that managers who thought of themselves as good listeners were often rated by their employees as poor listeners.[19] Many managers are good at *hearing* but poor at *listening.* Hearing is largely a passive activity; we even hear while we are asleep. Listening, on the other hand, requires involvement and action. Managers have to *decide* to listen.

Listening well requires hard work, but, fortunately, listening skills can be learned. People are usually poor listeners simply because they have not been taught to listen. People learn other communication skills in elementary schools, secondary schools, and college through reading, writing, and speaking classes. However, people rarely take listening classes. Despite this lack of formal training, a manager can become a better listener simply by learning and mastering listening techniques.

Listening Situations

Managers find themselves in a variety of listening situations. In the workplace, we usually find ourselves doing one of three types of listening: informational listening, evaluative listening, or empathetic listening.

Informational Listening. The goal of **informational listening** is to understand and remember what is important in a message. How well we understand and remember the message determines our success as an informational listener.

Most informational listening takes place in formal or semi-formal communication environments. Lectures, meetings, seminars, and conferences are all examples of situations in which you will practice informational listening.

Tips to help you become a better informational listener include the following:

- *Listen for the main idea.* You can't remember everything, so concentrate on what's most important.

- *Listen for the speaker's organizational method.* Determine whether the speaker is presenting a problem, a solution, or a case study, or using some other organizational approach. Identifying the organizational method can help you remember the information.

- *Identify significant details.* Pick out the most important details used to support the speaker's points and remember them.

- *Take notes.* If it's important, write it down.

- *Stay tuned even during familiar topics.* A poor listener tends to tune out speakers when they talk about things the listener already knows a lot about. If you do this, you can miss important information.

Evaluative Listening. The goal of **evaluative listening** is to make a decision or accept or reject an idea. Making the right decision often depends on how well you listen. Tips that will help you become a better evaluative listener include the following:

- *Judge the idea, not the person.* Even if you do not like the speaker, he or she might have something important to say.

- *Keep control of your emotions.* Concentrating on the issues, not your emotions, helps you hear important details.

- *Identify the speaker's position.* Listen for the main points of the speaker's message.

- *Consider the speaker's credibility.* Past experiences with the speaker can influence how you listen and how much credence you give to the message.

- *Determine whether the speaker's position is supported by facts.* Try to separate facts that support the speaker's position from the speaker's opinions.

- *Determine whether the speaker needs to do more homework.* Before making a decision, ask for more information if you need it.

- *If you do not agree with the speaker, decide whether there is room for compromise.* If you have an alternative position or idea, look for opportunities to compromise or otherwise reach common ground.

Empathetic Listening. A manager uses **empathetic listening** when acting as a sounding board for others' ideas or when coaching or counseling someone. Listening to the speaker's feelings is a very important part of this type of listening. Tips that can help you become a better empathetic listener include the following:

- *Avoid giving evaluative feedback.* Don't evaluate the speaker; help him or her explore the situation from his or her point of view. If a front desk agent comes to you for advice on how to address the pressure she feels when dealing with irritated guests, a good approach is to ask her to describe situations that made her uncomfortable and describe how she felt during those situations.

- *Don't provide direction.* Employees and other managers often want you to simply "hear them out" so they can determine what to do on their own. Offering suggestions is not helpful in these situations.

- *Provide good nonverbal feedback.* Using positive nonverbal feedback such as nodding your head or making appropriate eye contact can reassure speakers that you empathize with them.

- *Restate the speaker's idea in the form of a question.* Rephrasing what a speaker has said in the form of a question gives the speaker a chance to elaborate on and think through what he or she has said.

- *Listen for and paraphrase feelings.* The most important message you can send in empathetic listening is to reassure the speaker that you understand the feelings the speaker is conveying. **Paraphrasing** what speakers say helps them to confront their feelings.

- *Know your limitations.* Trying to help an employee, a manager, or a guest through a serious problem such as drug or alcohol addiction, a death in the family, or a similarly serious situation can do more harm than good. The best thing to do in this situation is to sympathize and then refer the individual to a specialist trained in counseling.

Before you read about obstacles to listening and techniques to improve listening, it may be useful to rate how effective you think you are at listening. Exhibit 8 is a managerial listening assessment you can use for this purpose.

Obstacles to Listening

Many people find that instead of listening while others are speaking, their minds wander. When this happens, they "tune out" what a speaker is saying. People are also poor listeners because they are easily distracted or because they simply do not try to listen better. Some people are poor listeners because they are easily bored when they try to listen. This is due in part to the fact that while speakers generally speak at a rate of 125 to 150 words per minute, most people can listen and comprehend at twice that rate.

Developing Listening Skills

You can become an effective listener if you want to do so. All it takes, in most cases, is learning how to concentrate and use listening techniques. The following sections provide some tips to improve your listening. Contrary to popular opinion, effective listening requires action on the part of the listener.

Active Listening. Passive listening requires only hearing. **Active listening** requires the listener to participate in the communication process. There are four principal requirements in active listening: intensity, empathy, acceptance, and a willingness to take responsibility for completeness.

Intensity helps you concentrate on what is being said and how it is being said. Empathy requires you to put yourself in the sender's shoes to better understand what the sender wants to communicate. Acceptance is listening without the

Exhibit 8 Managerial Listening Assessment

Listening Skills	Yes	No
Do you concentrate?		
Do you acknowledge?		
Do you exhibit emotional control?		
Do you structure your listening?		
Are you turned off if the speaker is anxious?		
Can you empathize with the speaker?		
Do you attach meaning:		
Through stories?		
Through memories?		
Do you evaluate the message?		
Do you respond and remember?		
Are you and the speaker exchanging non-verbals?		
Eye contact		
Facial feedback		
Gestures		
Do you judge content, not delivery?		
Do you take notes?		
Do you repeat information?		
Do you avoid:		
Interruptions?		
Prejudging?		
Do you provide feedback by paraphrasing?		

distractions of agreement or disagreement. Taking responsibility for completeness means the receiver is willing to do what's necessary to get the sender's entire message.

Techniques to improve active listening skills. Active listening skills can be improved using techniques that encourage two-way communication. Experts have suggested many different techniques; each has its advantages. Authors Raphael Kavanaugh and Jack Ninemeier identified a four-stage model of active listening composed of focusing, interpreting, evaluating, and responding:

- *Focusing.* Focusing involves turning your attention to the speaker and putting all other matters aside. You should minimize distractions, maintain an appropriate amount of eye contact, and show that you are paying attention by mirroring the speaker's emotions, asking questions to get more information, and asking the speaker to repeat what you do not understand.

- *Interpreting.* Effective listeners try to interpret why speakers are communicating. A speaker might be casually conversing, blowing off steam, expressing an idea, trading information, or hoping to persuade you of something. Knowing why the speaker is communicating can help you understand the message. Confirm that you understand the speaker's meaning by paraphrasing what the speaker is saying.

- *Evaluating.* The goal of the evaluating stage of active listening is to confirm that a common understanding has been reached. This can be accomplished by gathering more information through concentrating on the speaker's words, body language, and tone of voice, and through asking for more details. You should determine whether the speaker is relaying facts or expressing opinions. The speaker's facts may disagree with what you know to be true. You can communicate your evaluation of the speaker's message by nodding in approval or leaning toward the speaker if you agree with what the speaker is saying; you can signal disagreement by leaning away or shaking your head.

- *Responding.* An active listener responds to the message and the speaker. You may need to ask questions to find out exactly what kind of response the speaker wants. Once that is determined, you have to consider your time, energy, and inclination before responding.

Robbins also has suggestions for improving active listening skills:

- *Be motivated.* Listeners unwilling to hear and understand cannot be communicated with. Try to hear and understand what is being said.

- *Make eye contact.* Research shows that while people listen with their ears, they show they are listening with their eyes.[20] Making eye contact also helps you focus your attention.

- *Show interest.* Nonverbal signals such as head-nodding and attentive facial expressions show that you are interested.

- *Avoid distracting actions.* Shuffling papers, looking at your watch, and so on show a lack of interest.

- *Show empathy.* Try to understand, from the speaker's perspective, what the message is and why it is being communicated in the way you are hearing it. Communicate your empathy through phrases such as "You must have been pretty upset by that" or "I've felt that same way at times."

- *Take in the whole picture.* Interpret feelings and emotions, not just what is being said. Look for nonverbal clues.

- *Ask questions.* Asking questions shows interest and allows you to clarify the message. Probing questions such as "What happened next?" and "How did you feel about that?" send the message that you are listening. The exercise in Exhibit 9 can help you learn this important skill.

- *Don't interrupt.* Interrupting shows disrespect and arrogance. It sends the message that "You are not worth listening to" or "I can say what you are

Exhibit 9   Sample Questions Exercise

Decide whether the following questioning techniques are effective communication strategies, then check your answers with the correct responses listed below.

Yes   No

☐   ☐   1. You should challenge speakers to defend themselves by asking questions such as, "Why would you say something like that?"

☐   ☐   2. You should ask "open-ended" questions requiring an answer of more than one or two words, such as, "How could that be done?"

☐   ☐   3. You should use "leading" questions such as, "Can you tell me more about that?"

☐   ☐   4. You should ask lots of questions, just so the speaker knows you're interested.

☐   ☐   5. You should "mirror" words back to the speaker with questions like, "The new program didn't work? What happened?"

Correct Responses

1. **No.** Avoid challenging or threatening a speaker—it only leads to defensiveness, an argument, or silence. "Why" questions are especially threatening.

2. **Yes.** "Open-ended" questions elicit more information. "Close-ended" questions, which can be answered in one or two words, limit the information you get.

3. **Yes.** "Leading" questions encourage speakers to build on their ideas. Speakers may then give information that wouldn't have been shared if you hadn't encouraged them.

4. **No.** Asking questions unnecessarily simply interrupts the speaker's train of thought. Ask questions only when you sincerely want clarification or more information.

5. **Yes.** "Mirroring" a speaker's words back as a question encourages the speaker to expand on the ideas.

Source: Adapted from *Hospitality Management Skill Builders: Interpersonal Communication* (Lansing, Mich.: American Hotel & Lodging Educational Institute, 1994), p. 36.

---

trying to say much better." Exhibit 10 contains an exercise that can help you stop interrupting others.

- *Make a smooth transition when responding to the speaker.* Effective listeners make smooth transitions between what the speaker has said and what they say. Introducing a new topic before responding to the speaker's topic is a sure sign that you did not hear or did not care about what was just said.

- *Be natural.* Don't exaggerate the actions of a good listener. Too much eye contact, intensity, empathy, and so on can backfire. Speakers may decide you are mocking them or are just pretending to be interested.[21]

- *Encourage suggestions.* Asking people to offer advice shows that you value their opinions. Questions such as "What would you recommend?" or "What do you think we should do?" facilitate communication.

Exhibit 10   Sample Exercise to Curb the Urge to Interrupt

Everyone gets the urge to interrupt. Unfortunately, some of us give in to the urge too often. To reduce the number of times you interrupt people who are talking to you, do the following two things:

1. Think of a person who repeatedly interrupts you, or think of the last time a person interrupted you when you were saying something important. How did you feel? What did you think of that person?

_____

_____

_____

_____

_____

_____

_____

_____

_____

_____

_____

_____

_____

_____

_____

_____

_____

_____

_____

2. At least twice a day, challenge yourself to keep quiet when you want to interrupt someone. As soon as you feel the urge to interrupt, think to yourself, "Stop! I'm going to hear this person out and give good nonverbal feedback to show him or her that I'm really listening."

Source: Adapted from *Hospitality Management Skill Builders: Interpersonal Communication* (Lansing, Mich.: American Hotel & Lodging Educational Institute, 1994), p. 34.

- *Summarize what the speaker has said.* **Summarizing statements** condense parts of what the speaker has said and stress what you understood to be the important points of the message.

- *Self-disclosure.* Telling the speaker how you feel about what he or she has said provides feedback that helps the communication process.

Writing Skills

Writing is a difficult form of communication for many managers to master. However, everyone in business must be able to communicate in writing. Because written communications are more permanent than oral ones, they may represent you for some time to come. Therefore, it is important to learn how to express yourself effectively in writing.

Good writing clearly communicates information or ideas, as briefly as possible, to readers. Good writing also obeys certain rules of grammar, spelling, sentence structure, and punctuation.

Guidelines for Better Business Writing

Writing is easier when it is well-planned. What follows are four guidelines that will help you become a better writer:

- *Have a specific reader or audience in mind.* Writing will take on different tones and forms for different audiences. A memo to your staff can be more informal than a memo to your boss.

- *Know your objective.* Why are you writing this memo, letter, or report? Establishing in advance your purpose—and sticking to it—helps focus your writing.

- *Decide which information is essential to include.* Business writing typically is intended to convey specific information. Sticking to the point will improve most business writing.

- *Decide how to present the information.* Many managers have trouble organizing their thoughts on paper. Preparing an outline or a list of significant points you wish to present can help you write more effectively.

A tri-level outline like the following one is usually sufficient for most business writing:

    A. Major Point
        1. Minor supporting point
            a. sub-point
            b. sub-point
        2. Minor supporting point

    B. Major Point
        1. Minor supporting point
        2. Minor supporting point
        3. Minor supporting point
            a. sub-point
            b. sub-point
            c. sub-point

    Etc.

Managers and Writing

Managers typically use memos, letters, e-mail, and reports as their methods of communicating with others in writing. Written communications for business are generally intended to inform or persuade the intended audience on a specific topic.

It is important for managers to know how well they are communicating when they write. A poorly written memo, letter, or evaluation can detract from or obscure the message being sent. Grammar, spelling, choice of language, and content are vital in written communication. When writing, some managers tend to add more and more and more, but brevity is a virtue in business writing.

If a manager uses handwritten messages, then handwriting and penmanship are also important. A handwritten employee schedule is of little use if the employees cannot read it because it is illegible.

Many managers rely on support staff for help with formatting and grammar problems. To have support staff is certainly a great asset; however, it does not mean that a manager does not need to be a good writer in his or her own right.

If you begin by creating a tri-level outline, you will probably find that writing is easier.

Better Business Writing Rules. You can write better by following some simple rules:[22]

- Use specific language.
- Use active voice.
- Use plain English and simple sentences.
- Follow the inverted pyramid rule.
- Use topic sentences.
- Avoid clichés.
- Avoid jargon.
- Avoid condescending statements.
- Avoid sexist language.
- Stress the positive.
- Take a stand.

Let's take a brief look at each of these rules in the following sections.

Use specific language. Specific or concrete nouns express meaning more powerfully than general or abstract nouns. Nonspecific nouns (area, individual, thing) are especially uninformative and uninteresting. It is better to write "Ms. Rodriguez met with four dining room supervisors in the Red Room" than it is to write "The general manager met with some individuals in an area of the hotel." "Recently some new employees were hired" is not as informative as "Last week the executive housekeeper hired two room attendants and a laundry worker."

Use active voice. Active verbs convey more meaning than passive verbs. They also enliven sentences and make writing more succinct:

Passive:	The decision was made by Jan.
Active:	Jan made the decision.
Passive:	The employee handbook was revised by the house committee.
Active:	The house committee revised the employee handbook.

Use plain English and simple sentences. Simple words and sentences are easy to read. Managers who want to become effective writers should make it a point to use words that are familiar to their readers. While some writers try to impress others by using complicated words and sentences, they usually accomplish the opposite. Short sentences are easier to understand than long ones, but not all sentences should be short. Instead, it is better to vary the lengths of your sentences so that your writing is more interesting to readers.

Follow the inverted pyramid rule. Novelists often take many pages to build an image of a particular character or event. However, business writing follows different rules. Most business readers have little time for reading. Therefore, you should use the **inverted pyramid** style of writing in most of your business communications. Newspaper reporters use this method.

The inverted pyramid style places the most important information at the beginning and leaves less significant information for later paragraphs. Newspaper reporters know that their final paragraphs may be deleted by an editor who must make their stories fit into the newspaper's available space. Business writers should assume that their readers will be too busy to read all the way through their report or memo. Putting your most important points in the first paragraph or two will make it more likely that readers will get your message.

Use topic sentences. Every paragraph should address a single topic, and each paragraph should begin with a topic sentence. The topic sentence presents the paragraph's main point. Short topic sentences are more powerful and easier to remember than long ones. The other sentences in the paragraph should relate to or support the point made in the topic sentence. A sentence that does not relate to the topic sentence should be moved to another paragraph or deleted. Paragraphs, then, should look something like this: topic sentence, sentence adding more detail, sentence adding more detail, sentence adding more detail.

Avoid clichés. Avoid clichés such as "input," "parameters," "utilize," "hopefully," "prioritize," and so on. Instead, be succinct with your writing. The following example illustrates how much easier it is to understand a message when the clichés are weeded out:

Incorrect:	Enclosed please find the information per your request. Hopefully, you can utilize our products to benefit your company within the parameters of your company's invoice-processing prioritization. We appreciate your input.
Correct:	We have enclosed the information you requested. Our product will speed your computer's invoice processing. Thank you for your suggestions.

Exhibit 11   Additional Writing Guidelines

1. Avoid informal writing for most business communications.

2. Ensure subject and predicate agreement.

3. Distinguish plurals from possessives.

4. Use proper punctuation.

5. Remember that periods and commas go inside quotation marks.

6. Consider using new words (for example, the expression "due" is often overused).

7. Use "try to" instead of "try and."

8. Use "different from" instead of "different than."

9. Distinguish between "affect" and "effect."

10. Distinguish between "principle" and "principal."

Source: Adapted from R. O'Halloran and C. Deale, "Writing Across the Hospitality and Tourism Curriculum," *The Journal of Teaching in Travel & Tourism* 4, no. 2 (Philadelphia: Taylor & Francis, Inc., 2004), pp. 61–78.

Avoid jargon. Too many business communications are full of jargon. Jargon may mean something within a department or company, but it often means little to outside readers. If your writing will be read by someone who won't understand your jargon, don't use it.

Avoid condescending statements. Whenever possible, write with warmth, from one human being to another.

Avoid sexist language. There are many more women in business today than in the past. Because of this, and because of changing social values, sexism has no place in business writing. Terms such as "busboy" and "maid" are sexist. Many managers make errors in the salutations they use when writing business letters. For example, "Gentlemen" was for many years an acceptable salutation, but not today. You can avoid using sexist terms in your salutations by being specific. For example, instead of "Gentlemen" or "Dear Sirs," you could write "Dear Stockholders" or "Dear Members."

Stress the positive. Instead of telling people what they cannot do, tell them what they can do. Stressing the positive is as important in business writing as it is in any other business setting. For example, instead of writing, "We cannot accommodate your request for a banquet facility on March 17," you should write "We're sorry we cannot accommodate your request for banquet facilities on March 17, but we have open dates on both the 16th and the 18th."

Take a stand. Some managers make the mistake of failing to commit to what they are writing. Phrases such as "sort of," "perhaps," "somewhat," and "I think" send the message that you are not quite sure of what you are saying.

Exhibit 11 lists additional writing guidelines that may be helpful to managers.

Exhibit 12   Sample Business Memo Format

To: Reader
From: Writer (followed by signature)
Date: (the date the memo is written)
Re: Subject

Body Paragraph 1: The first sentence should be a clear, concise topic sentence establishing why you are writing the memo. This sentence may also explain what you want readers to do when they finish reading the memo.

Body Paragraph 2: This paragraph should contain important proof or details supporting Paragraph 1.

Body Paragraph 3: Less important evidence or details go here. Some memos may not need a third paragraph.

Final Body Paragraph: In this paragraph you thank the reader for his or her time and request action or repeat an earlier request for action.

Memos

Many managers find that their writing is limited primarily to memos, business letters, and e-mails. Memos usually are issued to address a single point. Therefore, you should find it easy to write a clear and concise memo.

Memos follow a specific format. While a memo's format may vary somewhat among organizations, every memo should contain five elements: to whom the memo is addressed, who wrote the memo, the date of the memo, the subject of the memo, and the body of the memo. Most organizations use a memo format similar to the one shown in Exhibit 12. Memo writers write their names or initials next to their typed names (which appear after "From:" near the top of the memo) rather than at the end of the memo.

Business Letters

Like memos, business letters should be clear and concise. When writing a business letter, you should follow the writing rules discussed earlier: use short sentences, begin each paragraph with a topic sentence, and so on.

Exhibit 13   Sample Business Letter Format

> **AAA HOTEL COMPANY**
> 555 ADDRESS
> CITY, STATE, ZIP CODE
> PHONE NUMBER/FAX NUMBER
>
>
> (date you are writing the letter goes here)
>
>
> Addressee's Name
> Addressee's Title
> Company's Name
> Company's Address
> City, State Zip Code
>
> Dear Addressee:
>
> Paragraph 1: Explain why you are writing the letter.
>
> Paragraph 2: Provide evidence or details to support your purpose.
>
> Paragraph 3: Tell how and when the topic of the letter should be addressed or followed up.
>
> Final Paragraph: Thank reader for his or her attention/time.
>
> Sincerely,
>
> (signature)
>
> Name of Writer

One of the primary differences between memos and business letters is their formats. Essential elements of a business-letter format include: company letterhead, date, addressee's name and address, salutation, main body, and closing. The business letter format shown in Exhibit 13 is known as the **full block letter style**. It is a style commonly used in the business world. With the full block letter style, the date, addressee information, salutation, main body paragraphs, closing, typed name, and signature all begin at the left margin. You should allow from one to three blank lines between the date and the addressee information, a line above and below the salutation, a line between the paragraphs in the main body, a line between the last line of the final paragraph and the closing, and three to five lines between the closing and the typed name of the writer. The writer's signature always appears between the closing and the typed name.

E-Mails

When e-mail began in 1972 as a way for academicians around the world to easily and quickly communicate with one another, there were fewer than 100 people online. Now, millions of people in more than 100 countries have access to e-mail. It is the most widely used application of the Internet.

E-mail is popular with businesspeople for many reasons. It is less interruptive than a telephone call and faster than a letter. E-mail does not depend on both parties being available at the same time. You can read an e-mail and respond to it at a time convenient for you.

There are also drawbacks to e-mail. Many people wrongly assume that the recipient of an e-mail will read and respond to it immediately. Actually, it is common for people to set aside a certain time of day to read and respond to e-mails, which may be hours after you sent your e-mail to them. For that reason, sending an e-mail to a group of people announcing a meeting in one hour is not the best way to communicate that message, since some in the group may not read the e-mail until the hour is long past. On the other hand, if you announce the meeting for the next day, chances are high that everyone will get the message, since most businesspeople try to keep up with their e-mails on a daily basis. In fact, some companies have a policy that e-mails from customers must be answered within 24 hours of their receipt, since most customers use e-mail as a way of getting a fast response. If you need an immediate response, telephones are still best; regular postal mail or "snail mail" can be used when it doesn't matter if it takes a few days for the message to get there; expectations regarding response times to e-mails lie somewhere in between.

Another drawback to e-mails is that, despite the informal, conversational tone that many have, they don't convey emotions nearly as well as face-to-face or telephone conversations. E-mails strip the conversation of all facial expressions, vocal inflections, gestures, and other clues to meaning. Your e-mail correspondent may have difficulty telling whether you are happy or sad, serious or kidding. Trying to convey sarcasm via e-mail is especially problematic, and should be avoided.

Despite these drawbacks, e-mail is a mainstay of today's business world. It is also still a relatively new method of communication, and e-mail etiquette, customs, and conventions are still being formed. However, there are a few guidelines that seem to be generally accepted, as discussed in the following paragraphs. (For more e-mailing tips, see Exhibit 14.)

Don't use the "To" field when mailing to more than one person. When sending an e-mail to two or more people, some people simply place all of the addresses in the "To" field and send it off. However, some people do not want their e-mail address publicized to others without their permission. Unless you are absolutely sure this will not raise privacy concerns (all of the people you are sending the e-mail to are internal, company e-mail users, for example), this practice should be avoided. It is better to use the "Bcc" (blind copy) field.

Be sure to include a relevant "Subject" line. Most businesspeople receive many e-mails each day. It is very helpful to include a subject line that truly and succinctly tips off the recipient to the content of the e-mail. Some people wait until they have

Exhibit 14   More Tips for Writing Effective E-Mails

- Choose a readable font style
- Use a thoughtful salutation
- Be polite
- Keep a dictionary handy
- Take time to write a complete message
- Think of your e-mail as a summary—keep it brief and to the point
- Consider page layout—readability is important
- Limit jargon

Source: Adapted from Gerardo San Diego, "The Art of Writing E-mail," www. net-market.com/email.htm.

written the e-mail before creating the subject line, to ensure that the subject line is properly descriptive.

Don't overuse the "High Priority" option. Remember the story of the little boy who cried wolf? People stopped paying attention to him, and he failed to get a response when it really mattered. The same may happen to you if you overuse the "High Priority" option when you send out e-mails. The person who is constantly sending such e-mails may be looked upon as someone with an overdeveloped sense of self-importance. Another reason to use "High Priority" sparingly is that such e-mails come across as somewhat aggressive.

Messages should be concise and to the point. It is harder to read text on a screen than on paper, and long e-mails can discourage recipients from reading them. Therefore, e-mails should be short whenever possible and always to the point. Use short paragraphs, and blank lines between paragraphs to break up the text. If you are asking several questions, it is often helpful to number them; this increases the likelihood that the recipient will answer all of them, rather than just the first one.

Don't write in all capital letters. Writing in all capital letters is considered rude by e-mailers; it's seen as the equivalent of shouting. Also, it is harder to read text in all capitals.

Check for writing errors. Since e-mails are less formal than other written communication, there is a tendency to pay less attention to such writing mechanics as proper grammar, punctuation, and spelling. However, when you are sending e-mails to customers and others outside the company, you should strive to uphold the company's image (and your image as a professional) and send out e-mails that are free of typos, errors in grammar, and so on. It not only looks better, it makes the message easier to read and understand. Running the spell-checker is a good idea, but it is not a substitute for actually giving the e-mail a quick read before sending it. There are many writing problems—even spelling errors (using the word "hear" when you meant "here," for example)—that the spell-checker cannot catch. Remember, some people—especially customers—might feel insulted to receive an e-mail filled with grammar mistakes and misspelled words. They may conclude that such sloppiness spills over into your company's products and customer service as well.

Simple formatting is best. Using HTML so that you can use fancy fonts or various colors and graphics for your e-mail messages will be totally lost on the person who receives the e-mail if his or her e-mail program does not read this format. The message will appear on your recipient's screen, not with fancy fonts and colors, but with the words interrupted by computer codes, making the message either hard to read or completely unreadable. Sometimes such a message can crash the recipient's e-mail system. So, at least when corresponding with people external to your business, you should choose Plain Text for your e-mail messages. If your internal e-mail system supports HTML, you can safely use the fancy fonts and colors for internal correspondence, but you will have to remember to switch over to Plain Text when e-mailing outsiders.

Don't send attachments unless absolutely necessary. Attachments can annoy e-mail recipients. Some large attachments have been known to crash e-mail systems, and many recipients are wary of attachments, fearing hidden computer viruses. Many e-mail users will not open any attachment, even from someone they know, unless the sender informs them beforehand that an attachment is coming. Some users have inboxes with limited space, so a large attachment may either take up most or all of their inbox—making it impossible for them to receive messages from others—or cause the message to be rejected and returned as undeliverable.

Keep abbreviations to a minimum. Some abbreviations are universally understood, such as "FYI" for "for your information." Others, less so—does everyone know that "BTW" stands for "by the way"? Informal e-mailers have developed a lengthy list of abbreviations for use in e-mail, but few people know very many of them. Experienced e-mailers will probably know that "LOL" stands for "laugh out loud," but even some of them might be confused by "ROTFL" ("rolling on the floor laughing"), and we enter even more arcane territory with "TTFN" or "TNSTAAFL" ("ta-ta for now" and "there's no such thing as a free lunch"). For this reason, abbreviations should be kept to a minimum, even with casual correspondence. Abbreviations should not be used when e-mailing customers and other external business correspondents, not only because of the possibility of confusion, but because they are too informal for business correspondence.

Limit "smilies" to casual correspondence only. Because e-mails seem to exist somewhere along the continuum between the informality of spoken speech and the formality of the written word, e-mailers have tried to introduce into e-mail messages the visual cues we send each other when speaking face-to-face, through what are termed "smilies" or "emoticons": simple strings of characters that usually mimic the human face. These range from the simple:

> :-) = smile, happy
> :-(= frown, displeasure

to the more esoteric:

> :-/ = perplexed
> :-O = shock, surprise, or yell
> ;-) = wink, light sarcasm

These are typically found at the end of sentences and will usually refer to the prior statement. Because there are literally scores of smilies and their translations are by no means universal, it is best to use them sparingly, if at all, even in casual correspondence.

Include a brief signature at the end of your e-mails. Many e-mail software programs allow you to automatically include a signature at the end of each e-mail message. You should take advantage of this option, since this will help identify you to people to whom you are sending an e-mail message for the first time, and can contain information that all recipients might find useful to know, such as your telephone number. Keep your signature brief—three to five lines is a good guide—and include your name, title, company name, and other helpful information, such as a telephone or fax number. Using a scanned image as part of your signature should be avoided—image files tend to be large, so to include one with your signature will slow message transmission and might even crash the software of less sophisticated e-mail systems. Some people like to include a saying or quote with their signature. Keep in mind that you will correspond with many people for weeks, even months or years, via e-mail, so before long that pithy saying or meaningful quote will be worn very thin.

Because your signature automatically appears, it is easy to forget about it. It is a good idea to check it periodically to make sure that all of its information is current.

Read before you send. The importance of reading over your e-mail before sending it has been mentioned earlier, but this tip is so important it bears repeating. This not only gives you a chance to correct errors, it allows you to make sure you are really saying what you intended to say.

Think before you send. E-mails are not private. Employers generally have the right to read any e-mails sent or received through the company e-mail system. Some companies routinely monitor e-mail messages to make sure employees are not wasting time on frivolous e-mails, or leaking company secrets, or sending messages that could get the company in trouble due to their content (sexist or racist jokes or comments; offensive comments, jokes, or pictures of a sexual nature; and so on). E-mails are sometimes misdirected (that "funny" joke sent to a co-worker might end up in the boss's inbox); e-mail systems are not hacker-proof; and the person to whom you sent the e-mail can forward it without your knowledge or permission to anyone with an e-mail address (your spouse, your boss, prospective employers, etc.). Therefore, it is very important to think before you send. Read the e-mail over carefully. Is the tone appropriate? Did you say anything that you might regret later? If it were posted on the company bulletin board or published in the newspaper, would you be embarrassed, or worse, fired? If it's not safe enough for the newspaper, it's not safe enough for e-mail.

Maintain the thread. Once you send an e-mail, you will probably get a response. If you want to reply to that response, you should hit the "Reply" button, not start a new e-mail message. That way the link (called the "thread") between your original e-mail and the ensuing responses will not be broken, and it will be easier to follow the correspondence. If responses are sent via new e-mails, it can be difficult for you and for your corresponder to follow the sequence of messages. Should you need to file the e-mail correspondence, it is much easier to find and file one e-mail consisting of a continuous thread than track down several separate e-mails for filing.

If you want to start a brand new subject, you should not hit the "Reply" button, because you would be introducing something irrelevant into the current conversation (thus "breaking the thread"). A new subject should be started off with its own e-mail and subject line.

Other e-mail guidelines do not have anything to do with creating messages. For example, forwarding chain letters and other "junk" e-mail is considered rude by many e-mail users. Almost without exception, e-mails of the "Please send this e-mail to everyone you know" variety—because "this is a new computer virus and we must get the word out quickly," or "it's the wish of a dying little girl," or "it will bring you good luck (or payment from someone)"—are *hoaxes* and should be deleted. If you want to check on the legitimacy of such e-mails, there are several sites on the Internet that can help, such as:

> www.snopes.com (for urban legends)
> www.symantec.com/avcenter/hoax.html (for computer virus hoaxes)

Also, it is a good idea to not leave your computer with your e-mail account still open. Anyone could sit down at your keyboard and send out an embarrassing or offensive message under your name.

Conclusion

As we have seen throughout the chapter, communication in any form needs to be effective. Strategies for ensuring effective communication in a business organization include providing education and training opportunities for managers and employees, fostering a corporate culture that values clear communication, and clearly articulating the organization's standards for communication. Organizations should provide their staffs with training and examples to follow that encompass all forms of effective communication—nonverbal communication (body language), speaking, listening, and writing.

To be effective, business communication must be clear and to the point. Many people have a tendency to keep adding more to the message being communicated. Unless there is real substance to the additional material, more is just more, not better. That's why this chapter will now draw to a close!

Endnotes

1. Christine Kay and John Russette, "Hospitality Management Competencies: Identifying Managers' Essential Skills," *Cornell Hotel and Restaurant Administration Quarterly* 42, no. 2 (2000): 53.

2. Henry Mintzberg, *The Nature of Managerial Work* (New York: Harper & Row, 1973).

3. C. Downs and C. A. Conrad, "A Critical Incident Study of Effective Subordinacy," *Journal of Business Communication*, Vol. 19 (1982), pp. 27–28.

4. C. A. Conrad, *Strategic Organizational Communication* (New York: Holt, Rinehart and Winston, 1985).

5. Portions of this section were adapted from Richard C. Huseman, et al., *Business Communications: Strategies and Skills*, 2d ed. (Chicago: Dryden Press, 1985), pp. 27–32.

6. Portions of this section were adapted from Raphael R. Kavanaugh and Jack D. Nine-meier, *Supervision in the Hospitality Industry*, 3rd ed. (Lansing, Mich.: Educational Institute of AH&LA, 2001), pp. 32–34.

7. Adapted from David A. Whetten and Kim S. Cameron, *Developing Management Skills* (Glenview, Ill.: Scott, Foresman and Co., 1984), p. 200.

8. Gary Yukl, *Skills for Managers and Leaders: Text, Cases and Exercises* (Englewood Cliffs, N.J.: Prentice-Hall, 1990), p. 108.

9. Some of the barriers in this list were adapted from Kavanaugh and Ninemeier.

10. Chad T. Lewis, Joseph P. Garcia, and Sarah M. Jobs, *Managerial Skills in Organizations* (Boston: Allyn and Bacon, 1990), p. 27.

11. P. Ekman, *Telling Lies: Clues to Deceit in the Marketplace, Politics, and Marriage* (New York: Norton, 1985).

12. A. Mehrabian, *Tactics of Social Influence* (Englewood Cliffs, N.J.: Prentice-Hall, 1972).

13. Lewis, Garcia, and Jobs, p. 27.

14. Edward T. Hall, *The Hidden Dimension* (New York: Doubleday, 1966).

15. K. Jensen, "Training Teachers to Use Verbal Intimacy, "*Communication Research Reports* 16, no. 3 (1999): 223.

16. Cyril R. Mill, "Feedback: The Art of Giving and Receiving Help," in Larry Porter and Cyril R. Mill (eds.), *The Reading Book for Human Relations Training* (Bethel, Maine: NTL Institute for Applied Behavioral Science, 1976), pp. 18–19.

17. Edwin A. Locke and Gary P. Latham, *Goal-Setting: A Motivational Technique That Works* (Englewood Cliffs, N.J.: Prentice-Hall, 1984).

18. Stephen P. Robbins, *Training in Inter-Personal Skills: TIPS for Managing People at Work* (Englewood Cliffs, N.J.: Prentice-Hall, 1989), p. 66.

19. Judi Brownell, "Perceptions of Effective Listeners," *The Journal of Business Communication*, Fall 1990, pp. 412–413.

20. Philip P. Hunsaker and Anthony J. Alessandra, *The Art of Managing People* (Englewood Cliffs, N.J.: Prentice-Hall, 1980), p. 33.

21. Hunsaker and Alessandra, pp. 32–34.

22. Some of these rules were adapted from Susan L. Brock, *Better Business Writing* (Menlo Park, Calif.: Crisp Publications, 1988), pp. 24–26.

Key Terms

active listening—Requires the listener to participate in the communication process by concentrating intensely on what the speaker is saying, listening with empathy and acceptance, and taking responsibility for getting the full message from the speaker.

body language—Signals sent from a person's face, arms, hands, legs, and posture that indicate his or her thoughts or mood.

devil's horns effect—Forming an overall negative impression of someone based solely on one undesirable quality that the individual is perceived to possess.

downward communication—Communication with those below you in the organization.

empathetic listening—Listening with an emphasis on understanding the speaker's feelings or acting as a sounding board for the speaker.

evaluative listening—Listening with an emphasis on understanding an argument or gaining enough information to make a decision or accept or reject an idea.

feedback—Any communication in which a person provides information about some aspect of another's message, work, or behavior.

full block letter style—A business-letter format in which all of the letter's elements—the date, addressee's name and address, salutation, main body, and closing—begin flush with the left margin (no indentations).

halo effect—Forming a positive impression of someone based solely on a single, positive attribute of the individual.

hidden agenda—A personal goal, expectation, or plan affecting your interactions with others that you do not reveal to others.

informational listening—Listening with an emphasis on understanding information. The goal of informational listening is to understand and remember the important information contained in the message.

intimate space—An area that ranges from skin contact to two feet (.6 meters) from an individual.

inverted pyramid—A style of writing in which the most important points are placed at the beginning of a written work, with lesser points included in the order of their importance.

lateral communication—Communication with those on the same level as you in the organization.

nonverbal communication—Information or messages conveyed through a person's dress, personal appearance, gestures, body movement, stance, and facial expressions.

paraphrase—To restate a message in your own words.

passive listening—Listening without really participating in the communication process.

personal space—An area two to four feet (.6 to 1.2 meters) from an individual.

project—To attribute or assign something in your own mind or a personal characteristic of yours to a person, group, object, or message.

public space—A nonthreatening area over 12 feet (3.7 meters) away from an individual.

sender-receiver model—A diagram that depicts the sending and receiving of communication between two parties.

social space—An area four to twelve feet (1.2 to 3.7 meters) from an individual.

summarizing statements—A part of active listening in which the listener condenses and restates parts of what the speaker has said in order to confirm that he or she correctly understands what the speaker is saying.

upward communication—Communication with those above you in the organization.

 # Review Questions

1. What are some myths about communication?

2. What are some barriers to effective interpersonal communication?

3. What is body language, and how can managers use it more effectively?

4. How can managers get better at communicating upward, downward, and laterally?

5. What are some of the strategies managers can use to give effective presentations?

6. What are six characteristics of effective feedback?

7. What are some techniques managers can use to improve their listening skills?

8. How do informational listening, evaluative listening, and empathetic listening differ from one another?

9. How can managers improve their business writing?

Chapter 7 Outline

Competencies

1. Explain the importance and nature of goal setting in an organization. (pp. 211–213)

2. List and briefly describe characteristics of effective goals. (pp. 213–216)

3. Identify guidelines managers should keep in mind when setting performance goals with employees. (pp. 216–219)

4. Summarize the challenges managers face and an important tool they can use when setting goals for themselves. (pp. 219–220)

5. Describe the nature of and need for coaching in today's hospitality organizations and identify potential barriers to coaching. (pp. 221–223)

6. Explain the use and significance of feedback when conducting coaching sessions. (pp. 223–224)

7. Explain why conflict occurs in organizations and describe positive and negative aspects of organizational conflict. (pp. 224–226)

8. Describe skills and list guidelines that can help managers handle organizational conflict. (pp. 226–227)

9. Summarize five conflict-management strategies, describe the four keys to principled negotiation, and outline strategies managers can use for third-party interventions. (pp. 227–230)

7

Goal-Setting, Coaching, and Conflict-Management Skills

GOAL SETTING, COACHING, AND CONFLICT MANAGEMENT are important skills for managers and leaders. Something to remember as you learn how to use the skills discussed in this chapter is that they should be used with one another. Effective managers master all of these skills and use them to get the most out of themselves and their employees.

Goal Setting

Lewis Carroll wrote the following in *Alice's Adventures in Wonderland:*

> Alice (to the Cheshire Cat): "Would you tell me, please, which way I ought to go from here?"
> "That depends a good deal on where you want to get to," said the Cat.
> "I don't much care where—" said Alice.
> "Then it doesn't matter which way you go," said the Cat.[1]

The same is true for managers and employees. If you do not care where you are going, developing goals is an irrelevant task. The creation of goals is only important and necessary if you do care where you are going. Without goals, you're like a dried leaf in autumn, blown wherever the winds take you.

Managers and employees should have a clear idea at all times of what they are trying to accomplish. Those who do are more likely to achieve their goals than those who do not. However, as anyone who has made a New Year's resolution knows, sticking to a goal is not easy.

Research has shown that there is a great monetary value to those organizations whose managers and employees set goals.[2] Research has also shown that in the hospitality industry, organizations' bottom lines increase between 10 and 20 percent as a direct result of goal setting. Furthermore, goal setting was found to benefit hospitality organizations by directing employees' attention, encouraging high-level performance, fostering innovation and persistence, and reducing stress.[3] Those organizations that insist on greater participation by their employees in the goal-setting process have also experienced increased employee motivation and improved performance.[4]

The authors wish to acknowledge the contributions to this chapter made by Misty Johanson, Ph.D., Associate Professor, School of Hospitality Leadership, DePaul University, Chicago, Illinois.

Exhibit 1   Sample Model for Setting and Attaining Goals

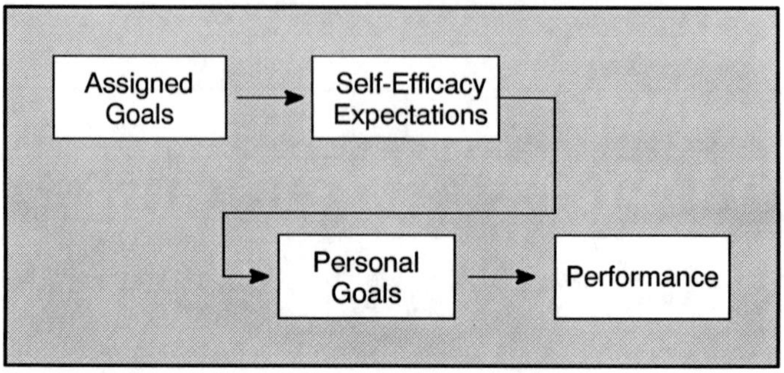

Source: Adapted from Edwin A. Locke and Gary P. Latham, *A Theory of Goal-Setting and Task Performance* (Englewood Cliffs, N.J.: Prentice-Hall, 1990).

Effective **goal setting** requires understanding how the goal-setting process works and identifying the skills that will help you attain goals. Edwin A. Locke and Gary P. Latham developed a widely accepted model for setting and attaining goals. This model, depicted in Exhibit 1, contains four distinctive steps: assigned goals, self-efficacy expectations, personal goals, and performance.[5]

In the "assigned goals" step, a goal is assigned to someone. Goals can be either self-assigned or assigned by others. "Self-efficacy expectations" refers to the beliefs the person has about being able to complete the goal. Goals serve as motivators because they cause people to compare their present capacity to perform with the capacity they need to succeed at their goals. If people believe that they will fall short of their goals, they feel dissatisfied and will work harder to attain them. As someone works to achieve an assigned goal, often it becomes a personal goal. Once this happens, the person is more likely to perform to whatever level is necessary to achieve the goal.

This model works only if people believe the assigned goal is attainable and they have the resources necessary to achieve the goal. If the goal is seen as unattainable, or if resources are not available, people usually will not work to achieve the goal. In other words, if goals seem to be reachable, people will work hard to reach them and feel bad if they don't, but they will not work hard for unreachable goals.

In addition to attainability, there are several other key ingredients to effective goal setting. For example:

- Difficult goals are more likely to lead to higher performance than easily attainable ones (but only if the difficult goals are thought to be attainable).

- Specific goals are more likely to lead to higher performance than vague or general ones (goals must have criteria for measurement).

- It is more likely that people will be motivated to work harder if they are informed along the way of the progress they are making toward reaching their goal (if left uninformed, many will lose interest).

- Goals are most likely to lead to higher performance when people have the abilities and skills required to reach them.

- When people accept goals as their own, the goals are more likely to lead to higher performance.

- Participation in setting goals helps people achieve higher performance.[6]

What do these findings mean to you as a manager? Some suggestions to keep in mind when setting goals for employees include the following:

- Difficult goals will do a better job of inspiring employees to perform at higher levels than easy goals (assuming employees believe the difficult goals are attainable). Therefore, setting easily attainable goals does not motivate as much as setting difficult goals.

- It's important to be specific when setting a goal. A goal such as "increase the number of rooms cleaned per day by 10 percent" is more effective than "clean more rooms." Without measureable criteria, the employee cannot judge whether he or she is improving and can become disheartened.

- Employees should be informed about the progress they are making toward attaining their goals. This information can motivate them further. The effect of feedback on goal attainment is shown in Exhibit 2. As you can see, consistent feedback significantly improves effectiveness.

- Unattainable goals do not motivate employees. A goal such as "increase the number of rooms cleaned per day by 50 percent," although specific, may be considered too high by employees and therefore will not motivate them. This is one reason why asking employees to help set their own goals is effective.

A good way to think about setting goals is to use the acronym SMART; a goal should be Specific, Measureable, Attainable, Realistic, and Timely. We will delve more deeply into the characteristics of effective goals in the following section.

Characteristics of Effective Goals

Gary Yukl says that effective goals share certain characteristics.[7] According to Yukl, goals must:

- Be clear and specific
- Be measurable
- Be verifiable
- Have time limits
- Be challenging
- Be relevant
- Be cost-effective
- Have controllable rather than uncontrollable outcomes
- Balance needs

Exhibit 2   Performance Without and With Feedback

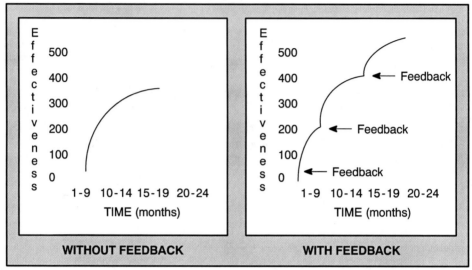

Source: R. D. Pritchard, R. S. D. Jones, P. L. Roth, K. K. Stuebing, and S. E. Ekeberg, "Effects of Group Feedback, Goal-Setting, and Incentives on Organizational Productivity," *Journal of Applied Psychology* 73 (1988): 337–358.

- Be measured over time
- Have objective measures

Each of these characteristics must be present for a goal to work effectively. Now let's take a closer look at each of these characteristics.

Clear and Specific. Goals must be clear and specific. Sometimes this is not easy. Sometimes goals are not completed, or are incorrectly completed, by employees simply because they did not understand the message. Therefore, when you discuss goals with others it is important to remember the lessons you learned about communicating clearly.

Specificity relates to the exactness of a goal. Goals such as "Do your best" or "Improve" are not specific. However, goals such as "Increase food sales by $1 per guest over the next two months" or "Decrease the number of days you are late for work to one per month beginning next month" are specific. Specific goals motivate; nonspecific goals do not motivate.

Measurable. Goals should be stated in terms that are easy to measure. The more measurable, the better. For example, the goal to "Increase food sales by $1 per guest over the next two months" is more measurable than "Increase food sales per guest" and is more easily measured than "Increase food sales per guest by a third" (this, while measurable, would be harder to calculate). "Experience a 10 percent decrease in guest complaints on guest comment cards over the next six months" is more measurable than "Make guests happier."

Verifiable. If a goal cannot be stated in measurable terms, it should be stated in verifiable terms. For example, a goal of "Rearrange the storeroom satisfactorily by 3:00 P.M." is not measurable. However, it is verifiable if both parties agree in advance on exactly what must be done to rearrange the storeroom satisfactorily.

Time Limits. Many goals are neglected or completed unsatisfactorily simply because the manager and the employee did not agree on a time limit in advance. "As soon as possible" is not specific enough. Neither is "soon," "right away," or "on high priority." Goals that include statements such as "by 2:00 P.M.," "by tomorrow at noon," "by June 1," and so on establish specific time limits.

Challenging. Goals should stretch a person's abilities, but not too far. Easy goals do not motivate because they seem unchallenging or childish; goals that are too hard to accomplish frustrate people.

A single goal for all employees probably will not work, because some employees perform at higher levels than others already. Therefore, while a goal for all the servers in a restaurant such as "Increase dessert sales to one dessert sold for every three adult guests served tonight" is measurable, clear, and specific, it may not motivate all servers. Some servers may already serve that many desserts or find it easy to do so. Others may believe that serving that many desserts is impossible. Managers must remember that their employees perform at different levels, so they should set employee goals at different levels, depending on the employee.

Relevant. Many managers set goals that employees consider irrelevant or trivial. For example, some managers set goals just to keep an employee busy. This makes it harder for employees to attain meaningful goals, since employees may become unable to distinguish the meaningful goals from the trivial ones. Setting unmeaningful goals is like "crying wolf"—after a while, nobody listens. Therefore, goals should be relevant to all concerned.

Cost-Effective. Given enough time, money, and people, almost any goal can be accomplished. However, some goals cost the organization too much to accomplish. Managers must consider how important a particular goal is and devote the appropriate resources to achieve it. The more important the goal, the more resources that can be devoted to it.

Controllable versus Uncontrollable Outcomes. Most managers and employees control only part of their jobs. Therefore, neither managers nor employees can control all aspects of many goals. For example, a hotel's maintenance department may be assigned a goal of decreasing expenses by 10 percent over three months. However, the rooms division manager may initiate room renovation projects to be carried out by in-house maintenance personnel. These two goals are in conflict with one another. The maintenance department will probably not reach its goal, due to a variable (the room renovation projects) over which it had no control.

This same principle applies to team goals. Individuals on a team should not be held solely accountable for the team's performance because they do not control all aspects of the team's performance. When evaluating a team, a manager should evaluate an employee's individual performance as well as the team's performance as a whole. Allowing each team member to evaluate the performance of all team members can motivate the team and help raise its overall performance, if done fairly.

Balance Needs. When setting goals, managers must keep the big picture in mind. A hotel manager is responsible for many different departments. A goal such as "Improve the hotel's overall profitability by 10 percent in June" may be attainable, but setting such a goal might risk hurting some departments in the hotel. When setting goals for several departments or units, managers must balance the needs of all the departments/units.

Measure Over Time. It is almost always better to measure goals over time than it is to measure them at a single point in time, because measurement over time (number of rooms cleaned every day for a week, sales per guest each day for a month, and so on) is a more accurate measurement of performance. Measuring a housekeeper's performance based on how many rooms he cleaned today is clearly not as accurate as measuring his performance based on how many rooms he cleaned each day over the last two weeks. A single day's performance does not take unusual circumstances into consideration.

Objective Measures. It is sometimes impossible to measure goals objectively. For example, restaurant and hotel chains like to set goals for all their units and compare one unit's performance to the average of the whole chain or to other units. This may not be a fair comparison. A restaurant in a high-traffic area might easily outperform a restaurant in a more out-of-the-way location, even though the staff of the out-of-the-way restaurant is just as talented and works just as hard. When Marriot opened the Fairfield Inn & Suites chain, the company installed computers for guest use at the front desks of the units. While the front desk agent computed a guest's bill, the guest completed a survey rating employee performance during his or her stay. The aggregated results of these surveys helped determine employee pay. The company had to abandon this approach, however, because a hotel next to Disneyland would always get higher marks than one, say, in Jackson, Mississippi.

One method of ensuring objectivity when evaluating managers or employees is to measure them against their own past performances. In this way, factors that might influence the performance of others do not work for or against the manager or employee being evaluated.

Setting Employee Goals

Managers are involved in setting two types of goals with employees: performance goals and self-improvement goals. Performance goals relate to attaining specific results at work; self-improvement goals relate either to the acquisition of knowledge or the development of skills by employees. In this section we will focus primarily on performance goals.

The number of performance goals set for or with an employee is important. Most research indicates that employees can work on no more than five to nine performance goals at one time.[8] This range has proven most effective because there are enough goals in it to capture the complexity of a work task, but there are not so many that employees become confused or think that they are being asked to accomplish too much.

An eight-step process for setting performance goals with employees is as follows:[9]

1. *Specify the objective or tasks to be completed.* Goal completion depends on establishing specific objectives or tasks. Objectives that are too general, such as, "I will do better at my job," are not specific enough.

2. *Establish difficult but attainable goals.* Be sure to establish goals that will require effort, yet be attainable.

3. *Specify how the employee's performance will be measured.* Be specific about whether the measures will include productivity, observations of changed behavior, or other measures.

4. *Specify the outcome to be reached.* Establish and discuss with the employee exactly what outcome you expect.

5. *Specify the deadline.* Remember, when setting deadlines, it is important to allow enough time for goals to be accomplished.

6. *Set priorities if there are multiple goals.* In the case of multiple goals, be sure to discuss and agree on which goal or goals are the most important. Be sure to use active listening skills to make sure that the employee understands the priorities.

7. *Determine coordination efforts.* If the employee needs the cooperation of others to attain a goal, be sure to arrange for this cooperation and explain to the employee how it will work. This is an especially important consideration when you set goals for teams.

8. *Establish a plan of action.* A step-by-step action plan makes goal attainment much easier. Since the steps of an action plan often represent "mini-goals," accomplishing them can encourage employees to keep progressing toward their goal.

Exhibit 3 is a self-assessment tool you can use to gauge how well you use goal-setting techniques when setting goals with employees.

Getting Employees to Accept Goals. There is a great deal of difference between goal creation and goal acceptance. Some suggestions for managers interested in encouraging employees to commit to goals are as follows:[10]

- *Provide support for goal completion.* You must support your employees' attempts to reach goals. Sometimes employees view goals as threatening or intimidating. Providing the necessary equipment, supplies, and other resources sends a strong message to employees that you are willing to help them attain the goals you assign to them. Positive managerial support leads to greater employee commitment to an organization and its goals.[11]

- *Encourage employees to participate in each step of the goal-setting process.* Managers must convince employees that their participation throughout the goal-setting process is accepted and valued. Too often, managers pay only marginal attention to employee suggestions about which goals should be set and

Exhibit 3   Setting Goals with Employees

Goal-Setting Checklist

When setting goals with employees:

	5	3	1	Points
I clearly state the purpose of the meeting.	usually	sometimes	seldom	_____
I review the employee's past accomplishments.	usually	sometimes	seldom	_____
I listen carefully to the employee.	usually	sometimes	seldom	_____
We create goals that are measurable, achievable, and relevant.	usually	sometimes	seldom	_____
I describe how I will measure the employee's progress.	usually	sometimes	seldom	_____
I obtain commitment from the employee and ask for an action plan.	usually	sometimes	seldom	_____
I use appropriate body language in the following areas:				
- Facial expression	usually	sometimes	seldom	_____
- Eye contact	usually	sometimes	seldom	_____
- Posture and movement	usually	sometimes	seldom	_____
- Gestures	usually	sometimes	seldom	_____
- Avoiding distracting visual mannerisms	usually	sometimes	seldom	_____
			Total Points	_____

If your score was between . . .	*Then you . . .*
55 and 41	use goal-setting techniques effectively.
40 and 26	use a number of goal-setting techniques well, but could improve in some areas.
25 and 11	need to work on improving many of the techniques used to set goals.

Three skills that I want to improve are:

1. _____

2. _____

3. _____

how they can be accomplished. When employees set the goal, they are more likely to attain it than when their boss sets it for them.

- *Pay attention to each employee's capabilities when setting goals for or with employees.* Employees are individuals. As a manager, you should make sure each employee has goals that are appropriate for him or her. People are unique—you should ensure that goals for each individual take into account that individual's unique personality, skill set, and so on.

- *Reward those who complete their goals.* Perhaps the most important step in the goal-setting process is to reward those who successfully complete their goals, whether they be performance or self-improvement goals. Giving employees who reach their goals a reward—be it recognition, a promotion, time off, or a salary increase—sends the message that you consider goal completion an important accomplishment. Word travels fast in most workplaces. If one employee receives rewards for attaining goals, you can bet others will hear about it quickly.

Setting Your Own Goals

In addition to setting goals for employees, managers must also set goals for themselves. While the process is essentially the same as that of setting goals for others, there is one major difference: there is no one helping you during the goal-setting process. When managers set goals for employees, the process involves two parties—the manager and the employee. The interaction helps manager and employee establish meaningful goals and inspires the employee to accomplish them. When setting goals for themselves, managers do not receive this feedback. This can be overcome by sharing your goals with others and listening to their feedback. Your boss, other managers, and even employees can help with this task.

One effective way for you to set your own goals is to use **SWOT analysis**. "SWOT" stands for *Strengths, Weaknesses, Opportunities,* and *Threats.* Adapted from strategic planning, the steps in the SWOT analysis technique for personal goal setting are as follows:[12]

- Make a list of personal strengths, or things you do well.

- Make a list of personal weaknesses, or things you do not do well.

- Make a list of opportunities for enhancing your capabilities (opportunities are drawn from the environment in which you work and live).

- Make a list of threats you face at work and in your personal life (threats are negative external forces that may affect you).

- Compare your strengths, weaknesses, opportunities, and threats (for example, strengths could offset weaknesses, enhance opportunities, and minimize threats).

- Create goals that you would like to achieve, taking into account your strengths, weaknesses, opportunities, and threats.

- Create a time line for accomplishing your goals (three months, one year, three years, and so on).

- Create action plans for accomplishing your goals. Action plans are the "baby steps" that eventually lead to goal attainment.

Carefully planned goals can help you improve your job performance. However, goal setting is not an easy task. As we discussed in the previous pages, you must pay attention to the various steps that make goals attainable. Before setting a goal for themselves, managers should review these steps.

Goals: Dreams Taken Seriously. What goals, personal as well as professional, would you like to achieve? Most people dream of accomplishment, success, and happiness. As publisher Malcolm Forbes once said, "When you cease to dream, you cease to live." Dreams are important; however, dreams do not come true unless you take action to achieve them. A good first action to take is to write your dreams down; this list can act as a constant reminder of what it is you want and should be working to achieve. Dreams become goals when you take the time to define them and then take action to achieve them.

Answering the following questions will help you determine which goals you would like to accomplish:

- Who am I?

- What do I want?

- How do I get it?

The first question can be answered through completion of the personal SWOT analysis just mentioned. By listing your strengths, weaknesses, opportunities, and threats, you can get a pretty good start at defining yourself. The second question, "What do I want?" can be analyzed by making a list, or several lists, of what it is that would make your life easier, more complete, or simply more fun. This list should include not only your professional life but as many other facets of your life as possible. "How do I get it?" helps you zero in on what kinds of action steps are necessary in order to accomplish your goals. A person cannot move an entire mountain all at once; however, any mountain can be moved one rock at a time. Making a list of action steps is like making a plan to move the rocks, one by one. Visualizing the end result can also help you attain your goals.

Goal attainment often involves other people. They can be bosses, co-workers, employees, family members, and friends. Knowing who to turn to for help and how to engage them in your action steps will help you attain your goals. In business, the people who support us are often referred to as our **"network."** Good goal-setters rely on their networks to help them reach their dreams.

In *Atlas Shrugged*, Ayn Rand wrote, "To me, there is only one form of human depravity—the man without a purpose." This begs the question, what do you do each morning if you have no goals? An employee without goals is likely not a good employee, while a manager without goals is likely not a good manager. Both are just passing the time, day by day.

As George Eliot said, "It is never too late to be who you might have been." It's all a matter of setting goals.

Coaching

The great Notre Dame football coach Ara Parseghian once said, "A good coach will make his players see what they can be rather than what they are." That statement captures a lot of what coaching in the workplace is about—i.e., getting the absolute most out of your team of players (employers, supervisors, and managers).

Coaching has been defined as "a directive process by a manager to train and orient an employee to the realities of the workplace and to help the employee remove barriers to optimum work performance."[13] Management's objective when coaching an employee is to help the employee become better at his or her job by identifying performance problems and helping the employee correct them. As the hospitality industry has redirected its management focus from controlling to empowering, coaching has become an imperative management skill.[14] Coaching is an ongoing process. To be a successful coach, a manager must provide employees with constructive feedback and assess each employee's performance on a regular basis.

There are three primary misconceptions about coaching in the hospitality industry:

- "Coaching is reactive and is either a form of discipline or reward." *False.* Coaching involves "assisting employees as they become empowered and begin to take on greater responsibilities. It does not consist of warnings and it does not involve managers keeping control of all power and responsibility. Furthermore, coaching is neither a reward system nor a component of a compensation or benefits package."[15]

- "Coaching is training." *False.* Training is different from coaching, but training and coaching are complimentary activities. While training is essential, "90 percent of all training objectives will be lost without follow-up coaching."[16]

- "Coaching requires only part-time attention." *False.* Coaching is "an ongoing function, as managers continually look for opportunities to coach their employees through feedback on performance problems or praise them on successful completion of a responsibility."[17]

It is critical for the future success of hospitality managers and their employees that these myths are addressed and proper training given so the practice of coaching can be used as a vital management tool.

Managers as Coaches

John Wooden, the great coach of UCLA basketball, once said, "A coach is someone who can give direction without causing resentment." To coach effectively, managers must learn how to coach others without provoking resentment from them. This is not always easy to do, but it is an attainable goal.

Generally speaking, most employees are one of three types: (1) those who have no problems completing their work in an acceptable fashion, (2) those who have problems completing their work and go to their manager for help with the problems, and (3) those who have problems but do not tell their manager. Unfortunately, many managers think they have too few of the first type, not enough of the second type, and too many of the third type. While some managers wish for a workplace in which employees never come to them with problems, this should not be their goal. In fact, this is perhaps the opposite of what managers should want. A manager's dream should be the employee who comes to him or her with a problem. Why? Because employees who identify problems for their managers actually make a manager's job easier in the long run. This is because problem identification is always the hardest part of finding solutions and making things better.

Helping employees solve problems builds the manager's reputation as a leader. It can increase opportunities for the manager to help employees motivate themselves, increase the employees' creativity and innovation, build team cohesiveness, and add to a manager's authority. It can also help the manager and employees avoid embarrassing surprises in performance evaluations. A manager who helps an employee solve a problem also helps establish what can become a long-term relationship between the company and the employee.

Why Employees Don't Ask for Help

Creating an environment in which employees feel that they can ask for help with their problems is a major first step in building a quality hospitality operation. However, no matter how often a manager emphasizes that he or she has an open-door policy, some employees will not ask for help. There are several reasons for this. Some employees believe that asking for help will make their manager think that they are incapable of doing their work. They likely think this either because their manager has criticized others in this way or because a former boss did so. Others believe that it is better to figure things out for themselves. Some employees are afraid that asking their manager for help with work problems may make co-workers believe that they are trying to "get in good with the boss." Some employees believe that managers don't have time to help them with their problems. And some employees may not come to their managers with problems because their cultural background discourages such action.

Managers also sometimes inadvertently discourage their employees from coming to them with problems through words or actions. For example, managers who praise employees who consistently make decisions on their own may be sending the message to other employees that this is expected of all employees.

Because employees often will not ask for help, managers must become proficient at identifying employees who need help. Declining work performance or productivity; disinterest; lack of cooperativeness; defensiveness with supervisors, co-workers, or guests; disorganization; absenteeism; irritability; lack of enthusiasm; and increased complaining are all signs that an employee needs coaching.

Why Managers Don't Want to Become Coaches

Managers have many reasons for not wanting to coach their employees. Some managers think that if they take the time to coach one employee, they may end up having to coach all of their employees (although many managers would say that having employees eager to be coached would be a good thing). Some managers believe that employees will feel threatened by the attention a manager gives to their problems (although employees rarely feel this way). Other managers think it is better for employees to figure things out on their own (coaching employees in how to make decisions will lead to this in the long run, and this is what managers want; the best managers are people who literally work themselves out of a job—i.e., they are no longer needed because all employees do the right thing all the time). Managers who hold these anti-coaching beliefs are missing golden opportunities to enhance their relationships with employees and improve the organization's performance.

The Importance of Feedback

Employees fail to perform effectively for three principal reasons:

- They do not know how to do their jobs
- Something or someone is keeping them from doing their jobs
- They do not want to do their jobs

Employees who fail to perform because they do not know how to do their jobs generally need feedback on their performance. Employees who fail to perform because something or someone is keeping them from it may not have the right equipment (or equipment that does not work properly). The activities of other employees may prevent some employees from doing their jobs effectively, or the boss may not be giving an employee enough time to do a job properly. Employees who do not want to do their jobs sometimes feel this way because they have a bad attitude. Unfortunately, many managers tend to think that all employees who fail to perform have a bad attitude. This is usually not the case, however. A study conducted at Cornell University of turnover among hospitality employees found that most employees leave their jobs for one of two reasons: an inability to work with their managers, or an inability to work with their co-workers—*not* because they either did not like their jobs or because they did not like to work at all.[18]

While feedback is the strongest weapon in a coach's arsenal for turning employee performance around, managers often use it in ways that cause more harm than good. For example, managers who provide their employees primarily with negative feedback can sour employee attitudes about their jobs, which can lead to lower productivity. Managers can also cause more harm than good by saying nothing. While the "strong, silent type" may be desirable in some professions, management is not one of them. Managers who say little or nothing to their employees are sending the message that all is well, whether it is or not. Consider, for example, what a restaurant cook must think at the end of a shift if his or her boss provides no feedback. Since nothing was said, the cook would go home thinking that everything must be okay, even if several problems occurred during the shift that the cook contributed to and the manager knows about but the cook is unaware of. To employees, when a boss says nothing, that means all is well.

There are four types of feedback: silence, criticism, advice, and reinforcement. Each of the four is likely to produce different results. Silence on the part of a manager generally sends the message that everything is going well or that the status quo should be maintained. Criticism is useful in stopping undesirable behaviors or results in the short run. Advice helps to shape or change behaviors or results. Only reinforcement is useful in increasing desired performance or results over the long term. Exhibit 4 further illustrates the impact of each of these four types of feedback.

Exhibit 4   Types of Feedback

TYPE	DEFINITION	PURPOSE	IMPACT
Silence	No response	Maintain status quo	• Decreases confidence • Reduces performance • Creates surprises later • Can create paranoia
Criticism	Identifies behaviors or results that are undesirable	Stop undesirable behaviors/ results	• Causes excuses or blaming of others • Decreases confidence • Leads to escape and avoidance • Hurts relationships
Advice	Identifies highly regarded behaviors or results; specifies how to use them	Shape or change behaviors/results to increase performance	• Improves confidence • Improves relationship • Improves performance
Reinforcement	Identifies desirable behaviors or results	Increase desired performance/results	• Increases confidence • Increases performance • Increases motivation

Source: Marianne Minor, *Coaching and Counseling: A Practical Guide for Managers* (Menlo Park, Calif.: Crisp Publications, Inc., 1989), pp. 28–29.

Conducting Coaching Sessions

Exhibit 5 provides tips for conducting a coaching session. These are general guidelines only. Unexpected events may occur during a coaching session that a manager will have to adapt to at the time. Therefore, managers must remain flexible when coaching.

Employees can react both positively and negatively to advice provided during a coaching session. One employee may welcome advice and immediately consider ways in which he or she can put the advice to use; another may become argumentative or emotional. The manager must remember that the purpose of coaching is to provide advice and assistance that will improve an employee's performance. If an employee becomes argumentative or emotional, much of the potentially positive benefits of the session will probably be lost. In such cases, it is best for the manager to terminate the coaching session, ask the employee to carefully consider why he or she is responding in a negative manner, and plan a second session to discuss this topic. The success of coaching depends on good communication. Sessions that are interrupted by tears, angry outbursts, or other emotional displays probably will not produce good results.

Conflict Management

Differences of opinion are natural. So, too, is conflict over such differences. The key to minimizing conflict is how such differences are handled. Conflict occurs often in organizations, but not all of it is based on actual ill-feeling by one party for another. Conflict sometimes occurs simply because one person or group wants resources that another person or group also wants. For example, front office managers may want to use training funds for training their employees to use the front

Exhibit 5   Tips for Conducting a Coaching Session

Before the Session
1. Establish a clear agenda in advance.
2. Make sure the employee knows about and understands the agenda.
3. Clear your calendar to allow ample time for the coaching session.
4. Find a quiet and private place to conduct the session.
5. Ensure that there will be no interruptions during the session.

At the Session
1. Greet the employee promptly and warmly.
2. Put the employee at ease by using receptive body language and lots of eye contact.
3. Allow the employee to become comfortable by beginning with small talk.
4. Describe the performance problem or issue that you want to address.
5. Ask open-ended questions about the employee's thoughts or feelings on the issue.
6. Encourage the employee to discuss the issue.
7. Encourage the employee to identify alternative solutions to the issue.
8. Offer suggestions to improve on the employee's solutions or thoughts on the issue.
9. Agree on appropriate goals.
10. Agree on appropriate action plans to accomplish the goals.
11. Establish a specific timetable for accomplishing the goals.
12. Schedule a follow-up session for reviewing progress.
13. Thank the employee for his or her interest, suggestions, and attention.

office computer system more effectively, while the human resources department may want to use the funds for training front office employees in other skills. This conflict is typical of the types of conflicts that occur in businesses.

Business theorists used to preach that all conflict was negative.[19] This is not true, however. Conflict can also enhance creativity and innovation when managed properly, and it has been shown to be an effective force in both organizational cohesiveness and team effectiveness.[20] Conflict can also help parties with divergent opinions to work together more closely.[21]

This does not mean that all conflict is positive. Sometimes conflict can be very destructive. The key for managers is to know how to manage conflict in such a way that the positive is emphasized and the negative is minimized.

Causes of Conflict

The first step in knowing how to manage conflict is understanding why conflict occurs. Conflict within organizations usually occurs because of one or more of the following reasons:[22]

- *Competition for resources.* Resources in organizations are always limited. The more limited they are, the more likely conflict is to occur. Conflict can occur over major resources such as funding for projects, facilities improvement, and so on. However, conflict can also occur over such issues as work space and office supplies.

- *Task interdependence.* Conflict is most likely to occur between individuals or groups that are dependent on one another. This dependence can be one-way or two-way. For example, servers in a restaurant regularly rely on cooks. In some ways, the cooks also rely on the servers (for example, for correct orders).

- *Jurisdictional ambiguity.* Overlapping responsibilities often lead to conflict. This can occur when one party takes responsibility that another can also claim. This could be cured by carefully designing the organization to ensure that no one's responsibilities overlapped. However, the result would likely be a highly bureaucratic and segmented organization, which is undesirable. Organizations should encourage employees to work as teams to solve problems. A strategy some organizations use to ensure teamwork is to create overlapping responsibilities. Managers must be prepared to help solve problems that arise from such an organizational design.

- *Status struggles.* Status struggles can result from perceived inequities. Status struggles can also occur when one person or group believes that it should be giving recommendations or instructions to another person or group instead of receiving them. This can happen between managers of different departments in a hotel, for example. It can also occur among employees—when bartenders believe that they should be giving orders to servers, not vice versa.

- *Communication barriers.* Conflicts regularly occur because two people or groups do not speak the same "language." Technical language can lead to confusion, which can lead to conflict about who said what or what meaning was intended. Insufficient communication or communication problems that lead to lack of understanding about organizational goals and how they relate to individuals or groups also can cause conflict.

- *Differences in values and beliefs.* Conflict is more likely between groups with differing social, ethnic, racial, or cultural values or beliefs.

Conflict-Management Skills

Managers can develop conflict-management approaches that fit their personalities and responsibilities. Development of these approaches depends on mastering conflict-management skills. Some of the skills important to **conflict management** include the following:

- *Listening skills.* Active listening can help managers understand what the party or parties involved in the conflict are really saying. Sometimes conflict can be resolved simply by achieving a better understanding of a situation by listening carefully to the party or parties.

- *Feedback skills.* Knowing how to provide constructive feedback to those in conflict can help soothe the confrontation.

- *Conflict-management styles.* There are a variety of conflict-management styles managers can use to help resolve a conflict (conflict-management styles will be discussed later in the chapter). Most managers have a favorite style. Knowing what it is can help you recognize when you should use it and when some other approach may be necessary. Knowing your own preferred style also helps you anticipate how you are likely to behave in a conflict.

Other tips for effectively handling conflicts include the following:

- *Be selective about the conflicts you get involved in.* Not every conflict requires your intervention. Sometimes minor conflicts are simply not worth your time and effort. Letting employees resolve their own conflicts often enhances their overall performance and abilities. Picking the battles you want to fight is especially important in personal conflicts.

- *Evaluate the participants in a conflict.* Knowing who is involved, why they are involved, what their interests and positions are, and what they hope to gain from a conflict will help you resolve the conflict.

- *Assess the source of the conflict.* Earlier we discussed some reasons why conflicts occur. Competition for resources, task interdependence, jurisdictional ambiguity, status struggles, communication barriers, and differences in values and beliefs all can cause conflict. Knowing a conflict's cause can help a manager evaluate the facts and criteria for resolving it.

- *Know your conflict-management options and select the best one.* Managers can use a variety of conflict-management strategies. Managers tend to use their favorite conflict-management option all of the time, but that option may not be the best approach in a given situation. You should base your selection of a particular conflict-management strategy on the situation at hand, not on your personal preferences.

Conflict-Management Strategies

Authors T. L. Ruble and K. W. Thomas classified the various approaches to conflict management into five strategies: avoidance, accommodation, compromise, collaboration, and competitiveness.[23] These classifications are still appropriate today. Exhibit 6 shows the Ruble and Thomas model.

According to Exhibit 6, it would appear that collaboration is always the best approach to use because it is high in both assertiveness and cooperativeness. However, this is only the case when several conditions exist: namely, that both parties are willing to ignore political or power issues, both parties are open-minded, and both parties are aware of the potential for conflict with the other.[24]

Sometimes, accommodation and avoidance are effective in circumstances when collaboration is not. Both accommodation and avoidance can work when you have to handle a temporary situation. You may want to simply accommodate a rude customer, for example. Accommodation takes the least amount of energy and effort. Therefore, at times when it is not worth the trouble to do anything else, accommodation may be a very appropriate response. Avoidance is useful in

Exhibit 6   Conflict Management Strategies

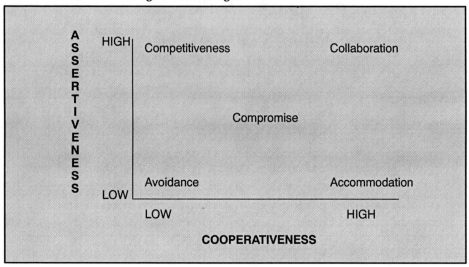

Source: T. L. Ruble and K. W. Thomas, "Support for a Two-Dimensional Model of Conflict Behavior," *Organizational Behavior and Human Performance* 16 (1976).

temporarily handling emotional situations, because this approach allows people time to "cool off."

The competitive strategy for managing conflict may be useful when something important is at stake. For example, it may be necessary to assert yourself more and accommodate less when conflict occurs over an issue that is particularly important to you or your company. Managers who use this approach too often, however, often get the reputation of being too hard-nosed or disagreeable. The competitive approach should be reserved for truly important issues.

Compromise is the best approach in many situations—especially in situations in which it is necessary to work with the other party in the future and therefore it is especially important to maintain good relations.

Principled Negotiation. Authors Roger Fisher and William Ury identified a process that helps people resolve conflicts in such a way that all parties can gain something from the interaction.[25] They refer to this process as **principled negotiation.** There are four keys to principled negotiation:

- *Separate the people from the problem.* Personal relationships often interfere with negotiations. Those in conflict often attack one another rather than the problem. When this occurs, any chance at resolving the conflict disappears quickly. Sticking to the issues is the best way to avoid this problem.

- *Focus on what people* really *mean.* It may be necessary to read between the lines of what someone is saying to find out what he or she really means.

- *Invent options for mutual gain.* Using techniques to create options that are mutually acceptable can solve many conflicts. Creativity-enhancing techniques (brainstorming, nominal group technique, free association, and so on) engaged in together by both parties might result in the creation of alternatives neither party thought of alone.

- *Use objective criteria.* Using objective criteria involves identifying a set of criteria that seem fair and reasonable to all parties and then applying those criteria to the conflict. For example, a conflict between managers from two departments over resources might be resolved if they agree to compare the current resource levels of the two departments against those of other properties in the chain, or against industry averages.

Strategies for Third-Party Interventions. Managers are often called on to resolve conflicts involving employees, other managers, or an employee or manager and a guest. Three third-party intervention strategies that are available to managers are mediation, process consultation, and organizational changes.

Mediation. The role of a mediator is to help the parties in conflict arrive at a resolution. Therefore, it is extremely important that mediators are impartial and trusted by both parties. The difficulty of this role depends on how polarized the parties have become. In an extremely polarized conflict, the two parties may no longer even be attempting to work out a resolution. When this is the case, mediators can either attempt to bring the two parties back together face-to-face to discuss issues or relay messages back and forth between the parties. A mediator can also create hypothetical solutions and suggest them to both parties in an attempt to reach common ground. Coming up with possible solutions is an extremely important function a mediator can perform in polarized conflicts, because typically neither party wants to look weak by suggesting alternative solutions.

Data collection is another important role mediators often play. When two parties are polarized to the extent that a mediator is required, they often have failed to recognize or discuss the facts pertinent to the conflict. Introduction of new information by the mediator can help overcome this impasse. It is very important that a mediator know as many of the facts about the conflict situation as possible.

Process consultation. While the focus of mediation is on issues, the focus of **process consultation** is on the attitudes the conflicting parties hold toward one another. Conflicting groups are sometimes unable to reach agreement because of distrust or hostility. Process consultation attempts to improve the relationship between the groups to the point that they can resolve the conflict themselves.

A primary objective in process consultation is to help each side understand why the other side holds the opinions that it does and is seeking the solutions it is seeking. Yukl suggested a variety of methods to accomplish this.[26] One method is to ask each group to describe how it perceives itself and the other group. These descriptions should include goals, intentions, attitudes, and behaviors relevant to the conflict. When this approach is used, the groups should first prepare written descriptions, then share them with the other group; then each group should examine its own self-perception versus that held by the other. Usually a meeting is then held so that the groups can discuss their different perceptions. The facilitator of this meeting should promote active listening to ensure that each side fully understands the other's perspective. Ideally, this meeting results in identifying the issues that must be resolved and the action plans needed to resolve them.

The same process can be used for individuals, with slight modifications. Used often by marriage counselors, process consultation for individuals begins with the written descriptions and the reviews of the written descriptions, as does group consultation. However, after this the two parties are encouraged to openly discuss what the other party does that disturbs them. During this process one person speaks and the other must listen without interruption. When finished, the listener must repeat what the speaker said (an active listening technique). Then the roles are reversed. Finally, each person is asked to describe actions that he or she can take that would facilitate reconciliation.

Organizational changes. Sometimes the best way to reduce or eliminate conflict is to change organizational policies, procedures, or rewards. For example, instead of rewarding competition, a manager might create a system to reward cooperation. In this way, employees are rewarded for working toward common goals. Other organizational changes managers can make include transfers, promotions, or organizational design changes that reduce or increase interaction, physical distances, and so on.

Guidelines for third-party interventions. Yukl provided a list of guidelines for third-party interventions that can help managers effectively reduce, eliminate, or solve conflicts. These include the following:[27]

For Problem-Oriented Conflicts

- Ask each party to explain how it views the problem.

- Provide factual information to help all parties understand the issues.

- Encourage parties to openly state their real needs and priorities (conflicts often focus on nonrelevant issues).

- Encourage parties to identify shared objectives and values.

- Encourage parties to generate solutions that meet the needs of all parties.

- Suggest compromises.

- Ensure commitment by all parties.

For Relationship-Oriented Conflicts

- Remain impartial and show respect for both parties.

- Discourage nonproductive behaviors (insults, stereotyping, and so on).

- Ensure that each party has the opportunity to speak.

- Encourage active listening.

- Ask both parties to describe how they view the other party's actions.

- Ask both parties to describe how they view their own actions.

- Ask both parties to select one to three items they would be willing to change.

- Use humor to break the tension.

Endnotes

1. Martin Gardner, *The Annotated Alice: Alice's Adventures in Wonderland & Through the Looking Glass* (New York: Clarkson N. Potter, Inc., 1960), p. 88.

2. David E. Terpstra and Elizabeth J. Rozell, "The Relationship of Goal Setting to Organizational Profitability," *Group and Organization Management* 19, no. 3 (1994): 285–294; and Nikos Mourkogiannis, "The Return in HR from Purpose-Focused Organizations," *Employee Relations Today* 35, no. 2 (2008): 25–30.

3. Edward A. Merritt and Florence Berger, "The Value of Setting Goals," *Cornell Hotel and Restaurant Administration Quarterly* 39, no. 1 (1998): 40–49.

4. Frederick J. De Micco, Steven J. Dempsey, Fulton F. Galer, and Martin Baker, "Participative Budgeting and Participant Motivation: A Review of the Literature," *FIU Hospitality Review* 6, no. 1 (1998): 77–94; and James L. Perry, Debra Mesch, and Laurie Paarlberg, "Motivating Employees in a New Governance Era: The Performance Paradigm Revisited," *Public Administration Review* 28, no. 2 (2006): 505–514.

5. Edwin A. Locke and Gary P. Latham, "Goal Setting Theory: Theory Building by Induction," in *Great Minds in Management: The Process of Theory Development*, eds. Ken G. Smith and Michael A. Hitt (New York: Oxford University Press, 2007).

6. Gary P. Latham and Timothy P. Steele, "The Motivational Effects of Participation versus Goal-Setting on Performance," *Academy of Management Journal* 26, no. 3 (1983): 406–417.

7. Gary Yukl, *Skills for Managers and Leaders: Text, Cases and Exercises* (Englewood Cliffs, N.J.: Prentice-Hall, 1990), pp. 131–134.

8. Yukl, p. 131.

9. Edwin A. Locke and Gary P. Latham, *Goal-Setting: A Motivational Technique That Works!* (Englewood Cliffs, N.J.: Prentice-Hall, 1984).

10. Adapted from Stephen P. Robbins, *Training in Inter-Personal Skills: TIPS for Managing People at Work* (Englewood Cliffs, N.J.: Prentice-Hall, 1989), pp. 51–52.

11. Douglas A. Amyx and Bruce Alford, "Salesperson Performance and Organizational Commitment: An Empirical Model," *Journal of Personal Selling and Sales Management* 25, no. 4 (2005): 345–359.

12. Joseph E. Garcia, "Reflections on Teaching Diversity," *Journal of Management Education* 18, no. 4 (1994): 430–431.

13. Marianne Minor, *Coaching and Counseling: A Practical Guide for Managers* (Menlo Park, Calif.: Crisp Publications, Inc., 1989), p. 2.

14. Michelle Krazmien and Florence Berger, "The Coaching Paradox," *International Journal of Hospitality Management* 16, no. 1 (1997): 3–10.

15. Krazmien and Berger, p. 7.

16. Krazmien and Berger, p. 8.

17. Krazmien and Berger.

18. Robert H. Woods and James F. Macaulay, "R for Turnover: Retention Programs That Work," *Cornell Hotel and Restaurant Administration Quarterly* 30, no. 1 (1989): 70–90.

19. Karen A. Jehn, "A Quantitative Analysis of Conflict Types and Dimensions in Organizational Groups," *Administrative Science Quarterly* 42, no. 2 (1997): 238–256.

20. Amanuel Tekleab, N. R. Quigley, and P. E. Tesluk, "A Longitudinal Study of Team Conflict, Conflict Management, Cohesion, and Team Effectiveness," *Group and Organization Management* 34, no. 2 (2009): 170–180.

21. Gerrard Macintosh and Charles Stevens, "Personality, Motives, and Conflict Strategies in Everyday Service Encounters," *International Journal of Conflict Management* 19, no. 2 (2008): 91–110.

22. Yukl, pp. 283–286.

23. T. L. Ruble and K. W. Thomas, "Support for a Two-Dimensional Model of Conflict Behavior," *Behavior and Human Performance* 16 (1976): 143–155.

24. Charles B. Derr, "Managing Organizational Conflict: Collaboration, Bargaining, and Power Approaches," *California Management Review* 21, no. 3 (1978): 76–90.

25. Roger Fisher and William Ury, *Getting to Yes* (New York: Viking-Penguin, Inc., 1981).

26. Yukl, p. 294.

27. Yukl, p. 296.

 # Key Terms

coaching—A directive process used by a manager to train and orient an employee to the realities of the workplace and to help the employee remove barriers to optimum work performance.

conflict management—A process in which a manager attempts to resolve a conflict by applying listening skills, feedback skills, and one or more of a variety of conflict-management strategies.

goal setting—A process in which objectives are created to improve one's work performance or personal skills.

network — The group of people who provide support to goal setters. This group can comprise friends, family, co-workers, bosses, etc.

principled negotiation—A process that helps conflicting parties resolve conflicts in such a way that all parties gain something from the resolution. Four keys to principled negotiation are to separate the people from the problem, focus on what people *really* mean, invent options for mutual gain, and use objective criteria.

process consultation—A process for resolving conflict that emphasizes understanding the attitudes the conflicting parties hold toward one another. Process consultation attempts to improve the relationship between the parties to the point that they can resolve the conflict themselves.

SWOT analysis—A brainstorming technique. "SWOT" stands for Strengths, Weaknesses, Opportunities, and Threats.

Review Questions

1. What are some of the keys to effective goal setting?
2. What are some of the characteristics of effective goals?
3. How can managers encourage employees to accept goals?
4. What are some techniques managers can use when setting their own goals?
5. Why do employees hesitate to ask their managers for help?
6. How should managers conduct coaching sessions with employees?
7. What are some of the causes of conflict within organizations?
8. What are some strategies managers can use to manage organizational conflict?

Chapter 8 Outline

Competencies

1. Identify forces of change that have made team-building a high priority for many hospitality organizations. (p. 235)

2. Describe ways in which teams can solve specific hospitality-related problems. (pp. 235–236)

3. Describe the kind of organizational support that is necessary for teams to succeed. (pp. 237–241)

4. Indicate the best size for a team and explain how a mission statement and a code of conduct increase the effectiveness of a team. (pp. 241–244)

5. Describe the basic role of the team leader and list some factors to consider in assessing an individual's leadership potential. (p. 245)

6. List the stages a team goes through during its development, summarize typical team-member characteristics at each stage, and describe how the role of the team leader changes as a team passes through the different stages of team development. (pp. 245–255)

7. Identify positive and negative roles that individuals may play in groups. (pp. 255–257)

8. Summarize tips on how to plan, conduct, and evaluate meetings effectively. (pp. 257–264)

9. Define a consensus decision and describe techniques that teams can use to reach decisions by consensus. (pp. 264–266)

10. Outline criteria by which high-performance teams can be evaluated. (pp. 266–267)

8

High-Performance Teams

BUSINESS ORGANIZATIONS have traditionally been led by hierarchical management systems that designed jobs for individuals.[1] Jobs were engineered as compartmentalized functions made up of simple, repetitive, fragmented tasks performed by workers on assembly lines. Managers and supervisors made all the decisions; employees simply followed orders.

Hospitality organizations followed the systems and structures of manufacturing firms. The compartmentalization of hotel functions began as basic operational distinctions: the front of the house and the back of the house. From there, departmental boundaries were drawn, standard operating procedures were set in stone, and turf wars began between the dining room and the kitchen, between convention sales and the rooms division, between housekeeping and engineering, and so on. These silos hurt the organizations. Yet, somehow, the employees made the system work. Meals were prepared and served, convention groups were booked, and broken vacuum cleaners were repaired. Individuals found ways around a cumbersome system to get the job done, while meeting and—at times—exceeding guest expectations.

Today's team-oriented hospitality organizations have reengineered jobs to fit a new business environment, one marked by increased competition, rapidly changing market demands, and higher productivity and quality goals. They found that the old, top-heavy hierarchical management system limited a hospitality organization's ability to make decisions fast enough to keep up with changing guest needs and expectations. They turned to team-based decision-making and problem-solving to improve the efficiency and overall effectiveness of their organizations.

The responsibility for addressing critical issues, solving operational problems, and improving productivity is no longer management's alone. These goals are best achieved through teamwork involving those employees who are closest to the problems and closest to the guests.[2]

Examples of Hospitality Teams

Team-oriented organizations support a variety of teams: departmental work teams, **cross-functional teams** (with members from several different departments),

---

This chapter was originally written by Sheryl Fried Kline, Ph.D., Associate Dean, College of Hospitality, Retail, & Sport Management, University of South Carolina, Columbia, South Carolina.

continuous-improvement teams, and specially designated **task-force teams**. Teams can be made up of members from a single department or from several departments. Teams can be temporary or permanent aspects of a department, division, or organization. And team meetings can be formal and routinely scheduled or casual and scheduled only on an as-needed basis. In other words, teams can take many shapes. The following examples briefly describe the efforts of several teams at different hospitality properties.

Will the Real Las Vegas Style Please Set Up? A meeting planner requested a Las Vegas–style banquet setup. The director of catering instructed the setup crew appropriately; however, when the banquet manager inspected the room after setup, he was appalled. "This is not Las Vegas–style seating!" he exclaimed. The setup crew rearranged the room. Once again, when the banquet manager inspected the new setup, he cried, "This is not Las Vegas style!"

As a result of these communication problems, a team was formed comprising the banquet manager, the director of catering, the executive steward, and the supervisor of the setup crew. All agreed that banquet event orders contained information that was often incomplete, vague, and sometimes wrong. The team held brainstorming sessions and eventually produced a list of every type of banquet setup and the proper terms that should be used to describe them. Next, the team diagrammed each type of setup and distributed copies to every department involved in the sale or service of banquet functions. It soon became much easier for these departments to communicate effectively with one another.

Distributing the setup diagrams to prospective banquet customers helped ensure that hotel employees and prospective guests were speaking the same language. This eliminated unwelcome surprises and assured prospective guests that their expectations would be met.

Housekeeping and Maintenance Finally Get Together. Housekeeping room attendants were frustrated by the lack of response to work orders that they submitted to the maintenance department. They often had to send two or three requests for each guestroom repair. Room attendants felt that maintenance failed not only to respond to work orders quickly enough, but, more importantly, that they also failed to understand how prompt repair work significantly increased guest satisfaction.

Managers decided that better communication and cooperation were needed from both departments and formed a team consisting of room attendants and maintenance employees. The first problem the team tackled was the maintenance department's alleged slow response to repair requests from housekeeping. At team meetings, each department finally got the opportunity to hear the other side of the story. The team agreed on priorities for handling different types of work orders. It also instituted a reply system by which maintenance could keep housekeeping informed about the current status of work orders, including the status of parts or furniture that had to be ordered. In addition, maintenance formed a "Do It Now" Squad that consisted of maintenance workers with moveable carts stocked with parts and tools for most minor repair work. The housekeeping and maintenance departments are no longer at odds with each other because the team opened the communication channels between the two.

Organizational Support for Successful Teams

The fundamental premise of team-oriented organizations is that the performance level of teams exceeds that of individuals.[3] High-performance teams are examples of synergy in the workplace: the productivity of a team can be greater than the sum of the productivity of its members working alone. Especially in decision-making situations, teams consistently outperform the average individual.

However, successful teams do not develop in a vacuum. High-performance teams thrive only in organizations that are willing to provide the resources teams need to achieve their goals. Exhibit 1 is an example of a survey managers can fill out to help them determine whether organizational conditions are right for forming teams.

In addition to visible support from the top, basic resources that team-oriented organizations supply for teams include:

- Direction and guidelines for team activities

- Access to information and facilities

- Team training

- Award and recognition systems

Direction and Guidelines for Team Activities

The primary resource provided by team-oriented organizations is a leadership commitment that clearly defines the direction of teams within the organization and provides principles and guidelines for team activities.

Leaders within the organization must provide direction for teams by answering fundamental questions that employees will have about team participation. Questions that leaders should be able to answer before developing teams include:

- What will be the purpose of teams in this organization?

- What issues will teams address?

- What areas of the organization will be affected by the work and decisions of teams?

- Should teams be structured on a departmental basis, a cross-functional basis, or both?

- Should teams be temporary or permanent?

- Should membership be voluntary, strongly encouraged, or required?

- What is the optimum number of people our teams will need to accomplish their goals?

Most successful team-oriented organizations start forming teams first at the level of department managers. When these teams demonstrate success and receive the necessary support from their superiors, teams are established at the supervisory level. When teams of supervisors become successful and receive the necessary support from their department managers, employee teams are formed.

Exhibit 1   Team Readiness Survey

Question: When does it make sense to start work teams in your organization?

Answer: When the conditions are right.

This team readiness survey can help you determine if conditions are right for forming work teams in your organization. Using the scale below each item, give yourself a "5" for *yes* (if you strongly agree with the item), a "1" for *no* (if you strongly disagree with the item), or a "2," "3," or "4," depending on how close you are to either end of the scale. When you are finished, total your scores and consult the scoring guide for an indication of your organization's readiness to accept work teams.

1. Management believes that front-line employees can and should make the majority of decisions that affect how they do their work.

1	2	3	4	5
Strongly Disagree			Strongly Agree	

2. Employees can suggest and implement improvements to their work without going through several levels of approval.

1	2	3	4	5
Strongly Disagree			Strongly Agree	

3. The union is likely to agree to renegotiate traditional work rules and job classifications to permit greater flexibility and autonomy.

1	2	3	4	5
Strongly Disagree			Strongly Agree	

4. The nature of the work in your organization lends itself to a team-based approach rather than to individual effort.

1	2	3	4	5
Strongly Disagree			Strongly Agree	

5. Your technology is flexible enough to permit restructuring or reorganization based on the needs of your teams. The physical design of your workplace lends itself to working in teams.

1	2	3	4	5
Strongly Disagree			Strongly Agree	

6. It is possible to organize work so that teams of employees can take responsibility for entire jobs.

1	2	3	4	5
Strongly Disagree			Strongly Agree	

7. There is enough complexity in jobs to allow for initiative and decision-making.

1	2	3	4	5
Strongly Disagree			Strongly Agree	

8. Your employees would be interested or willing to organize into teams.

1	2	3	4	5
Strongly Disagree			Strongly Agree	

Exhibit 1   *(continued)*

9. Your overall organizational culture, vision, and values support teamwork and empowerment.

1	2	3	4	5
Strongly Disagree			Strongly Agree	

10. Your organization has a history of following through on initiatives such as empowerment.

1	2	3	4	5
Strongly Disagree			Strongly Agree	

11. Management in your organization is willing to adjust responsibility downward and radically change its own roles and behavior.

1	2	3	4	5
Strongly Disagree			Strongly Agree	

12. Your company is secure enough to guarantee a period of relative stability during which the teams can develop.

1	2	3	4	5
Strongly Disagree			Strongly Agree	

13. You have adequate support functions, such as human resources, engineering, and maintenance, that can help teams by providing information, coaching, and training.

1	2	3	4	5
Strongly Disagree			Strongly Agree	

14. Management understands that developing teams is a lengthy, time-consuming, and labor-intensive process. It is willing and able to make the investment.

1	2	3	4	5
Strongly Disagree			Strongly Agree	

15. Your organization has systems that provide timely information to front-line employees.

1	2	3	4	5
Strongly Disagree			Strongly Agree	

Scoring Guide

65–75 points:
Implementing teams is most likely to succeed. Focus resources on any items rated as "1" or "2" to accelerate the process.

50–64 points:
Implementing teams is possible but may be difficult, especially if you have low scores in relation to items assessing management's readiness for teams (Items 1, 9, 10, 11, 12, and 14).

Below 50 points:
Implementing teams will be difficult, if not impossible. Focus instead on raising awareness and increasing understanding of team-based processes.

Source: Richard S. Wellins, William C. Byham, and Jeanne M. Wilson, *Empowered Teams: Creating Self-Directed Work Groups That Improve Quality, Productivity, and Participation* (San Francisco: Jossey-Bass Publishers, 1991), pp. 95-97. © 1991, Jossey-Bass Inc., Publishers.

Successes at the managerial and supervisory levels help leaders within the organization determine the number of additional teams to form.

The direction provided by leaders within the organization helps individual teams develop mission statements and codes of conduct (mission statements and codes of conduct will be discussed later in the chapter). Guidelines for team activities help ensure that teams do not tackle problems or address issues that are inappropriate or counterproductive to achieving the overall goals of the organization. Teams do not set goals in a vacuum. The goals must represent the mission of the team, which in turn must represent the mission of the organization. Many team-oriented organizations place limitations on their teams' goals. For example, compensation, benefits, corporate policies, and other such issues are commonly declared off-limits. In general, teams focus on work issues that directly relate to their areas of responsibility. This includes solving work-related problems and finding ways to do their jobs faster and better.

Another resource that the organization must supply to teams is the time and attention of its managers. In some team-oriented organizations, team members make a proposal to the appropriate managers. The proposal defines the issue that team members tackled, recaps their analyses, and seeks approval to implement their recommendations. Since the managers have been kept informed of the team's progress from the start, there are usually no surprises at these meetings. However, proposals are often revised before implementation.

Access to Information and Facilities

Teams need resources and access to data and information from other employees in the organization to make well-informed decisions and achieve their goals. The productivity of a team is often a function of the degree of support it receives from all department managers in this regard. For example, unless the accounting manager supports the team concept and has communicated this support to the accounting department, a continuous-improvement team investigating how to reduce glass breakage might have to wait several weeks for the accounting department to supply basic data on breakage costs.

Team Training

Team-oriented organizations also supply the necessary training for team leaders and members. Substantial training is essential during the early stages of a team's development. Periodic training sessions to improve member performance are also needed throughout the life of a team. The types of team training required depend on the scope of team activities within an organization but generally include topics such as:

- Communication skills
- Stages of team development
- Roles individuals play in groups
- Tools for effective meetings
- Steps in the analysis of issues or problems

- Consensus decision-making
- Quality tools and techniques
- Work flow and process analysis
- Presentation skills

Teams do not need all of this training before they begin to contribute effectively to an organization's goals. In fact, for many topics and team tools, training may be most effective on an as-needed basis—in other words, **just-in-time training**. Few things can destroy the enthusiasm of a new team quicker than starting out with long, drawn-out training sessions on how to use Pareto charts and histograms.

Award and Recognition Systems

An award and recognition system is another essential resource provided by organizations with effective teams. Such a system communicates within the organization the successful efforts of teams. Awards and forms of recognition do not have to be expensive. Some of the more effective include:

- Certificates
- Badges and service pins
- Plaques
- T-shirts
- Coffee mugs
- Free team dinners
- Lunch with the general manager

Whatever form of recognition is selected, it should have one primary message: quite simply, "Thank you."

One forum for recognizing team contributions and distributing awards is a quarterly or annual banquet. A standing ovation from fellow employees is a memorable experience that rewards team accomplishments. A quarterly newsletter can also acknowledge team successes while extending recognition to supportive groups and individuals. Bulletin boards, updated on a regular basis, can display team accomplishments as well as photographs of new team members or employees from other departments who are currently assisting a team in its problem-solving effort.

Characteristics of Successful Teams

The size of a team can greatly affect the quality of a team's efforts. Effective teams range in size from three to seven members. Managers or others attending team meetings as advisers or experts on specific issues related to the team's work are not considered members of the team. It may be helpful to limit the number of visitors to each meeting.

Given the necessary support from the organization (including team training sessions), three important characteristics of successful teams are:

- A team mission statement

- A team code of conduct

- Effective team leaders[4]

Team building is a process that demands active team member participation; it is not a spectator sport. The team mission statement and code of conduct encourage productive contributions from team members and foster a cooperative team spirit. A mission statement should guide the team in setting goals, establishing priorities, and connecting with the overall goals of the organization. A team's code of conduct states norms and rules for interacting. High-performance teams also have leaders with flexible leadership styles that meet the team's need for guidance and facilitate the members through the stages of team development.

Team Mission Statement

A team **mission statement** is a brief statement explaining why the team exists and how it contributes to the overall goals of a department or organization. A clear, well-defined mission statement rallies members around a shared vision of what the team stands for and strives to accomplish. The statement clarifies the direction of the team and suggests the type of work that lies ahead. The team mission statement also communicates the importance of the team's efforts in relation to the ongoing operations of a department or organization. Exhibit 2 presents three levels of mission statements—a property-level mission, a departmental mission, and a team mission within that department—and illustrates how the three relate to one another.

One of the first tasks facing a newly formed team is to develop a mission statement. In the case of a task-force team, the mission is simply a statement of what the team has been formed to achieve. For example, a hotel might assemble a task force to draft procedures that will reduce the time department heads take to analyze and respond to weekly guest comment cards and other forms of guest feedback. The mission of this team is crystal-clear.

In the case of departmental problem-solving teams and cross-functional continuous-improvement teams, the development of mission statements can be much more involved and challenging. A mission-writing session should be conducted either by the team leader or by a facilitator who is not a member of the team. One way to conduct this kind of session is to first **brainstorm** the elements of a mission statement. Generally, a mission statement should answer the following questions:

- What do we do?

- How do we do it?

- For whom do we do it?

The session leader can write each question at the top of a separate flip chart sheet and record the answers brainstormed by the team. With these sheets posted on the wall for all to see, individual team members may then write their own versions of a mission statement on flip chart sheets. These sheets can then be displayed to

Exhibit 2   Three Mission Statement Levels

Sample Property-Level Mission Statement

The ABC Hotel is a health-oriented resort that leads the hospitality industry in service excellence through employee development and innovation.

Sample Housekeeping Department Mission Statement

The mission of the housekeeping department at the ABC Hotel is to ensure guest satisfaction through a clean and healthy environment provided by efficient and well-trained employees.

Sample Housekeeping Team Mission Statement

The mission of the housekeeping continuous-improvement team is to increase guest satisfaction by identifying and solving problems that disrupt a clean and healthy environment for our guests and fellow employees.

---

the group, and the leader or facilitator can help the team come up with a single statement.

Once a draft of the mission is written, the team can test the value of the statement by answering the following questions:

- Does this mission statement foster common goals within our team?
- Can anyone outside our team read this mission statement and understand what we do?
- Can we use this mission statement to evaluate our team's performance?

If the team answers "yes" to all three questions, the mission statement is complete. "No" answers to any of the questions should prompt appropriate revisions to the statement.

Mission writing is not a dry, mechanical exercise; it's an important team-building activity. The interaction required demonstrates how important everyone's participation is to the team's success. In future meetings, if team members become confused or begin to lose their sense of purpose, the team leader can refocus their efforts by reminding them of the team's mission statement.[5]

Exhibit 3   Sample Team Code of Conduct

As a member of this team, I agree to:

- Focus on the mission of the team.
- Use the team tools presented during training sessions.
- Contribute to team discussions.
- Listen to and consider input from other members.
- Criticize ideas, not individuals.
- Make decisions by consensus.
- Confront, not ignore, conflict.
- Arrive on time for all scheduled team meetings.
- Keep to the agenda set for each team meeting.
- Ensure that minutes are taken at each team meeting.
- Complete assignments on time.

Date _____

Team Member _____

Team Leader _____

Team Code of Conduct

Effective teams adopt a **code of conduct** that members are expected to abide by. The conduct code establishes ground rules for behavior on the team and may also include guidelines for team meetings, such as requiring agendas and minutes. The code may include the team's expectations about the quality and type of group interaction. It may also indicate the attendance, level of participation, and preparedness expected of each team member. Exhibit 3 presents a sample team code of conduct. Some organizations may secure the commitment of team members to the ground rules of behavior by presenting the code in the form of a personal pledge or promise.

The code of conduct helps establish the team's norms. These stated norms must be positive and must contribute to the mission and goals of the team, the department, and the organization. Norms that promote competition instead of cooperation or suspicion instead of trust will be detrimental to the team's overall effectiveness.

The team must monitor itself to ensure that the code is followed. While at times the team leader functions as the disciplinarian, members of effective teams enforce the code themselves. The more actively a team participates in the development of a code of conduct, the more likely its members will be to police behaviors within the team.

Effective Team Leaders

The primary role of a team leader is to function as the servant, not the master, of the team. Team leaders should not strive to build power based on their position, and must avoid any temptation to impose their wills on the team's efforts. This is not an easy role to play. Like everyone else, team leaders like to follow their own ideas. However, the leader's role is not to direct a team toward achieving goals that he or she thinks are in the best interest of the team, but rather to assist the team in reaching the goals that it sets for itself. Team goals should result from the decisions of the team, not from the needs, wants, or desires of the team leader.

Some team-oriented organizations have found that supervisors and department managers are not necessarily the best team leaders within their own work areas. Depending on the cultural characteristics of an organization, supervisors and department managers may experience role conflicts as team leaders. Team members may also feel that the presence of their boss inhibits their full participation in team discussions. These are matters for each organization to settle before forming teams. However, since supervisors and department managers provide team leaders with essential support and necessary guidance, they should be actively involved in selecting individuals who will serve as leaders. Exhibit 4 presents a sample form that organizations can use to assess the leadership potential of individuals.

Once individuals are selected for team leader training, completing an initial evaluation of their own leadership skills can be enlightening and create an awareness of a need for further training and development. Exhibit 5 presents a sample team leader self-evaluation form that individuals can use to determine important areas that need their attention during their training sessions. The self-evaluation form should be completed periodically as individuals fulfill their roles as team leaders. The initial assessment can serve as a **baseline measurement** against which team leaders can measure their growth and progress.

Stages of Team Development

Just as there are stages in the development of an individual (infancy, childhood, adolescence, adulthood, maturity, and death), so there are identifiable stages in the development of a group or team. Like individuals, groups cannot be forced to mature. High-performance teams do not spring from the will of a corporate executive, a department manager, or a team leader. However, the group development process can be shortened when team leaders and members are guided through structured training sessions based on the principles of team development.[6]

Within team-oriented organizations, team leaders and members are trained to recognize behaviors associated with each developmental stage. This training provides a team with a common vocabulary by which to (1) understand their own developmental process, (2) discuss issues that arise throughout the life of the group, and (3) better prepare the team for resolving conflict, building consensus, and making quality decisions.

While there are probably as many models of group development as there are team-building consultants, a basic model created by B. W. Tuckman has served as the basis for a great deal of research on team building in manufacturing and service

Exhibit 4   Sample Form for Assessing Leadership Potential

Use the following rating scale to assess the leadership potential of _____ :
(name of employee)

    1 point—Demonstrates the behavior rarely
    3 points—Demonstrates the behavior occasionally
    5 points—Demonstrates the behavior consistently

The individual:

____ 1. shows interest and enthusiasm about working in a team environment.

____ 2. demonstrates commitment, responsibility, and optimism.

____ 3. commands the respect of peers and has established credibility in the organization.

____ 4. exercises good judgment and is competent, thorough, objective, and open-minded on the job.

____ 5. is cooperative, congenial, and relaxed in the work environment.

____ 6. speaks clearly and listens actively.

____ 7. demonstrates the ability to plan, organize, and coordinate job-related activities.

____ 8. is experienced, knowledgeable, and suggests insightful improvements.

____ 9. is an independent and innovative thinker.

____ 10. is interested in self-development.

____ 11. has an acceptable attendance record.

____ 12. sets and achieves goals.

Scoring Guide

50–60 points:
    Individual demonstrates strong leadership potential.

40–49 points:
    Individual needs to improve in several areas during team leader training.

Less than 40 points:
    Individual may not be appropriate for team leader training at this time.

Source: Adapted from Stephen J. Shriver, *Managing Quality Services* (Lansing, Mich.: American Hotel & Lodging Educational Institute, 1988), p. 216.

industries.[7] Variations of this model are used in team training programs within some hospitality organizations. The following sections explore the behaviors associated with the five stages of group development according to Tuckman's model: forming, storming, norming, performing, and transforming (see Exhibit 6).

Stage 1—Forming

The first stage of team development, **forming,** begins the transformation that takes place when individuals become members of a group. Team members at this stage

Exhibit 5   Sample Team Leader Self-Evaluation Form

Think about your leadership experiences and use the following scale to rate yourself on each of the items listed below:

   1 point—Weak
   3 points—Unsure
   5 points—Strong

___   1.   When speaking before a group, I can project my voice and display enthusiasm.

___   2.   While listening to a speaker, I am able to observe other people's behavior.

___   3.   I am able to understand both spoken messages and nonverbal gestures.

___   4.   I am able to ask open-ended questions that encourage others to share their ideas, feelings, or interests.

___   5.   I can use effective openers to generate a lively group discussion.

___   6.   I can focus a group's discussion by discriminating between significant and irrelevant information and comments.

___   7.   I can restate or clarify another person's ideas.

___   8.   I can take an unexpected incident or event and use it to teach a concept.

___   9.   I am able to give constructive pointers to individuals in a nonjudgmental manner.

___ 10.   When working with a group, I can share my own feelings about the topic under discussion.

___ 11.   I am able to elicit participation from most people in a group.

___ 12.   I have a sense of timing for pacing discussions and planning activities.

___ 13.   I can accept anger or criticism from a person or a group without becoming defensive.

___ 14.   I am able to help others comfortably display their emotions or relate their feelings.

___ 15.   I have a sense of humor and can laugh at myself.

Scoring Guide

65–75 points:
   You have solid team-leader skills.

55–64 points:
   You need to work on several areas to become a better team leader.

Less than 55 points:
   You need to enhance your skills before becoming a team leader.

Source: Adapted from Stephen J. Shriver, *Managing Quality Services* (Lansing, Mich.: American Hotel & Lodging Educational Institute, 1988), p. 218.

are anxious about their roles and responsibilities; they may be concerned about fitting into the group and about their ability to contribute to the team. Some of the questions that individuals may have at this stage include:

•   Why am I on this team, and how will I fit in?

Exhibit 6   Five Stages of Group Development

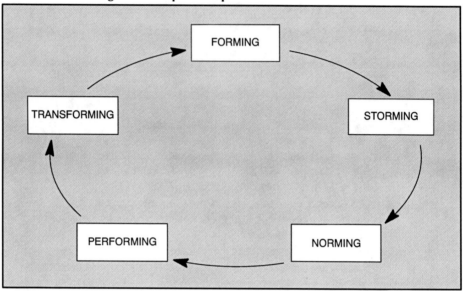

- What do the other team members expect from me?
- Can I trust the other team members?
- How will I benefit from working on this team?
- What can I contribute in order to be accepted by the others?
- What is really important to this team?
- Are the team's goals the same as mine?
- What are the rules?

During this stage of team development, individuals test various behaviors and are dependent on formal or informal group leaders to guide them into their roles as team members. Individuals enter a group with some tension, anxiety, and even suspicion about this new situation. They think about how they will fit into the group and to what extent they want to belong. They are generally more concerned with establishing relationships within the group than they are on setting direction for the team or assigning tasks.

At this stage, members may be hesitant to participate in discussions. Communication is often polite and tentative, with participation limited to one or two of the more vocal members. Often, members seem to wish to avoid the work at hand and instead discuss irrelevant and nonthreatening issues such as the weather, news, or common acquaintances. During this stage, productivity is low and working relationships are cautious and noncommittal.

Members rarely act independently at this point. Many may be confused about what they are supposed to do and how they will accomplish tasks as a group; they therefore tend to be dependent on the leader for support and direction. Their

Exhibit 7   Characteristics of Teams at the Forming Stage

- Low group structure, low member involvement
- Must be prodded into action
- Impersonal, watchful, guarded, and cautious
- Tentative attachment to the team
- Members cautiously explore boundaries of acceptable individual and team behavior
- Tendency to avoid others—to be "loners"
- Very little real communication
- Suspicion, fear, and anxiety about the task ahead
- Some anxiety about why they are there, why others are there, who'll lead the group, and what they'll do

Source: Adapted from Anthony R. Montebello and Victor R. Buzzotta, "Work Teams That Work," *Training and Development*, March 1993, p. 63.

implicit assumption is that the leader is competent and benevolent, and few, if any, attempts are made to challenge him or her. Exhibit 7 summarizes some of the characteristics of teams at the forming stage of development.

The leader's responsibility during the forming stage of a team's development is to assist people with the transition from individuals to team members. This can be done effectively by working with members of the team to develop the team mission statement. The team leader can also establish direction for the team and clarify the roles of individual members by setting goals and determining methods for documenting progress toward those goals. The team leader can alleviate some of the members' anxieties simply by presenting administrative team tools that will help structure interactions within the group. These tools include the code of conduct and the formats to be used for creating meeting agendas and for taking minutes of meetings. The more the group participates in creating the code of conduct, the easier it is to manage the conflicts that naturally arise in the next stage of team development.

Stage 2—Storming

The second stage of team development, **storming**, is marked by conflict within the group. Team members push boundaries and challenge authority in an attempt to clarify the team's goals, values, and norms. Some of the questions that individuals may have at this stage include:

- Who has the most power to influence people on this team?
- Who's really in charge of this team?
- Why can't team members criticize ideas instead of each other?
- Do we need to reach a consensus on everything we do?
- How can we keep departmental politics out of the team process?

Exhibit 8   Characteristics of Teams at the Storming Stage

- High group structure and direction—low member involvement
- Getting things done without regard for the needs of team members
- Dominated by one or two team members
- Overstructured, with tight control
- Impatient with lack of progress; overly competitive and confrontational
- Self-serving—"look out for yourself"
- One-way communication prevails
- People become testy, blameful, and overzealous
- Frustration, anger, and resistance to goals
- Defensiveness, competition, and choosing sides; subgroup polarization and infighting

Source: Adapted from Anthony R. Montebello and Victor R. Buzzotta, "Work Teams That Work," *Training and Development,* March 1993, p. 63.

- How are we going to resolve the conflicts in this team?

At this stage, members may find that their initial expectations of the team are far different from the realities of trying to accomplish something together. Consequently, some may feel frustrated, angry, and disillusioned. Members may become competitive with one another, grow impatient with the team's slow progress, or become overly zealous in their individual roles. Establishing a pecking order within the group becomes more important than accepting productive roles in achieving team goals. Team meetings can become confrontational, with members blaming one another and acting defensively. Exhibit 8 lists some of the characteristics of teams at the storming stage of development.

The leader's responsibility during the storming stage of a team's development is to manage, not suppress, the conflict. It is important for the leader not to take member rebellion personally. Although conflict and tension may be considered negative emotions, they should not be avoided during this stage. This behavior may be essential for the development of group cohesion and for the clarification of the group's structure and goals. Conflict in and of itself is neutral; how it is handled makes it either a positive or negative factor within a team.

Conflict needs to be managed so that it does not become counterproductive or destructive. The leader must redirect the energies of the team without smothering the initiative, ideas, and talents of individual members. Revisiting the team's mission, code of conduct, and goals can help reinforce the team concept. The leader should also encourage open communication and interaction among group members. By providing positive feedback for productive behaviors and focusing the group on its task and goals, the leader will be better able to guide the team through the storming stage and further prepare members to work together to accomplish their mission.

Exhibit 9   Characteristics of Teams at the Norming Stage

- Low group structure—high member involvement
- Builds toward a friendly and social team climate; high concern for the needs of team members
- Unfocused, irrelevant communications
- Informal information exchanges and social encounters
- Feelings of mutual trust, respect, and harmony
- Avoidance of conflict
- Focus on harmony and conformity; competitive relationships become cooperative
- Sense of team cohesion and close attachment to the team

Source: Adapted from Anthony R. Montebello and Victor R. Buzzotta, "Work Teams That Work," *Training and Development*, March 1993, p. 63.

Stage 3—Norming

During the third stage of team development, **norming**, relationships become cooperative and mutually supportive. The team establishes itself as a functioning unit with its own patterns of communication and behavior. In this stage, members learn that they can work effectively together as a cohesive unit. They are more tolerant of each other and accept the diverse perspectives and personalities that each brings to the group. Conflicts occur less frequently, and the team is better able to cope with differences of opinion.

Questions that blocked productive teamwork in the previous stages are answered. Goals are more clearly defined and a group structure becomes evident. Members recognize how each individual contributes to the group's efforts. Roles within the team are founded on the demonstrated talents and skills of individual members rather than on previous assumptions based on appearance, stereotypes, or job titles. Each member understands the group's mission and how to contribute to achieving the team's goals. As mutual trust and acceptance grow among the members, the team becomes much more productive and focused on task-oriented activities rather than on building relationships within the group. Exhibit 9 indicates some of the characteristics of teams at the norming stage of development.

The leader's responsibility during the norming stage of a team's development is to facilitate the group's decision-making and problem-solving activities. The leader blends into the group as an equal participant and, while not forcing direction upon the team, ensures that productive group norms and member roles are applied to the tasks at hand.

As team cohesiveness and spirit grow, pressures to conform also increase. The danger at this stage is that the team might sacrifice valuable differences of opinion for the sake of team unity, a phenomenon called "**groupthink**." This emphasis on conformity can stifle the team's ability to make good decisions and solve problems effectively. Acting to preserve its newfound harmony by avoiding conflict, the team might become too sure of itself. Members can become complacent and less open to innovative ideas about accomplishing team goals. Groupthink is especially likely to occur when groups are highly cohesive and under considerable pressure to make a quality decision. Also, teams can sometimes become isolated from outside opinions; when this happens, they sometimes believe that the "truth" lies only within their group and groupthink is more likely to occur. Some of the negative characteristics of groupthink include the following:

- Examining too few alternatives
- Not being critical of each other's ideas
- Not examining alternatives
- Not seeking expert opinion
- Being too selective in gathering information
- Not having contingency plans

Symptoms or warning signs of groupthink include:

- Having an illusion of invulnerability
- Rationalizing poor decisions
- Sharing stereotypes that guide the decision
- Exercising direct pressure on others
- Not expressing true feelings
- Maintaining an illusion of unanimity

Several historical events in which groupthink led to disastrous results include the bombing of Pearl Harbor (pilots reported seeing the Japanese Navy closing in on Hawaii, but U.S. admirals and generals did not believe that this was possible and dismissed the warnings as false); the Kennedy-planned invasion of Cuba (Kennedy's cabinet was convinced the invasion would be simple, but it ended badly at the Bay of Pigs, in which the forces sent to occupy Cuba were easily defeated); and the 1986 *Challenger* explosion (where the U.S. spaceship disintegrated shortly after takeoff, killing all astronauts on board, because the management team that ordered the liftoff did not listen to engineers who said there could be problems with the rubber "O" rings in the spaceship).

To avoid groupthink, the team leader must keep the team focused on its task and facilitate open communication. Signs of complacency or rigid conformity should be met with prodding questions and suggestions that push the team to explore alternatives. The leader must encourage members to investigate all options before making decisions.

Stage 4—Performing

The fourth stage of team development, **performing**, finds the team functioning at its highest level of productivity. The team's norms become standards for evaluating the performance of individual members and the team's progress toward its

Exhibit 10   Characteristics of Teams at the Performing Stage

- High group structure and direction—high member involvement
- Gets things done by working collaboratively with each other
- Agreement on who they are, what they're doing, and where they're going
- Team has clarified relationships and performance expectations
- Participation by all team members in achieving challenging goals
- Cooperative and productive climate
- Open, direct, and relevant communications
- Ability to prevent or work through team issues

Source: Adapted from Anthony R. Montebello and Victor R. Buzzotta, "Work Teams That Work," *Training and Development*, March 1993, p. 63.

goals. The focus of each member shifts completely from individual to group concerns, and members are more likely to phrase their concerns in terms of the full group: the word "we" replaces "I." Questions that team members may have at this stage include:

- What is the ideal way for our group to function most effectively?
- How can we best measure progress toward our goals?
- Are we constantly improving as a team?
- How can we be sure that we are making the best decisions?

At this stage of development, members come to value their differences more than their similarities. The team is eager for conflict of ideas rather than conflict of personalities. Personal conflicts are avoided, and members are able to speak freely and respond to criticism as honest feedback. Members know they can learn from one another, and they take advantage of opportunities to grow personally and professionally. Exhibit 10 outlines some of the characteristics of teams at the performing stage of development.

The leader's role at this stage is to ensure that the organization provides the resources that the team needs to accomplish its goals. The leader serves primarily as the communication channel between the team and the organization, with minimal interaction with the team itself. Many tasks previously performed by the leader are now the responsibility of other team members. The empowered team, with its rules, norms, roles, and goals, applies its full energies to the challenges at hand.

Stage 5—Transforming

The last stage of team development is often called the **transforming** stage because, at this point, the group is either preparing to disband or facing a major change in its mission, membership, or environment. Many teams have predetermined ending points. Even permanent teams have various types of endings, such as the period between completion of one task and initiation of another, or the loss of a team leader or a team member. Questions that team members may have at this stage include:

- What will the new team leader expect from us?

- Will we be as productive a team as we were before?

- How are we going to replace the talents and skills of the member leaving the team?

- How will the new team member fit in with our way of getting things done?

- How fast can we bring the new team member up to speed?

During this stage, members often regress to the unproductive team behaviors characteristic of the forming and storming stages of development. For example, when the composition of the team changes, the carryover members may lose enthusiasm and go back to depending on the leader for direction and motivation. Conflicts may arise again, and members may need to resume active roles in resolving them. Throughout the development of the transforming team, the members should keep in mind that while regressive behaviors will arise, progress back to the performing stage of development will probably be much faster than with the original group.

When a team disbands, it may be appropriate to have a recap meeting at which members can review their work and discuss their development as a team. This brings closure to the team's efforts, provides members an opportunity to learn from their experiences, and may help motivate individuals to accept future team challenges.

Realities of Team Development

It is important to remember that any model of human behavior is not necessarily a direct reflection of reality. The model of team development just presented is a theoretical tool for understanding what happens during the life cycle of a team. Pigeonholing a team into a specific stage of development greatly oversimplifies the complexities of human behavior, however.

Few groups move smoothly through developmental stages. Some groups are unable to progress through a certain stage. For example, a team stuck in the forming stage may always rely on the group leader to solve problems and make decisions for the group. Another team may never get beyond the storming stage, with its members constantly fighting among themselves or with the team leader. A group in the norming stage may be so pleased with itself and its early successes that it forgets its mission, relaxes its efforts, and never reaches the performing stage.

Other groups may fluctuate between stages, bouncing back and forth without ever fully developing. For example, a group may move from the forming stage to the storming stage, then regress to the forming stage. This may occur when the fighting in the storming stage produces so much anxiety that members wish to retreat back to the safe, polite, nonthreatening conversations typical of the forming stage.

It is a mistake to expect that a team at a specific stage of development will exhibit only the behaviors characteristic of that particular stage. The reality of team dynamics is such that, at any given time, a team may display behaviors from any of the five stages of development. The criteria used to determine a team's stage of development are the *predominant* types of behavior displayed by the team.

Roles Individuals Play in Groups

Training programs within team-oriented organizations often address the roles that individuals play in groups. Team leaders and members are trained to recognize behaviors associated with both positive and negative roles. This training enables a team to advance its development as a group, have better discussions at meetings, and resolve conflicts.

Exhibit 11 identifies seven positive roles individuals may play in a group. Also identified are three dominant characteristics and some typical comments of individuals in each of these roles. As team members become aware of these roles, they can more easily recognize, appreciate, and encourage the positive roles played by other members on the team.[8]

An awareness of positive roles helps a team to assess the talents of its individual members. It also alerts individuals to specific roles that they can comfortably adopt within the team.

Just as individuals play positive roles, they also play negative ones. Exhibit 12 describes five negative roles that individuals may adopt in group situations. When individuals play negative roles, their behavior decreases the team's productivity and may even prevent the team from reaching its goals. As team members become aware of negative roles, they are better able to recognize and discourage these behaviors.

Being aware of negative roles also helps a team predict potential conflicts within the group. A team leader can ask members to rate themselves on how likely they are to behave in any of the ways outlined in Exhibit 12. Even if some members are not completely honest, the resulting information helps the leader identify the types of conflict likely to emerge in different situations. The exercise may also help individuals become more aware of themselves; some may recognize the roles they need to shed during the norming stage of development and may be more likely to control their own behavior.

When members can recognize negative roles that individuals play in groups, they are able to exert a friendly form of peer pressure to discourage unproductive behavior. For example, a "Dominator" or "Cynic" at a team meeting might represent a potentially explosive situation at any time, especially during the storming stage of group development. But if other team members use some gentle humor to prod the individual toward self-awareness, conflict can be avoided. When individuals persist in negative roles, discussion may be necessary. Beyond that, the leader and team must recognize when to "give up" and ask the individual to leave the team.

It is important to note that these roles are not personality types. One person can play several roles during a single team meeting. The topic of discussion, the stage of the group's development, and the influence of the team leader can all affect the roles that members may play at any given time.

Exhibit 11   Positive Roles Individuals Play in Groups

The Inquirer

1. Is concerned with the basics of reasoning.
2. Focuses the group's attention on the facts of a situation.
3. Encourages the group to interpret the facts in different ways.

Typical Comments:

- "Just how many times does this happen?"
- "Does this happen with just certain people or does it apply to everyone in that department?"
- "Does the problem arise because of the worker or because of the work method?"
- "Whose responsibility is this?"

The Contributor

1. Submits factual information.
2. Attempts to build a basis for sound decision-making.
3. Offers considered opinions about facts.

Typical Comments:

- "I think our decision should be based on the figures Denise got from the accounting department."
- "Let's see if we can combine that idea with the feedback we received from the dining room manager."
- "I think that we should listen to the facts and discuss what we should do about this later."
- "Let me give you the feedback I got from maintenance and housekeeping."

The Elaborator

1. Translates generalizations into concrete examples.
2. Builds on the ideas of others.
3. Projects a picture of what might happen if a solution is implemented.

Typical Comments:

- "Let's imagine what it would be like if we tried that idea in my department."
- "What do you think other employees would say about that?"
- "How do you think that would work at the front desk?"
- "How would this affect our guests?"

The Reviewer

1. Summarizes the progress of the group.
2. Clarifies relationships among the ideas that are being discussed.
3. Identifies points that the group agrees upon.

Typical Comments:

- "Let's recap what we've done so far."
- "Let me list the points that we seem to agree on."
- "Matt, let me try to rephrase what you just said and combine it with points that Andrew brought up at the last meeting."
- "So far we have identified five reasons why we need to do this. Let me list them and see if we all agree."

Exhibit 11 *(continued)*

The Evaluator

1. Judges the group's thinking by its own standards.
2. Raises questions about facts and figures.
3. Explores the practical applications of proposed solutions.

Typical Comments:

- "Let's check these figures against the invoices in accounting."
- "Maybe we need a second and third opinion about this problem."
- "There could be another side to this story that we don't know about. We always try to get all of the information."
- "I think that we've tried things like this before and found out that we were on the wrong track."

The Energizer

1. Keeps the group's discussion moving along.
2. Stimulates new ideas that are pertinent to the topic.
3. Prods members to decide on a specific course of action.

Typical Comments:

- "Okay, we get the point, but what about this other idea?"
- "Let's move on to the next idea and come back to this later."
- "Let's wait on this point until we get the feedback we need from other departments. What's next?"
- "We've discussed this enough. Let's make a decision."

The Gatekeeper

1. Encourages non-participating group members to talk.
2. Opens the door for new views.
3. Encourages the inclusion of all group members.

Typical Comments:

- "Mary, you haven't voiced your opinion yet—what do you think?"
- "Let's go around the group and ask each person to share their perspective on this."
- "Thanks for your comments, Kendall; now I'd like to hear from other members of the group."
- "Does anyone have a different viewpoint that they'd like to share?"

Source: Adapted from Stephen J. Shriver, *Managing Quality Services* (Lansing, Mich.: American Hotel & Lodging Educational Institute, 1988), pp. 209–210.

Team Meetings

Almost everyone has attended a meeting at which nothing was accomplished. People talked and talked, but at the end of the meeting, the group was no closer to achieving its objectives than it was before the meeting began. Meetings can fail for a variety of reasons. If the meeting's objectives are not clear, participants don't understand what they are supposed to accomplish. If one person dominates the meeting, few others participate in discussions and most sit wondering why the

Exhibit 12   Negative Roles Individuals Play in Groups

The Dominator

1. Demands attention and tries to run the show.
2. Constantly interrupts other people.
3. Imposes personal opinions on the group.

Typical Comments:

- "Now, I've had a lot more experience at this sort of thing, so let me tell you what to do."
- "The only way we're going to make progress here is by following up on my idea."
- "Hold everything, I know exactly what to do."
- "You're wasting everyone's time discussing these things; let's just do what I suggested earlier."

The Blocker

1. Is a frustrated dominator.
2. Repeats arguments and refuses to listen to anyone else's reasoning.
3. When ignored by the group, the person becomes stubborn and resists everything the group wants to do.

Typical Comments:

- "None of you really understands what I'm trying to say."
- "We went over that idea at the last meeting and I didn't like it then either."
- "Well, that's my opinion and I think it's better than yours, so listen more carefully to me this time."
- "Why are we voting on this issue? There's a lot more I have to say."

The Cynic

1. Scoffs at the group's progress.
2. Tries to start conflicts and arguments among members of the group.
3. Is always negative.

Typical Comments:

- "I don't care what you do."
- "Do what you want; management won't approve it anyway."
- "You're just wasting your time if you're going to do that."
- "This whole thing is stupid; nobody cares what the team wants to do anyway."

The Security Seeker

1. Wants sympathy or personal recognition.
2. Always has it worse than anyone else.
3. His or her personal experiences are always more important than anyone else's.

Typical Comments:

- "I wish somebody would have told me what to do when that happened to me."
- "I never know what to do when that happens in my department."
- "The situation is so bad in my department that even this solution won't work."
- "I always have so many things going on, I'll never have time to do that."

Exhibit 12   *(continued)*

The Lobbyist

1. Always plugs pet theories.
2. Is only concerned with problems that involve his or her own department.
3. Will keep talking about his or her own ideas even though the group has decided to do something entirely different.

Typical Comments:

- "I've been pretty open-minded about this, but don't you think we're being unfair to the people in my department?"
- "That's okay if that's what you guys want to do, but I don't think you really understand my idea."
- "That's a good idea you have, but I think you forgot to consider the things that I said last week."
- "I agree with everything you say, but I just can't buy your conclusion."

Source: Adapted from Stephen J. Shriver, *Managing Quality Services* (Lansing, Mich.: American Hotel & Lodging Educational Institute, 1988), pp. 211–212.

meeting was called in the first place. If key people do not attend the meeting, everyone argues uselessly about facts that the absent parties could easily clarify.

Ineffective meetings bore participants and are costly to organizations. Eight people wasting one hour at a meeting is equivalent to one person losing an entire work day. Five unproductive meetings in a month is equivalent to paying one person a week's wages to do nothing. If this pattern persists for a year, the lost productivity is equal to two months' worth of one person's time and wages.

Team-oriented organizations cannot afford ineffective meetings. But with the proper tools, team meetings can be productive and worthwhile. The sections that follow describe techniques for planning, conducting, and evaluating meetings. While many functions are addressed as the responsibilities of a team leader, exactly who does what is determined primarily by the stage of a team's development. In the early stages, the team leader will indeed assume responsibility for managing meetings effectively. However, in the later stages of a team's development, those same responsibilities become shared among all members of the team.

Planning the Meeting

The first step in planning a meeting is to determine the meeting's objectives. As the team leader thinks about what the meeting should accomplish, it may become apparent to him or her that a meeting is not really necessary. For example, in the case of task-force teams, it might be possible for the team to achieve some of its objectives by simply having one of its members network with a few individuals and then report to the team. In the case of regularly scheduled meetings for a continuous-improvement team, meeting objectives are determined in advance by the team leader based on the team's progress toward addressing the issue or solving the problem at hand.

Once meeting objectives are established, the team leader prepares an **agenda**. An agenda is essentially a plan for a successful meeting; it lists the meeting's

Exhibit 13   Sample Meeting Agenda Format

Meeting Agenda

Meeting Room _____   Date _____

Starting Time _____   Ending Time _____

Meeting Objectives	**Time**

Review:

1.
2.
3.
4.
5.
6.
7.

Summary:

Source: Adapted from Stephen J. Shriver, *Managing Quality Services* (Lansing, Mich.: American Hotel & Lodging Educational Institute, 1988), p. 224.

objectives and a time limit for accomplishing each of them. Stating time limits for discussion on the agenda keeps participants on track and prevents them from dwelling too long on minor issues. An agenda also lists the location and date for the meeting, as well as the starting and ending times. The time frame for most meetings is usually between one hour and an hour and a half, particularly for teams that meet on a weekly basis. Team meetings that run longer tend to be less productive, because some members lose interest and become inattentive.

Exhibit 13 presents a sample format for an agenda. Most agendas include a "review" section as the first item. This represents the time when the team leader reviews the agenda for the meeting and any appropriate items from previous meetings. The last item on the agenda is a summary. Just before adjourning the meeting, the team leader summarizes the discussion, reminds team members of any assignments, and announces the date, time, and place of the next meeting.

Careful consideration should be given to the sequence of a meeting's activities. Generally, the first 20 minutes of a meeting are livelier and more creative than the last 20 minutes. Those items requiring energy, bright ideas, and clear heads should be placed at the top of the agenda. Occasionally it may be effective to deal with an important item near the end of a meeting; this may keep participants alert during the first half of the meeting as they gear up for the later activity.

Before distributing a meeting's agenda, the team leader usually reviews it with the property's quality manager or appropriate department managers. These managers may offer tips on how to conduct portions of the meeting, or they may suggest changes in the meeting plan. For example, if a major objective of a house-keeping team's meeting is to analyze data gathered on linen usage, a manager might suggest that the team leader invite a visitor from the accounting department or laundry area. This visitor could help interpret data as well as discuss with the team current procedures in his or her work area.

Once the agenda is set, the team leader distributes copies to all prospective attendees. This should be done early enough so that everyone is able to schedule time for the meeting. Adequate notice is also necessary to ensure that everyone can properly prepare.

Depending on the meeting's objectives and the issues to be discussed, the team leader may test the reactions of some team members to items on the agenda before the actual meeting. With some idea of what to expect at the meeting, the team leader can plan ways to facilitate discussion. Even who sits where can help determine a meeting's outcome. Typically, in meetings around a table, the chief antagonist of the team leader will sit at the opposite end of the table from the leader. The leader's biggest supporters will usually sit to his or her right (bringing to mind the phrase "right-hand man"), while detractors will often sit to his or her left. Mixing the seating arrangement can defuse antagonism during meetings.

Conducting the Meeting

During team meetings, one member should be assigned the responsibility of taking **minutes**—a written record of the events and actions at the meeting. Exhibit 14 presents a sample format that can be used to record the minutes of a meeting.

The first items recorded are the place, date, and starting and ending times of the meeting. The minutes also list the names of members present, late, or absent, along with any visitors. Recording late arrivals encourages members to be on time and to participate in the entire meeting. The next section of the minutes lists the meeting's objectives as they appear on the agenda.

Meeting minutes are not word-for-word transcriptions of what transpires at a meeting; rather, they are a synopsis of the essential events and actions. The "events" section of the minutes summarizes discussions and records decisions made. Since discussions and decisions are team activities, exactly who said what is not important and therefore does not appear on the minutes. The "actions" section lists actions that the team has decided to take. Names of individuals may be listed here to indicate assignments and responsibilities. Within a few days of the meeting, copies of the minutes should be distributed to all those who attended and, as appropriate, to others concerned with the team.

During a meeting, the team leader's primary responsibility is to keep the meeting on track and ensure that its objectives are achieved. When members talk about lunch in the cafeteria, a co-worker, or other topics not on the agenda, the team has lost its focus and the team leader must redirect the team back to the appropriate agenda item. Leaders should encourage the team to examine different sides of each issue. Leaders must also ensure that a clash of ideas does not become a battle of personalities.

During discussions, the team leader's responsibility is to facilitate the exchange of ideas and make sure that all members participate and understand the issues.

Exhibit 14   Sample Meeting Minutes Format

Meeting Minutes

Meeting Room _____   Date _____

Starting Time _____   Ending Time _____

Members Present:

Late Arrivals:

Members Absent:

Non-Members Present:

Objectives:
1.
2.
3.

Events:
1.
2.
3.

Actions:
1.
2.
3.

Responsibility:
1.
2.
3.

Source: Adapted from Stephen J. Shriver, *Managing Quality Services* (Lansing, Mich.: American Hotel & Lodging Educational Institute, 1988), p. 225.

Some effective techniques for controlling a team member who wants to do all of the talking are:

- Nodding quickly to indicate the point is taken and understood
- Writing down the idea and referring to it if it is raised again
- Interrupting the person and stating, "We have to move on"
- Asking the person a closed question requiring a simple "yes" or "no" answer
- Summarizing the person's point of view and asking for input from others

Team leaders also need to draw out the quiet members of their team. Silence may indicate shyness, hostility, or a lack of understanding. Techniques for encouraging quiet team members to speak up include:

- Restating the meeting's objectives

- Asking silent members for explanations or elaborations

- Complimenting normally quiet members when they do speak

- Asking each team member for his or her thoughts on the issue under discussion

Members of a new team and new members of an already established team may not feel confident enough to participate fully in discussions. Sometimes young team members hesitate to express their thoughts and opinions in the presence of older team members. Team leaders can overcome these barriers by asking such members for their ideas before consulting the older or more experienced members of the team.

Discussions at meetings do not simply end by themselves. Team leaders must learn when to stop discussions and move the team forward. It is important to stop a team's discussion when the team needs an expert opinion, more facts, or technical advice before it can make a decision. If members need time to discuss an issue with their co-workers, or if events beyond the team's control will change or clarify the situation under discussion, then the discussion should be postponed until a more appropriate time. If two or three members can settle an issue outside the meeting, a discussion involving the entire team is a waste of time.

Side conversations disrupt and hinder a meeting's progress. The team leader must know how to handle such situations with the following methods:

- Asking the talkers if they wish to share their conversation with the whole team

- Leaning forward and making eye contact

- Calling on the talkers and asking them an easy question or asking them to restate the last comment and give an opinion

- Discussing their behavior with them after the meeting

Evaluating the Meeting

The work involved in a successful meeting is not over when the meeting ends. The minutes must be distributed to team members and to appropriate managers and department heads. The team leader may also wish to discuss the meeting's accomplishments with a department head or other managers. The team leader must also begin to prepare for the next meeting.

After each meeting, or on a regularly scheduled basis, team members should complete a meeting evaluation form similar to the one presented in Exhibit 15. Managers and team leaders can use this feedback to identify areas for improvement. Items on the evaluation form can be phrased in such a way as to remind members of the team-related values that make meetings productive for the organization and satisfying to themselves as individuals.

Exhibit 15   Sample Meeting Evaluation Form

Meeting _____

Date _____

Evaluate each statement below according to the following scale:

    1 = Strongly disagree
    2 = Disagree
    3 = Undecided
    4 = Agree
    5 = Strongly agree

_____ 1. I was notified of this meeting in sufficient time to prepare for it.

_____ 2. At the start of the meeting, I understood its purpose and agenda.

_____ 3. I understood what was expected of me as a participant and what was expected of the other participants.

_____ 4. I understood how the meeting was intended to flow and when it would end.

_____ 5. Most participants listened to each other.

_____ 6. Most participants expressed themselves openly, honestly, and directly.

_____ 7. Agreements were explicit and clear, and conflicts were openly explored and constructively managed.

_____ 8. The meeting generally proceeded as intended and achieved its stated purpose.

_____ 9. My participation contributed to the ends achieved by the meeting.

_____10. Overall, I am satisfied with this meeting and I feel my time was well-spent.

Scoring Guide

40–50 points:
    We did well in this meeting.

30–39 points:
    We could perform better. Let's discuss how to improve as a team.

Less than 30 points:
    We may need to refocus or retrain in certain areas.

Consensus Team Decision-Making

In carrying out their mission, teams make many different kinds of decisions. For example, continuous-improvement teams must decide what problems need their attention, which of these problems they should work on first, what types of data they must collect and analyze, what solutions they should test, and how they should evaluate the solutions they implement. Task-force teams face similar decision-making situations as they tackle the problems they have been charged to solve.

If the team leader makes all of these decisions, there is no team—just a group of individuals who carry out someone else's orders. There is also the danger that a clique or subgroup within the team might become a ruling majority. Simply voting on decisions is not enough, as the majority decision is not necessarily the best decision; too often, a majority decision represents a group of individuals forcing its will upon others.

For important, final decisions, the goal of every team should be to reach a **consensus** and make decisions that reflect the best thinking of every team member. A **consensus decision** is not a unanimous decision. A unanimous decision is one that everyone in the group agrees with; there is no conflict. Unanimous decisions are rare. Little would get done if a team needed unanimous decisions at each stage of its work.

A consensus decision, on the other hand, may involve conflict within the team. In fact, a conflict of ideas is encouraged so that all sides of an issue are acknowledged and discussed before members make a decision. Consensus means that, while all members may not believe that an idea or a decision is the best one, no one has major reservations about it, and all agree that the idea or decision can be supported without significant reservations.

In order for consensus decision-making to work effectively, the views of each member must be given fair consideration and be evaluated critically by the entire team. This is where the gatekeeper's role of encouraging all viewpoints becomes important. Conflict, or disagreement, is a natural and essential part of this process. The very idea of discussion presupposes different points of view about the best way to resolve a problem or address a concern. If a team stifles discussion by discouraging disagreement, it is more likely to make superficial or unwise decisions. Consensus decision-making grows out of a clash of ideas and the serious consideration that members give to different alternatives. Teams thereby broaden their understanding of a problem, identify a greater number of alternatives from which to select a final solution, and stimulate productive interaction involving everyone in carrying out the team's mission.

Conflict can be disruptive when team leaders and members don't know how to channel it toward constructive discussion. Competition can foster disruptive conflict; in a competitive environment, team members see conflict and disagreement as a game in which someone will win and others must lose. "Getting my way" becomes more important than finding the best solution to the problem at hand. When members become locked in disruptive conflict, feelings and perspectives polarize, and individuals may be unable to see value in the ideas of others. In such situations, members frequently resort to personal attacks and criticisms instead of focusing their disagreement on the issues.

Cooperation is the key to consensus decision-making and constructive discussion. This fundamental team value must be stressed in the team's mission, code of conduct, and training sessions. Constructive conflict develops when members understand the value of disagreement. In cooperative environments, team spirit is high and all are committed to the team's mission and goals. Members assume that disagreements arise from sincere involvement with the facts and issues surrounding a problem. They also believe that by discussing different ideas they will eventually reach an agreement that is better than any single individual's initial suggestion.

Evaluating High-Performance Teams

Management evaluates high-performance teams on the basis of significant results produced by team activities. Significant results are commonly measured in terms of either increased revenues or reduced expenses. The following is a partial list of success indicators that would be suitable for evaluating the results of high-performance teams in a hotel:

- Increased occupancy percentage
- Increased average daily rate (ADR)
- Increased market penetration
- Increased rate yield
- Increased gross operating profit
- Increased net operating income
- Increased sales dollars per hour
- Lower unit cost
- Reduced dollar expenditures
- Lower cost per occupied room
- Lower cost per cover
- Fewer FTEs (full-time equivalent employees)
- Fewer shifts per day
- Shorter cycle time for work processes
- Higher rate of return customers
- Better comment card scores
- Higher inspection scores
- Fewer guest complaints
- Lower recovery costs (fewer meals or drinks given free to dissatisfied customers)

Organizations may also wish to monitor the activities of teams. Summary statistics for each team and overall team activities may include:

- The number of issues or problems tackled
- The number of recommendations or solutions successfully implemented
- The cycle time between tackling issues or problems and successfully implementing recommendations or solutions
- The number of new team leaders and members currently in training

- Team turnover statistics
- Individual and composite comments from exit evaluation forms completed by people leaving teams

Self-Evaluation

A team that is experiencing difficulty in achieving results, or a team that is producing good results but feels there is room for improvement, might find it useful to evaluate itself. A sample team-effectiveness inventory is presented in Exhibit 16.

To complete the team-effectiveness inventory, the team leader and each team member individually rate the team on 20 items. After each person has completed the inventory, a team member should average the team members' answers to each question. The team leader's ratings should not be included in the average; these ratings should be held out as separate measures.

The team should then transfer the team members' average for each item to the team-effectiveness scoring sheet and total the numbers for each of the five areas. The team leader's scores should also be transferred to the scoring sheet and added up. This will provide a rating for each area—from the team's perspective and from the team leader's perspective—as to the effectiveness of the team in that area.

The team can add together the ratings for all the areas to calculate the total team-effectiveness rating—again, both from the team members' perspective and from the team leader's perspective. A total of 100 points—or 100 percent effectiveness—is the ideal. But teams must realize that 100 percent effectiveness is virtually impossible to achieve.

The similarities and differences between the team members' ratings of the team and the team leader's scores are an important topic for discussion. Before beginning an effort to improve team effectiveness, the team leader and team members should agree on the team's current state. Without that agreement, the team and its leader may head down different paths, harming the team environment rather than enhancing it. The team and team leader can use the team-effectiveness scoring sheet to compare the team members' perceptions to the team leader's perceptions. If the members and leader scored an "effectiveness area" (such as "Team Mission") the same, the rating can be recorded in the "consensus rating" column on the chart. If differences exist, team members and the team leader should explore the reasons for those differences, citing specific examples to support their ratings. Once team members and the team leader have agreed on a rating, it can be recorded in the consensus rating column. As teams develop and mature, the inventory items and scoring sheet can be revised to encourage member-member comparisons rather than member-leader comparisons.

Self-Directed Work Teams of the Future

In most team-oriented hospitality organizations, managers, supervisors, and employees spend the vast majority of their time at their "regular" jobs. These jobs are, for the most part, the same as those in hospitality organizations that have not formed teams; they are task-oriented and reflect a traditional organizational hierarchy with clear boundaries between departments and functional areas.

Exhibit 16   Sample Team-Effectiveness Inventory

Using the scale below, circle the number that corresponds with your assessment of the extent to which each statement is true about your team.

1	=	Strongly disagree
2	=	Disagree
3	=	Undecided
4	=	Agree
5	=	Strongly agree

Team-Effectiveness Inventory

1.	Everyone on my team knows exactly why the team does what it does.	5	4	3	2	1
2.	The team leader consistently lets team members know how we're doing on meeting our customers' expectations.	5	4	3	2	1
3.	Everyone on my team has a significant amount of say or influence on decisions that affect his or her job.	5	4	3	2	1
4.	If outsiders were to describe the way we communicate within our team, they would use such words as "open," "honest," "timely," and "two-way."	5	4	3	2	1
5.	Team members have the skills they need to accomplish their roles within the team.	5	4	3	2	1
6.	Everyone on the team knows and understands the team's priorities.	5	4	3	2	1
7.	As a team, we work together to set clear, achievable, and appropriate goals.	5	4	3	2	1
8.	I would rather have the team decide how to do something than have the team leader give step-by-step instructions.	5	4	3	2	1
9.	As a team, rather than ignore destructive conflicts, we are able to work together to solve them.	5	4	3	2	1
10.	The role each member of the team is expected to play makes sense to the whole team.	5	4	3	2	1
11.	The team understands how it fits into the organization.	5	4	3	2	1
12.	If my team doesn't reach a goal, I'm more interested in finding out why we failed to meet the goal than I am in reprimanding team members.	5	4	3	2	1
13.	The team has so much ownership of the work that, if necessary, we would offer to stay late to finish a job.	5	4	3	2	1
14.	The team leader encourages every person on the team to be open and honest, even if people have to share information that goes against what the team leader would like to hear.	5	4	3	2	1
15.	There is a good match between the capabilities and responsibilities of each person on the team.	5	4	3	2	1
16.	Everyone on the team is working toward accomplishing the same thing.	5	4	3	2	1
17.	The team has the support and resources it needs to meet customers' expectations.	5	4	3	2	1
18.	The team knows as much about what's going on in the organization as the team leader does, because the team leader always keeps everyone up to date.	5	4	3	2	1

Exhibit 16   *(continued)*

19. The team leader believes that everyone on the team has something   5 4 3 2 1
to contribute—such as knowledge, skills, abilities, and information—
that is of value to all.

20. Team members clearly understand the team's unwritten rules of how   5 4 3 2 1
to behave within the group.

Scoring Sheet

THE FIVE EFFECTIVENESS AREAS	RATINGS ON NUMBERED INVENTORY ITEMS		TEAM RATINGS	TEAM LEADER RATINGS	CONSENSUS RATING
Team Mission Average of team members' ratings Team leader's ratings	1 6 11 16 ___ + ___ + ___ + ___ = ___ + ___ + ___ + ___ =	_____		_____	=========
Goal Achievement Average of team members' ratings Team leader's ratings	2 7 12 17 ___ + ___ + ___ + ___ = ___ + ___ + ___ + ___ =	_____		_____	=========
Empowerment Average of team members' ratings Team leader's ratings	3 8 13 18 ___ + ___ + ___ + ___ = ___ + ___ + ___ + ___ =	_____		_____	=========
Open, Honest Communication Average of team members' ratings Team leader's ratings	4 9 14 19 ___ + ___ + ___ + ___ = ___ + ___ + ___ + ___ =	_____		_____	=========
Positive Roles and Norms Average of team members' ratings Team leader's ratings	5 10 15 20 ___ + ___ + ___ + ___ = ___ + ___ + ___ + ___ =	_____		_____	=========
	Total Team-Effectiveness Rating				

The successful work of "part-time" teams helps an organization keep pace with guest needs and expectations without changing the fundamental structure of the organization.

The ever-increasing empowerment of teams in a few of today's hospitality organizations suggests that we may see more self-directed hospitality teams in the future. Some organizations have taken "regular" jobs that were designed for individuals and transformed them for teams. Such jobs integrate duties and tasks from several areas and may include responsibilities previously reserved for supervisors and managers. The "regular" job is membership on the team.

A **self-directed team** manages itself and its work. The team makes job assignments, plans work schedules, and makes service- and production-related decisions. The team designs and implements its own compensation system and hires, trains, appraises, disciplines, and fires its own members. (As a side benefit, it's been proven that self-directed teams have a positive effect on work ethics as well.[9]) Supervisors and managers assume entirely new kinds of responsibilities centered on supporting and providing resources for the organization's teams on a full-time basis. Moving toward self-directed teams means changing not only job descriptions but also the fundamental structure of an organization, including its information patterns, its rewards and compensation systems, and its career paths.

While some team-oriented hospitality organizations may not choose self-directed teams as their future, many of them are focusing on similar issues. More and more companies are rewriting job descriptions and cross-training employees to function effectively in several different positions. Department supervisors and managers receive training and development opportunities that span areas traditionally reserved for other departments. And all staff members receive fundamental training in how their day-to-day actions affect the financial performance of the organization as a business.

Endnotes

1. Portions of this chapter have been adapted from Stephen J. Shriver, *Managing Quality Services* (Lansing, Mich.: American Hotel & Lodging Educational Institute, 1988).

2. Peter Senge, *The Fifth Discipline: The Art & Practice of the Learning Organization* (New York: Random House, Inc., 2006).

3. David J. Cooper and John H. Kagel, "Are Two Heads Better than One? Team versus Individual Play in Signaling Games," *American Economic Review* 95, no. 3 (June 2005): 477–509; Debra Adams and Catherine Waddle, "Evaluating the Return from Management Development Programmes: Individual Returns versus Organizational Benefits," *International Journal of Contemporary Hospitality Management* 14, no. 1 (2002): 14–20.

4. Greg Stewart, "A Meta-Analytical Review of Relationships Between Team Design Features and Team Performance," *Journal of Management* 32, no. 1 (2006): 29–55.

5. Dana Tesone, "Development of a Sustainable Tourism Hospitality Human Resources Management Module: A Template for Teaching Sustainability Across the Curriculum," *International Journal of Hospitality Management* 23, no. 3 (2004): 207–237.

6. Simon Taggar and Robert Ellis, "The Role of Leaders in Shaping Formal Team Norms," *The Leadership Quarterly* 18, no. 2 (2007): 105–120.

7. B. W. Tuckman, "Developmental Sequences in Small Groups," *Psychological Bulletin* 63, no. 6 (1965): 383–399.

8. Daniel Levi, *Groups Dynamics for Teams* (Thousand Oaks, Calif.: Sage Publications, Inc., 2001). Includes a discussion of 64 different roles team members can play in groups.

9. Gregory C. Petty, Doo Hun Lim, Seung Won Yoon, and Johnny Fontan, "The Effect of Self-Directed Work Teams on Work Ethic," *Performance Improvement Quality* 21, no. 2 (2008): 49–63.

Key Terms

agenda—A written plan for a meeting that indicates the date, time, and place for the meeting and the issues to be addressed.

baseline measurement—A measurement used as a basis for comparisons or for control purposes; a beginning point in an evaluation of output observed over a period of time. A baseline measurement represents how a process performs prior to any improvement effort.

brainstorming—An idea-gathering technique that uses group interaction to generate as many ideas as possible within a given time period. Brainstorming taps into the collective brainpower of the group and yields greater results than could be achieved if each individual in the group worked alone.

code of conduct—Expectations of behavior mutually agreed upon by team members.

consensus—Expectations of behavior mutually agreed upon by team members.

consensus decision—A decision made after all aspects of an issue, both positive and negative, have been reviewed or discussed to the extent that everyone openly understands, supports, and participates in the decision.

continuous-improvement team—A permanent work team formed to implement incremental improvements in an organization on an ongoing basis. It can be either functional or cross-functional in nature.

cross-functional team—A team of individuals from different organizational units or functions that solves problems and develops solutions affecting the organization as a system.

forming—The first stage of team development, characterized by cautious, limited member participation, dependence on the leader, and low productivity.

groupthink—The tendency of a group to stifle differences of opinion in an effort to preserve group unity and harmony; may arise during the norming stage of team development.

just-in-time training—A process that provides training when it is needed.

minutes—A written summary of the events and actions of a meeting.

mission statement—A statement of the mission of an organization or team that describes the organization's or team's reason for existence. Mission statements are broad and expected to remain in effect for an extended period of time.

norming—The third stage of team development, during which relationships become cooperative and supportive as members learn that they can work together as a cohesive unit. The team becomes more productive during this stage.

performing—The fourth stage of team development, during which a team achieves its peak productivity: individual members share the desire to achieve the team's common goals and appreciate each other's individual contributions toward that end.

self-directed team—A work team that manages itself and its work, making job assignments, planning work schedules, and making service- and production-related decisions.

storming—The second stage of team development, characterized by conflict within the group as team members push boundaries and challenge authority. Member interaction becomes confrontational, and productivity remains low.

task-force team—A temporary work team formed to solve a specific problem that usually involves several departments or areas within an organization.

transforming—The fifth and final stage of team development, when the group is either preparing to disband or facing a major change in its mission, membership, or environment. The team often regresses to behaviors characteristic of earlier stages of development as it struggles to cope with the changes.

Review Questions

1. Successful teams need what types of resources from their parent organizations?

2. What are three important characteristics of successful teams?

3. What are the characteristics of a team in the forming stage? the storming stage? the norming stage? the performing stage? the transforming stage?

4. What are some of the positive roles individuals may play within a group? What are some of the negative roles?

5. What are some of the keys to planning a successful meeting?

6. What are some of the strategies team leaders can employ to conduct a successful meeting?

7. How does a consensus decision differ from a unanimous decision?

8. How can work teams be evaluated?

Chapter 9 Outline

Managing Diversity
    Why Diversity Must Be Managed
    The Benefits of Diversity
    Diversity Within the Hospitality
        Industry
The Changing Work Force
    Women in the Workplace
    Minorities in the Workplace
    Older Workers
    Undereducated Workers
    Workers with Disabilities
Fostering Diversity in Your Organization
    Understand Your Organization's
        Diversity
    Strengthen Top Management
        Commitment
    Acquire Diverse Talent
    Retain Diverse Staff
    Conduct Diversity Training
    Disseminate Diversity Materials
    Maintain Forward Momentum
A Final Note on Diversity

Competencies

1. Explain why diversity must be managed and how diversity management benefits hospitality organizations. (pp. 275–283)

2. Identify the ways in which the work force is changing and how it is becoming more diverse. (pp. 283–296)

3. Describe ways to foster diversity within an organization and the key issues that must be addressed. (pp. 296–305)

9

The Challenge of Diversity

INTEREST IN WORK FORCE DIVERSITY has grown steadily over the past several decades.[1]
Rapid and often unpredictable changes in work force demographics have been
primary drivers in motivating executives to develop new management strategies
that embrace the new reality of diverse workplaces. In recent years, the need for
greater financial growth and increased market share has led many hospitality
companies to encourage diversity in the workplace, the supply chain, and in ownership structures.

The declining number of white male workers entering the work force and the
rapid increase in the number of female, minority, seasonal international, immigrant refugee, and older workers have caused managers to reconsider how they
manage their businesses and relate to their employees. Diversity no longer refers
only to ethnicity and gender; rather, diversity encompasses the many ways in
which people differ from one another—age, educational background, sexual orientation, level of financial success, and so on. Walk into any hotel, restaurant, or
other hospitality business in almost any U.S. city and you will realize that the
hospitality industry consists of diverse groups of people. Even in small rural communities you will find, if you dig a little deeper, that there is wide diversity among
a seemingly homogenous work force. Behind the scenes, even in predominantly
Caucasian regions of the United States such as Vermont, a variety of people from
many parts of the world are working to ensure guest satisfaction and quality customer service. In Burlington, Vermont, for example, one can find in the housekeeping departments of local hotels Bosnians working alongside Hmong people, or
Polish housekeepers supervising part-time housekeepers in their fifties who need
work to supplement their retirement benefits. In Stowe, Vermont, during the busy
ski season, resorts and hotels employ international workers from countries such
as Chile, Peru, Argentina, Jamaica, Lithuania, and Romania, to name a few. On the
surface, differences in color and ethnicity are apparent; what isn't apparent are the
often subtle differences among employees in values, beliefs, cultural characteristics, educational levels, perceptions of life, and so on.

The hospitality industry is a leader in employing people from diverse backgrounds at all levels of lodging accommodations, from large, full-service resorts
to roadside limited-service hotels. Diversity is not only found among hospitality employees; hospitality managers, owners, and suppliers are also coming from
increasingly diverse backgrounds. Minority-owned businesses have become
prominent in supplying the hospitality industry, and minority-owned hotel management companies fly the flags of all the major hotel chains.

As work force diversity continues its rapid pace in the hospitality industry
of the twenty-first century, traditional management practices are becoming less

effective. No longer can managers expect that the way they learned to manage in the twentieth century will work well today. During the late twentieth century, management practices were transforming, trying to keep up with the changing nature of the work force as well as the work environment. Today a more integrated approach to management is necessary, rather than merely focusing on the traditional management tasks of planning, controlling, organizing, and so on. Managing a diverse work force requires putting a human face on the management challenges posed by diversity. Managers must come out of their offices to engage one-on-one with employees at all levels and build a community of people whose main purpose is achieving the goals of the organization.

The aim of diversity management is to create a high-performance organization where the focus is on guest satisfaction and business success. To achieve success in the highly competitive hospitality marketplace, a comfortable work environment that brings out the best in all employees, regardless of background, is required. Today, diversity has become a significant business and management strategy rather than simply a goal to employ people of diverse backgrounds in order to create a workplace with minority representation, as was often the focus in the past.

In this chapter, a variety of ideas will be presented on how to foster and celebrate diversity in a hospitality organization. First we will examine why diversity must be managed and identify the benefits of diversity. Next we will discuss some of the major groups that are changing the work force and have made diversity such an important topic. Finally, the chapter concludes with a look at some of the ways that organizations can successfully foster diversity.

Managing Diversity

What does "managing diversity" mean? According to one definition, managing diversity refers to using "management policies and techniques that enable a heterogeneous work force to perform to its potential in an equitable work environment where no one group has an advantage or disadvantage."[2] As just mentioned, diversity in the twenty-first century refers not only to gender and race but to numerous other personal characteristics, including age, educational background, sexual orientation, physical abilities or qualities, social status, economic status, religion, and virtually any other characteristic that makes a person unique (see Exhibit 1).

Simply stated, the philosophy of managing diversity suggests that organizations make whatever changes are necessary to their systems, structures, and management practices to eliminate any subtle barriers that might keep people from reaching their full potential.[3] Again, the goal of diversity management is a high-performance organization.

According to R. Roosevelt Thomas, Jr., founder of the American Institute for Managing Diversity, Inc., at Atlanta's Morehouse College, "Managing diversity does not mean controlling or containing diversity, it means enabling every member of your work force to perform to his or her potential. Managing diversity means: How do we build systems and a culture that unite different people in a

Exhibit 1 Diversity Characteristics

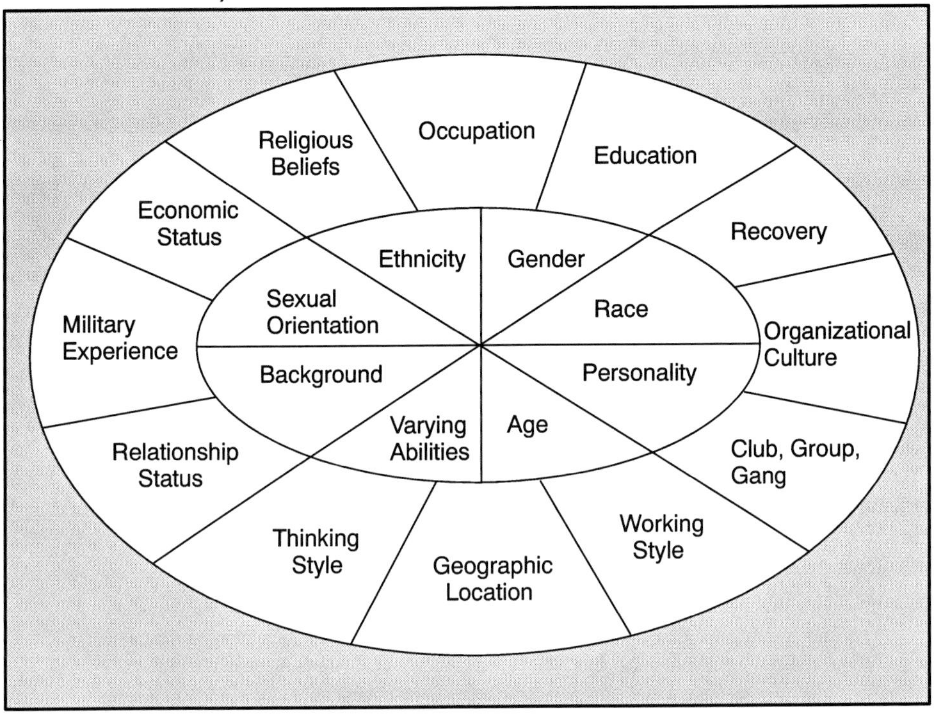

common pursuit without undermining their diversity? It's taking differences into account while developing a cohesive whole."[4]

"Managing diversity" is something of a misnomer. "Managing" diversity does not mean controlling it, or doing whatever it takes to make people less diverse. Managing diversity requires managers to look at people as individuals, and to see individual strengths and weaknesses instead of bothersome variances from arbitrary corporate norms. Trying to fit round people into the corporation's square holes is not what managing diversity is about. Managing diversity means finding ways to get groups of people with different backgrounds and values to work harmoniously together and share their different perspectives in a way that furthers the goals of the organization.

Why Diversity Must Be Managed

There are two major reasons for managers to be concerned with diversity. The first is demographics. Managers are going to have to deal with a diverse work force whether they like it or not, because the makeup of today's work force is much different than it was in the past. "A diverse work force is not something your company ought to have; it's something your company does have, or soon will have," says Thomas.[5] The second reason is productivity. As Ellis Cose, author of a book on equality in America, puts it: "It is going to be awfully hard to forge a globally competitive work force if [people from different backgrounds] can't learn to work together."[6]

We'll take a closer look at each of these issues in the following sections.

Demographics. The number of minorities and immigrants entering the U.S. labor force continues to increase. By 2020, the number of ethnic minorities is projected to be 31 percent of the work force—up from 24 percent in 1995. The percentage of white men in the work force continues to decline. The percentage of women in the work force is rising; today, approximately 50 percent of the work force is made up of women, up from 30 percent in 1960. These statistics vary somewhat from source to source; however, disagreements about the specific numbers should not obscure the main point: the work force is always changing, with the numbers of women, minorities, elderly, disabled, and international temporary visa holders entering the work force dramatically increasing, while the number of white males entering the work force is steadily decreasing. In many cases, organizations are hiring different people than they are accustomed to hiring.

Productivity. The second major reason to be concerned about diversity is that once you have a diverse work force, simply throwing different people together does not create a productive work environment—or even a genuinely diverse one. Why? Because:

> people tend to cluster with people like themselves, those with whom they feel comfortable and who confirm old stereotypes. It is harder to manage a group of people who have different wants and ideas about how work is to be done. Prejudice and cultural misunderstandings cause conflict, bad decisions, and poor results. Productivity may decline unless diversity is deliberately managed and managed well.
>
> The reality today is that most organizations must deal with diversity at entry levels simply because of the demographics of the labor pool. At the same time, organizations need diversity at the top where more complex tasks and decision-making need different perspectives. The upshot is that effective managing of diversity is a requirement at all levels.[7]

Until recently, Thomas argues, the tendency for people to assimilate—that is, blend in with the mainstream culture and the culture of the particular organization where they worked—made it unnecessary to manage diversity. The corporation dictated a mold for up-and-comers to fit: always arrive early and work late, never turn down a transfer to another city, dress like so, talk like so, express the right opinions. "Managing" was largely a matter of enforcing the mold and rewarding those who fit it best.[8]

But the workers entering the work force today are different. Thomas notes that "more and more employees, including white males, are coming to the workplace inclined to celebrate their differences and less willing to adapt blindly. They want to keep the traits that are unique to themselves and not unnecessarily compromise who they are."[9] This has meant that organizations must change the way they manage workers if they want to have a work force that is as productive as it can be:

> "There is more interest in expressing our pride in who we are by adopting the dress or speech patterns associated with our own ethnic groups," according to Ayala Esnard, Marriott Management Services (MMS) human

resources manager for the University of Miami and other Miami-area MMS accounts. "The danger in that kind of display of pride is polarization. Everyone goes to his own cultural corner and stands around talking to other members of his same ethnic group. What we're trying to do [with diversity management] is get them out of those corners and onto the dance floor so they can all work together."[10]

The problem for women and minority workers wanting to get out onto the corporate dance floor is that they are not as familiar with the music as are their white male counterparts. Each organization has its own culture that reflects attitudes about what is important, how work is done, and how employees should behave and be rewarded, and these unwritten rules or values, for most U.S. companies, are male, white, and based in European traditions.[11] Women and minorities aren't as aware of many of the unwritten rules as are their white male co-workers. White men may not share these rules with others, either because (1) the rules are so obvious (to them) that it seldom occurs to them that others don't know them, too, or (2) because the white male managers are themselves only subconsciously aware of the unwritten rules.

To help their staffs become more productive, managers must learn to identify the norms of the organization and pass them on to those entering the workplace. Through effective orientation and training programs, entrants into the workplace such as teenagers, recent college graduates, women, and minorities have an opportunity to learn about career advancement, communication, organizational culture, power, networking, and all the other unwritten rules for success. This does not mean that young people, women, and minorities must do all the changing, however. A large part of managing diversity is helping the organization change the rules to accommodate differences in style and perspective among workers from different backgrounds. The purpose of sharing the current set of unwritten rules is not to impose them on people but to give everyone a chance to understand the organization as it currently exists and how they can succeed within it. Employees who know the unwritten rules can proceed with building their careers while helping the organization change its culture to adapt to a more diverse work force and a more multicultural society.

The Benefits of Diversity

Organizations can realize substantial benefits from dealing successfully with diversity issues. Benefits include giving customers better service, reducing costs, increasing productivity, and improving the quality of management, among other benefits.

Better Service to Customers. When hospitality organizations value and embrace diversity, their customers benefit. Walk into any Starbucks coffee shop and observe how the staff serving the coffee reflects the demographics and lifestyle choices of the customer base. Hiring employees who speak more than English is critical in major international destinations such as Miami, Los Angeles, San Francisco, Boston, and New York, because guests from around the world feel much more welcome and comfortable when they can speak in their native language when checking into hotels, ordering food in a restaurant, or discussing service-related issues. A hotel that has no minorities at the front desk or in sales or management may be less attractive to a black or Hispanic group than one that does. A hotel gift shop that does not have ethnic products such as special hair care items or diverse periodicals on the shelves risks sending the message that the hotel's management is not sensitive to the needs of different groups.[12]

When a hospitality business uses marketing materials with photos of guests from only one ethnic background, it limits its potential markets. One such firm that organizes upscale walking tours was told by a potential customer that, since no people of color were on the brochure, they wouldn't be booking with the company. The company, however, didn't have any photos from its archives of guests from different backgrounds, and it was reluctant to purchase photos that weren't of real tours, just to put people of different ethnic groups in its marketing materials. This is an ethical dilemma that must be grappled with by operations and marketing people alike.

Hospitality organizations such as Wyndham International, Starwood Hotels & Resorts, and Hilton have made great strides in building a diverse work environment, resulting in extraordinarily diversified business models that greatly benefit their customers. Of Wyndham's workforce, 61 percent of employees are from minority groups, with 64 percent of all new hires from minority populations. Of Starwood's new hires, 58 percent are from minority groups; 32 percent of Starwood's current management staff is made up of minorities. In early 2007, Marriott announced historic benchmarks reached in its company-wide diversity initiatives: $400 million spent with women- and minority-owned businesses; 400 hotels opened, or in the pipeline, owned or managed by minorities or women; and an all-time high in diverse appointments to management positions.[13] This diverse business model gives Marriott a strong advantage in today's global hospitality marketplace. With guests from around the world, Marriott and the other major hotel companies have the ability to meet the variety of tastes, service requirements, and general communication patterns of their guests, because their employees and suppliers represent the cultural characteristics of their customers, resulting in a better understanding of customer requirements than if the companies' work forces were all Caucasian.

Reduced Costs. Costs associated with recruiting, training, relocating, and compensating employees are major expenses for organizations. Increased diversity practices save money by reducing unwanted turnover and providing non-monetary reasons for employees to stay with an organization. A company with no sensitivity to diversity issues may hire women and members of minority groups and invest money in training them, only to have them leave because the company doesn't have a welcoming atmosphere. Lower discrimination lawsuit costs are just one more example of the savings an organization that promotes diversity might enjoy. Furthermore, it has been shown that companies attract more applicants of diverse backgrounds when advertisements feature employees from a richly diverse workplace.

Increased Productivity. People who enjoy coming to work generally produce more. People who believe that their work will be valued or that their work will lead to advancement are also inclined to work harder. Research has proven that

Diversity and the LISTEN System

Diversity is much more than skin deep. Good managers begin with the understanding that all people are individuals and should be treated as such. An organizational culture that values diversity will bring out the best in its people.

Hospitality organizations that are successful in the twenty-first century have standard operating procedures that help guide employees in day-to-day tasks. Setting standards, training to standards, evaluating performance, and retraining are all tools that managers use to manage others. However, employing standard operating procedures by themselves may not be adequate when managers must work with people who come to the workplace with a wide variety of cultural characteristics, personality traits, values, languages, and beliefs. Additional tools are needed for managers to effectively guide a diverse work force. New tools that have more to do with interpersonal and emotional management skills are required, tools that help managers develop patience, active listening skills, tolerance for uncertainty and ambiguity, the ability to empathize with others, and the sensitivity to honor feelings as well as ideas.

Listening is one of the first steps in developing an understanding of others. The acronym "LISTEN" stands for a number of actions that managers can employ to interact successfully with staff members while simultaneously directing them toward achieving the goals of the organization. "L" stands for listen, "I" represents inquiry, "S" stands for solutions, "T" stands for tolerance of ambiguity, "E" asks managers to encourage employees to focus on goals, and "N" stands for Negotiate for win/win outcomes.

The first few letters of LISTEN can help guide managers in learning about their staffs. Listening to employees is an important step in gathering information. Listening can include non-verbal cues that tell managers how an employee is feeling. Asking questions of employees gives them the feeling that their manager cares about who they are and what they think. Inquiry is the basis of learning; when combined with listening, inquiry becomes a way to show respect for others.

The LISTEN system can be used not just by managers, but by all members of the organization, from the boardroom to the dish room. As part of a diversity training program, new employee training, and ongoing training initiatives, the LISTEN system can become a cornerstone of the company's culture.

diverse groups of people are generally more creative and innovative than homogeneous groups.

Ernest H. Drew, then CEO of Hoechst Celanese, a giant chemical firm, became an advocate of diversity after a conference for Hoechst's top 125 officers, mostly white men, and 50 or so lower-level women and minorities. The group split into problem-solving teams. By chance, some teams were mixed by race and gender, others were all white and male. The main issue was how the corporate culture affected the firm and what changes might be made to improve results. When the teams presented their findings, "it was so obvious that the diverse teams had the broader solutions," Drew recalls. "They had ideas I hadn't even thought of. For the first time, we realized that diversity is a strength as it relates to problem solving. Before, we just thought of diversity as the total number of minorities and women in the company, like affirmative action. Now we knew we needed diversity at every level of the company where decisions are made."[14]

At the University of North Texas, ethnically diverse teams of business students were pitted without their knowledge against all-white teams for 17 weeks. At first the all-white teams sprinted ahead, but by the study's end the more diverse groups were viewing situations from a broader range of perspectives and producing more innovative solutions to problems. Said one of the professors who conducted the experiment, "Cultural diversity in the U.S. work force has sometimes been viewed as a dark cloud. Our results suggest that it has a silver lining."[15]

Improved Quality of Management. Including nontraditional employees in competition for managerial positions can improve the pool of applicants. It also may unblock some highly qualified individuals who may have been unable to advance due to policies that discriminated against them for one reason or another. The additional competition can also encourage members of the dominant group to work harder to retain their positions. Moreover, exposure to colleagues from different backgrounds can help managers develop new ways to solve workplace problems.

Improving the quality of management also means improving the quality of management decisions. Making sure you have a diverse work force on the levels where important decisions are made is perhaps where diversity can benefit an organization the most. If you doubt it, just ask General Motors. A single Spanish speaker in the decision-making loop could have saved GM the expense of trying to market the Chevrolet Nova in Mexico. ("No va" means "won't go" in Spanish.[16]) If you are designing a product for an Asian customer, having at least one person on the design team that is Asian or is familiar with Asian cultures would help you discover, for example, that many Asians consider white, blue, and yellow to be funeral colors and might reject products in those colors.[17]

Additional Benefits. Taylor Cox and Stacy Blake reported additional benefits that organizations realize from increased diversity: increased creativity and innovation, enhanced organizational flexibility, increased resource acquisition abilities, and enhanced social responsibility.[18]

Organizations that learn to use diversity as an asset "will stride ahead of those that don't. The payoff will be in productivity (greater output), quality (fewer errors), flexibility (faster response to change), and innovation (more creativity). Organizations that don't learn to respect, value, and utilize individual differences (including differences in sex, race, age, education, function, and other areas) will continue to be socked with discrimination and harassment lawsuits, low morale, high recruitment costs, high turnover, and a lack of creativity."[19]

If diversity is so great, why is it such a hard issue to deal with? "Managing diversity is not natural," according to Theodore E. Payne, a manager in the corporate affirmative action and equal opportunity department at Xerox Corporation. "There's a synergy among likes. Lots of things go unsaid. There's a breakdown in synergy when people are unlike."[20]

People with similar backgrounds, values, and interests tend to congregate together; most of us prefer to have lunch or socialize after work with people most like ourselves. Even the way the human mind operates works against diversity management:

The growing consensus from psychological experiments is that racial and ethnic prejudices are an unfortunate by-product of the way the mind categorizes all experience. Essentially, the mind seeks to simplify the chaos of the world by fitting all perceptions into categories. Thus it fits different kinds of people into pigeonholes, just as it does with restaurants or television programs.[21]

To manage a diverse group of people, managers must confront their pigeonholes—that is, better understand their prejudices and tendencies to stereotype others. Although that is hard work, the rewards can be great.

Diversity Within the Hospitality Industry

Many hospitality companies are working hard to better diversify their work forces. *Fortune* magazine listed five hotel companies and three restaurant companies in its annual list of "America's 50 Best Companies for Minorities." Hilton Hotels Corporation topped the list at number 13, followed by Hyatt at number 18, Starwood at number 32, Wyndham at number 35, and the MGM Mirage Las Vegas at number 42. McDonald's has been ranked at or near the top of this list many times in recent years.[22] Marriott's great strides in diversity management have already been mentioned.

What is it that these companies do to successfully build and maintain a diverse work force? An important first step is hiring minorities, followed by active training and development. Promoting from within is critical to increasing diversity in the management ranks. At Hilton Hotels, for example, more than 60 percent of new hires are minorities, and its diversity efforts endeavor to make sure that those minorities are given every opportunity to climb the company ladder. Non-whites make up only one-third of employees enrolled in succession plans, according to the report in *Fortune*. At Starwood Hotels & Resorts, the company Intranet encourages staff members to submit anonymous comments on diversity issues, which management receives for review. And English-language-speaking courses abound across the hospitality sector, as demonstrated by Darden Restaurants, Marriott International, and many other leaders in the industry.

The Changing Work Force

Some of the major groups that are changing the demographics of the work force are women, minorities, older workers, undereducated workers, and workers with disabilities. We will take a look at each of these groups in the following sections.

Women in the Workplace

During the 1980s and 90s, one of the biggest societal changes was the increasing number of women who were joining the work force. In 1985, women made up approximately 36 percent of the U.S. work force, up from 30 percent in 1960.[23] Today, as mentioned earlier, about 50 percent of the work force is women.

The number of women in management is also increasing dramatically. One of the reasons that women are making up a larger and larger percentage of both employees and managers is that they are continuing their education after high school in much greater numbers. In fact, today there are more women in college

Gender's Impact on Communication in the Work Place: A Quiz

Answer the following questions by circling "T" for "True" or "F" for "False."

T F 1. Male managers praise women more than they do men.

T F 2. Women are more likely than men to answer questions not addressed to them.

T F 3. In an open discussion, women talk more than men.

T F 4. Male managers tend to interrupt women more frequently than they do men.

T F 5. Female managers interpret nonverbal cues better than male managers.

T F 6. Women use more polite forms of communication than men.

T F 7. Men use more tag questions than women. (Example: "It's a nice day, isn't it?")

T F 8. Men criticize women more frequently than they do men.

T F 9. Men work harder to keep a conversation going than women.

T F 10. Women communicate with more emotion and drama than men.

T F 11. Women are touched more often than men.

T F 12. Women reveal more personal information than men.

Answer Key

1. F	5. T	9. F
2. F	6. T	10. F
3. F	7. F	11. T
4. T	8. F	12. T

Scoring Guide

10–12 correct	You are sensitive to gender issues in the work place.
5–9 correct	You are sensitive to some gender issues, but may experience gender-related communication problems.
4 or less correct	You need to enhance your awareness of gender issues.

Source: Quoted by Ellen Cooperperson, "How to Manage a Culturally Diverse Workforce," Corporate Performance Management, Inc., Babylon, New York, from the work of Dr. Hazel Rozema and John Gray, Professors, the University of Arkansas.

than men. To put this in perspective, consider that 95 percent of all graduate degrees and 90 percent of all undergraduate degrees were earned by men in 1960.

The increasing number of women in the work force means that managers must find new ways to deal with new types of problems. For example, business today is attempting to cope with the issue of sexual harassment in the workplace.

Sexual harassment can be any behavior of a sexual nature that makes workers uncomfortable, including:

- Sexual innuendos

- Inappropriate touching

- Off-color jokes

- Sexually explicit pictures or photographs

- Unwanted flirting

- Inappropriate conversations or comments

- Revealing apparel

Sixty-four percent of the female managers in a study of gender issues in hospitality management reported that they had been subjected to sexual harassment at work; the number of female employees subjected to such treatment may be much higher. In addition, nearly 90 percent of the female managers reported that they believed sexual discrimination occurred on a frequent basis, most often in promotion-related situations, although the prevalence is high in other situations as well.[24] The fact that both male and female managers reported high levels of sexual discrimination confirms that this is a substantial problem for hospitality managers.

How much managers earn is also a gender issue. Female hospitality managers earn, on average, only about 80 percent of what male managers in similar positions earn. More than 60 percent of the females participating in a study of hospitality management earned salaries lower than the mean average salaries of male managers in similar positions. This amounted to about a $6,500 per year gap (males earned $42,306; females, $35,919).

Other issues related to the increased number of women in the work force include the following:

- *Less flexibility by managers and employees.* The rapidly increasing number of dual-income families in the United States has resulted in many employees and managers being less willing to relocate.

- *More variety in benefits offered.* In the past, companies were able to offer a single benefit package to employees. As the number of women in the work force grows, companies must develop new packages that take the needs of female managers and employees into account.

- *Changed and more flexible leave policies.* Both men and women are demanding more leave time to care for newborns or other family members and take care of other personal obligations. This will likely increase as more women enter the work force.

- *Part-time and work-at-home jobs.* More and more women are joining the work force on a part-time or work-at-home basis. As a result, hospitality managers today must develop methods of addressing the particular needs of these employees.

Minorities in the Workplace

The number of minorities and immigrants entering the U.S. labor force is increasing significantly. Richard Judy and Carol D'Amico predicted that by 2020, racial minorities will make up 31 percent of the work force, up from 24 percent in 1995.[25] Among the issues today's managers must address is how to enhance communication between culturally diverse groups. In the future, a manager's job may depend on the extent to which he or she can communicate effectively with people from a variety of cultural and ethnic backgrounds. Managers will also face the problem of how to ensure that their organizations are sensitive to the needs and rights of each employee. This was difficult even when the work force was predominantly white men; it will be much more difficult as the work force becomes increasingly diverse. At the same time that managers are coping with how to ensure that individual rights are protected, they must also develop systems and methods of ensuring that all employees work toward the common goals of the company.

Among the issues managers must address because of the increasing number of minorities in the work force are the following:

- How to develop and institute cultural awareness training for their employees.

- How to increase the verbal skills for frontline hospitality employees for whom English is a second language.

- How to develop and institute reward systems that meet the varying needs of employees from different cultural backgrounds.

- How to motivate people to want to achieve corporate and unit-level goals who have different values about time, money, service, and achievement.

In the past, managers were encouraged to ignore differences among their workers. Advocates of civil rights downplayed cultural heritage, because differences from the mainstream were regularly used as evidence of the inferiority of minority groups. Consequently, "we are all equal" came to mean "we are all the same." Even now, many who say they value diversity are offended when actual differences among different ethnic groups are discussed.

Diversity asks managers not to ignore differences among people, but to value them. Managers must move from "We are all the same; let's cooperate," to "We are all different; let's capitalize on those differences."

Communicating with Employees Who Do Not Speak English or Do Not Speak It Well. Sometimes managers must work with employees from various minority groups who do not speak English or can only speak it brokenly. In such cases, managers are often reduced to relying on body language to figure out whether they've been understood by an employee. Managers must keep in mind that, although nonverbal signals can be very helpful in assessing how much of a message has been understood, body language is by no means universal.[26] A blank expression may be a sign of poor understanding for many people, but for someone from Asia, a blank expression might reflect a desire to avoid an overt display of emotion. Similarly, someone who avoids eye contact while you are speaking to him or her might be having trouble understanding you, or could be simply indicating respect, depending on his or her cultural background.

Five Ways to Help Non-English-Speaking Room Attendants Be More Productive

Communication within a hotel's housekeeping department is especially challenging if some employees do not speak English. Here are five things managers can do to help a non-English-speaking employee become part of the team.

1. **Hire more than one person of the same nationality.**

    If possible, hire more than one person of the same nationality; this can make the work environment less intimidating. It is comforting to have someone to talk to while you eat lunch or learn new tasks.

2. **Make it easy for employees to communicate with each other.**

    One way to make it easier for the housekeeping staff to communicate is to use flash cards. For example, housekeeping supervisors can carry cards with simple requests printed in different languages. If a room attendant neglects a task, the supervisor can pull out the appropriate card. The card might ask the employee to dust, vacuum, change the bedspread—whatever the task might be. As the non-English-speaking employee gains work experience and a better grasp of English, the cards will be needed less and less. A local school, employment agency, or library can provide the resources necessary to make the flash cards, or a bilingual employee can translate a list of housekeeping tasks. You may be able to use drawings instead of words to indicate tasks.

3. **Make it easy for guests to communicate with employees.**

    Non-English-speaking employees often have difficulty understanding guest requests. A variation on the flash card idea might help. All room attendants can carry on their cart a clipboard with the 15 to 20 most common guest requests, such as more soap, more towels, or the location of the hotel's restaurant. When a guest approaches a non-English-speaking room attendant and makes a request, the attendant can get out the clipboard and invite the guest to point to the appropriate request. The attendant can then take immediate action. This means faster service for the guest and eliminates the need for the guest to call the front desk.

4. **Offer classes in English.**

    Many non-English-speaking employees want to learn English. Most local education and community centers offer classes designed for people for whom English is a second language. Hotels can offer classes on-site as well.

5. **Learn about non-English-speaking employees.**

    It is comforting to non-English-speaking workers when their supervisor learns a few words of their native language. Saying "please," "thank you," "have a nice evening," and "well done" in the employee's language can dramatically increase morale. It is also important for managers and other employees to learn the basics of the non-English-speakers' cultures. Honoring their holidays, acknowledging their customs, and encouraging them to share their cultures with the rest of the staff can make them more loyal and productive employees.

Source: Adapted from Mary Friedman, "Five ways to help non-English-speaking room-keepers be more productive," *The Rooms Chronicle* 3, no. 4 (1995): 4.

What follows are suggestions to help you assess how much of what you said was actually understood by someone who does not speak English very well:

- *Be wary of a lack of interruptions.* Although no interruptions can mean that someone is really listening, a complete lack of interruptions sometimes means that you are not being understood.

- *Notice efforts to change the subject.* If a listener is eager to change the subject, this could indicate that the listener can't understand what you are saying and is trying to talk about something more familiar.

- *Note the complete absence of questions.* If a listener doesn't ask any questions, it could indicate that he or she doesn't understand what you are saying, not that he or she understands you perfectly.

- *Watch out for inappropriate laughter.* A self-conscious giggle can indicate poor comprehension. Do not interpret laughter as a sign of disrespect—it is more likely the listener's way of covering up embarrassment.

- *Invite questions in private or in writing.* By providing someone with the opportunity to ask questions in private or in writing, you spare him or her the humiliation of having to admit a lack of understanding in front of co-workers. This suggestion is especially valuable during training sessions, when the number of people present can make it difficult for a trainee to admit to being confused.

- *Allow enough time for people to formulate questions.* If someone doesn't speak English very well, it might take him or her a long time to construct a question— people who speak English as a second language often think of the question in their own language, then must translate it into English. A worker who is rushed may be denied the chance to clear up an important point.

- *Make sure that "yes" is really yes.* In Asia, it is appropriate to answer any question with an initial "yes." This response is often merely an acknowledgment that the question has been heard and understood; it is not an answer to the question.

  Native English speakers know that when someone asks, "You don't understand, do you?" the appropriate response (if they do not understand) is "no," as in "no, I do not understand." In many Asian languages, however, the way of communicating a negative response to this question would be to say "yes," as in "yes, I agree with you that I do not understand." If you are speaking with an Asian immigrant, it is therefore important to phrase all questions in the positive, as in, "Do you understand?" rather than "You don't understand, do you?" If you are asked a negatively phrased question by an Asian employee, you should answer it with a complete sentence. If you just say "yes" or "no," the meaning of your response could easily be taken as the opposite of what you intended.

- *Beware of the tentative "yes."* If the reply to your question, "Do you understand?" is a hesitant yes, or, "Yes, I think so," the listener may not understand and may be trying to cushion the abruptness of a negative response. A tentative yes could be the listener's way of saying, "No, I do not understand, but I am uncomfortable coming right out and saying so."

- *Have the listener repeat what you have said.* This is a simple way of assessing understanding. However, some workers may feel that asking them to repeat something makes them look foolish in front of co-workers. If possible, you should make such a request in private. If you get a word-for-word recitation of what you said, your listener may be displaying a good memory rather than real comprehension.

- *Observe behavior and inspect production.* For example, if the procedure you were teaching is done correctly the first time, the chances are good that the listener understood your instructions.

Not only do you have to worry about whether you have been understood; sometimes it is a challenge to understand what a nonnative English speaker is saying to you. The challenge depends in part on the thickness of the accent, the country of origin, and the manager's own familiarity with a particular accent. Keep in mind that it is easier to understand a foreign language than to speak it; just because someone has trouble speaking English doesn't mean that he or she doesn't have a good grasp of English vocabulary and grammar.

Do not be discouraged if you find it difficult to understand the accents of some of your employees. The more you hear a particular accent, the easier it will be to understand. Our ears and minds gradually adapt to new sounds and new ways of pronouncing words, and eventually even the thickest accent becomes decipherable. In the meantime, however, there are some techniques that can help you better understand nonnative English speakers:

- *Ask the speaker to speak more slowly.* Foreign accents are especially hard to understand if the speaker is talking rapidly.

- *Repeat what you believe the speaker has said.* Saying, "As I understand it, you mean—" or something along those lines can be a quick way to establish whether you have understood the speaker correctly.

- *Encourage nonnative English speakers to write when written communication can be appropriately substituted for oral communication.* For many for whom English is a second language, it is easier to write English than to speak it. This works the other way, too—it can be easier to read English than to hear it, so you should use the written word when appropriate as well. Some nonnative English speakers have a highly developed knowledge of English vocabulary but have difficulty with pronunciation. The written word gets around this problem.

- *If necessary, ask the speaker to spell difficult words.* It can be embarrassing to ask a speaker to spell out what he or she is trying to say, but this technique can also shorten what could otherwise be a long, painful, and even more embarrassing exchange.

- *Give the speaker plenty of time to communicate.* Create an atmosphere in which the conversation is leisurely and relaxed, with plenty of pauses for collecting one's thoughts.

- *Listen to all that the speaker has to say before assuming that you do not understand.* You may be confused by the speaker's first few words or sentences, but often it is better to let the speaker continue rather than cut him or her off with a question. The chances are good that, if allowed to continue, the speaker will eventually say something that makes everything click into place.

- *Observe body language.* Although the meaning of body language varies from culture to culture, it can still provide general clues as to what is being said. For example, if employees wring their hands, it is usually safe to assume they are nervous or upset. As you get to know your employees as individuals, the meaning of their body language should become clearer.

- *Expect to understand the speaker.* When we hear a foreign accent, there is a danger of thinking, "I'll never understand what this person is saying," and therefore tuning out the speaker. Or, we listen to the accent rather than to what is being said. Be aware of your listening habits. Are you truly listening to the words?

While much of this section presents generalizations only, they can give you a place to start if you are having trouble managing or communicating with a minority co-worker.

Older Workers

The U.S. work force is aging. In 1970, the median age for U.S. employees was 28; by 1989 it was 36; by 2000 it was 39; and by 2020 the median age will have increased to over 41.[27] In 2000, 33.9 percent of the work force was 45–64 years old; by 2025, it is projected to be 36.7 percent.[28] On the other end of the age spectrum, employees age 16 to 24 years—one of the most predominant age groups employed by the hospitality industry—constituted only about 16 percent of the work force by 2000; in contrast, during the mid-1970s this group accounted for approximately 25 percent of the work force. The decrease in the 16–24 age group will result in much stiffer competition for employees among hospitality companies.

The dramatic increase in the number of older workers will result in significant changes for hospitality managers. For example, today many hospitality companies have programs designed to recruit and motivate young entry-level personnel. These programs likely will not work for older employees. Another issue managers may face is the higher demand for part-time jobs from older workers interested in augmenting their incomes. Managers will also have to address the issue of how to cope with younger managers managing older employees.[29] Many young managers hold negative biases about older workers. In fact, negative opinions about older workers are so prevalent that the term "ageism" has been coined. Among the commonly held negative perceptions are that older workers:

- Lack ambition and motivation
- Are unlikely to keep up with new ideas and technology
- Have more problems with interpersonal relationships
- Are less competent as managers

- Are less creative

- Have higher accident rates

- Take longer or are more difficult to train

- Are absent more often

- Are less productive and exhibit poorer performance

- Tend to express lower job satisfaction

- Are less loyal to their companies

- Are inflexible and resistant to change

- Have higher turnover rates

- Cost more to employ[30]

Researchers who studied these perceptions found them to be largely untrue. Unfortunately, the fact that these perceptions are more myth than reality has not yet changed the opinions of a significant portion of managers and employees about older workers.

A study published in *Senior Journal* showed some possible compatibility issues concerning older and younger workers that employers need to be prepared to appropriately address. Results of the study indicated that:

- Only 20 percent of workers believe that their older co-workers energize them and bring new ideas to the table.

- While 90 percent of employed U.S. adults surveyed stated that people over age 50 are "with-the-times," 70 percent think that their company does not value older workers.

Many older workers, on the other hand, think their companies do not discriminate based on employees' ages. In fact, more than half of employed adults aged 55 or older agreed that their company treats employees of all ages fairly (58 percent) and that their company values employees over the age of 50 (54 percent). That is a good thing, considering that one-fifth of employed adults said they are older than their boss. Exhibit 2 outlines varying perspectives of how the oldest and youngest workers surveyed viewed each other in the workplace.

Ideas managers can use to help them bridge the generation gap at work include the following:

- Avoid any age-based assumptions and recognize that all of your colleagues and employees will potentially bring different and insightful ideas to the table.

- Be open-minded to learning new ways of doing things and be receptive to time-tested ideas.

- Create an environment where all employees have a meaningful opportunity to contribute. By fostering effective communication and collaboration among staff members, you may be surprised at how many good ideas develop.[31]

Exhibit 2   How Older and Younger Workers View Each Other

Oldest Workers' Viewpoint (age 55+)	Youngest Workers' Viewpoint (ages 18–34)
• 75 percent said they relate well to younger co-workers	• 54 percent said they relate well to older co-workers
• 43 percent said they learn from younger co-workers	• 64 percent said they learn from older co-workers
• 54 percent said their company values employees over age 50	• 25 percent said their company values employees over age 50
• 42 percent said their younger co-workers energize them and bring new ideas to the table	• 23 percent said their older co-workers energize them and bring new ideas to the table
• 32 percent agreed that younger employees seek advice and guidance from employees over age 50	• 22 percent agreed that younger employees seek advice and guidance from employees over age 50

Source: *Senior Journal*, April, 26, 2006.

Other problems hospitality managers must address as their work force ages include the increased need for health care benefits and wellness activities, the need to develop more lateral career opportunities, and the need to address family and work life issues important to older workers.

Recruiting Older Workers. After working a lifetime, why do older people want to return to work?[32] Some of the most common reasons include the following:

- To earn money
- To earn health insurance and other benefits
- To develop new skills
- To use time productively
- To feel useful and needed
- To stay in touch with current developments
- To provide structure to their days
- To do something worthwhile

Older workers in the job market are a highly diverse group of individuals. Major subgroups include the following:

- *Mid-life career changers.* Mid-life career changers are what could be called younger older workers—workers from age 50 to 62—who have plateaued in their current positions or believe that economic conditions threaten their current job. Typically, they want a chance to advance, develop new skills, and earn more money. Mid-life career changers tend to look for full-time work with full benefits. They want to maintain health insurance coverage and continue to build pension and Social Security credits.

- *Displaced older workers.* Displaced older workers are workers who have been fired or laid off from their jobs. They usually have recent work experience but receive no Social Security benefits and probably no pension benefits. These workers may identify with their former job title, and they may have been told that their skills are obsolete. Displaced older workers have a strong need to work full time and receive full benefits, maintain health coverage, and build retirement security.

- *Retirees age 62 or younger.* These individuals aren't receiving Social Security benefits but may have pensions and some health coverage as part of an early retirement deal. These retirees are frequently bored. They are looking for some structure in their lives and a sense of belonging as well as a meaningful job. They also may identify strongly with their former job title. Their objectives range from full-time work to part-time work for supplementary income.

- *Retirees age 62 to 69 who are on Social Security.* This group may think employers are not interested in them, that their skills are obsolete, or that they can't compete with younger workers. They may also have health conditions that they think will limit their usefulness. This group generally wants part-time work with flexible hours in order to supplement Social Security earnings.

- *Retirees age 70 or older who are on Social Security.* These workers need to supplement retirement income and may be looking for various psychological and social benefits. They usually share the concerns of the 62- to 69-year-old retirees and are also typically interested in part-time work with flexible hours.

Undereducated Workers

The rising functional illiteracy rate in the United States has resulted in more companies developing educational programs for their workers. Currently about 20 million people in the United States are functionally illiterate. Companies that have turned to this potential employee group to fill their labor needs have found that one of the keys to successfully recruiting and retaining the undereducated is offering work-based education systems. The need for such systems will increase as more companies find it necessary to hire undereducated employees.

The first place illiteracy takes its toll is in the application process. Many undereducated people don't even seek employment because they're afraid of filling out forms. If undereducated individuals are hired, often they cannot advance simply because their performance suffers due to the everyday problems caused by their poor reading and writing skills, or because they are too embarrassed to take training classes or competency tests that can lead to advancement and higher pay.

One of the challenges facing hospitality managers is the wide gap between the educational levels of their employees. While managers must address the needs of their undereducated employees, they must also find ways to satisfy the needs of educated workers who typically want creative and stimulating work with less supervision and more self-management.

Workers with Disabilities

The Americans with Disabilities Act (ADA) was passed by Congress in 1990 and became law in 1992. It forbids discrimination against people with disabilities, and has been described as the most sweeping U.S. civil rights legislation since Title VII of the Civil Rights Act of 1964. Approximately 43 million U.S. citizens are covered by the ADA. Two-thirds of these people are between the ages of 16 and 64, and therefore are considered part of the potential work force. Most are either under-employed or unemployed altogether.

The ADA considers individuals to have disabilities for a wide variety of reasons. For example, according to the ADA, the word "disability" refers to:

- A physical or mental impairment that substantially limits one or more major life activities

- A record or history of such impairment

- A perception that an individual is impaired

Under this definition, anyone who suffers any impairment of his or her major life activities has a disability. Most people think of the disabled as people who use wheelchairs or walkers. These are not the only types of disabilities covered by the ADA. The ADA also recognizes the following disabilities: speech, vision, and hearing impairments; mental retardation; specific learning disabilities; emotional illnesses; obesity problems; cosmetic disfigurement; diseases that substantially affect an individual's life (cancer, heart disease, palsy, epilepsy, multiple sclerosis, arthritis, asthma, diabetes); contagious diseases, including HIV and AIDS; and drug and alcohol addictions.

To employ these persons, hospitality managers must make what the ADA refers to as "reasonable accommodations" in the work environment. While many managers still think that making reasonable accommodations is extremely difficult, in most cases it is not. For instance, the Equal Employment Opportunity Commission considers the following to meet the ADA's reasonable accommodation requirements in most cases:

- Making facilities wheelchair-accessible (widening aisles, raising or lowering work stations, etc.)

- Restructuring jobs by eliminating nonessential elements difficult for individuals with disabilities to perform

- Reassigning workers to other jobs (if necessary) if they become disabled after employment

- Modifying work schedules to allow for medical appointments

- Modifying equipment to allow persons with disabilities to work

- Modifying training materials and policies to accommodate employees with disabilities

Many companies have already realized the value of hiring workers with disabilities. Those that have not yet done so will be required, either by law or by the

Tips for Interacting with People with Disabilities at Work

- Treat a disabled person like an individual. Respond to a person who happens to have a disability, rather than to a disability that happens to be attached to a person.

- If you think a disabled individual might need help, it's okay to offer—your offer can always be declined. But ask first, don't presume. Then ask how you can be of help.

- Disabled individuals with upper extremity involvement may need assistance in opening doors or turning the pages of a memo or report.

- Using words such as "see" and "look" around visually impaired people is acceptable. These words generally mean to perceive, and avoiding their use could lead to strained or awkward conversations.

- Give specific directions, using north, south, east, and west, when orienting someone to a distant location, and give them an idea of the distance to the location.

- When guiding blind people, allow them to grasp your elbow; don't take their arm and push them ahead of you.

- Don't pet guide dogs when they are in harness and working. Petting them interferes with their concentration on the task at hand—guiding the blind person.

- Speak directly to disabled individuals rather than to the people accompanying them. Avoid starting statements with "Would he like to—" or "Does she want—"

- When describing diagrams, be specific. Avoid "Over here, we have a description of—" Rather, say "In the upper left-hand corner there is a description of—"

- When meeting a person with a hearing impairment, speak slowly and distinctly and make appropriate eye contact.

- Some hearing-impaired individuals read lips. This is more difficult if speakers chew gum, have their hands near their mouths, move around unnecessarily, or turn around while talking.

- If you have trouble understanding someone's speech, try writing notes—it can save time and frustration.

- When speaking with people in wheelchairs, kneel or sit next to them. If you stand, they might strain their necks trying to continually look up at you.

- It's okay to invite disabled individuals to events that they can't physically participate in. Even if they can't play tennis, for example, they can watch, keep score, and cheer their friends on.

- When calling a hearing-impaired individual, let the phone ring longer than usual. Turn off distracting appliances (a dishwasher, vacuum, television, etc.) on your end. Pause after each sentence to make sure the person is keeping up with you.

Sources: Adapted from "Dealing with the Disabled," from *Communication Briefings*, March 1991; and "Tips for Accommodating Handicappers," from the Office of Programs for Handicapper Students, Michigan State University, February 1989.

need for employees, to develop programs to accommodate such workers in the near future.

Fostering Diversity in Your Organization

Although there are some things managers can do on an individual basis to further the cause of diversity, for most organizations, fostering diversity amounts to changing the organization's culture, something that individual managers can't do on their own. An organization's cultural values are deeply rooted and widely held, making them extremely difficult to change. Many organizations have attempted to find quick fixes for diversity enhancement, but sooner or later those companies learned that there is no such thing. Turning an organization from one that just has a diverse work force into one that harnesses the opportunities of workplace diversity requires a comprehensive and carefully planned recruitment, training, and professional development program. With a strong diversity program in place, a hospitality organization has the potential to ultimately change the company culture.

Fostering diversity within an organization may mean that most if not all staff members must go through a diversity training program. This initial step will bring all employees into alignment with regard to their understanding of the diversity issues relevant to the organization. In the long run, however, diversity training programs for new hires as well as ongoing diversity training programs for existing employees should be created, so that diversity training is not a one-time event. Institutionalizing diversity training will help to ensure that the organization truly creates a workplace culture that values diversity. The goal of diversity programs is to create and nourish a culture where everyone feels accepted and valued, where people come to work every day and feel assured that they are truly a welcome part of the work community.

There are many processes a company can use to develop and sustain a culture which values and celebrates diversity. An example of one process is illustrated in Exhibit 3. Ann Morrison developed this five-step process for creating a diversity program after researching the way many organizations approached the diversity issue. The program is designed to increase an organization's awareness of its own unique diversity issues and help it create measurable diversity goals. Whatever model is chosen, there are several general issues an organization must address.

Understand Your Organization's Diversity

Before a company can foster diversity, it must determine where it is in terms of diversity issues. Morrison refers to this initial step as a "discover and rediscover" step, because she wanted to emphasize that the process is ongoing. A company should not try to conduct diversity training before it understands its own unique diversity issues. For example, one diversity training consultant created a diversity training program that focused on racial issues for a San Francisco company, only to find out after the training began that racial issues were not a problem at that particular company, but homophobia was (the company had a large number of gay and lesbian employees). The training didn't help the company deal with its

Exhibit 3   Five Steps for Achieving Diversity

Step 1
Discover and rediscover diversity problems in your organization.

Step 2
Strengthen top management commitment.

Step 3
Choose solutions that fit a balanced strategy.

Step 4
Demand results and revisit goals.

Step 5
Use building blocks to maintain momentum.

Source: "A Special Report on Diversity," *Training & Development*, April 1993, p. 42.

problems, and gay employees left the training thinking management didn't consider their issues to be important.[33]

Different organizations also define diversity in different ways. Generally speaking, it is defined as understanding, respecting, valuing, and accommodating human and cultural differences.

An organization's diversity mix and related problems cannot be discovered using what one author termed the BOWGSAT Method—a Bunch of White Guys Sitting Around a Table.[34] Information should be collected through a variety of means: interviews of selected employees and managers; focus groups of employees and managers (careful attention should be paid to ensuring diversity in the focus groups); employee surveys asking employees about the concerns they have about racial, gender, and lifestyle differences among people at work; employee attitude or satisfaction surveys; and statistical reviews of the demographics of the current work force. Organizations should collect more than just the facts; perceptions count, too.

No single individual should be in charge of data gathering; it is too large and too important an undertaking. Instead, a diversity management team representing the makeup of the entire organization should be empowered to collect and interpret data. While the task of designing and developing a diversity program can be delegated to a single person, it is best driven by a committee of employees and managers.

The objective of understanding the organization's diversity is to come up with a comprehensive overview of the current work force. With this information, an employer can customize an initial diversity program to fit the organization's particular needs.

A final word of advice: don't get bogged down in collecting or analyzing information. Collecting information will make employees aware that you intend to develop a diversity program; once they are aware of this fact, they'll want something to happen right away.

Strengthen Top Management Commitment

Hospitality organizations such as Hilton, Hyatt, and Marriott that succeed in managing a diverse work force have top management commitment. At Darden Restaurants, minorities are in decision-making roles, with 36 percent of the board of directors and 19 percent of management consisting of minorities. Top management commitment to the diversity program is critical to a program's success. Without open support from top management, diversity management will flounder at best.

The push for diversity training should begin with top management. If the desire for diversity training is not coming from top managers, then the advocates of such training—from the human resources department, perhaps, or from a coalition of middle managers—must sell the benefits of diversity training to them. Diversity requires a commitment and "buy in" from upper managers so that issues involving time, cooperation, and funding can be more easily resolved. Hospitality organizations with strong diversity programs indicate that improved attitudes, lower turnover, and greater upward mobility are the positive business outcomes. To encourage commitment by top managers, diversity training should be linked to business benefits; social or moral motivations alone usually will not suffice. Effective diversity management will improve the organization's marketing position, establish it as a preferred employer for an increasingly diverse work force, and increase staff morale and productivity—these are the types of business reasons top managers will listen to.

Once top managers are on board, they must model a commitment to diversity for their employees. A good start is for top managers to release a statement outlining their commitment. Having a high-level manager kick off diversity training helps, too. For diversity training to truly succeed, top management must understand the value of a diverse work force, direct strategies to support diversity, and model appropriate behaviors.

Acquire Diverse Talent

Smart managers and heads of human resources departments understand that diversity is required at all levels of their organizations in order to demonstrate commitment to diversity in their workplaces. Organizations need to make their selection criteria position-specific and not based on any diversity issues, however. The "best candidate for the job" is being sought, not one of any particular diverse group. The goal is to attract a more diverse group of candidates overall from which to select. Firms that are successful in attracting and retaining a diverse labor force are those that walk the talk. Firms are more likely to recruit from diverse groups if

Tips for Fostering Diversity Within an Organization

- Show a videotape on diversity at a meeting and discuss it afterwards.
- Mentor someone with different gender, ethnic, racial, lifestyle, or age-group status.
- Form a diversity task force to investigate diversity issues and suggest changes.
- Give feedback in a way that recognizes diversity of cultures and values.
- Make sure the organization's advertising and internal communications respect diversity.
- Establish rewards and incentives for managers who do a good job of managing diversity.
- Be consistent—for example, don't publicly support sexual harassment policies and privately tell sex jokes.
- Form pairs of employees from different gender, ethnic, racial, age, and lifestyle groups to work together.
- Identify organizations that do a good job of managing diversity and emulate some of their better actions.
- Involve people who are not part of the organization's dominant culture in succession planning and promotion planning sessions.
- Make sure your management style encourages healthy disagreement.
- Learn how to effectively interview people from different cultures or who hold different opinions about lifestyles.
- Subscribe to one or more newsletters on diversity and circulate them to your staff.
- Ask employees whether they feel they are being treated fairly.
- Observe social interactions to see whether some employees are excluded, and then make room for them.
- Make sure biases are removed from performance measures.
- Invite employees with diverse opinions and backgrounds to participate in management decisions.
- Include a declaration about diversity in your company's mission statement.
- Attend diversity workshops that focus specifically on how to manage diversity.

Source: David Farkas, "Solving the Diversity Puzzle," *Restaurant Hospitality*, March 1994, p. 58.

they display images of their diverse workplace. Also, if an organization's application and interview process is designed by a diverse group of managers for a broad cross-section of the population, there is a greater chance that the organization will successfully recruit talent from a variety of demographic and lifestyle groups. With a diverse applicant pool, it makes sense for organizations to have interviewers from a variety of backgrounds. During big recruitment drives, interviewers should reflect the demographic characteristics of the area in which recruiting is taking place. This will put prospective employees at ease and help them feel that they are speaking with peers.

Demand and Measure Results. If an organization has a goal of making its work force more diverse, it should hold its managers accountable for achieving some hard numbers. "Diversity efforts that don't have statistical goals are doomed," says Morrison. "The reluctance of managers to hold themselves and others to some numbers has probably done more damage to diversity efforts than anything else."[35]

Top management and the diversity management team should agree on a modest start; an organization will not become more diverse overnight. It is important for the organization to develop both long- and short-term goals. Attaining short-term goals shows employees that progress is being made.

At one manufacturing company, work force diversity is one of four equally weighted performance criteria used to determine managers' salaries and bonuses. As one manager observed, "When [the company CEO] started hitting people in the pocketbook, they began to value diversity."[36]

Retain Diverse Staff

Retention of a diverse staff is vital to creating and sustaining a diverse work environment. Personnel policies and procedures must ensure that the organization is providing a quality work experience for all. Managers who learn to cross over gender and ethnic lines in order to develop a deeper understanding of the people who report to them will have better luck at retaining a diverse work team.

Retention efforts that promote diversity must focus on:

- Keeping all competent employees, regardless of background.

- Getting to know what motivates and demotivates employees as individuals.

- Providing training opportunities for personal growth as well as skills and knowledge.

- Showing employees a career path and providing the tools for them to achieve the next level.

- Creating an environment to keep the best people.

- Employing people of diverse backgrounds at all levels of the organization.

- Minimizing the effect of people who are barriers to the diversity program's success.

- Telling potential employees that you consider diversity a business necessity.

Career advancement opportunities are essential to retaining a diverse work force. Ensuring that all employees have accurate and timely information pertaining to advancement opportunities, as well as the training and coaching that precedes promotion, will help ensure that all employees can develop individual career plans and develop an understanding of the skills and knowledge necessary to succeed. Furthermore, employees need to receive the message that advancement is a reality for them within the organization. To do this, an organization must first identify promotion opportunities. This can be done by providing career flow charts to all employees illustrating how one can advance in a given career. Finally, an organization must demonstrate its commitment to retaining its employees by promoting talented and qualified individuals from within, so that all groups see that their efforts have the potential to be rewarded with advancement.

Career advancement for many workers may be stymied by a limited education, however. In order to encourage talented people to make a career in the hospitality industry, hospitality companies may want to consider educational funding mechanisms to encourage diverse talent to seek higher education in hospitality management. Developing a mentoring program can also aid staff members who might be unfamiliar with how to navigate the corporate waters. Mentoring or buddy programs for new recruits will result in greater retention and increased diversity in supervisory and management positions.

Conduct Diversity Training

As mentioned earlier, diversity training should be integrated into orientation and training programs for all new employees. When any kind of training is provided for current staff and management, it is important that diversity be a segment whenever appropriate. Management training on interpersonal skills such as coaching, communication, and performance feedback are essential when the work force is diverse.

It should be noted at the outset that, although diversity training is important, it can only achieve so much; it is personal connections through working and playing together that result in a changed work culture. Project teams are one method of bringing diverse groups of people together, so that they can get to know each other on a personal level as they work together. Another strategy to complement formal training is to create social events that are fun for everyone. The more people become connected through shared experiences that engage them, the more they begin to bond. Inviting employees' families to workplace social activities for special celebrations such as holiday parties and summer picnics is a great way to build community and allow co-workers to see each other in a broader human context rather than just as company employees. When people work and play together, negative diversity issues tend to melt away.

Diversity Training as a Stand-Alone Program. Diversity training as a stand-alone training program is important when problems such as harassment and discrimination occur. When signs of tension and conflict appear, targeted diversity training can be part of the solution. Extensive diversity training may even be required by a court if discrimination in the workplace is found. In conflict situations, training not only in interpersonal skills is important, but also training that helps staff members see the negative impact such conflict has on the company. The negative impact might include reduced employee morale, higher turnover, potential for sabotage, reduction in customer satisfaction, and difficulty in recruiting talented employees due to negative word of mouth on the street.

Ideas for Diversity Training

Managers can incorporate a variety of methods into a diversity training program to help people engage in conversation about diversity topics and issues. Some diversity training methods managers may employ include the following:

1. *Show a film and discuss its messages.* The film *Crash* is an example of a film that explores cultural clashes, communication breakdowns, and the dangers of stereotyping. A film like this can be used to break the ice and initiate conversations about interpersonal communication and the perspectives of people from diverse backgrounds.

2. *Talk about guests.* Talking about the diverse characteristics of their guests helps staff members better understand diversity issues as well as the people they are serving. Managers can ask the question, "Who are our customers, and what are some of their distinguishing characteristics?" At most properties, guests are very diverse, even when many of them share the same ethnic origins. For example, a diversity training session at a New England lodging property revealed that the property's guests were very diverse, even though the vast majority of them were Caucasian. The brainstorming session revealed that, among the property's guests, the staff was serving gay and lesbian visitors, Hasidic Jewish visitors, elderly people, people with disabilities, people traveling from foreign lands who didn't speak English, deaf people, and even famous people traveling in chauffer-driven vehicles. To the employees of this property, their guests seemed very different from each other after this discussion. Yet, when the guests' needs as travelers were analyzed, similarities rather than differences were revealed. This brainstorming session resulted in a serious discussion about what it is to stereotype and prejudge, and how, in the end, it is very rewarding to serve the traveling public.

3. *Celebrate diversity through food.* During a diversity training program, managers can serve food from the different cultures represented in their workplace and lead a discussion about the various foods and the ways in which food is used in cultural traditions.

4. *Share personal stories.* Managers can place employees in pairs or small groups and invite them to answer questions such as, "How do you like to spend your free time?" "What music do you enjoy?" "What are your favorite restaurants?" "What is your family like?" etc. Sharing personal stories helps people understand one another and discover that they have many things in common.

Diversity training shouldn't be just about demographic facts and figures or stories from other organizations engaged in diversity management. Diversity training should also be about *your* organization and the way in which *your* people can work together better to achieve organizational goals. Sometimes diversity training is about your customers—who they are, what they require, and how they may be different in many ways from your employees. When designing a diversity training program or integrating diversity training into existing orientation and training, managers and others involved need to keep in mind the information gathered during the initial assessment process. Using this information as a launching pad for deep reflection and interpersonal communication will be helpful. Diversity training that really gets results inspires deeper thinking not only between the participants, but within each participant as well.

Who Should Conduct Diversity Training? Deciding who should conduct your company's diversity training is one of the most important decisions your company will ever make. The wrong choice can do great damage. For example:

> In one case, the managers at a small Midwestern manufacturing company hired diversity consultants to help employees uncover racial tensions in the workplace and learn to deal with them. The consultants split employees into two groups: employees who felt oppressed (minorities) and people who made employees feel oppressed (Caucasian men and women). Employees in the group that felt oppressed shared their resentment and anger toward the Caucasian employees, who listened without responding.
>
> Far from bringing the groups closer together, the exercise outraged the Caucasian workers. In addition, members of the group that felt oppressed left feeling vulnerable. This drove a wedge between employees, which made working relationships at the company worse than ever.[37]

The first decision to make is whether an in-house trainer or an external trainer/consultant should conduct the training. An external consultant might be more objective and may be more likely to receive respect from employees than an in-house trainer would. On the other hand, in-house trainers will likely better understand the company's culture.

If you use an outside consultant, review his or her credentials thoroughly. Ask for references and check them. Ask the consultant how he or she will adapt the training program so that it addresses the organization's unique culture and diversity needs. You should also meet with the consultant personally before hiring him or her, to get a feel for his or her training philosophy, sense of humor, and ability to deal with delicate issues. Another good idea is to have the consultant conduct a pilot program with a small group of employees first. That way, you can test whether the consultant is right for your organization before signing a long-term contract.

Some companies have management positions specifically devoted to diversity management and training. Others use diversity teams, diversity centers, diversity advisory boards, or rotate diversity training responsibilities among various staff positions.

Diversity Training Techniques. There are many training techniques for teaching diversity issues, but most of them can be summarized by the following general guidelines:

- Give trainees information on the demographics, contributions, culture, and values of different groups.

- Provide information on the historical and current effect of prejudice on the opportunities for full participation in the workplace for some groups.

- Have several representatives of the various groups within the organization explain their personal perspectives.

- Use exercises that remind trainees (or let them experience) what it feels like to be different.

- Arrange for staff members to do volunteer work in community or social-service centers.

- Provide references that link employee questions and needs with community resources.[38]

Organizations should not plan freewheeling, encounter-group types of sessions where participants are encouraged to say whatever is on their minds. Not only can employees come away from such sessions feeling angrier and more isolated from co-workers than when they started, but such sessions might come back to haunt you in court.[39] Some companies question the need for this kind of emotional purging in a work setting, and have shifted the focus of diversity programs away from stereotypes and racial and gender issues to the broader topic of differences.

Disseminate Diversity Materials

All types of media are needed to communicate a property's diversity message. Some properties include a diversity brochure in their orientation packets to reinforce the property's position on diversity, and to answer frequently asked questions. Ongoing company communications via newsletters, flyers, bulletin boards, and e-mails can include diversity messages.

Once diversity programs are initiated, managers often create a notebook or workbook and keep diversity notes and materials in it. This information can become train-the-trainer material and help provide consistency in the company's diversity programs.

A central area for collecting and holding diversity information can provide all employees access to the information that the property collects. A diversity resource library can consist of a binder of information, a diversity newsletter, a bulletin board, or an area of an office with diversity resource materials.

Maintain Forward Momentum

Organizations should design their diversity programs so that they maintain forward momentum. A good strategy for most organizations is to use short-term successes or "building blocks," such as the recruitment of nontraditional employees or the completion of sensitivity training, to help the organization achieve long-term success. Rewarding departments or individuals who deserve recognition for their successes in diversity enhancement sends the message that the culture is changing.

An important building block for success is the ability to motivate people to participate and take action. Top managers must engage and encourage both employees and lower-level managers to take action. In order to maintain interest, activities and training should be pertinent, compelling, and available as needed.

Managers should use changes in the business climate to change or eliminate traditional practices that have hindered diversity in the past. Shifting markets, changes in the labor supply, and so on all create opportunities for managers to illustrate through hiring, promotion, and marketing practices that diversity is important in their organization.

As mentioned previously, sex and race represent only two aspects of diversity. They are also the two that most organizations address first. Successes in these areas should be used as building blocks for entry into more complex diversity training programs (behaviorally based diversity, the different value systems held by different groups, sexual orientation issues, and so on).

Generic diversity programs generally do not work. Organizations should tailor their diversity programs to their own unique needs. A successful long-term diversity strategy includes three ongoing main elements: education, enforcement, and exposure. Education increases the sensitivity of managers and employees. Enforcement of standards ensures that discrimination and harassment will be quickly extinguished. Exposure of traditional managers and employees to nontraditional managers and employees increases understanding and provides evidence that diversity is working.

A Final Note on Diversity

Diversity is an emotion-laden topic for many people. As a result, even the best-intentioned managers and employees can sometimes offend others, even though they are attempting to develop a sound diversity program. Merely using statistics or examples of cultural differences to illustrate the diversity among groups can be misconstrued by some as perpetuating biases or stereotypes, for example. Managers and employees must be very careful, even when they are promoting diversity, not to offend others.

Endnotes

1. Judi Brownell, "Relational Listening: Fostering Effective Communication Practices in Diverse Organizational Environments," *Hospitality and Tourism Educator* 6, no. 4 (1994): 11–19.

2. Cresencio Torres and Mary Bruxelles, "Capitalizing on Global Diversity," *HR Magazine*, December 1992, p. 31.

3. Beverly Geber, "Managing Diversity," *Training*, July 1990, p. 24.

4. Karolyn Schuster, "Managing Cultural Diversity," *Food Management*, September 1992, p. 122, and Jack Gordon, "Rethinking Diversity," *Training*, January 1992, p. 23.

5. Schuster, p. 122.

6. Faye Rice, "How to Make Diversity Pay," *Fortune*, August 8, 1994, p. 86.

7. Lennie Copeland, "Learning to Manage a Multicultural Work Force," *Training*, May 1988, p. 51.

8. Jack Gordon, "Rethinking Diversity," *Training*, January 1992, p. 24.

9. Michael Mobley and Tamara Payne, "Backlash! The Challenge to Diversity Training," *Training & Development*, December 1992, p. 50.

10. Schuster, p. 123.

11. Copeland, p. 49.

12. Amy Tiebel, "Diversity: Meaningful Change Is Critical for Survival," *Convene,* November 1993, p. 30.

13. PRNewswire, "Marriott Ranks Highest in Lodging Industry for Diversity," March 21, 2007.

14. Rice, p. 79.

15. Rice, p. 79.

16. Gordon, p. 27.

17. Marcia Forsberg, "Cultural Training Improves Relations with Asian Clients," *Personnel Journal,* May 1993, p. 84.

18. Taylor Cox and Stacy Blake, "Managing Cultural Diversity: Implications for Organizational Competitiveness," *Academy of Management Executives* 5 (1991): 45–54.

19. Mobley and Payne, p. 52.

20. Gretchen Haight, "Managing Diversity," *Across the Board* 27, no. 3 (1990): 23.

21. Haight, p. 23.

22. *Fortune,* June 28, 2004.

23. Laurie Ashmore Epting, Saundra H. Glover, and Suzan D. Boyd, "Managing Diversity," *Health Care Supervisor* 12, no. 4 (1994): 73–83.

24. Robert H. Woods and Raphael Kavanaugh, "Gender Discrimination and Sexual Harassment as Experienced by Hospitality Managers," *Cornell Hotel and Restaurant Administration Quarterly* 35, no. 1 (1994): 16–21.

25. Richard W. Judy and Carol D'Amico, *Workforce 2020* (Indianapolis, Indiana: Hudson Institute, 1997), 109.

26. Much of the following material was adapted from material provided by Howard Johnson Franchise Systems, Inc., Parsippany, New Jersey.

27. Patricia J. Silfies, Frederick J. DeMicco, Raphael R. Kavanaugh, and Stuart H. Mann, "Attitudes of Hospitality Management Students Toward Older Workers: A Follow-Up Study," *Hospitality and Tourism Educator* 6, no. 1 (1994): 7–15.

28. Michael C. McKeon, "The Aging Work Force" *UI News* 12, no. 4 (2001).

29. T. Murphy, "Generation Gaps," *Working Women,* July 1991, pp. 41–45.

30. Silfies et al., p. 8.

31. *Senior Journal,* April, 26, 2006.

32. Much of the following material was adapted from Joan L. Kelly, "Employers Must Recognize that Older People Want to Work," *Personnel Journal,* January 1990, pp. 44–47.

33. Shari Caudron, "Training Can Damage Diversity Efforts," *Personnel Journal,* April 1993, p. 58.

34. Ann Perkins Delatte and Larry Baytos, "Guidelines for Successful Diversity Training," *Training,* January 1993, p. 59.

35. Catherine M. Petrini, "The Language of Diversity," *Training & Development,* April 1993, p. 36.

36. Patricia Galagan, "Leading Diversity," *Training & Development*, April 1993, pp. 42–43.

37. Caudron, p. 51.

38. Allison Rossett and Terry Bickham, "Diversity Training: Hope, Faith and Cynicism," *Training*, January 1994, p. 42.

39. Much of the following information about Lucky Stores was adapted from Kathleen Murray, "The Unfortunate Side Effects of 'Diversity Training,'" *New York Times*, August 1, 1993.

Review Questions

1. What is meant by "managing" diversity?

2. What are some of the benefits of diversity for organizations?

3. What are some of the challenges businesses face due to the increasing number of women in the workplace?

4. How can managers do a better job of communicating with employees who do not speak English or do not speak it well?

5. Businesses that want to recruit older workers face what kind of challenges?

6. How does the Americans with Disabilities Act define "disability"?

7. How can an organization foster diversity in the workplace?

8. What are some diversity training strategies and techniques?

Internet Sites

For more information, visit the following Internet sites. Remember that Internet addresses can change without notice. If the site is no longer there, you can use a search engine to look for additional sites.

American Association of Retired Persons
www.aarp.org

American Council on Education
www.acenet.edu

American Institute for Managing Diversity
www.aimd.org

Chinese for Affirmative Action
www.caasf.org

Diversity.com
www.diversity.com

DiversityInc Media LLC
www.diversityinc.com

Diversity Officer Magazine
www.diversityofficermagazine.com

DiversityWorking.com
www.diversityworking.com

International Reading Association
www.reading.org

Multicultural Foodservice & Hospitality Alliance
www.mfha.net

National Association for the Advancement of Colored People
www.naacp.org

National Association of Negro Business and Professional Women's Clubs
www.nanbpwc.org

National Coalition for Literacy
www.national-coalition-literacy.org

National Council of La Raza
www.nclr.org

National Council on Aging
www.ncoa.org

National Puerto Rican Coalition
www.bateylink.org

National Urban League
www.nul.org

Office of Disability Employment Policy
www.dol.gov/odep

Office of Equal Opportunity & Diversity Management
http://oeodm.od.nih.gov

Opportunities Industrialization Centers of America
www.oicofamerica.org

SER—Jobs for Progress National
www.ser-national.org

Chapter 10 Outline

Realizing You Must Make a Decision
Understanding Yourself
    Skills
    Interests
    Values
    Personality Type
    Personal Vision Statement
Understanding Your Options
    Information Interviewing
    Publication Research
    University Opportunities
    Internships and Field Experiences
    Expanding and Narrowing Options
Choosing an Occupation
Implementing a Choice
    Networking
    Creating an Effective Résumé
    Cover Letters
    Interviewing for Jobs
    Parameters of Negotiation
Professional Development
    Reach Out to Others
    Planning Your Development
    Create the Plan
    Execute the Plan
    Professional Certification

Competencies

1. Create a personal vision statement after analyzing your skills, interests, values, and personality type. (pp. 311–316)

2. Describe how to research hospitality career options and specific companies. (pp. 316–324)

3. Identify ways to choose an occupation and implement your career choice. (pp. 324–348)

4. Explain how to develop and implement a professional development plan for your entire career. (pp. 348–352)

10

Strategic Career Planning

This chapter was written by Michael P. Sciarini, Ph.D.,
Associate Professor, *The* School of Hospitality Business,
Michigan State University, East Lansing, Michigan.

CREATING A PLAN FOR CAREER SUCCESS can seem overwhelming. Career planning involves a series of decisions. Finding and using a good decision-making model can help you take control of your career rather than leaving it to chance. Creating a vision statement helps you know what it is you want to do and for whom. Knowing this makes it easier to know what the right decision is—even if it is still difficult to make that decision.

We aren't typically trained in decision-making. We make things up as we go along, believing that "experience is the best teacher." While experience is a good teacher, it is an awfully expensive and painful one. The bills of experience are high. Using a model lets you look ahead and realize that there are things you can't control, but that you're more likely to end up in a good place if you use a good process. You don't have to eliminate spontaneity or creativity. Instead, you are framing the problem and figuring out what you need to decide.

In this chapter, we look at strategic career planning using a model for good decision-making that was developed by Sampson, Peterson, Lenz, and Reardon.[1] This model is a circular one with the following steps:

- Realizing I need to make a decision
- Understanding myself and my options
- Expanding and narrowing my list of options
- Choosing an occupation or field of study
- Implementing my choice

Realizing You Must Make a Decision

The first step in this decision-making model is realizing that you need to make a choice. This realization can come about through many different means. There may be events in your life, such as graduation, a job loss, or a need to choose a course of study. This realization may also be triggered by comments from friends or relatives, the way you feel, an increased amount of procrastination, or physical problems brought on by the need to make a decision.

Part of this step is realizing the scope of your decision. For example, thinking of your career in terms of "I want to be a hotel general manager" may be too short-term. Becoming a hotel general manager may be an objective for your career, but first you have to understand the bigger picture of "for whom you want to do what." Ideally, career planning is more than just an occupation or a title. It is a holistic process that is balanced and takes into account what you want to do for the rest of your life.

While comments from parents, friends, and relatives can be a trigger to let you know you need to make a decision, it is important to understand their influences and the pressures that they bring to bear. Well-intended people may try to pressure you into work or a process that was right for them. You need to find out what is right *for you*. This can especially be true in hospitality, where some people have a negative image of the industry. They may discourage you because of what they perceive the industry and its careers to be.

Understanding Yourself

Once you have come to the awareness that you need to make a choice about your career, it is time to ask the question, "What do I know about myself?" The answers to this question provide the foundation for the remainder of the career-planning process. While this question is short and simply worded, the answers lead to a series of more complex and directed questions that will reveal your strengths, weaknesses, interests, values, and personality type.

Regardless of your current status (18-year-old first-year college student, graduating college senior, mid-life career changer, or about anywhere in between or beyond), you need to understand yourself before you can begin a search for a job. Understanding yourself will help you discover what sort of jobs you are best fitted for, what you want to do with your life, and what you would most enjoy. Understanding yourself involves cataloging your skills, interests, values, personality type, and developing a personal vision statement.

Skills

An excellent way to begin analyzing your skills is to create a list of things you are proud to have accomplished. (This list will also prove useful later when you create résumés and a career portfolio.) This list should be extensive and cover your adult life. It should not be restricted only to paid or professional work experiences. Include *everything*—for example, school accomplishments, volunteer work, hobbies, church work, extracurricular activities, solving a problem, managing a project, handling a difficult situation, and so forth. Seeking the input of friends, family, and co-workers can help you lengthen and refine the list.

Input from others is also useful in the next step of the process. After you have listed your accomplishments, evaluate the root causes of the accomplishments. These causes—personal qualities, characteristics, skills, and abilities—are your strengths. Exhibit 1 presents a form that will help you rate yourself with regard to a number of skills and personal qualities.

After you create your list of accomplishments and rate your skills and personal qualities, match your strengths (those skills and qualities you rated as 4 or 5 in Exhibit 1) with your list of accomplishments. For example, if you gave yourself

Exhibit 1   Self-Rating Tool

Key: 5 = Strongest   1 = Weakest

Basic Skills						Hospitality/Technical/Other					
Reading	1	2	3	4	5	Complaint/Conflict Management	1	2	3	4	5
Writing	1	2	3	4	5	2nd Language (or more)	1	2	3	4	5
Listening	1	2	3	4	5	Hospitality Technical					
Speaking	1	2	3	4	5	(that is, food prep, hotel					
Math	1	2	3	4	5	operations etc.)	1	2	3	4	5
Computer Literacy	1	2	3	4	5						
						Personal Qualities					
Thinking Skills						Work Ethic	1	2	3	4	5
Creative Thinking	1	2	3	4	5	Self Esteem	1	2	3	4	5
Critical Thinking	1	2	3	4	5	Sociability	1	2	3	4	5
Visualizing	1	2	3	4	5	Dependability	1	2	3	4	5
Knowing How to Learn	1	2	3	4	5	Initiative	1	2	3	4	5
Reasoning	1	2	3	4	5	Honesty/Integrity	1	2	3	4	5
Analyzing	1	2	3	4	5	Cooperation	1	2	3	4	5
						Persistence	1	2	3	4	5
Leadership/Management Skills						Flexibility	1	2	3	4	5
Self-Management	1	2	3	4	5	Service Orientation	1	2	3	4	5
Communication	1	2	3	4	5	Attention to Detail	1	2	3	4	5
Teamwork	1	2	3	4	5	Enthusiasm	1	2	3	4	5
Leadership	1	2	3	4	5	Optimism	1	2	3	4	5
Negotiation	1	2	3	4	5	Other _____	1	2	3	4	5
Problem Solving	1	2	3	4	5	_____	1	2	3	4	5
Listening	1	2	3	4	5						
Budget Management	1	2	3	4	5						
Decision-Making	1	2	3	4	5						

Source: Adapted from *Life Work Portfolio*, developed by the National Occupational Information Coordinating Committee, Washington, D.C.

a 5 in self-management, you might match this to the accomplishment that you have a perfect attendance record at work. With this process, you are in essence documenting your strengths. If someone asks you, "Why do you consider X a strength?" or "In what ways have you used this strength in the past?" you will have a ready list of examples to share.

This documentation should be a source of self-esteem and confidence for you. When later you use this documentation in résumés, job search correspondence, and interviews, it also helps potential employers decide whether to extend job offers to you.

Interests

Knowing your skills is very important, but it is not enough. You should also identify the activities and experiences you find interesting. Your skills do not necessarily reflect your current interests. Your proficiency in any given area may be a result of past interests that have little connection to your present ones.

There is published evidence in support of pursuing authentic interests; for example, researchers who conducted a study of 120 top performers across a variety of fields reported that one's motivations and interests (i.e., extraordinary drives) are more significant variables in achievement than family background, education, or talent.[2]

To help identify your interests, review your accomplishments and skills, focusing on your preferred leisure-time pursuits, then think about them in relation to the opportunities and demands of the hospitality industry. Interests that have links to hospitality industry careers include traveling, cooking, acting and performing, organizing events, participating in team activities, and learning and speaking languages.

While you are examining your interests, note areas of strong *dis*interest or *dis*like. Acknowledging an aversion (to, for example, food preparation or travel) is also important and useful in career planning.

Sincere interest and genuine enthusiasm are vital for balanced success in any career. They can provide the impetus for accomplishing great things. Don't worry about the practicality of your interests yet. Starting with what you really enjoy can lead to a variety of career possibilities.

There are a variety of interest assessments available through career services/ placement offices and online. One online example of a career guidance program can be found at www.iccweb.com.

Values

You should also examine your values during the self-assessment process. Carefully consider the relationships, objects, and activities that you value most highly and give special thought to how they do or do not fit into the workplace.

Simply pondering the question, "What matters most to me?" can be very thought-provoking. As you consider your values, keep in mind that it is usually difficult to find a career that easily and clearly provides everything you desire. There are typically some trade-offs. Exhibit 2 presents an exercise to help you clarify your preferred work environment and work-related values.

This chapter began with an acknowledgment of the seemingly overwhelming nature of career planning. However, the systematic self-assessment activities presented to this point demonstrate that what may start out as overwhelming can in fact become exciting and appealing. This necessary self-assessment step provides the information you'll attempt to make sense of during the remainder of the career-planning process. The commonalities that exist among your values, interests, and strengths shed light on which direction you should pursue next.

Your image of the future should be clearer after you go through the self-assessment step, although you still probably won't know exactly what you want to do. However, having detailed answers to the question, "What do I know about myself?" allows you to compare your strengths, interests, and values with the exciting and challenging careers and occupations of the hospitality industry.

Personality Type

People gain the most satisfaction from careers that are aligned with their personalities and psychological preferences. All types of personalities make contributions to hospitality and play important roles in making a property successful.

As an individual, understanding your personality type may guide you toward the type of work you will feel most comfortable with. Generally speaking, people feel most comfortable, energetic, and competent when they are doing things that

Exhibit 2   Values at Work

The following is a list of some possible characteristics of work environments. The list is arranged in a forced-choice format to assist you in prioritizing as you evaluate potential careers. There are no correct answers. Rather, each alternative may be valued differently by different people.

Read each pair of characteristics below. If you could have one but not both of these choices as part of your next job, which would you select? (Circle your preference.)

Freedom and autonomy	vs.	Clear direction and close supervision
Managing/delivering service	vs.	Creating a tangible product
Managing a crisis	vs.	Planning a strategy
Success measured by earnings, position, promotions	vs.	Success measured by balance of career, family, friends, and social responsibilities
Owning my own business	vs.	Working in someone else's business
Working individually	vs.	Working with a team
Working in a large group	vs.	Working in a small group
High risk for high reward	vs.	More security with moderate rewards
Managing the details	vs.	Shaping the big picture
Working 10- to 12-hour days	vs.	Time for nonwork activities
Co-workers similar to me	vs.	Co-workers not similar to me
Multicultural diversity	vs.	Homogeneous environment
Stable long-term career with one organization	vs.	Fast-paced career with variety of companies
Consistency of daily work and pace	vs.	Variety of work and changing pace
Living in one area for an extended period	vs.	Frequent relocation, opportunity to move
Adherence to moral/ethical standards	vs.	Achieving financial results at any cost
Working Monday-through-Friday, few weekends, no holidays	vs.	Working when necessary, including weekends and holidays

If you could be certain of having only five of these characteristics in your next job, which would they be? Highlight or underline them.

match their preferred personality type. If they are in a position that does not align with their personality, it can be very painful. They may want to stretch and do a lot of different things—it is limiting to stereotype or pigeonhole oneself—but people are generally more successful within their comfort zones. By finding out what you like and how you prefer to make choices and interact with others, you'll be able to identify the path that energizes you.

There are several different instruments available that measure personality type. You don't have to spend a lot to find a useful tool. An example of a free online personality assessment may be found at www.typefocus.com.

Personal Vision Statement

Creating a personal vision statement—or mission statement—ties everything together and is the blueprint for all of your career planning. It helps to make sense

Exhibit 3   Vision Statement Checklist

An empowering mission statement:

- Represents the deepest and best within you.
- Is the fulfillment of your own unique gifts.
- Transcends yourself.
- Addresses and integrates all four fundamental human needs and capacities (physical, social, mental, and spiritual).
- Is based on principles that produce quality of life results.
- Deals with both vision and principle-based values.
- Deals with all the significant roles in your life, representing a lifetime balance.
- Is written to inspire you—not to impress anyone else.

Source: Stephen M. Covey, A. Roger Merrill, and Rebecca Merrill, *First Things First* (New York: Fireside, 1996), p. 113.

of the distinct elements. Once you know your skills and interests, what you value, and what your personality type is, you need to summarize or compile this in a way that you can use so that the information is valuable to you.

Viktor Frankl was an Austrian psychologist who survived Nazi concentration camps during World War II. He watched others to try to determine what helped people survive and came to the conclusion that it was the people who had a mission or a vision. They were able to look past their current circumstances and see a reason to go on. They were looking ahead to things they wanted to accomplish, to being with their family, to living their life.

A vision statement can help you in every step of career and life planning. It helps you determine which life roles you want to take on. If you want to be a general manager, what do you have to do to become one? If you want to also be a parent or a partner, what do you need to do to be a successful parent or partner? Is that in conflict with what you need to do to become a successful general manager? Your vision statement will answer the question, "What do I want to do and for whom?"

The actual structure and appearance of your vision statement will be as unique as you are. An artistic and tactile person will build a vision statement differently than a visual or auditory person will. Create a statement that works for you and is meaningful to you. Stephen Covey developed a checklist (Exhibit 3) for an empowering mission statement in his book, *First Things First*. It can help you think through your mission and summarize what you want to do and for whom. To access a mission-builder website, go to www.franklincovey.com/missionbuilder.

Understanding Your Options

Now that you better understand yourself, you need to understand what options are available to you. Begin by identifying your ideal work conditions. Try describing your dream job. What is the typical day like? Who would you want to work with? Who is your boss? Where do you want to work? What type of tasks do you want to do? What are the pay and benefits? The hours? What would you wear?

Then, knowing what you would really love doing, start finding out what the work environment is actually like. You can find this out via networking, information interviewing, or through reading industry articles.

Once you have an idea of what you want to do, start finding out more about specific companies. Look for the organization's mission statement. Is there overlap between its mission statement and your vision statement? Look at the company's behavior, its history, ownership structure, key players, competition, how it advertises itself, its financial performance, and its long-term objectives. Make a critical analysis of the company to determine whether it is behaving the way its mission statement says it wants to.

Information Interviewing

You should supplement the picture of the hospitality industry presented in the books, magazines, newspapers, reports, and so on found in a library or online with information from *people*, especially those who are currently doing the sort of work you find interesting. Getting up-to-date information from practicing professionals may be accomplished through **information interviewing**.

The goals of information interviewing center on career exploration, *not* employment. An information interview is not intended to result in a job offer (at least in the short term), but rather in firsthand information on possible career paths and specific occupations. The personal contacts you make and the information you collect about a specific company may eventually result in a job offer, but the immediate goal of information interviewing is to get a general sense of what a career is like and how individuals have gotten into particular careers and jobs.

Information interviewing provides a number of benefits, including the following:[3]

- It helps you grow through shyness or inhibition about talking to others.

- It helps you clarify your goals as you learn more about specific jobs, personality traits of successful individuals, and so forth.

- It helps you establish or expand a professional network and increases the likelihood that you will be an impressive candidate when you actively seek employment later.

If you identify contract services management as a career path of interest (to name one possibility), you should seek to identify people employed in that area to interview. Be sure to collect a variety and sufficient quantity of information from these interviews to create a balanced perspective. Basing a decision on any single opinion is risky.

Don't assume that information interviews require the persons being interviewed to do something they don't want to do. Students especially seem to feel that information interviews are intrusive and burdensome to the interviewees. The opposite is often true! Many people enjoy talking about themselves. They are not only willing to discuss their background, industry, and job; they are usually flattered when asked to do so.

A useful method for overcoming the fear of bothering others involves making a preliminary list of potential people to contact. Start with any family, friends, or

Exhibit 4   Sample Information Interviewing Questions

- Describe what you do.
- How did you become interested in _____? (Fill in the blank: hospitality, hotels, restaurants, clubs, contract service, etc.)
- Which part of your job is most interesting, challenging, fun, difficult, etc.?
- What personal attributes are most important for success as a _____? (Fill in the blank: hospitality manager, hotel manager, restaurant manager, etc.)
- How did you get your job?
- What experiences have been most valuable to you in your career?
- What specific skills are required of you on a day-to-day basis?
- How often do you work late? weekends? holidays?
- Does your job require travel? How much?
- How does your job affect the rest of your life?
- What's the best educational preparation to become (whatever you are interested in)?
- Which professional journals, books, and organizations do you recommend?
- Who offers the best training in this field?
- What qualities and qualifications do you look for when hiring new employees?
- What reasons do you see for people leaving the industry?
- What do the next five years look like for your organization? the industry?
- If you were me, what would you do to get started in this industry?
- Whom else could I speak with to learn more?

neighbors you know in the hospitality industry. If none of the people you know work in hospitality, ask them if they know anyone in the business. Friends of friends are usually easier to approach than complete strangers. Alumni of your school are also excellent interview candidates, and you have at least one thing in common with them. If, after enlisting the assistance of others, you still cannot identify anyone in the industry (which is unlikely), you have at least recruited friends, family, and neighbors into the process and they can be on the lookout for contacts.

Recommended additions to your contact list include faculty at your school, classmates who've completed internships, staff members of chambers of commerce in the geographic areas you prefer, staff members of convention and visitors bureaus in the geographic areas you prefer, members of student clubs and organizations, and staff members of hospitality professional and trade organizations. You should begin making contacts from almost your first day on campus. If you work at it, by the mid-point of your college career you can easily have a lengthy and focused list of contacts to manage.

While you are compiling your potential contact list, also make a list of the information you want to find out and develop questions to use in interviews. Exhibit 4 includes a list of possible questions.

Always be courteous and professional when requesting interviews. Write a brief letter or call to ask for an appointment. Don't forget that this is a business contact. Thank the interviewee in advance for the consideration, explain your purpose, and promise to be brief.

After an interview, follow up by sending a sincere and personalized thank-you note. In addition, keep a record of the interview and what you learned from it. This information will be useful later in the career-planning process.

Publication Research

Today, much research is done via the Internet. Many companies post information about their company and its performance, as do many business and trade magazines. Many career sites offer links to help research the performance and history of individual companies. The web can provide a wealth of information once you know what you want to know and how to learn it. Bring to your research a healthy skepticism about what you find on the web and whether it is reliable, however.

General Sources. One of the best web-based resources for occupation and career information is the *Occupational Outlook Handbook* (www.bls.gov/oco). This resource, compiled by the U.S. Department of Labor, provides information about many jobs. Other general links that may also be helpful include:

- www.quintcareers.com
- www.nationjob.com
- www.careerbuilder.com
- www.careers.org
- www.jobweb.com
- www.jobstar.org
- www.monster.com
- www.careers.wsj.com

An ever-growing list of hospitality management books (from introductory overviews to narrowly focused texts) may also be found in the library. Information published by the major hospitality trade associations is useful for gathering general career information. (See Exhibit 5 for a list of major hospitality trade associations.)

There are also a variety of industry-related news sites, some of which include free e-mail subscriptions you can sign up for to conveniently stay up-to-date with what's happening, such as:

- Hospitality Net at www.hospitalitynet.org/index.html
- Hotel Online at www.hotel-online.com
- STR Global at www.strglobal.com/home.aspx
- Hotel Interactive at www.hotelinteractive.com
- Foodservice.com at www.foodservice.com/newsletter
- Nation's Restaurant News at www.nrn.com
- NRA Smart Brief at www.smartbrief.com/nra

Exhibit 5   Major Hospitality Trade Associations

What follows is a list of associations that can provide you with additional information about the segment of the hospitality industry they represent.

American Culinary Federation (ACF)
180 Center Place Way
St. Augustine, FL 32095
www.acfchefs.org

American Dietetic Association (ADA)
120 South Riverside Plaza, Suite 2000
Chicago, IL 60606-6995
www.eatright.org

American Franchisee Association (AFA)
53 West Jackson Blvd., Suite 1157
Chicago, IL 60604
www.franchisee.org

American Hotel & Lodging Association (AH&LA)
1201 New York Avenue, NW, Suite 600
Washington, DC 20005
www.arda.org

American Hotel & Lodging Educational Institute (AH&LEI)
800 North Magnolia Avenue, Suite 300
Orlando, FL 32803
www.ei-ahla.org

American Society of Baking (ASB)
765 Baywood Drive, Suite 339
Petaluma, CA 94954
www.asbe.org

American Society for Healthcare Food Service Administrators (ASHFSA)
455 South Fourth Street, Suite 650
Louisville, KY 40202
www.ashfsa.org

American Society of Travel Agents (ASTA)
1101 King Street, Suite 200
Alexandria, VA 22314
www.asta.org

Asian American Hotel Owners Association
7000 Peachtree Dunwoody Road, Building 7
Atlanta, GA 30328
www.aahoa.com

Association for Linen Management
2161 Lexington Road, Suite 2
Richmond, Kentucky 40475
www.almnet.org

Association of Retail Travel Agents (ARTA)
2692 Richmond, Suite 202
Lexington, KY 40509
www.artaonline.com

Club Managers Association of America (CMAA)
1733 King Street
Alexandria, VA 22314
www.cmaa.org

Council of Hotel & Restaurant Trainers
741 Carleton Road
Westfield, NJ 07091
www.chart.org

Council on Hotel, Restaurant and Institutional Education (CHRIE)
2810 North Parham Road, Suite 230
Richmond, VA 23294
www.chrie.org

Cruise Lines International Association, Inc. (CLIA)
910 SE 17th Street, Suite 400
Fort Lauderdale, FL 33316
www.cruising.org

Dietary Managers Association (DMA)
406 Surrey Woods Drive
St. Charles, IL 60174
www.dmaonline.org

Food Marketing Institute (FMI)
2345 Crystal Drive, Suite 800
Arlington, VA 22202
www.fmi.org

Foodservice Consultants Society International (FCSI)
144 Parkedge Street
Rockwood, Ontario N0B 2K0
www.fcsi.org

Hospitality Financial and Technology Professionals
11709 Boulder Lane, Suite 110
Austin, TX 78726
www.hftp.org

Hospitality Sales and Marketing Association International (HSMAI)
1760 Old Meadow Road, Suite 500
McLean, VA 22102
www.hsmai.org

International Association of Conference Centers
243 North Lindbergh Boulevard
Saint Louis, MO 63141
www.iacconline.org

International Association of Reservation Executives
7400 East Arapahoe Road, Suite 211
Centennial, CO 80112
www.iare.com

Exhibit 5   *(continued)*

International Executive Housekeepers
   Association (IEHA)
1001 Eastwind Drive, Suite 301
Westerville OH 43081-3361
www.ieha.org

International Food Service Executives
   Association (IFSEA)
Synergy Communications
500 Ryland Street, Suite 200
Reno, NV 89502
www.ifsea.com

International Franchise Association (IFA)
1501 K Street, NW, Suite 350
Washington, DC 20005
www.franchise.org

International Hotel & Restaurant Association
   (IH&RA)
Rue de Montbrillant 87
CH-1202 Geneva, Switzerland
www.ih-ra.com

International Society of Hospitality Consultants
411 6th Street South #204
Naples, FL 34102
www.ishc.com

Meeting Professionals International (MPI)
3030 Lyndon B. Johnson Freeway, Suite 1700
Dallas, TX 75234-2759
www.mpiweb.org

National Association of Black Hotel Owners,
   Operators & Developers, Inc.
3520 West Broward Boulevard, Suite 218B
Fort Lauderdale, FL 33312
www.nabhood.net

National Association of Catering Executives
   (NACE)
9891 Broken Land Parkway
Suite 301
Columbia, MD 21046
www.nace.net

National Association of College & University
   Food Services (NACUFS)
2525 Jolly Road, Suite 280
Okemos, MI 48864-3680
www.nacufs.org

National Association of Concessionaires (NAC)
35 East Wacker Drive, Suite 1816
Chicago, IL 60601
www.naconline.org

National Black McDonald's Operators
   Association (NBMOA)
www.nbmoa.org

National Club Association
1201 15th Street NW
Suite 450
Washington, DC 20005
www.nationalclub.org

National Restaurant Association (NRA)
1200 17th Street NW
Washington, DC 20036
www.restaurant.org

National Restaurant Association Educational
   Foundation (NRAEF)
175 West Jackson Boulevard, Suite 1500
Chicago, Illinois 60604-2702
www.nraef.org

National Tour Association (NTA)
546 East Main Street
Lexington, KY 40508
www.ntaonline.com

Professional Convention Management
   Association (PCMA)
2301 South Lake Shore Drive, Suite 1001
Chicago, IL 60616-1419
www.pcma.org

School Nutrition Association (SNA)
700 South Washington Street, Suite 300
Alexandria, VA 22314
www.asfsa.org

Small Luxury Hotels of the World (SLHW)
370 Lexington Avenue, Suite 1506
New York, NY 10017
www.slh.com

Society for Foodservice Management (SFM)
15000 Commerce Parkway, Suite C
Mount Laurel, NJ 08054
www.sfm-online.org

The Travel Institute
148 Linden Street, Suite 305
Wellesley, MA 02482
www.thetravelinstitute.com

U.S. Travel Association
1100 New York Avenue NW, Suite 450
Washington, DC 20005-3934
www.tia.org

Women's Foodservice Forum (WFF)
1650 West 82nd Street, Suite 650
Bloomington, MN 55431
www.womensfoodserviceforum.com

Company-Specific Sources. It is inevitable that your search for information will narrow to specific organizations. Researching specific companies will help you determine if your interests, strengths, and values fit those companies. Also, it is common for an interviewer to ask applicants about their knowledge of his or her company. Researching a specific company may also help you identify ways that you can add value to the company and may result in questions about the company that you'll want answers to during the interviewing process.

The quantity of information available on hospitality organizations is almost as varied as the companies themselves. If an organization is large, has been around a while, and is traded on a major stock exchange, there will likely be a great deal of information available. Publicly held companies must file annual reports with the Securities and Exchange Commission that contain detailed financial information. EDGAR, the Electronic Data Gathering, Analysis, and Retrieval system, performs automated collection, validation, indexing, acceptance, and forwarding of submissions by companies and others who are required by law to file forms.[4]

Publicly held companies also will be listed in directories and may be written about extensively in books, journals, and magazines. Companies typically receive press coverage for extraordinary performance or events. However, it's not necessarily a bad sign if the company you are interested in lacks this type of coverage.

Privately held hospitality companies (not traded on stock exchanges) are not required to file annual reports. Information beyond directory listings (directory listings typically contain the company's name, address, number of units, and so forth) is generally tougher to find for privately held companies.

Examples of directories that may be useful when researching specific hospitality organizations include the following:

- *AH&LA/STR Directory of Hotel & Lodging Companies,* from Smith Travel Research and the American Hotel & Lodging Association.

- *High Volume Independent Restaurants Database,* from Chain Store Guide (CSG).

- *Ward's Business Directory of U.S. Private and Public Companies* lists approximately 110,000 companies in alphabetic, geographic, and industry arrangements. It is an excellent source of information on small and mid-size companies.

- *International Directory of Company Histories* includes the historical development of many public, private, and nonprofit companies. Each directory entry generally provides basic company information; a discussion of the company's mission, goals, and ideals; key milestones; principal subsidiaries and operating units; key competitors; and a short bibliography for further reading.

- Standard & Poor's industry surveys and stock reports include company financials, market information, recent developments, and a brief profile of each company's business, including major products lines, research and development efforts, and marketing information.

- *D & B Business Rankings* from Dun & Bradstreet, Inc., includes the top 25,000 U.S. public and private companies ranked by overall sales volume and number of employees.

When researching more than one company, keep separate files for each one. These files might hold annual reports, copies of business articles, and other information. Mixing company information only adds confusion to an already complex process.

Annual reports and financial statements. The annual reports of hospitality organizations are important research tools that can give you detailed company information. Most annual reports include photos, financial statements, and text. The text is usually fairly understandable and the photos tend to make the report more interesting. The financial statements—specifically, the income statement, balance sheet, and various supporting exhibits—are where many people run into trouble. Simply stated, the income statement presents profit or loss levels—in effect, how the company did that year. The balance sheet shows what the company owns and what it owes at a particular point in time. When analyzing these statements, you should remember that a historical record for a series of years gives a much more accurate picture of the financial health of a company than do the numbers for any single year. Many corporations now include multi-year financial summaries as part of their annual reports. Comparing financial information from year to year can reveal important trends. While it is nice to learn about past and current performance, it is desirable to be able to make some prediction of future performance, since you are considering becoming an employee of the organization!

University Opportunities

Students enrolled in hospitality management programs have several opportunities available to help expand their options. For example, they can tap into the networks of previous graduates of their school through student and industry mentor programs. They can also attend career fairs that provide excellent opportunities to gather information and make personal contacts with a relatively large number of organizations in a short time. Companies invited to a career fair set up table-top or booth exhibits and disseminate information about their organizations while collecting information from students and other participants.

For students interviewing on campus, participating in a company's presentation or "open house" can prove invaluable. Corporate presentations are intended to help students learn more about the company—what it is, what it does, and why it would be great to work for. The presentations convey general background information about the company and give students opportunities for one-on-one contact with company representatives.

Internships and Field Experiences

Most college hospitality management programs require their students to gain industry experience via internships or field experiences. These experiences provide many potential benefits to both the student interns and the employing organizations. The employer usually gains an enthusiastic (albeit short-term) employee and the opportunity to evaluate the employee in a realistic work environment. For students, internships are excellent opportunities to learn what it's really like in the work world. Even when a student intern decides that a particular industry segment or employer is not a great career match, he or she is better informed on what direction to head next.

To reap the full benefits of an internship, treat it as an extended information interview. In other words, when opportunities present themselves, ask your co-workers questions about the industry, their careers, and so on. For the intern who starts with a desire to learn and a strong work ethic, even the most difficult circumstances can lead to a positive outcome. Perhaps the best way to get the most out of an internship is to be the type of employee you would like to manage someday.[5]

Expanding and Narrowing Options

Now that you have determined who you are and what options are available, you need to compare the two to see where there is overlap. Which occupations and career choices fit your values, interests, skills, personality, and vision? If the list is long, you'll need to narrow it down to three to five; if the list is short, you may need to expand it by doing further research.

Choosing an Occupation

According to career counselor Patricia Carr, when evaluating job choices, you should consider the FACTS—Fit, Advancement, Compensation, Training, and Site.[6]

Fit. Reflect upon the self-assessment portion of your career planning process. Is this occupation a good match with your strengths, values, and interests? Objectively assess what attracts you to this choice. Keep in mind that prestige, reputation, and beautiful work surroundings won't hold much long-term appeal if the work pace and job requirements don't fit your skills and interests. If the company's mission and values aren't congruent with your personal values, there is probably not enough money in the world to keep you feeling satisfied. No matter how impressed your family and friends are with a company, you have to be able to perform the work that will be demanded of you.

Advancement. What are the realistic career paths that lead from this job? Consider how the company has presented advancement opportunities in its literature and throughout the interviewing process. Try to balance this presentation with what might be a different reality. Ask about promotion from within (including examples), turnover rates, and organizational structures and reporting relationships. Consult your network contacts. A commitment to employee development means more than merely saying, "We promote from within."

Compensation. When it comes to compensation, there is usually a great deal more to consider than just the starting base salary. Taking a long-term perspective will help you evaluate the compensation offer. Be aware of the following items that may be included as part of your compensation package:

- *Insurance policies.* Medical, dental, optical, life, and disability insurance may be offered. "Cafeteria-style" plans that allow you to select the type and amounts of coverage and benefit levels you want are becoming more popular. Trying to make sense of the written materials available on these programs may be tough. Don't hesitate to ask for clarification from the company, and consider input from more experienced family members and network contacts as you evaluate your choices.

- *Bonuses or profit sharing.* Financial compensation over and above base salary may be available based on meeting performance goals for your position, property, or unit. Examples of performance goals include increased market share, higher guest or cover counts, higher occupancy percentage, higher average daily rate, more revenue per available guestroom, and others.

- *Stock options.* Employees may be offered the opportunity to purchase shares of company stock, often at below-market prices. The risk is usually small, the potential payoff great.

- *Paid vacation, emergency, and family leave.* Hospitality organizations may offer one to two weeks of vacation and similar amounts of paid sick/personal leave annually. While current federal law (the Family and Medical Leave Act) requires employers to grant twelve weeks of *unpaid* family or medical leave to employees under certain circumstances, some employers offer paid maternity, paternity, or family leave.

- *Retirement programs.* Some organizations offer tax-deferred, fund-matching 401(k) plans, in which the employer matches employee contributions up to a predetermined limit. Be aware of any vesting requirements—you may have to be on the job for a good length of time before you are eligible for the benefit. If a 401(k) or similar retirement plan is available to you, keep in mind the impact of compound interest over the length of a career and begin investing early. Payroll deduction options make investing in a 401(k) virtually painless, and one day you could wake up with a large retirement fund.

- *Educational and training assistance.* Beyond the company-specific job training you receive, some organizations may offer reimbursement for college classes or other training opportunities you pursue outside of work.

- *Paid relocation expenses and other benefits.* Your company may also provide assistance and relocation expenses associated with transfers and promotions. Hospitality companies are also known for offering discounted or free hotel stays to employees. Company vehicles, paid parking, laundry services, and paid professional association or club memberships are not usually part of initial job offers.

Training. Some companies require new management hires to complete a six- to eighteen-month training program. Others offer more flexible and self-directed programs. Still others may take a "sink or swim" approach with new hires—that is, offer no training at all. It is vital that you understand the company's training philosophy and how it suits your needs and expectations. A company's commitment to training must be considered in relation to your current skill and experience levels. You want to make sure you choose a company with a supportive work environment that maximizes your chance at success.

Site. Where you work can have an enormous effect on how you work. Many (but not all) hospitality companies expect you to relocate for promotions and career growth. Newly hired managers sometimes discover that sadness over leaving behind family and friends quickly replaces the initial excitement of a new job in a new location. Some managers develop a good old-fashioned case of homesickness, which may affect their job performance. Having chosen a hospitality career, you need to realize that moving is not usually all fun and excitement; it also involves change and the necessity to build new relationships. Tapping into your network can help ease any transition difficulties you experience when you relocate.

Multiple Rating System. A multiple rating system can help bring some objectivity to the important decision of choosing among different career choices. A multiple rating system uses the same criteria to judge each job offer. The criteria consist of those issues that you consider to be of critical importance. After determining the critical issues, you rate each job offer on each issue, using a scale of 1 to 100. The higher the rating, the better you think the job offer covers that issue.

Simply totaling these ratings may not identify the best job offer, because you will undoubtedly feel that some issues are more important than others. In order to more accurately identify the best offer, you should assign to each issue a percentage value that reflects its relative importance to you. Then, multiply the rating for each issue by its percentage value and total the points to yield an overall score for each job offer. The offer receiving the highest overall score identifies the company that you should seriously consider as your future employer.

The following example illustrates how you can use a multiple rating system to evaluate job offers. Assume that Steve receives three job offers. Also assume that Steve chooses to evaluate these offers on the following five key issues and that he weights the issues as follows:

Critical Issues	Percentage Value
Fit	35%
Advancement	25%
Compensation	20%
Training	15%
Site	5%
Total	100%

(When evaluating actual job offers, you can use these criteria or develop your own list of critical issues.) Exhibit 6 shows the results of Steve's evaluation of the job offers. Steve will probably not give further consideration to the offer from Company C because it did not score well on any of the key issues. Since the overall scores of Company A and Company B are so close, Steve may want to further analyze the differences between these companies before making a final decision. For example, the job offer from Company A scored relatively high on compensation and site. On the other hand, Company B had better scores in the areas of fit, advancement, and training. Steve's final decision may well hinge on the importance he gives short-term career goals (compensation and site) versus long-term considerations (fit, advancement, and training).

Exhibit 6   Evaluating Job Offers Using the Multiple Rating System

Issues	Company A Points/Value/Total	Company B Points/Value/Total	Company C Points/Value/Total
Fit	60 × .35 = 21.0	70 × .35 = 24.5	50 × .35 = 17.5
Advancement	50 × .25 = 12.5	60 × .25 = 15.0	40 × .25 = 10.0
Compensation	85 × .20 = 17.0	55 × .20 = 11.0	60 × .20 = 12.0
Training	40 × .15 = 6.0	70 × .15 = 10.5	60 × .15 = 9.0
Site	100 × .05 = 5.0	50 × .05 = 2.5	40 × .05 = 2.0
Total Score	**61.5**	**63.5**	**50.5**

Implementing a Choice

Getting a job is much like any other sales process. It is important to realize, however, that while you are not really selling *yourself,* you are making a bargain to trade a substantial portion of your time/effort/behavior for some sort of compensation package. In terms of pursuing this deal, you should at this point in the chapter have a better understanding of what you have to offer (your strengths, interests, values, and accomplishments) and have identified targeted "buyers" (potential employers). It is time to create a personal sales plan based on all of the marketing research you've already done. The key question is, "How will I get from where I am now to where I want to be?"

Networking

"Networks" are generally defined as interconnected systems. Just as computers are sometimes networked so they can share information, people form networks for sharing social and business information. Employment **networking** has been identified as the primary source by which most jobs are found.[7] Just as researching the hospitality industry required a multi-level approach (from the broad and general to the narrow and specific), so it is with getting from where you are now to where you want to go next. Information interviewing was the broader form of networking, which is now narrowed to seeking specific employment opportunities.

You might want to start your employment networking by calling people on the list of contacts you created during the information interviewing phase of your career search. Or, if you have decided on some specific organizations that you might want to work for, you can expand your contact list by adding people from your targeted organizations and people who may know individuals within those organizations.

Before you proceed with the networking process, it is important to be aware of some common self-defeating perspectives and practices associated with employment networking:

- *The "I need a job, not a network" perspective.* Expecting results overnight is unrealistic. Networking is not intended to replace interviewing. Instead, networking augments the selection and interviewing process. Why walk into an interview as a stranger, known only by a résumé and cover letter, when meeting and communicating with the recruiter in advance increases the likelihood of achieving your desired results? Furthermore, what if your targeted employers don't recruit on campus? Networking is often the best way to reach employment decision-makers.

- *Fear of rejection.* Realistically, what is the worst thing that can happen to you if you attempt to contact someone? The risk of your request being rejected or ignored is a small price to pay for the benefits that may result from making one good contact. Most professionals know that the roles of information "gatherer" and "disseminator" have a tendency to switch back and forth over time. The person you approach for help today may be approaching you for help in the not-too-distant future. Therefore, many of the people you contact will be interested in establishing a business relationship.

- *Aversion to "manipulating" others.* The notion that networking requires you to use others, in a negative sense, is mistaken. Again, successful hospitality professionals recognize the importance of networking, and most like to be "well connected." As service-oriented individuals, most of them enjoy the chance to help others and know they can expect reciprocity.

- *The "they owe me" perspective.* Just because someone is a family friend or an alumnus of your school does not mean he or she owes you a job or anything else. On the other hand, if approached with respect and courtesy, such people will probably help when possible.

How do you begin a networking telephone call? If you are calling someone you have kept in touch with throughout the information interviewing stage of your job search, a good way to begin is to let them know you are about to graduate, or—if it's been a while since graduation—give them an update of how your job search is going. If you have developed a relationship with them over the past several months (or even years), they will be interested in your news and will probably quite naturally begin talking about possible job openings or individuals who may be of help to you.

If you are attending an industry trade show or professional conference, don't let the fact that you're now actively looking for a job lead you into a social faux pas such as the following: "Hi, my name is Ted Johnson. I'm graduating soon, and I really need a job. Can I give you a copy of my résumé?" Even though you are looking for a job, you should call on the skills you learned when you were asking people for information interviews. Why? Because the best way to look for a job is to look for additional contacts, and the best way to make additional contacts is to request information interviews. People are much more open to a request for advice or a future meeting than to a request for a job or for help in finding a job.

When you are at a social function and you want to make networking contacts, introduce yourself to someone—don't wait to be introduced, or for someone to approach you. Extend your hand for a handshake, look the other person in the eye, smile, and say something like the following: "Hello, my name is Joanna Rodriguez. I'm from Syracuse, New York, and I'm just finishing my studies at State University." By telling the other person more than just your name, you are volunteering information that can help start the conversation. The other person will probably respond in a similar way. As Frank Doyle, former director of human resources at the National Restaurant Association and current vice president of professional development for the American Society of Association Executives, points out:

> There are three things people want to talk about: themselves, their work, and their company. You need to create a parallel between yourself and the other person, and you make this connection by getting them to talk: "So, when was your company founded?" or "You're from Chicago? I visited there last summer." Then proceed to talk about your trip to Chicago, or ask about where exactly they are from.[8]

Learn more about the individual's organization as well as his or her place in it. Stay clear of potentially troublesome topics, such as religion and politics, and don't launch into funny stories about the pranks you pulled during your college career. In fact, it's a little risky to attempt jokes or humor of any kind during first meetings, because what may seem funny to you may not be funny to others.

After you've spent enough time (perhaps 10 to 15 minutes) to have a meaningful conversation, you should try to further the relationship before parting. Marilyn Goldman, a national certified career counselor, suggests that you be direct. "Ask them when you can come to see them to further discuss your career goals."[9] Asking contacts if you can call them in the near future will usually prompt them to give you a business card. This gives you the information you need to send your résumé and a cover letter to them. In the cover letter, remind them of how you met and inform them that you will call within the next few days to see if you can arrange another personal meeting.

As you can see, the main difference between information interviewing and employment networking is that the interval between meeting someone and beginning to talk about specific job possibilities is much shorter when you are employment networking.

Networking takes effort and practice. The good news for students is that hospitality professionals are sometimes more likely to extend an extra effort on behalf of a student, because they may see a bit of themselves reflected in the student or because they see the student as a potential protégé. Hospitality professionals, by the very nature of the business, enjoy providing service and exceeding expectations. Many of these individuals take great pride and satisfaction in assisting the career development of others. It's good for them and the industry as a whole.

It is important to create a networking plan that corresponds to your employment timetable. As graduation approaches, you can establish goals in terms of the number of networking contacts you want to make per week and have a schedule for attending career fairs, company presentations, industry trade shows, professional conferences, alumni association events, and guest lectures and seminars on campus.

Additionally, pay attention to the general media and hospitality trade press to learn who is receiving publicity and awards. If you spot an industry award recipient employed by a targeted employer, why not drop a note of congratulations and a request for advice? By following up on these and other leads, you can learn a great deal and improve your employment prospects.

Modern technology has offered the ultimate in networking via the Internet. Be aware of the international, cost-effective communications capabilities that exist via the World Wide Web. The possibility of reaching anyone almost anywhere is becoming a reality, and access to people and information online creates a heretofore unheard of potential for employment networking.[10]

While there are large and popular examples of web-based social networking sites such as Facebook and MySpace for students and LinkedIn for professionals, many more narrowly focused sites have recently emerged, including Who is Who in Hospitality (www.wiwih.com), that are aimed at those wishing to concentrate their networking efforts on members of the global hospitality industry.

An additional note about social networking sites like Facebook: employers can and do use these sites when checking backgrounds of employment candidates. Students and others would be well served to only post information and photographs that they would feel comfortable being viewed by their own mother or the most conservative person they know.

Employment websites help employers find job seekers and recruit staff. There are both generic and hospitality-specific job sites. Some sites even have a feature called a "job agent" or "job detective." This feature will send an e-mail to you every time a new job is posted on the site that matches your search criteria.

Creating an Effective Résumé

An excellent résumé does not guarantee an employment offer, but a poor résumé may prevent one. Résumés are useful in the following ways:

- They help you obtain employment interviews.

- They set you up to interview effectively by allowing you to emphasize your talents and accomplishments.

- They help recruiters and interviewers to remember you and share your capabilities with others who influence or make hiring decisions.

Simply put, a résumé is a personalized direct-marketing piece. Like any good direct-marketing piece, it should show the *targeted* audience members what the subject (you) could offer to them. Like a well-designed restaurant menu or hotel rack brochure, a résumé should prompt inquiries and result in sales opportunities (that is, interviews). What you put on the résumé helps establish what questions you'll be asked in an interview. Provide context to the interviewer instead of just listing responsibilities or duties. Explain what you accomplished—quantifying it whenever possible.

The main components of an effective, one-page, chronological résumé are listed below:

- *Personal details.* Personal details should go at the top of your résumé. These include your full name, address (or addresses—school, home, and e-mail), and phone number(s). Make it *easy* for an employer to get in touch. Remember to professionalize your phone answering-machine message. Your friends probably love the jokes and sound effects, but such a greeting may not create the desired impression on a recruiter calling to arrange an interview.

- *Educational background.* The next section should outline your educational background. Include the name and location (city and state) of your school, the degree you earned or expect to earn, and your actual or planned graduation date. On your first résumé, you may want to include your grade point average if it is a 3.0 or above (on a 4.0 scale). As with any other element of a résumé, accentuate the positive and be prepared to discuss and explain the negative (especially grades). Most hospitality recruiters do not overemphasize grades, but they do view academic performance as another component of a well-balanced candidate. Transfer students or those who have attended other institutions should include this information if it enhances their résumés. High school accomplishments are generally left off, especially after the first year of college.

- *Professional experience/employment.* This is the most important section. Refer to your accomplishments and strengths. Do not forget internships or any employment at all relevant to your career goals. Provide a brief summary of each experience, including the name of the organization, its location (city and state), the dates employed, and your title or position. It is not necessary to provide a complete address or the name of your boss/supervisor. Enhance the impact of each individual employment description by using bullet points, emphasizing accomplishments rather than just describing your work, maintaining consistency in format and phrasing, avoiding "I" and "me," and quantifying when possible (for example, "increased sales by X percent," "reduced expenses by Y percent," "supervised Z employees").

- *Activities, special skills, honors.* Indicate relevant information such as professional memberships and affiliations, foreign language capabilities, computer skills, scholarships and awards, and appropriate extracurricular activities (especially involving leadership positions). Determining what to include in this section is a function of space (it's usually best to limit your early résumés to one page) and relevance to your career and current employment goals.

Don't include irrelevant personal information like marital status, height, weight, and health status, and don't include the phrase "references available upon request." Employers will assume this to be true. Be prepared to provide a list of references to employers if they request one, but make it a separate document from your résumé. (While we're on the subject of references, be sure to choose them wisely, and obtain academic, work, and personal references. Always ask permission before using a reference, and provide each reference with a copy of your résumé. Do not forget to keep references updated on the status of your employment search and to thank them appropriately.)

You do *not* have to include an objective on your résumé. Unless the objective is very specific and targeted, it is better to put it in a cover letter. Alternatively, you may develop multiple versions of your résumé with an objective tailored to each targeted employer.

Many employers scan (in about 30 seconds each) hundreds or even thousands of résumés each year. Keep this in mind as you create yours. Use words efficiently and effectively. Look at the keywords employers use in their ad, on their website, in the job description, etc. Make sure you use those same key words in your résumé whenever appropriate. Print the résumé on high-quality paper and beware of exotic color choices.

If you think that your résumé might be electronically scanned into a database, follow these guidelines:[11]

- Limit your résumé to a maximum of two pages and include your name on each page.

- Use standard-size business-correspondence paper (in the United States, 8 ½-by 11-inch paper) of at least medium thickness (20-pound paper or above) to print original laser copies in black ink.

- Use 12 to 14 point fonts in Helvetica, Times, or a similar typeface for clear and distinct letter and word separations.

- Do not use italics, underlining, shading, boxes, columns, or fancy graphics. Careful use of bold lettering is fine.

An employer typically accesses computerized résumés by searching for key words that describe the employer's selection and evaluation criteria (that is, experience, accomplishments, skills, and abilities). To find out which key words matter to your targeted employers, you could:

- Check the recruitment advertising, brochures, and position descriptions of the companies you've targeted.

- Ask the recruiters/employers directly.

- Check with the job bank service that manages the résumé and recruitment database (if appropriate).

There is no perfect and exclusive format for creating a résumé. Based on the input of hospitality recruiters, the chronological format provided in Exhibit 7 is preferred because it's easy to scan. Still, other formats exist, including personal brochures, résumés organized by function, threefold menus, and even matchbook covers and labels on wine bottles. (The references at the end of this chapter include books on résumé development.) With alternative approaches comes risk; you should know your targeted employers well before undertaking a creative approach. A résumé is only effective if it produces the desired result—an interview. If you want to try a creative format, make sure it is not so creative as to cause premature or unnecessary rejection. Since how someone reacts to a résumé is so subjective and unpredictable, it is usually best to stick with a conservative approach.

No matter what format you use, proofread your résumé with extreme care, even if you use spell-checking software. (A spell-checker will not flag certain spelling mistakes, such as "I received a degree form Worldclass University." Since "form" is spelled correctly, the spell checker will not catch that you meant to type "from.") Why risk elimination from consideration simply because of spelling or typographical mistakes? Ask friends, faculty, staff members at campus career centers, and so forth to give you feedback about your résumé. Starting work on your résumé early in the career-planning process will give you plenty of time to create a flawless one.

Exhibit 7   Sample Résumé with a Chronological Format

CHRIS JONES

School Address:
123 Maple Avenue #1
Anytown, USA 48824
Telephone: 123-555-1234
E-mail: success@wmb.edu

Home Address:
1234 Oak Road
Anytown, USA 48824
Telephone: 123-555-4321

EDUCATION
State University, Anytown, USA
College of Business
School of Hotel, Restaurant & Institutional Management
Bachelor of Arts, June 20X4
Self-financed 90% of college expenses through internships and part-time employment

EXPERIENCE
Resident Assistant
Department of Residence Life, State University, Anytown, USA. August 20X3 to Present.
- Coordinated and implemented educational, multicultural, and recreational programs
- Mediated conflicts and enforced Residence Life hall rules and regulations
- Acted as a resource agent for student residents and staff members

Management Intern
Fancy Hotel and Towers (800 rooms, 4 Star), Anytown, USA. May to August 20X3.
- Directly supervised the daily activities of 15 Guest Service Agents
- Created and implemented a new-hire training guide for Guest Services
- Designed and implemented full valet service for the property, including accounting procedures and cash control

Sales and Marketing Intern
Luxurious Hotel (500 rooms, 5 Star, 5 Diamond), Anywhere, USA. May to August 20X2.
- Created a comparative analysis of local competitors
- Planned and executed client appreciation functions
- Executed telemarketing and sales blitzes

Prep and Line Cook
Lettuce Stuff U Restaurant (125 seats, family dining), Anycity, USA. May to August 20X1.
- Sautéed, grilled, baked, deep-fried, and assembled all menu items to order
- Assisted with the creation of menus and production methods
- Responsible for opening and closing the restaurant

Assistant Manager
Melting Ecstasy (10-seat ice cream parlor), Anycity, USA. August 20X0 to May 20X1.
- Performed opening, closing, finance, customer service, and inventory duties

ACTIVITIES
Vice President of Human Resources, Hospitality Association, 20X3
Director of Corporate Ambassadors, Career Expo 20X3
Student Hospitality Sales Organization, active member, 20X1–20X4

HONORS
National Restaurant Association Scholarship, 20X4
Hospitality Association, Student of the Month, October 20X3

SKILLS
Proficient in use of IBM and Macintosh computers and associated software
Fluent in Spanish

A recent development in résumé building is the "video résumé."[12] Video résumés are possible because of increasingly widespread broadband Internet usage, higher-quality video technology, and increased enthusiasm for online video sharing. An individual need only have access to a digital video camera and the Internet in order to post a video online, which he or she can then e-mail anywhere in the world that has Internet access.

Whichever format is used, keep in mind that a résumé is simply a tool. Like any tool, it is well suited for some situations, but not all. The most effective résumés are usually hand-delivered, or at least arrive from someone familiar to the employer. If you rely on résumés alone to secure employment interviews, you lower your chances of success. Use all the tools and strategies available to maximize the results of your employment search.

Cover Letters

Tom Jackson, a noted career and job search authority, suggests that the purpose of cover letters is "to communicate a specific personalized message to a particular employer, answering the most fundamental employment question of all: 'Why should I hire you?'"[13]

Jackson's position is that the responsibility for effective communication lies entirely in the hands of the job seeker. In other words, if an employer fails to read or make sense of your résumé or cover letter, it is self-defeating and useless to blame the employer. You must accept full responsibility for ensuring that communication occurs. All written correspondence associated with your job search reveals not only your credentials and past accomplishments, but also your ability (or lack thereof) to communicate in writing.

If you are like most people, a job search is often the first time you have had to write something that will be evaluated by someone other than a teacher or professor. The tasks themselves—applying for jobs, writing thank-you letters to busy executives, and so on—are difficult enough, but most of the time you don't know (or don't know very well) the people you are writing to. The challenge of determining what to write can be intimidating, especially since there is no chance to rewrite for a "higher grade." The written component of applying for employment, expressing gratitude, and accepting or rejecting job offers is similar to résumé design and construction in the sense that, rather than a single correct model or formula for these types of correspondence, there is a range of effective strategies and techniques you can use. In general, effective job-search correspondence conveys to the reader why you are writing and how you will add value to his or her organization. It also specifies how you plan to follow up your correspondence (with a phone call, for example).

Jackson suggests five rules for writing effective cover letters:

- *Rule 1: Address it to a particular person by name.* Target each cover letter to a specific person. Call the company to obtain the correct name and title if necessary.

- *Rule 2: Communicate something personal.* One of the most effective strategies is to include the name of the person who referred you; this lets the recipient of your letter know of a common acquaintance. You might also, for example, mention that you noticed that the company recently received positive publicity in the trade or general press, or that you recently learned of a new company unit opening near your home.

* *Rule 3: Answer the question, "Why should I see you?"* A common error is to express *your* needs rather than conveying what you will do for the employer. Keep the employer's perspective in mind at all times. The decision to hire you will be based on the value (the skills and ability to produce results) you will add to the organization, not on your need for a job or rent money. The degree of assertiveness you use in pointing out the value you can add must be balanced against the risk of sounding overconfident to the reader. Research and networking should help you decide how far to go in a cover letter.

* *Rule 4: Use their language.* Your knowledge of the industry and the specific company you are writing to should guide your choice of words. If you desire to become an "associate" or "cast member" (because this terminology applies to a targeted organization), then say so.

* *Rule 5: Ask for the interview.* Do not write something like "hope to hear from you soon." Request a personal interview. Employers expect you to suggest a time *and* volunteer to confirm the arrangements. Requesting the interview and stating your intention to call and follow up on the request do not guarantee an interview. However, failing to do so substantially increases the likelihood that you will be ignored. Without some sort of follow-up, you can't even be sure your letter reached the intended recipient.

Appropriate print and paper quality and color are just as important for your business correspondence as for your résumé. In fact, ideally the paper and typeface used for your business correspondence should match that used for your résumé. Think twice before using a creative or bold approach.

Be sure to keep a copy of each letter you send, and deliver on any promises you make to follow up. Failure to call when you said you would will not be viewed favorably. Keep this in mind when sending out a quantity of cover letters and résumés. It may be a better strategy to stagger the mailing—and therefore the follow-up phone calls you'll have to make—to ensure that you are able to call everyone as promised.

Beware of copying phrases and formats from other people's cover letters. Consider what an employer might think who receives copies of virtually the same letter from different students at the same school. Use formats and samples (like those in Exhibit 8) as illustrations and guidelines only. Any letter should be a direct and unique reflection of the person signing it.

As a final caution, be careful when utilizing e-mail to send cover letters. Attaching or including a cover letter in the body of an e-mail seems to be a generally accepted practice; however, with the advent of instant messaging, some students have developed a tendency to assume a casual tone and expect recruiters and employers to be familiar and comfortable with abbreviations, lack of punctuation, incomplete sentences, and animated background images. E-mailing correspondence can be an efficient strategy, but, again, it must be done with appropriate consideration for the perceptions and expectations of the recipients.

Exhibit 8   Sample Cover Letter Format/Sample Cover Letter

Your Address

Date

Employer's Address
(Use an individual's name, if possible)

Dear _____ :

First paragraph: State why you are writing, explain the type of work you are interested in, and indicate how you learned about the employer or the specific job opening.

Second paragraph: Be specific about why you are interested in the position. Briefly summarize some of your strongest qualifications to do the work. Remember to consider this from an employer's point of view. Show what you have to offer the employer, don't merely daydream about what the employer can offer you.

Closing paragraph(s): Refer the reader to the résumé (or application form) you are enclosing. Declare your interest in an interview and offer to provide more information upon request. Invite a response by asking a question or indicating what follow-up you have in mind.

Sincerely,

[signature]

Your Name (Typed)

Enclosure

4321 Pine Street
Anysuburb, USA 54321

January 10, 20XX

Ms. Terry Smith, Director
Voguefoods, Inc.
1234 East Cedar Street
Anymetropolis, USA 12345

Dear Ms. Smith:

Recently I spoke with your director of food services, Gordon Burger. He informed me of your intention to implement a more health-conscious food program at Voguefoods, Inc., and suggested that I contact you. My credentials in the food science industry would enable me to successfully promote the growth of such a program.

In the spring of next year, I will be receiving a Master's Degree in Hotel, Restaurant and Institutional Management from State University. In addition to my degree I will have over four years of work experience in the field of food service. This work experience has familiarized me with diet therapy, food chemistry, menu planning, and food administration.

The American Institutions Food Service Association recently recognized me for my achievements in menu planning with the Midprice Hotels Corporation. I am health-conscious and enjoy working closely with others. I feel very positive about your organization, and I believe I could make a significant contribution to it.

I would like the opportunity to meet with you and discuss how I might be able to promote the growth of a nutritional food program at Voguefoods. I will call you on Monday, January 17, to determine your interest and, if appropriate, arrange for a personal meeting.

I am looking forward to meeting with you.

Sincerely,

[signature]

Pat Smith

Enclosure

Source: Adapted from materials prepared by the Career Development and Placement Services Center at Michigan State University, East Lansing, Michigan.

Interviewing for Jobs

Interviewing is an intimidating and stressful activity for most people. This need not be so. In fact, if you use the career exploration and planning process outlined to this point, you will have a lot of assets to draw upon (namely, self-assessment and company information) to ensure that you are at your best when it comes time to interview.

To help manage the stress you may feel about interviewing, keep in mind this straightforward list of goals you want to accomplish before and during your initial meeting with a recruiter:

- Find out what the employer is looking for in new hires for the position you've targeted.

- Clearly present what you can add to the company by being ready to answer questions about your qualifications and experiences.

- Collect more information about the company during the interview to help you evaluate whether this company is right for you.

A few fundamentals to keep in mind as you prepare to interview include the following:

1. *Be on time.* A sure way to upset an interviewer is to show up late for (or, worse yet, cancel) an interview. If you are unfamiliar with the interview location, check it out in advance. Plan for traffic and allow extra travel time. You should arrive at least ten minutes before the interview.

2. *Your appearance matters.* A properly fitting, comfortable business suit (this goes for women as well as men) is usually best. Your research on the company should help you figure out its expectations. Jewelry, cologne, hair style, and facial hair should usually be kept conservative. Tom Jackson suggests that you dress so that you feel successful. As with résumés, being creative with your personal appearance may backfire. The interviewer will probably remember you if you show up with purple hair, but that does not mean you will get a job offer.

3. *A positive attitude may be the most important thing to bring.* Leave behind thoughts about bad luck, horrible bosses, crazy professors, the terrible morning you had, or any other negatives when you head out to interview. Keep your focus on present and future opportunities, not past problems. Strive always to present yourself in the most favorable and positive light possible.

4. *Bring paper, a pen, extra résumés, and your reference list.* The pen and paper will be useful for making notes either during or (more likely) right after the interview. You may also be well served by jotting down a few key questions you want to ask the interviewer (more on this later). The list of references and extra résumés need not be shared unless they are requested.

5. *Practice interviewing with friends, family, and others.* Interview with anyone who is willing to help you sharpen your interviewing skills. On-campus career centers often offer videotaping services, which is a great way to analyze yourself in action.

Your research on the company will have already revealed important information. Before you interview, you should also find out as much as you can about the specific job you're interviewing for. Then, you can focus on presenting the ways that your strengths, values, and interests will fit the job.

It is also useful to find out more about the specific interviewer if you can. The correct spelling and pronunciation of the interviewer's name, his or her background with the company or industry, and his or her interviewing style are examples of useful information you should seek. To find information relative to the last two points, go through the research you've collected to this point. Question classmates who've recently interviewed, faculty at your school, and other contacts to be sure you know all you can before you sit down to interview. Your goal should be to never walk into an interview as a stranger. If you do your homework, you may be able to meet and get to know the recruiter before the interview (for example, at trade shows, conferences, guest lecture appearances, company presentations, career fairs, and the like).

The point of preparing for an interview is to control all that you are able to control. Recognize, however, that you cannot control everything—for example, the interviewer's mood, the number of openings the company has, the other candidates who will be interviewed, and so forth.

Salary and Cost of Living. Salary is certainly not the only consideration when it comes to compensation (as noted earlier), but it is worthwhile to at least get a sense of the ranges available for the positions/companies/locations you are considering. You can find information about general salary levels at websites such as:

- www.hcareers.com
- www.collegejournal.com/salarydata
- www.salaryexpert.com
- www.cbsalary.com

Your school's career services center might have data on starting salary levels for recent graduates. You can also check directly with classmates or alumni for insights they may have. Asking the recruiter directly at this early stage isn't usually recommended, but as the interviewing process proceeds it will inevitably need to be discussed, and the more you know as a candidate, the better prepared you will be when it comes time to make a decision.

Cost of living at the location(s) in which you might relocate for work is another factor you must take into consideration. For cost-of-living information, you can check websites such as:

- www.homefair.com
- www.accra.org

You may also find it useful to read local newspapers or access websites such as www.REFdesk.com (a resource for national and international news sites) to check on cost-of-living information. And, again, don't neglect to ask family members, friends, and others in your social network who may know about the cost of living and other quality-of-life factors in the geographic areas you are targeting or considering.

Pre-Employment Testing. It is not uncommon for employers to utilize one or more of a variety of pre-employment measures in an effort to increase the likelihood of making the best hiring decisions. According to a survey conducted by the National Association of Colleges and Employers (NACE), more than half of employers conduct some sort of pre-employment testing of the new college graduates they consider for employment.[14] The most commonly utilized test was for substance abuse, followed by personality assessments, aptitude tests, background checks, and, when appropriate to the job, tests of the candidates' physical abilities.

Anticipating Interview Questions. Too many people spend too little time preparing to interview and are therefore less effective than they would like to be. The prevailing attitude seems to be, "Since I don't know what the interviewer will ask, I'll just give it my best shot."[15]

The problem with this attitude is that it assumes you can't figure out what sorts of questions an interviewer will ask you. By putting yourself in the position of the interviewer and thinking carefully about all you've learned up to now (about yourself; the hospitality industry; and the specific recruiter, company, and job you're interested in), you can reasonably anticipate nearly every type of question you will be asked. Some recruiters believe that all interviewing questions flow from three core questions: Why should I hire you? Will you fit in my organization? and, Are you interested in and able to effectively do the job? Armed with this information, you can practice and improve your ability to interview effectively. A list of more specific interview questions is included in Exhibit 9.

As you anticipate what you will be asked, be sure to avoid memorizing your answers. Memorized answers usually end up sounding rehearsed and insincere. Also, memorizing can result in total confusion if you lose your place during your answer. Rather than planning your exact words, use the notepad you will bring to the interview to create brief key-word outlines of the points you want to make in response to a specific question. Refine these outlines later as you practice interviewing with roommates, friends, and others. Your confidence level will grow as you practice. Clearly, this level of preparation takes time, but without a significant investment of time and effort, you cannot expect a reasonable rate of return. There are no quick fixes or short-cuts.

Preparing for Behavior-Based Interviews. Many hospitality employers use an interviewing technique that is intended to determine how you have behaved under specific circumstances in the past. This is known as **behavior-based interviewing**. This type of interviewing is rooted in the belief that the best predictor of your future behavior is your past behavior. Having done well under specific conditions in your past is considered a good indicator of your potential for succeeding in the future (given similar conditions). Exhibit 10 provides a list of typical behavior-based interview questions.

The types of behavior-based interview questions you will be asked are determined by the requirements of the job you are seeking. The employer analyzes the job and determines what qualities and skills are needed for success. During your research, you should also analyze the job. You may then ascertain the skills and qualities necessary for success and, therefore, the sorts of behavior-based questions you will probably be asked. Armed with this knowledge, you can examine

Exhibit 9   Sample Interview Questions

- Tell me about yourself.
- What do you really want to do in life?
- Why should I hire you?
- Where do you see yourself in five years? How will you get there?
- How much will you be making in five years? ten years?
- What are your strengths? weaknesses?
- What motivates you?
- Would you work if you were independently wealthy?
- What's the funniest thing that ever happened to you?
- If you could, how would you change your past?
- Describe your perfect job.
- Why have you chosen this career/job?
- Describe your best/worst boss.
- Do you prefer to work alone or on a team?
- Do you have a geographical preference?
- Are you willing to relocate?
- What was the best/worst thing about your last job?
- If you had it to do over, would you still pick your school?
- What did you learn in school that will help you on the job?
- How do you feel about your grades?
- How did you spend your school vacations?
- Describe your best/worst professor.
- Describe your favorite/least favorite course.
- Tell me about your extracurricular involvement.
- Have you ever quit a job or been fired? Why?
- Who has been the most influential person in your life?
- What makes you angry? How do you express your anger?
- How would your last boss describe you?
- What books and magazines do you read?
- What sort of person annoys you?
- What are your interests outside of work?
- How do you handle stress?
- If you were hiring a person for this job, how would you make your decision?
- How much do you know about our company?
- Why are you interviewing for this position?
- If you joined our company, what is the first thing you'd recommend we change?
- If you joined our company, what is the one thing you'd recommend we never change?
- If you joined our company, what would you plan to accomplish during your first week? day? hour?
- Where else are you interviewing?
- What do you think determines a person's progress in our company?
- How will you decide which company to go to work for?
- Was there anything that you were afraid I was going to ask you today? Why?

Exhibit 10 Sample Behavior-Based Interview Questions

- How did you do in school? Which courses were the hardest? the easiest? Why?
- How did you decide to major in hospitality? What other areas did you consider? Would you make the same decision if you had to make it over again?
- What are some obstacles you had to overcome to complete college and get where you are today? How did you handle them?
- Give an example of a time when you had to achieve consensus in a group disagreement. What was your approach? What was the outcome?
- Tell me about a time you saw an opportunity to improve something when no one else thought it needed improving. What did you do?
- What was the toughest decision you had to make in the last year? How did you go about making this decision? What was the result?
- Tell me about a time when you were given a job or assignment where you had no prior training. How did you learn to do it?
- Tell me about a time when you failed at something. What did you learn from it? How did you do it differently next time?
- How flexible and adaptable are you? Can you give me examples?
- Tell me about a time when you worked with others who did not work well together. How did you deal with that?
- Describe a time in which you had to take an unpopular stand on an issue. How did you do it and what was the outcome?
- Describe a situation when you had the responsibility for completing something but you didn't want to. What did you do and what was the result?
- Describe a time when you felt strong in your convictions and the majority of people felt a different way. What was the issue and how was it resolved?
- Describe a situation where you had to motivate a group of people to accomplish a difficult goal. How did you help them set objectives and overcome obstacles?
- Tell me about a time when you had to gain cooperation from an individual or a group in order to accomplish something.
- Give me some examples of people who come to you for advice. How do you help them?
- Have you ever been asked to do something you didn't think was right? What did you do?
- Tell me about a time when you came forward with the truth and put yourself in a difficult position. What did you do?
- How do you go about building trust with others you work with? Give me some examples.
- Do people trust you? How do you know?
- Tell me about a time when you convinced a peer (or a group of peers) to adopt your ideas. What did you do? What was the result?
- When you come up against a roadblock, what do you do?
- Would you describe yourself as a "take charge" person? What does that mean to you? Give me an example of when you took charge and describe the result.
- Tell me about a decision you made in the last year that you're not very proud of.
- Give me an example of when you worked the hardest and felt the greatest sense of achievement.
- Tell me about one or two long-term goals that you have. What have you done to reach them?
- How do you prioritize multiple and conflicting demands? Give me a recent example.
- Tell me about a time when you had to make a decision without having all of the facts.

Courtesy of ARAMARK.

your past behaviors to select the examples that best demonstrate the qualities and skills you want to share with the interviewer.

Failure to prepare for a behavior-based interview practically guarantees rejection. Few people are able to answer behavior-based questions effectively without having prepared for them.

Based on the job you are seeking and your research of the specific recruiter with whom you'll meet, create a list of the potential behavior-based questions you expect to be asked. As you consider the job description of the position for which you are interviewing, note what knowledge, skills, abilities, and experiences the company is looking for. Hospitality employers often use words and phrases such as "quality," "guest satisfaction," "attention to detail," etc. They usually want to know how you will help them do things like enhance guest satisfaction while increasing profitability for the company and keeping employees motivated.

Next, recall past experiences and behaviors and make a written list of those that might help you answer typical behavior-based questions the interviewer might ask (refer back to Exhibit 10). Then outline and organize your answers using a strategy such as STAR (situation, task, accomplishment, result) and practice telling others about those experiences until you can summarize them briefly (in about two or three minutes), yet retain the details that describe how your behavior exhibited the skills and attributes you know the employer values.

Sometimes descriptions of those skills and attributes can be included on your résumé, setting the interviewer up to ask you about them. For example, you might point out on your résumé that at Company A you increased sales revenues by a certain amount and reduced expenses by a certain amount, and at Company B you reduced guest complaints and improved guest tracking systems.

You may be selling your potential more than your past results when interviewing for your first job. Look for examples across all of your previous experiences—school, extracurricular activities, volunteer work, internships, and so forth. Review the lists of strengths, interests, values, and accomplishments you developed earlier to find the overlap between your accomplishments and what the prospective employer values.

You should expect to be asked to describe times when you were *un*successful. Such behavior-based questions probe for descriptions of times you were unable to resolve a conflict, handle a complaint, make a sale, and so forth. When preparing for these questions, consider why the interviewer would ask them. The interviewer does not expect and probably wouldn't believe an answer like, "I've never been unsuccessful." The interviewer probably wants to check your level of emotional stability and maturity when handling a disappointment.

Be careful not to sabotage yourself with negative responses, especially when describing an unsuccessful experience—conclude the response on a positive note with a summary of what you learned and how you will avoid mistakes or situations like the one you described in the future. You may also want to ask for feedback on your answer with a follow-up question, such as, "Is that the sort of information you were looking for?" Additionally, don't be afraid to ask for a moment to consider your answer and, if necessary, admit that nothing comes to mind at the moment—you can't invent experiences that you've never had.

Illegal Interview Questions. Laws at the federal, state, and even local levels specify that the questions employers may legally ask in interviews must be related to the position under consideration. Unfortunately, employers are not always aware of (or, in some cases, may choose to ignore) the law. You should be aware of the types of questions that are considered illegal. You may then be prepared to handle situations involving these sorts of questions.

The types of information that interviewers cannot legally ask you to provide include the following:

- Your national origin, race, or ethnicity
- Your social and religious affiliations or memberships
- Your age
- Your family and marital status
- Your height and weight
- Whether you are disabled and, if so, the nature of your disability
- Whether you have an arrest record and, if so, what you have been arrested for

Context and word choice are very important when it comes to the legality of interview questions. For example, while it is illegal to ask applicants where they were born or whether they are U.S. citizens, it is legal to ask if they are authorized to work in this country. It is illegal for an interviewer to ask you a general question about your arrest record, but the interviewer may be able to legally ask if you have ever been convicted for embezzlement if this crime might affect your performance of the job under consideration (for example, an embezzlement conviction might have a bearing on your fitness for a job in a hotel's accounting department).[16]

If you are asked an illegal question in an interview, it is important to recognize your options. The strategy you employ in answering an illegal question will depend in part on your interest in the company and how much you want the job. If asked an illegal question, you can:

- *Simply answer the question.* In most cases, you can assume that the interviewer had no harmful intent when he or she asked the question and was probably just not aware of the law. Answering the question will keep the interview on track and usually will not damage your candidacy. The risk you take in providing any information that is not job related is that the employer may consider it in making a hiring decision and therefore illegally discriminate against you.

- *Point out that the question is illegal and refuse to answer.* This is likely to embarrass or anger the interviewer and could result in a quick termination of the interview. Depending on the strength of your convictions, you may not want to work for a company that breaks the law anyway. However, if the interviewer was well intentioned and simply ignorant of the law, you may have just walked away from an excellent opportunity.

- *Politely ask the interviewer how the particular question relates to your ability to do the job.* In this way, you can better determine why the question was asked.

Exhibit 11   Questions Applicants Might Ask Interviewers

- How would your CEO describe your company's culture? Would a line-level employee give the same answer?
- How would you describe your company's culture?
- How long have you been with this company?
- Why did you join this company?
- What do you wish you had known before you joined the company?
- What do you like most/least about the company?
- What is the turnover history among new hires for the job under consideration?
- What are the biggest challenges/opportunities the company is facing in the next year? five years?
- How often will I be evaluated if hired?
- What types of people seem to do well with your company?
- What would you expect me to accomplish in the first month/year on the job?
- Why is the job I'm applying for open?
- When will the hiring decision be made? What comes next in the process?
- Is there any additional information or anything else you'd recommend I do to enhance my chances of receiving an offer?
- May I have one of your business cards?

You still must decide whether to answer, but you will likely have a better feel for the recruiter's intentions and this may influence your decision.

Questioning the Interviewer. Most recruiters expect you to ask them questions. This is only appropriate, as interviewing involves two parties trying to determine if an employment match exists. Asking questions of the interviewer might reinforce your interest in the company and can demonstrate to the employer that you've done your homework before the interview. Questioning the interviewer also provides the opportunity for you to clarify issues and collect useful information.

Avoid asking questions that you could have found answers to before the interview (for example, company mission, size, locations, and so forth). Also, despite the excitement and nervousness you may feel during an interview, try not to ask questions that were answered earlier in the interview. Don't be in a rush to ask too many questions early on, because answers to some of your questions will usually surface during the course of the interview. It is common for the recruiter to wait and ask if you have any questions near the end of the meeting. This allows you to integrate all that you've learned and ask intelligent questions. Exhibit 11 includes examples of questions to ask interviewers.

It is generally wise to avoid asking any questions related to compensation. As part of your company-specific research and networking efforts, you should be able to get a reasonable idea of how a company pays and what benefits it offers. Employers may provide salary ranges and vacation and benefit information in recruitment brochures and literature, for example. During initial interviews, your focus is best placed on answering the recruiter's "Why should I hire you?" question. There will be a more appropriate time to learn more about (and negotiate) the specific compensation associated with the job.

Recruiters close interviews in a variety of ways. Some save the "Why should I hire you?" question for last, to give you an opportunity to summarize your job-related skills and potential for success on the job. Others may say, "Any questions?" and then move to an explanation of how the process proceeds. Before you leave, be sure you understand the timetable for the employment decision. Ask questions if the recruiter does not specify this information. Close on a positive note by thanking the interviewer for the opportunity to be considered for the job.

Thank-You Letters. No matter how the process will proceed after the initial interview, it is wise to send a thank-you note to the interviewer. While it is customary to thank the interviewer in writing, not all interviewers expect a typewritten letter. A legible, handwritten note on paper that matches the paper you used for your résumé will generally be well received. It is important to send the letter in a timely fashion, usually within a day or two of the interview. If you interviewed on campus, it may be possible to deliver your thank-you note by hand to the site of the interview on the same day that you were interviewed. This approach can be very effective, especially if you follow it up after a few days with a phone call to reiterate your interest and ask if there is anything else you can do to maximize the chance of an offer. This demonstration of your initiative and enthusiasm might have a big impact on whether you are offered the job. In addition to being the polite thing to do, writing and sending a thank-you note is another networking tool—even if you are not offered the job, a thank-you note may contribute to an impression that you are a socially astute, strong job candidate whose name should be passed along.

Preparing for Second Interviews. Initial interviews are often followed by one or more additional interviews. From the employer's perspective, only those applicants who show substantial promise are invited to continue the process. For you, a second interview means an additional opportunity to explore the company and sell yourself. Do not assume a job offer is guaranteed simply because you are invited to a second interview.

When preparing for a second interview, be sure to confirm all of the arrangements in advance (by phone or in writing), including the handling of expenses (expenses are usually covered by the employer) and the names and titles of those with whom you'll be interviewing. Bring extra copies of your résumé—just in case—and remember to treat *every* person you meet the same way you'd treat the recruiter. The recruiter may ask all who come in contact with you for an opinion about you. Assume that virtually everything you do is being evaluated. In turn, carefully consider the environment and people you come in contact with. How does the work environment feel? Do you think you could fit in with the people you meet?

Some organizations may ask you to shadow a manager for a day or two or complete a **job preview**, during which you will actually work in a location for a short period. This allows a more complete opportunity for you and the employer to get to know each other. Should the opportunity for a job preview occur, remember the advice that was mentioned earlier: "Be the type of employee you'd like to manage." Show enthusiasm and ask questions.

Some interviewers will ask you to submit a sample of your writing as part of the second interview process. At least one hospitality employer requires all second interviewees to write a two-paragraph memo at the close of their second interview. The subject? "Why I would be an asset to your company."

Handling Rejection. Being turned down for a job can seem devastating. Whether the company's rejection letter arrives after the first interview or later in the process, it's painful just the same.

It is important not to take a rejection to mean you are a failure. A rejection only means that this particular employer at this particular time chose for whatever reason not to extend a job offer to you. The best thing you can do is try to objectively assess the situation and determine if your failure to receive an offer resulted from factors you control or factors that were beyond your control. If, for example, you failed to research the company thoroughly, you can control and improve on that aspect of the process. However, it may be that there was a more qualified candidate, a factor over which you have no control. Think back to the three core interviewing questions noted earlier: Why should I hire you? Will you fit in my organization? and, Are you interested in and able to effectively do the job? Did you enthusiastically present clear and compelling examples of how you could do the job under consideration? At the same time, were you careful to avoid coming across as a know-it-all? Consider, too, your feelings and perceptions after the interviewing process. Was there a good fit between you and the company? If you had doubts about working for the company, a rejection may be a blessing in disguise.

In any case, you should follow up a rejection letter by again contacting the interviewer. Send a letter thanking him or her and asking for any feedback he or she may provide to help you strengthen your position for future consideration (if you still think you'd like to work for that particular company). Demonstrating professional perseverance and assertiveness in this way has virtually no risk attached. It may, in fact, pay off in some constructive feedback. You might even be considered for future openings. Remember to step back from the anger or disappointment that might be your initial emotional reaction. Think about your specific career goals and remember that it is the *process*, not a single event, that matters. Most successful people use their failures as motivation to do what has been referred to as "failing toward success." A long-term perspective based on your understanding of yourself and your options will help you through the sting of any temporary failure to receive a job offer.

Before leaving the topic of rejection, we should discuss what you should do when *you* are doing the rejecting—that is, when you must turn down a job offer. If you determine that it is in your best interest to choose an alternative offer, it is important to notify in writing the interviewer you are turning down. Be conscientious and polite. Keep in mind the strong networks that exist among hospitality professionals. If you turn down a company in a discourteous way, your action might be communicated far and wide along the networks and ultimately come back to haunt you.

Parameters of Negotiation

As a new graduate of a hospitality management program, you may believe that you are not in a position to negotiate the terms and conditions of your first job offer. If you believe this, then you are certainly correct. If you believe otherwise, however, you may discover that there is some room to improve any job offer you receive. This is not to suggest that you should approach negotiations with an adversarial perspective. Rather, your goal is to sell your services at the best rate under conditions you and the company agree are best.

To negotiate effectively, you must know what someone with your education and experience is worth (you can find out through industry and company research) and what you want and need (discovered through self-assessment). You must also understand what the company needs and how much it is willing to pay for it. Specific areas to consider for negotiation include the following:

- Starting salary
- Timing of performance reviews
- Desired geographic location
- Relocation assistance
- Starting time (the date you must report for work)

Be sure you are selling your skills and accomplishments (how you will add value to the company) as the basis for your negotiations. *Your* needs (car payments, rent, loans) will seldom convince an employer to change an offer. Your understanding of the *company's* needs and how you can satisfy them is far more likely to lead to a bump in salary, strong consideration for your preferred geographic location, or whatever you are negotiating for. You may also consider leveraging your offer with a second offer from a competitor, although you should be cautious about trying to start a bidding war. Remember that your top priority is to start your career under the best conditions. Actions based on short-term thinking may have long-term negative consequences. On the other hand, if you approach negotiating your first offer with maturity and a sense of fairness, you are likely to enhance your employer's impression of you. As businesspeople, recruiters realize that negotiating is a part of life and business. The risk of offending or angering employers by attempting (in a professional manner) to convince them of your worth is minimal.

Accepting an offer of employment is a serious commitment. The pressures that are associated with making such a commitment can feel immense. Having to weigh multiple job offers sounds like a nice problem to have, but it can be very stressful, especially when decision timetables conflict.

Though you cannot control the timing of offers, you can ask for extensions on decision dates. This doesn't guarantee an employer will grant an extension, but this is a far better solution than accepting an offer and then later reneging. Even beyond the important ethical considerations, your reneging will be associated with you for a very long time. In the small world of the hospitality industry, you will probably someday cross paths with the individuals you lied to. At the very least, you will probably at some point have to do business with the company you jilted. To say nothing of how your reneging may damage relations between your school and the company in question. Why risk so much short- and long-term damage to yourself and others? Use your heart and head as well as your network of advisors (family, friends, industry contacts) to help you work through the stress of managing multiple offers. Compromising your personal integrity to gain a job is a destructive trade-off.

Professional Development

To borrow a particularly apt phrase, when it comes to professional development, you've got to own your own. The success or failure of your professional development lies primarily in your hands. No one else knows your skills, interests, and values as well as you do. Nor can anyone else as accurately gauge the development activities that will be most profitable and effective for you.

Professional development is the process by which an employee becomes proficient at the job he or she is doing. Professional development ensures that you continue to have the knowledge and skills necessary for success.

Professional development is also a never-ending process. There will never be a point at which you will be able to say that you have learned all there is to learn and are as skilled as it is possible to be. Taking control of your professional development is part of taking control of your career. What does professional development do for you? It:

- *Maintains your current position.* You have an obligation in a changing world to constantly update your skill set. Even if you want to do what you are doing for the rest of your life, what you are doing will evolve and change.

- *Enhances mobility options.* If you desire mobility, doing well in your current position enhances your prospects. Even if you are not formally promoted, professional development gives you enrichment, a higher degree of professionalism, and can help keep your interest in your job high.

- *Makes promotion a stronger possibility.* If you want to be promoted, it is important that you start developing the skill set you will need for the position you want. Employees who are high performers in one job sometimes find themselves promoted to a job for which they have no skills.

Reach Out to Others

While your professional development is wholly your responsibility, you don't have to do it alone. Indeed, you will be much more effective if you systematically involve other people, including your manager, your peers, your subordinates, hospitality professionals at other properties, and educators.

Nearly every person with whom you come into professional contact has something they can teach you. Try to find something to learn from each person, even if it is how *not* to do something. You can learn through observation, conversations, or presentations.

There are also people who can become more formally involved in your professional development. In the early stages of forming your professional development plan, talk to your manager and discuss your plan. Your manager may have advice about skills that he or she thinks are going to be important or be aware of resources to which you could have access. Find out what sort of formal opportunities are available from your property or corporate offices.

Fostering a mentor-protégé relationship with a skilled manager can also greatly accelerate your professional development. A mentor is someone who can act as a coach, an advisor, a teacher, and a role model. A mentor can give you feedback on your performance and encourage you in your development. He or she can help you reach your goals of excelling at what you are doing.

Planning Your Development

There is no such thing as a perfect professional development plan. But perfection is not really the goal. It is excellence and movement toward excellence that matters.

Once you have a job, you are ready to set goals for your professional development. In order to set goals, you need to know what you want to be good at and how good you are at it now. You also need to determine how good you want to get and how good your manager needs you to get.

There are many ways to conduct a self-assessment to determine where there are development needs. Some of the tools that exist include:

- Past performance reviews
- Conversations with your peers, managers, and subordinates
- Lists of strengths, weaknesses, values, and interests

Once you have conducted a self-assessment, you need to gather feedback from people around you. Gathering feedback will help you verify your skills and needs as well as identify what your organization's needs are now and in the foreseeable future. People who can provide feedback on your skills include your manager, your peers, and your employees.

You now need to determine in which direction you want your professional development to go. This involves writing goals for each of your strengths and weaknesses and then setting priorities for those goals. The next step is to focus on two or three of these goals and create a plan for reaching them. While your self-assessment may identify several areas in which you wish to develop, you will get more reward out of making real progress on two or three of your most important goals than if you make only a few steps toward all of your goals without reaching any of them.

There are several different methods for setting priorities:

- *Determine which skills and competencies your organization needs now and in the foreseeable future.* What does your organization need from you? What skills would most help your organization meet its goals?

- *Work on your weakest areas first.* This can be an effective way of setting priorities if the weaknesses you identify are so essential to your job that you will not be able to perform to standards unless you improve those skills.

- *Build up your strengths and highest interest areas first.* It is much easier to get motivated to learn about a skill in which you already have a great deal of confidence or interest. Getting an enthusiastic start in your professional development activities can create a momentum that will carry over when you begin working on other areas.

- *Combine the three methods above.*

It is also helpful to determine both your short- and long-term goals. Think about where you are and where you want to be in one year, five years, and ten years. Think about which skills you will need to arrive at where you want to be in those time frames.

Create the Plan

Once the groundwork has been laid and you know what you need to improve, what your goals are, and what your priorities are, it's time to create the plan that will get you where you want to be. Common steps for creating a professional development plan include: setting objectives, getting motivated, determining learning activities, establishing a timetable, identifying resources, and anticipating barriers and constraints.

Execute the Plan

Creating the plan draws a map for accomplishing your development. Once the map is in place, it is time to execute your plan.

Professional development activities must be scheduled. Pick a regular time that you can commit to on a daily basis. It might be right before work, at lunch, or at the end of the day—whatever time will work best for you. Evaluate what your energy level is and determine when you will be fresh and most amenable to learning. Consider your other time constraints so that your development activities aren't consistently sacrificed to other demands.

Look each day for development opportunities that are right under your nose. Take a careful look at your routine. Could you do something in a new way? For example, say your goal is to provide more specific employee feedback. In the past, you have coached only when your employees have needed correction. Determine instead that you are going to try to "catch someone doing good" each day this week and praise them with specific observations.

Learn to take calculated risks in your job. Experiment with the tasks that you do and the way you interact with your employees and your peers. Try to forecast what will happen if you do something differently. What is the worst-case scenario? Can you live with that? Often, taking risks pays off with greater opportunities and rewards.

Look also for opportunities to volunteer in your workplace. There is frequently more work to do than there are people to do it. While you probably also have a very busy schedule, making time to do things outside your normal job description can enhance your career and add to your skills and knowledge.

Professional Certification

A means of documenting your current professional competencies and skills and obtaining new ones is available through an array of professional hospitality certification programs provided by hospitality associations and other organizations (see Exhibit 12). These programs, which are rooted in the guilds of medieval times, are usually managed and administered by associations or governmental agencies. These sponsoring organizations have a vested interest in helping people learn management and other work practices in a specific hospitality area. Certification

Exhibit 12 **U.S. Hospitality Organizations Offering Professional Certifications and Designations**

American Culinary Federation (ACF)
www.acfchefs.org

American Dietetic Association (ADA)
www.eatright.org

American Hotel & Lodging Educational Institute (AH&LEI)
www.ahlei.org

American Society for Healthcare Food Service Administrators (ASHFSA)
www.ashfsa.org

Club Managers Association of America (CMAA)
www.cmaa.org

Convention Industry Council (CIC)
www.conventionindustry.org

Dietary Managers Association (DMA)
www.dmaonline.org

Hospitality Financial and Technology Professionals (HFTP)
www.hftp.org

Hospitality Sales and Marketing Association International (HSMAI)
www.hsmai.org

International Association of Exhibitions and Events (IAEE)
www.iaee.com

International Executive Housekeepers Association (IEHA)
www.ieha.org

International Food Service Executives Association (IFSEA)
www.ifsea.com

International Special Events Society (ISES)
www.ises.com

National Association of Catering Executives (NACE)
www.nace.net

National Restaurant Association Educational Foundation (NRAEF)
www.nraef.org

National Tour Association (NTA)
www.ntaonline.com

The Travel Institute
www.thetravelinstitute.com

is available at a variety of levels, from newly hired employees to senior managers. Hospitality certification provides a means of continuing and documenting your professional development over the length of a career.

Endnotes

1. J. P. Sampson Jr., G. W. Peterson, J. G. Lenz, and R. C. Reardon, "A Cognitive Approach to Career Services: Translating Concepts into Practice," *The Career Development Quarterly* 41 (1992): 67–72.

2. Benjamin Bloom, ed. *Developing Talent in Young People* (New York: Random House, Inc., 1985).

3. Martha Stoodley, *Information Interviewing: What It Is And How To Use It In Your Career* (Garrett Park, Md.: Garrett Park Press, 1990).

4. See www.sec.gov/edgar.shtml for more information on the SEC's EDGAR system.

5. Reg Foucar-Szocki, "The Top 10 Ideas For Successfully Surviving An Internship," *HOSTEUR Magazine*, Fall 1993, p. 14.

6. Patricia Carr, "Eeny, Meany, Miney, Mo," reprinted in *The Best of Managing Your Career: Rating Potential Employers (The College Edition of the National Business Employment Weekly)*, n.d.

7. Richard Beatty, *Job Search Networking* (Holbrook, Mass.: Bob Adams, Inc., 1994).

8. Cameron J. Heffernan, "Networking: A Key to Your Career," *HOSTEUR Magazine*, Spring 1994, pp. 12–13.

9. Heffernan, p. 13.

10. For more information, see James Gonyea, *The On-Line Job Search Companion* (New York: McGraw-Hill, 1995).

11. Peter Weddle, *Electronic Résumés for the New Job Market* (Manassas Park, Va.: Impact Publications, 1995).

12. Diana Ransom, "Video Resumes Are Taking Off," *Wall Street Journal* (1/1/2007), http://online.wsj.com/public/us; or www.resumebook.tv/press/Career_Journal.pdf.

13. Tom Jackson, *The Perfect Résumé for the 90's* (New York: Doubleday, 1990).

14. Results from the 2006 NACE Employer Benchmark Survey in NACE'S *College Relations & Recruiting Status Report*.

15. Tom Washington, *The Hunt: Complete Guide to Effective Job Finding* (Bellevue, Wash.: Mount Vernon Press, 1992).

16. A more detailed discussion of the legal issues surrounding interviewing may be found in Robert H. Woods, *Managing Hospitality Human Resources*, 4th ed. (Lansing, Mich.: American Hotel & Lodging Educational Institute, 2006).

 # Key Terms

behavior-based interviewing—A technique used by interviewers to determine how applicants have behaved under specific circumstances in the past. The theory behind behavior-based interviewing is that the best predictor of future behavior is past behavior.

information interviewing—A form of interviewing in which the goal is not to gain employment but to gain more information about a particular career.

job preview—A method used by some employers for evaluating job candidates, in which the candidates actually work for the employer for a short time.

networking—The practice of developing personal connections with friends, acquaintances, colleagues, associates, teachers, counselors, and others.

Review Questions

1. What are some triggers that let you know you need to make a choice about your career?
2. What do you need to understand about yourself to make good career decisions?
3. What should a personal vision statement include?
4. What sources can give you more information about a specific company?
5. What elements does an effective resume include?
6. How should you write a cover letter?
7. What can you do to prepare for an interview?
8. How can you create and execute a professional development plan?

Internet Sites

For more information, visit the following Internet sites. Remember that Internet addresses can change without notice. If the site is no longer there, you can use a search engine to look for additional sites.

CareerMag.com
www.careermag.com

Casino Careers Online
www.casinocareers.com

StarChefs
www.culinaryjobfinder.com

entreejobbank.com
www.entreejobbank.com

Hcareers
www.hcareers.com

Hospitality Jobs Online
www.hospitalityonline.com

Hoteljobs.com
www.hoteljobs.com

Improvenow.Com
www.improvenow.com

Job Profiles
www.jobprofiles.org

JobWeb
www.jobweb.com

Monster.com
www.monster.com

NationJob
www.nationjob.com

Quintessential Careers
www.quintcareers.com

ResortJobs.com
www.resortjobs.com

Yahoo Careers
http://careers.yahoo.com

Chapter 11 Outline

Competencies

1. Define ethics and discuss ethical issues, including ethical theories and how ethical values might be determined. (pp. 355–362)

2. Identify common ethical issues in the hospitality industry. (pp. 362–363)

3. Describe how hospitality managers define, communicate, and perceive ethics in the industry. (pp. 363–367)

4. Describe a code of ethics and explain its importance. (pp. 367–369)

11

A Look at Ethics

Portions of this chapter were written by Stephen S.J. Hall, Executive Director,
International Institute for Quality and Ethics in Service and Tourism (IIQEST).

IMAGINE IT IS A COLD, overcast day and you are in the middle of the Maine woodlands, shivering, with nothing in sight but trees. You've had a wonderful hike in the woods, but now it is dusk and you want to return to the road and your car. You know the road ran east and west and you started out hiking south. Now, though, you are completely lost and have no clue which way is north. You could start backtracking and hope to see familiar landmarks that would lead you out, but now the light is different and things don't look the same. You could take a wild guess at north and plod doggedly on, hoping you had guessed correctly. You could settle down, hoping it would not become too cold, and wait to catch a glimpse of the moonrise if the overcast skies permitted it—then you would know where east was and could then identify north. Or, you could wait until morning and see where the sun rose and that would tell you north. On the other hand, had you remembered to bring your compass, you could just consult it and start walking directly north and be on your way home in no time. Every seasoned hiker knows the value of a compass and how it can help a hiker make the right decisions.

Many ethical-decision moments in life can make you feel like you're lost in the woods. For example, what if you have evidence that a friend is taking materials home from work that he is not entitled to take? What if you know that your boss is deciding which contractor to choose based on the kickback received? Maybe a friend wants to add two days to a vacation, so she calls in sick at the last minute—should you tell her supervisor the truth if asked about the situation? What if the person on the sidewalk ahead of you pulls a handkerchief from his pocket and a fifty dollar bill falls out. Do you pick it up, call to him, and tell him what happened? Or do you pick it up, stick it in your pocket, and simply walk on? Maybe you're backing your vehicle and you bump into a parked car and break its taillight. Do you stop and leave a note with your name and telephone number, or do you go on your way, hoping no one saw the incident? Suppose someone tells you a vicious rumor about the daughter of an executive in your company whom you don't particularly like. Do you relish the idea of telling others, or do you keep it to yourself?

What actions do people usually take in such situations? What actions *should* they take? What decisions do we make and how do we make them? The compass that can help us determine the proper choices goes by the name of "ethics."

Ethics Defined

Ethics in its broadest sense comes from the Greek word *ethos,* meaning "character." Philosophers through the centuries have attempted to define **ethics**. Ethics can be described as choosing between right and wrong, or as making the better choice between two rights. It can be described as what ought to be. It can also be described as the study of moral principles concerning rightful behavior. Or, "Being ethical is doing the right thing when no one is looking."

Having a sense of ethics also means that you can see the larger principle involved in small actions. Most hospitality employees would recognize that accepting sexual advances from a guest, taking home equipment such as a property cell phone, or taking money out of the till is wrong, but would those same employees equally regard as wrong such "small" things as punching a time card for a co-worker who is running late, making personal calls on the property's toll-free phone lines, or taking cleaning products home?

Ethical discussions focus on the "right thing to do" or the "wrong thing to do." When used in this way, "right" and "wrong" are ethical terms. However, "right" and "wrong" are not always used in the ethical sense. For example, we could talk about the "right" way to log in lost-and-found items picked up in the hotel lobby. There is no ethical or moral dimension to the way the lost-and-found records are kept, but ethics are involved when we discuss *whether* lost-and-found items should be turned in, or how they should be disposed of after going unclaimed.

Ethical Theories

For thousands of years, philosophers and others have taken different approaches to ethics and have developed various theories. We will take a brief look at some of the most important of these in the following sections.

Utilitarianism. Some ethical theorists argue that the *consequences* of an action make it either moral or immoral. Thus, an action that leads to beneficial consequences is right and moral, and one that leads to harmful consequences is wrong or immoral. **Utilitarianism** holds that an action is morally justified to the extent that it maximizes benefits and minimizes harm or costs. Thus, the moral thing to do in any situation is that action that can be reasonably seen to provide the greatest net benefit for all concerned, when the expected costs are subtracted from the expected benefits. To do something else is to behave unethically, and the more an alternative action maximizes net costs or net harm, the more immoral it becomes. The phrase often used to describe utilitarianism is that it calls for "the greatest good for the greatest number of people."

Kantian Ethics. Immanuel Kant, an eighteenth-century German philosopher (1724–1804), developed an approach to ethics very different from utilitarianism. Kant argued that the consequences of an action are irrelevant to a moral evaluation of that action. His theory argued that actions are moral or immoral because of their very nature, not because of their consequences. For Kant, their nature stems from the type of rules they follow, and it is on the basis of the rules followed that an action can be morally judged.

For Kant, it is the motivation behind an action that makes it morally worth praising or condemning. Moral actions are undertaken out of a sense of *duty*—which means you do it because you know it is the "right thing to do." Actions that are undertaken simply because you enjoy them, for example, do not take on a moral character, even if they result in many positive benefits for others.

The Ethic of Justice. "Justice" is a word often used when making moral judgments. Most people believe in justice and oppose injustice, but what exactly is meant by terms like "justice" and "injustice"? Usually, justice is thought of as "being fair." Justice requires that people treat others fairly.

But, what does it mean to treat everybody fairly? In the first place, it requires that we treat like cases alike. Justice is a comparative term: it involves comparing cases and making sure that we are not discriminating or treating people differently who are alike in relevant respects. To a certain degree, our notion of justice is based on the notion of individual rights. A violation of an individual's rights is considered an injustice.

Social Responsibility. The concept of **social responsibility** suggests that "at any one time in any society there is a set of generally accepted relationships, obligations, and duties between the major institutions and the people. Philosophers and political theorists have called this set of common understandings 'the social contract.'"[1] This contract differs among societies and may change over time. For example, today we expect that businesses will take care not to pollute the air we breathe or the water we drink, will offer fair wages and employee benefits, will provide a satisfactory product or service at a reasonable price, and will in some way participate in making the community in which they operate a better place. These are not ethical considerations per se—they are part of a "deal" that says that we as consumers expect companies to act in this manner because they are part of the society we all share.

Many hospitality organizations recognize this and have stated publicly their belief that it is good business to be a good citizen. They support local arts, raise funds for charities, and try to put some of their profits into the communities that have made their success possible.

Determining Ethical Values

So what exactly puts something in the "moral" or "ethical" category? Ethical or moral norms concern a society's most deeply held values, the things it most cherishes and the things it most despises. As such, they concern actions that individuals believe either greatly benefit or greatly injure human beings. Ethical or moral norms are held to be more important than other values such as self-interest or material comfort. That is, if there is a conflict between "doing the right thing" and doing something that is wrong but makes us wealthier or more comfortable, we should do the "right" or ethical thing. Exhibit 1 lists six commonly held ethical values.

Ethics also affects our image or reputation—our character. Image and reputation most often refer to how others see us, not who we really are. Sometimes, people try to project an image that is different from who they really are. These

Exhibit 1   The Six Pillars of Character

The Josephson Institute identified six ethical values through research conducted with national leaders. These values are ones that can be used to develop good character and ethical behavior.

1. **Trustworthiness:** When others trust us, they don't monitor us to make sure we're going to do what we said we would do. It is a complicated trait that encompasses such qualities as honesty, integrity, reliability, and loyalty. Leaders exercise this value when they:

    a. Are honest
    b. Don't deceive, cheat, or steal
    c. Are reliable
    d. Have the courage to do the right thing
    e. Build a good reputation
    f. Are loyal

2. **Respect:** Respect is sometimes embodied by the Golden Rule. It excludes violence, humiliation, manipulation, and exploitation. It embodies such notions as civility, courtesy, decency, dignity, autonomy, tolerance, and acceptance. Leaders exercise this value when they:

    a. Treat others with respect
    b. Follow the Golden Rule
    c. Are tolerant of differences
    d. Use good manners, not bad language
    e. Are considerate of the feelings of others
    f. Don't threaten, hit, or hurt anyone
    g. Deal peacefully with anger, insults, and disagreements

3. **Responsibility:** Being responsible means being in charge of life's choices and one's own life. It means being accountable for what we do and who we are. It means recognizing that our actions matter and that we are morally responsible for the consequences. Leaders exercise this value when they:

    a. Do what they are supposed to do
    b. Persevere
    c. Always do their best
    d. Use self-control
    e. Are self-disciplined
    f. Think before they act and consider the consequences
    g. Are accountable for their choices

4. **Fairness:** Fairness implies adhering to a balanced standard of justice without relevance to one's own feelings or inclinations. Leaders exercise this value when they:

    a. Play by the rules
    b. Take turns and share
    c. Are open-minded
    d. Listen to others
    e. Don't take advantage of others
    f. Don't blame others carelessly

Exhibit 1 *(continued)*

5. **Caring:** Caring is the heart of ethics and ethical decision-making. It is not possible to be truly ethical and also unconcerned about the welfare of others. Ultimately, ethics is about good relations with other people. Leaders exercise this value when they:
   a. Are kind
   b. Are compassionate and show they care
   c. Express gratitude
   d. Forgive others
   e. Help people in need

6. **Citizenship:** Citizenship includes civic virtues and duties that prescribe how we ought to behave as part of a community. The good citizen gives more than he or she takes. Leaders exercise this value when they:
   a. Do their share to make their school and community better
   b. Cooperate
   c. Get involved in community affairs
   d. Stay informed and vote
   e. Are a good neighbor
   f. Obey laws and rules
   g. Respect authority
   h. Protect the environment

Source: "Making Ethical Decisions," by the Josephson Institute of Ethics (www.josephson-institute.org) and *ISPA Knowledge Network 2007: Leadership & Management*, with Larry Prochazaka.

people can often tarnish the reputation of people around them by giving their peers a bad name. For example, say you work as a guestroom attendant in a hotel and three of your fellow guestroom attendants are terminated because they stole guest property. People could say, "You just can't trust guestroom attendants these days—they'll all steal if given a chance." This is untrue, but you are blemished by the bad actions of a small number of your peers.

A person's image or reputation is a very precious thing. It is made up of three parts: who we really are, who we want others to think we are, and who others really do think we are. Ideally, all three of these views are the same. Sometimes we may want the views to be different by intent. For example, a boxer needs to project the image of a mean, tough warrior who cannot be defeated, because this plants fear and doubt in an opponent. Some managers have the philosophy that fear is a good motivator and portray a mean, tough image as well. This may work in the short run, but has not proven to be a good motivator over time. Trust and loyalty are powerful elements of good management, but they are not stimulated by fear. Instead, authentic leadership—leadership in which managers are who they appear to be—has proven to be most motivating to employees. Authentic leadership is achieved when the three parts that make up a person's image or reputation are identical (or are at least as identical as is humanly possible).

Ethics can also be defined as "knowing what is right and having the will to do it." That is, knowing what is right doesn't mean much unless the individual has the will to do what is right. If a person acts unethically, then by this definition there are two possible explanations: either the person did not know that the actions were unethical, or the person knew but lacked the will to do what was right. If lack of knowledge is the reason for the wrongdoing of an employee, then the wrongdoing might be due to improper supervision or lack of training. If there was knowledge but no will to do the right thing, then the unethical behavior is the responsibility of the employee.

Ethical Litmus Tests. One way to determine what is ethical or "right" is to apply the following seven litmus tests or filters to every decision that has an ethical component:

- Is the action legal?
- Does it hurt anyone?
- Is it fair?
- Am I being honest?
- Can I live with my decision?
- Would I be willing to share my decision with everyone?
- What if everyone did it?

These seven tests must be taken together; each one alone is incomplete. For example, concerning the "Is the action legal?" test, in the past in the United States, slavery was considered legal, as was denying voting rights to women. Both are, of course, highly unethical, and the laws were eventually changed. In the case of "Does it hurt anyone?" consider that during a severe economic downturn it may be necessary to hurt some employees through termination in order to save the jobs of many others. (There are, though, ways to terminate employees that are less painful than others, and that is where ethics again enters the picture.) In terms of the fairness test, it might be unfair to employees to outsource operations to another country where wages are lower, but in terms of profitability, this action could be considered most fair to the company's stockholders. As for honesty, it might not be ethical to be honest when a stock analyst asks you if it is true that your company is about to enter a major merger. Living with an unethical decision is often easier when there are financial gains involved, but more often than not, dishonest acts, however rationalized, result in more loss than gain. The sixth test asks whether you would be willing to share the decision you are about to make with *everyone*—your boss, your employees, your spouse, your children, your friends, etc. Another way that this test is often presented is, Would you be willing to have your decision, and all the details that went into it, published on the front page of your local newspaper? Immanuel Kant is responsible for the final test. He reasoned that if everyone was unethical—that is, if everyone was dishonest, unfair, untrustworthy, hurtful, etc.—society would collapse. Despite the fact that some people act unethically, the vast majority of businesspeople do act ethically.

As you can see, these seven tests for ethics, taken individually, often are not enough to enable you to determine the "right" behavior in a particular situation. However, when taken together and all applied to a decision, they will greatly enhance the probability that the decision you make will be ethical.

Simplifying Ethics

With all of these sometimes conflicting ideas about ethics, how does a hospitality manager determine what is ethical and what is not? What is the basis for ethics, and how can one determine which ethical compass is most effective or "best"?

People have struggled with these questions since the dawn of time. Some people believe that there is a source of absolute truth by which all people must live. For many people and civilizations, this absolute truth could be found in the precepts of their religions. The absolute truth was given to people by a higher power. However, others sought a more secular basis for ethics—one that could apply to everyone, regardless of their faith (or lack of any faith). One approach to finding something that might be readily accepted as logical and meaningful to everyone is to look at the concept of "human rights." One theory of human rights says that humans, regardless of race, creed, gender, sexual orientation, or religion, all have one universally guaranteed right: They have the right to control the property that is rightfully theirs.

"Property," when used in this sense, is defined more broadly than simply land or goods. Our prime property is the physical body that we are born with. As we grow, we add the property of our character, our image, and our reputation. We also accumulate material property such as clothing, a house, a car, and other goods. Assuming that we acquired our material wealth lawfully, it is ours to control.

Also included among each person's "property" is one's conscience. All people have a conscience, an intangible something that helps them differentiate right from wrong. However, because the conscience is personal and subjective, the evaluation of right and wrong, good or bad, moral or immoral, varies with the individual.

What are some examples of the relationship between ethics and property? A few examples include:

- *Bearing false witness.* When we talk negatively about other people, regardless of the accuracy of our words, we are eroding their reputation, which is a part of their property. Doing so is unethical behavior.

- *Theft.* Besides being illegal, taking someone's physical property is an unethical act.

- *Kickbacks.* Receiving gifts for favors granted in which there is the anticipation or expectation of an unwarranted gain is unethical. For example, a purchasing agent who accepts a gift for buying from a specific vendor is impacting the financial property of the owner, who expects fair and competitive bidding.

- *False advertising.* Advertising conditions that do not exist to attract business is unethical because you are diminishing the customer's financial resources (property) under false pretenses.

- *False claims.* Guests who falsely claim a loss, such as money missing from their guestroom, are affecting the reputation of the establishment (which is part of the establishment's "property") and therefore are acting unethically.

Ethical Issues in the Hospitality Industry

Talking about ethical theories in the abstract is one thing; acting ethically in the real world is something else. Hospitality leaders face many ethical issues that come up in the normal course of business operation—for example, handling overbooking situations, discovering a cashier has been pocketing money, or receiving an unexpected kickback from a supplier.

Linda K. Enghagen surveyed 113 four-year colleges and universities on ethical issues in hospitality and tourism. While a total of 35 different issues were raised, the ten that received the most mentions were:

- Managing an ethical environment
- Relations with guests and employees
- Honesty
- Employee privacy rights
- Alcohol and drug testing
- Environmental issues
- Relations with foreign governments
- Codes of ethics and self-governance
- Employee abuse of alcohol/drugs
- Conflicts of interest[2]

These issues reflect the academic perspective. Industry leaders have cited many other ethical problems that concern them. These include:

- Travel agent commissions
- Overbooking
- AIDS
- Employment discrimination by age, sex, or race
- Kickbacks
- Concealing income from the Internal Revenue Service
- Revenue management
- Advertising claims
- Raiding a competitor's staff
- Truth-in-menu laws
- Meeting the needs of guests and employees with disabilities
- Adequate safety and security measures

Kickbacks deserve some further discussion. Many people believe that kickbacks occur only in an organization's purchasing department; however, kickbacks can occur and cause problems elsewhere, too. Taking a hotel as an example, the chief engineer who accepts a gift from a contractor is more apt to approve invoices from that contractor without question; the catering manager who accepts gifts is more apt to provide services at less than full cost; the general manager who accepts gifts is more apt to approve special rates for convention rooms; and the sales and marketing manager who accepts kickbacks from an advertiser is apt to choose the advertising company for the wrong reason.

Research on the Ethical Views of Hospitality Managers

In late 2005, Stephen S.J. Hall, the founder and director of the International Institute of Quality and Ethics in Service and Tourism, conducted a survey among hospitality managers on the topic of ethics. The survey explored such things as how managers defined and communicated ethics, what the survey respondents' perceptions of ethics were, and whether people could be trained in ethical principles.

Hall sent a survey to 500 hotel members of the American Hotel & Lodging Association and received responses from 224 individuals representing 89 different properties and leadership positions from general manager to a variety of department heads in the areas of sales and marketing, food and beverage, accounting and finance, front office, housekeeping, personnel, security, engineering, and purchasing.

Why Ethics?

A fundamental question from Hall's survey explored why it was important to focus on ethics in the first place. Of those managers surveyed, the top five responses to the "Why ethics?" question were:

- It is part of doing business; every business should practice ethics.
- Ethics builds trust and integrity.
- Ethics makes for better service.
- Good ethics builds higher profits.
- Good ethics builds a better image.

"Trust" was a key word in all of the responses. For example, when guests trust that a lodging facility or restaurant will consistently deliver quality products and services, that trust helps generate repeat business, a vital key to business success. In every survey Hall has conducted worldwide, hoteliers have the awareness that ethics pays great dividends because trust from guests evolves from the practice of business ethics.

Defining Ethics

As part of the research, hospitality managers were asked how they would define ethics. The responses did not yield a single, common working definition. When analyzed, there were a total of 33 different approaches to the definition of ethics. There were some words that came up repeatedly in the definitions managers gave, however. The words getting the most use were "right" and "morality." It is also noteworthy that 20 percent of the respondents didn't answer the question at all.

The survey also asked respondents to give examples of unethical behavior that had the potential of occurring in their area of expertise or management. Responses were generally classified into such areas as kickbacks, lying and cheating (both outside the property and in-house), theft, personnel issues, procedures, and unlawful acts (see Exhibit 2 for a list of the unethical behaviors respondents identified).

Communicating Ethics

The survey also looked into how well ethics were communicated to all of the different **stakeholders** at the various properties.

One question asked was whether the property had a visible, published code of ethics. Ironically, given the survey's subject, Hall found reason to suspect that people were answering the survey based on what they thought was the correct answer, rather than giving a truthful answer. Of the 44 properties from which two or more responses were received, there was agreement on the question in only 52 percent of the cases. In 21 instances of disagreement, the general manager responded no. In two of the disagreement cases, the general manager left the answer blank. In a follow-up to the 29 properties who said they had a published code, only six of them were willing to share it with the researchers, although they claimed it was shared with everyone at the property. The survey's author concluded that many respondents said their properties had a code of ethics because they thought that was the better response, even though their properties didn't actually have one.

More than 80 percent of the respondents said that ethics had been discussed in department head meetings. However, while only three percent of the general managers acknowledged that "no," ethics was not discussed in meetings, department heads had a considerably higher rate of "no" responses. Out of 44 properties with multiple responders, 16 (or 36 percent) of them had disagreement among the responders as to whether ethics was ever discussed. It would appear that few general managers want it to be known that ethics is not ever discussed at their properties. This is an understandable reaction. Just about everyone wants to be perceived as an ethical person.

Another common theme among hospitality managers was the desire for greater knowledge about ethics—for themselves, their employees, and people entering the industry. Of the responders, 169 said they would like to personally learn more about ethics, while 64 said no. When asked whether their employees could be trained to act more ethically, 78 percent of the managers said yes, with only 4 percent giving an outright no (the rest said they were uncertain). Sixty-six percent of the managers agreed that hospitality schools should have a course in ethics for future hotel managers.

The strongest response to any question on the survey was whether managers thought it was important for the hospitality industry to focus on ethics and ethical understanding. The response to that question yielded a 98 percent response of "yes."

Exhibit 2   Examples of Unethical Behavior

KICKBACKS
- Room upgrades for tips
- Using hotel contractors for personal use
- Sharing bids with favorite vendor
- Upgrades for cash tips
- Theft by managers of vendor gifts
- Deliberately specifying noncompetitive brands
- Accepting gifts for reduced rates
- Hidden commissions to third parties

LYING AND CHEATING — OUTSIDE
- Guests who fabricate complaints for compensation
- Union contacting customers with lies to hurt hotel
- Meeting planner wrongly blames hotel
- Guest wrongly demanding compensation
- Price fixing
- Applicant falsifying information

LYING AND CHEATING — STAFF
- Sales manager creates bogus contracts
- False worker compensation claims
- Falsifying leaves or absences
- Overcharging guests who don't know better
- Advertising services that cannot be delivered
- Promising something undeliverable
- Entertaining friends on expense account
- Married manager dating
- Non-disclosure of conflict of interest

THEFT
- Pouring heavy or free drinks
- Stealing food products
- Not turning in found valuables
- Pocketing voided cash receipts
- Taking confiscated property
- Embezzling
- Selling free products to employees
- Cheating on time sheets
- Stealing personal guest info for fraud

(continued)

Exhibit 2 *(continued)*

PERSONNEL RELATED

- Favoritism in salaries and bonuses
- Improper relationship with staff
- Nepotism
- Gossiping about guests and co-workers
- Differential treatment of employees
- Giving out confidential information
- Bad mouthing competition to guests
- Sharing confidential information

PROCEDURAL

- Purposely overcharging
- Not honoring contracts with guests and suppliers
- Unauthorized rates given to clients
- Denying cancels due to a disaster
- Non-bid purchasing
- Verbally committing without written backup
- Allowing unauthorized entrance
- Overcharging on consumption events

UNLAWFUL

- Misappropriation of company assets
- Illegal substances in the workplace
- Invoice fraud
- Under-recording of liabilities
- Not enforcing safety measures
- Discussing rate setting with competitors
- Unfair compensation for women and minorities
- Balance sheet inaccuracy
- Price fixing

Perceptions of Ethics

Hall's survey on ethics also explored how hospitality managers perceived the ethics of their employees and the industry as a whole, and asked them how they thought ethical behavior could help a property.

On the survey, hospitality managers were asked to rank how ethical they thought particular hospitality-related entities were on a scale of zero to ten, with

Exhibit 3   Ethical Ranking of Hospitality Entities

Segment	Averages
Your department	8.939
Your owning corporation	8.544
Your hotel	8.478
The American hotel industry	7.365
Your competitors	7.283
Your employees	7.174
Your guests in general	7.060
Hotel labor unions	4.601

zero being the lowest in terms of ethical behavior and ten being the highest ethical behavior. Managers gave their highest rankings to their departments, the corporations that owned their hotels, and their hotels, with the lowest rankings given to guests and hotel labor unions (see Exhibit 3).

Managers were also asked whether they thought their employees behaved more ethically today than they did ten years ago—and if they didn't, why? This question was met with a great deal of ambiguity. Of the respondents, 90 said yes, 94 said no, and 31 did not know. Food and beverage department managers thought strongly that employees today are *not* more ethical, while the managers of sales and marketing departments felt strongly that today's employees *are* more ethical. When asked to give a reason why they perceived today's employees to be less ethical, 30 percent of managers cited "a decline in ethics," while 16 percent cited "a decline in family values." Hospitality managers also gave some ways they thought their properties would benefit if their employees acted more ethically. The largest response was that it would create a better environment at their property, followed by the belief that it would increase profits.

Creating a Code of Ethics

Ethical principles are most effective when they are written down. Writing them helps to clarify them and tends to establish commitment to them. One common way in which businesses record their ethical principles is in a code of ethics. A **code of ethics** is simply a statement of the principles by which an operation intends to conduct business. Done properly, a code of ethics serves as a unifier and a moral compass for the organization.

A written, published code of ethics clearly identifies the principles that guide management. Of course, a published code demands that it be followed. For example, a principle forbidding the taking of gratuities by any employee other than those for which gratuities are a stated part of their compensation is meaningless if the general manager accepts gifts for favors rendered. Likewise, a code of ethics that forbids all forms of pilferage is meaningless if the food and beverage manager takes food home for personal use. In short, managers must "walk their talk" for a code of ethics to be effective for themselves and their employees.

Codes of ethics can be written for every level of the organization, but they all stem from the organization's overall code. The first step in creating an organization-wide code of ethics is to identify the tasks of the organization in broad terms at every level. The tasks of a hotel, for example, are to:

- Sell rooms, food, and services

- Advertise the hotel's products and services

- Hire, train, and manage all employees

- Maintain the property in a safe and healthy condition

- Return an honest profit to the owners and shareholders

- Be a productive part of the local community

- Strictly adhere to all local, state, and federal laws

The next step is to think through the principles of management that govern each task. For example, a property may wish to practice total price transparency (no hidden costs) when selling goods and services. It may have an ethical principle regarding overbooking. Property management may choose to follow an ethical principle regarding adjusting guestroom rates during slow and peak business periods. In the area of advertising, managers may want to follow high principles of honesty regarding truthful descriptions of products and services, the types of "specials" that are offered, and so on. In terms of employee safety and health, property managers may want to emphasize the importance of strict adherence to all safety and health laws. They may also wish to place high importance on protecting the welfare of guests.

Codes of ethics shouldn't try to include everything, however. Simplicity trumps extensive listings. Ethical principles are guidelines or directions only; as such, they should be kept somewhat general. Policies, procedures, rules, and regulations can fill in the details. Exhibit 4 is a sample code of ethics for the service and tourism industry created by the International Institute for Excellence in Service and Tourism. It should be emphasized that this code is just an example of one approach and is not meant to be considered the last word on the subject. Property managers should develop their own codes for their own properties.

A code of ethics is simply a body of guiding principles. By following a meaningful code of ethics, managers and others within an organization can build trust in those they encounter while on the job, and trust is a fundamental building block of success for any business. Even with the best code of ethics, however, and the most comprehensive set of policies and rules, in the end ethical behavior is an intensely personal matter that every manager and employee must wrestle with. There are no easy guidelines that apply equally well in all circumstances.

Exhibit 4   Sample Code of Ethics

CODE OF ETHICS IN SERVICE AND TOURISM

1. We acknowledge ethics and morality as inseparable elements of doing business and we will test every decision against the highest standards of honesty, legality, fairness, and conscience.
2. We will conduct ourselves at all times, personally and collectively, so as to bring credit to the service and tourism industry at large.
3. We will concentrate our time, energy, and resources on the improvement of our own product and services and we will not denigrate our competition in the pursuit of our own success.
4. We will treat all guests equally regardless of race, religion, nationality, creed, or sex.
5. We will deliver all standards of service and product with total consistency to each and every guest.
6. We will provide a totally safe and sanitary environment at all times to every guest and employee.
7. We will, in words and deeds, develop and maintain the highest level of trust, honesty, and understanding among guests, employees, employers, and the public at large.
8. We will provide every employee, at every level, all of the knowledge, training, equipment, and motivation required to perform his or her tasks according to our published standards.
9. We will guarantee that every employee at all levels, engaged in the same or similar tasks, will have the same opportunity to perform and advance, and will be evaluated against the same standards.
10. We will actively and conscientiously work to protect and preserve our environment and natural resources in all that we do.
11. We will seek a fair and honest profit—no more and no less.

Source: International Institute for Excellence in Service and Tourism.

Endnotes

1. George A. Steiner, "Social Policies for Business," *California Management Review,* Winter 1972, pp. 17–24; cited by Donald P. Robin and Eric Reidenbach in "Social Responsibility, Ethics, and Marketing Strategy: Closing the Gap Between Concept and Application," *Journal of Marketing,* January 1987, p. 45.
2. Linda K. Enghagen, "Ethics in Hospitality/Tourism Education: A Survey," supplied by the author.

 # Key Terms

code of ethics—A statement of the principles by which an operation intends to conduct its business.

ethics—A guide for behavior. Ethics can be described in various ways—as choosing between right and wrong, as making the better choice between two rights, or as the study of moral principles concerning rightful behavior.

social responsibility—A concept suggesting that at any one time in any society there is a set of generally accepted relationships, obligations, and duties between the major institutions and the people.

stakeholder—Anyone who is affected by the outcome of a given decision.

utilitarianism—An ethical philosophy that holds that an action is morally justified to the extent that it maximizes benefits and minimizes harm or costs.

 Review Questions

1. In its broadest sense, how can ethics be defined?

2. How are ethical theories different in what they demand from a person and the person's actions?

3. What are some ways that ethical values can be determined?

4. What are some litmus tests that can be used to determine whether an action is ethical?

5. What is one way that ethics can be simplified?

6. What are some common ethical issues within the hospitality industry?

7. What are some of the ethical views and issues that were revealed by the Hall survey of hospitality managers?

8. What is a code of ethics, and how can it be created?

 Internet Sites

For more information, visit the following Internet sites. Remember that Internet addresses can change without notice. If the site is no longer there, you can use a search engine to look for additional sites.

Business Ethics: The Magazine of
  Corporate Responsibility
www.business-ethics.com

Codes of Ethics Online
ethics.iit.edu/codes/coe.html

Hospitality Ethics Blog
www.hospitalityethics.blogspot.com

International Business Ethics Institute
www.business-ethics.org

Josephson Institute
www.josephsoninstitute.org

Index